JOURNAL OF
Medieval Military History

Volume IX

JOURNAL OF MEDIEVAL MILITARY HISTORY

Editors

Clifford J. Rogers
Kelly DeVries
John France

ISSN 1477–545X

The Journal, an annual publication of De re militari: The Society for Medieval Military History, covers medieval warfare in the broadest possible terms, both chronologically and thematically. It aims to encompass topics ranging from traditional studies of the strategic and tactical conduct of war, to explorations of the martial aspects of chivalric culture and *mentalité*, examinations of the development of military technology, and prosopographical treatments of the composition of medieval armies. Editions of previously unpublished documents of significance to the field are included. The Journal also seeks to foster debate on key disputed aspects of medieval military history.

The editors welcome submissions to the Journal, which should be formatted in accordance with the style-sheet provided on De re militari's website (www.deremilitari.org), and sent electronically to the editor specified there.

JOURNAL OF
Medieval Military History

Volume IX

Soldiers, Weapons and Armies in the
Fifteenth Century

Edited by

ANNE CURRY
ADRIAN R. BELL

THE BOYDELL PRESS

© Contributors 2011

All Rights Reserved. Except as permitted under current legislation
no part of this work may be photocopied, stored in a retrieval system,
published, performed in public, adapted, broadcast,
transmitted, recorded or reproduced in any form or by any means,
without the prior permission of the copyright owner

First published 2011
The Boydell Press, Woodbridge

ISBN 978 1 84383 668 1

The Boydell Press is an imprint of Boydell & Brewer Ltd
PO Box 9, Woodbridge, Suffolk IP12 3DF, UK
and of Boydell & Brewer Inc.
668 Mt Hope Avenue, Rochester, NY 14620, USA
website: www.boydellandbrewer.com

A CIP catalogue record for this book is available
from the British Library

The publisher has no responsibility for the continued existence or accuracy
of URLs for external or third-party internet websites referred to in this book,
and does not guarantee that any content on such websites is, or will remain,
accurate or appropriate.
Papers used by Boydell & Brewer Ltd are natural, recyclable products
made from wood grown in sustainable forests

Typeset by
Frances Hackeson Freelance Publishing Services, Brinscall, Lancs
Printed in Great Britain by
CPI Group (UK) Ltd, Croydon, CR0 4YY

Contents

List of Illustrations	*page* vi
Preface	vii
The French Offensives of 1404–1407 against Anglo-Gascon Aquitaine *Guilhem Pépin*	1
The King's Welshmen: Welsh Involvement in the Expeditionary Army of 1415 *Adam Chapman*	41
Gunners, Aides and Archers: The Personnel of the English Ordnance Companies in Normandy in the Fifteenth Century *Andy King*	65
Defense, Honor and Community: The Military and Social Bonds of the Dukes of Burgundy and the Flemish Shooting Guilds *Laura Crombie*	76
The Battle of Edgecote or Banbury (1469) Through the Eyes of Contemporary Welsh Poets *Barry Lewis*	97
Descriptions of Battles in Fifteenth-Century Urban Chronicles: A Comparison of the Siege of London in May 1471 and the Battle of Grandson, 2 March 1476 *Andreas Remy*	118
Urban Espionage and Counterespionage during the Burgundian Wars (1468–1477) *Bastian Walter*	132
Urban Militias, Nobles and Mercenaries: The Organization of the Antwerp Army in the Flemish–Brabantine Revolt of the 1480s *Frederik Buylaert, Jan Van Camp and Bert Verwerft*	146
Military Equipment in the Town of Southampton During the Fourteenth and Fifteenth Centuries *Randall Moffett*	167

Illustrations

The French Offensives of 1404–1407 against Anglo-Gascon Aquitaine
Map 1 The first French offensive 1404   *page* 4
Map 2 The second French offensive 1405   11
Map 3 The third French offensive 1406–7   18

Defense, Honor and Community: The Military and Social Bonds of the Dukes of Burgundy and the Flemish Shooting Guilds
Map 1 Map of Flanders   78

Urban Militias, Nobles and Mercenaries: The Organization of the Antwerp Army in the Flemish–Brabantine Revolt of the 1480s
Figure 1 The financial costs of the Antwerp army (January–August 1489)   154
Figure 2 The distribution of the expenditures for the Antwerp army (January–August 1489)   154
Figure 3 The composition of the cavalry detachment (1489)   160

Military Equipment in the Town of Southampton during the Fourteenth and Fifteenth Centuries
Figure 1 God's House Gate (author's photograph)   172
Figure 2 Peak of God's House Gate (author's photograph)   173
Figure 3 The Arcade (author's photograph)   174
Figure 4 Arcade Gunport (author's photograph)   175
Figure 5 Southampton Breastplate (drawing by Stuart Quayle)   180
Figure 6 God's House Tower and Gate (author's photograph)   183
Figure 7 God's House Tower's Gunport (author's photograph)   184

Preface

This volume is largely derived from papers delivered at the 2010 Fifteenth Century Conference, held at the University of Southampton. One of the themes was "England's Wars 1399–c.1500," building on a similar event held at the University of Reading in July 2009 which had focused on the same topic in the previous century and resulted in two publications.[1] As it turned out, the subjects covered ranged much more widely than England, but proved highly complementary. Revised versions of these papers form the core of this guest-edited volume; we were delighted to be able also to include further submissions from Andy King and Randall Moffett (both linked to the University of Southampton), and Bastian Walter, whose article happily landed on the general editors' desk at the time we were putting together this special issue. We are grateful to them for allowing us the opportunity to act as guest editors.

The Welsh feature in two studies. Adam Chapman provided new insights, based on close reading of the surviving archival sources, of the Welsh archers recruited for Henry V's campaign of 1415. These archers have achieved almost mythical status, but as Chapman shows, the reality of the situation was rather different. As he notes, there is no mention of Agincourt in Welsh poetry of the fifteenth century, yet such poetry is an exceptionally valuable, and as yet underexploited, source for the study of warfare in the period. Barry Lewis shows its potential with respect to one of the battles of the Wars of the Roses (Edgecote or Banbury, 1469). Guilhem Pépin's essay sheds light on another topic which has hitherto escaped detailed scrutiny: the wars which the French conducted against English-held Gascony in the first decade of the fifteenth century. Whilst the later English tenure of Normandy is better studied, Andy King adds flesh to the bones of the ordnance retinue by drawing on the database (www.medievalsoldier.org) compiled as part of the AHRC-funded project The Soldier in Later Medieval England. Guns also feature prominently in Randall Moffett's study of weaponry in late medieval Southampton, which emphasises the role of townsmen themselves in military innovation. Three contributions at the conference shifted the focus

---

[1] A.R. Bell and A. Curry, with A. Chapman, A. King and D. Simpkin, *The Soldier Experience in the Fourteenth Century* (Woodbridge, 2011); *The Journal of Medieval History* 37 (3) (September 2011).

to the Low Countries. Laura Crombie brought to light the archer and crossbow guilds of the area, showing not only their popularity but also their importance to the dukes of Burgundy, their immediate lords, at a key period of state formation. The significant contribution of towns to the armies of the Low Countries provides the subject of the essay by Frederik Buylaert, Jan Van Camp and Bert Verwerft, concentrating on the city of Antwerp in the 1480s. Towns are also the focus in the comparative study of descriptions of military engagements of the second half of the century in the London Chronicles and in Swiss chronicles by Andreas Remy. And it is the records of the towns of the Swiss confederation and Upper Rhine which inform Bastian Walter's discussion of spying and the transmission of military information during the Burgundian Wars of the 1480s. Together all of these papers confirm the strength of research activity in Britain, the USA and Europe on late medieval warfare as well as showing the potential for further study in quite remarkable archival collections.

Anne Curry
University of Southampton
Adrian R. Bell
University of Reading

The French Offensives of 1404–1407 against Anglo-Gascon Aquitaine

Guilhem Pépin

From 1396 the realm of England was at peace with the kingdom of France, thanks to the long truce signed by Richard II and Charles VI and the marriage of the former with Isabella, daughter of the latter. However, the deposition of Richard by Henry of Lancaster in 1399 changed the situation. Charles's brother, Louis, duke of Orléans, had considerable influence over the sick king, and became the staunchest supporter of a new war against England. Although Orléans had entered into an alliance with the duke of Lancaster in 1399 in order to gain support against John the Fearless, duke of Burgundy, after Henry's accession he became the English king's most determined opponent at the French court. The exact reasons for his hostility towards Henry are difficult to establish. Perhaps the deposition of Richard II, who was son-in-law of Charles VI, was sufficient in itself, but we may also suspect that Orléans exploited an anti-English line to reinforce his own hold on the French royal government against the Burgundians.

The attention of Louis of Orléans was logically focused on the duchy of Aquitaine (known in French as Guyenne). At this point Gascony, the western part of the duchy, was the only possession of the king of England on the mainland of France save for Calais. But Orléans' interest was also personal. As count of Angoulême he was one of the most important lords of the duchy. In 1400 he obtained the county of Périgord which had been seized by the king from its legitimate count, Archambaud VI. Furthermore, the two most important native lords of Guyenne within the French party were in Orléans' patronage: his first cousin, Charles, lord of Albret, who was nominated as constable of France in 1403, and his more distant cousin, the count of Armagnac, Bernat VII. It appears that the aims of the duke of Orléans were straightforward enough: he aspired to conquer all the possessions of the king of England on the continent, an aim never accomplished by previous French governments, even if it had been on occasion almost reached.

Curiously, the story of the French offensives designed by the duke of Orléans against Anglo-Gascon Aquitaine between 1404 and 1407 has been overlooked until now. No works study them as a whole, despite the fact that they were the first episodes of the fifteenth-century phase of the Hundred Years War. Furthermore, as many errors have been made on the dating of these offensives it is necessary to write a coherent narrative. It is very difficult to reconstruct the exact chronology of each offensive as we have to rely on chronicles, particularly the Chronicle of the Monk of St-Denis, and on later reports of the events. However, despite the general lack of chronological reference points, it is possible to obtain a fairly good idea of what happened during the French offensives.

The origins of the conflict, 1400–1404

Louis of Orléans was unable to convince the French government to declare war against Henry IV. This was because Isabella of France, daughter of Charles VI and wife of the late Richard II, was not handed back to the French until July 1401, and because the Anglo-French truces had been renewed until March 1404.[1] Nonetheless, Orléans encouraged and also initiated activities designed to increase tension between the two monarchies. He was probably behind the decision to grant on 14 January 1401 the title of duke of Guyenne to the Dauphin Louis, a clear act of defiance against Henry IV.[2] Similarly, he organized a fight in Montendre,[3] situated at the limit of Anglo-Gascon Guyenne where, on 19 May 1402, seven "French knights" of the duke's household – the most famous being the Gascon Arnaut-Guilhem de Barbazan and the Breton Guillaume du Chastel – were victorious over seven English knights.[4] In the same year the French government provided an unofficial French fleet to the admiral of Scotland, David Lindsay, earl of Crawford, and a state of undeclared war persisted at sea between the French and English in the following years.[5] During the same period Orléans also tried in vain to provoke a war with England by sending two letters of challenge to Henry IV.[6] Locally, an important blow was struck against Anglo-Gascon Guyenne when on 28 March 1401 Charles VI obtained the homage of Archambaud de Grailly, captal de Buch, for the county of Foix which he claimed as husband of its heiress Ysabe de Foix.[7] On 4 April 1401 Archambaud also paid liege homage to Louis

---

[1] *Foedera, conventiones, litterae et cuiuscunque generis acta publica*, ed. T. Rymer, 1st ed. (London, 1704–35), viii, pp. 306–09. Charles VI renewed the treaties with England on 29 January 1400. See Jules de la Martinière, "Instructions secrètes données par Charles VI au sire d'Albret pour soulever la Guyenne contre Henri IV (fin octobre 1399–janvier 1400)," *Bibliothèque de l'École de Chartes* 74 (1913), 331, n. 2.

[2] Françoise Lehoux, *Jean de France, duc de Berri*, 4 vols. (Paris, 1966–68), 2:516 [hereafter *Berri*].

[3] Montendre, ch[ef]-l[ieu de] c[anton], arr[ondissement de] Jonzac, dép[artement de] Charente-Maritime.

[4] Jean-Bernard de Vaivre, "Le rôle armorié du combat de Montendre," *Journal des Savants* 2 (1973), 99–121.

[5] Chris J. Ford, "The Crisis in the Channel, 1400–1403," *Transactions of the Royal Historical Society*, 5th series 29 (1979), 71–77.

[6] *La chronique d'Enguerran de Monstrelet*, ed. L. Douet-d'Arcq, 6 vols. (Paris, 1857–62), 1:43–66. See Chris Given-Wilson, "'The Quarrels of Old Women': Henry IV, Louis of Orléans, and Anglo-French Chivalric Challenges in the Early Fifteenth Century," in *The Reign of Henry IV. Rebellion and Survival, 1403–1413*, ed. G. Dodd and D. Biggs (York, 2008), pp. 28–47.

[7] *Histoire générale de Languedoc* [HGL], ed. Dom Devic and Dom Vaissette, 16 vols. (Toulouse, 1872–1904), 9:982. He was also vicomte of Bénauges and Castillon and lord of Puy-Paulin in Bordeaux.

of Orléans, promising to serve him against everybody excepting the king of France and the Dauphin.[8] As a token of his good faith he delivered his castle of Bouteville in Angoumois to Orléans around April 1401.[9] According to the Monk of St-Denis the count of Foix had taken this castle by trickery from the "English" routiers who held the castle from him.[10] The castle of Chalais, on the other hand, did not surrender to Archambaud because Peyroat Dupuch, its captain, preferred to remain English in order to keep his right to levy *patis* (ransoms) on the surrounding region.[11]

The first French offensive (1404)

Overview

The first expedition of this year against Anglo-Gascon strongholds was led by the constable Charles d'Albret, first cousin of the king, in Limousin and Périgord between mid-August and October 1404. The main military event was the seizure of the castle of Courbefy after a siege of seven weeks. In October the count of Clermont, son of the duke of Bourbon, led another expedition together with the vicomte of Castellbò, son of the count of Foix, against the Anglo-Gascon garrisons of Lavedan (south Bigorre) under the authority of the captain of Lourdes. Clermont was able to seize all the latter's castles except for Lourdes and Les Angles. Subsequently Clermont and the vicomte of Castellbò attacked the Chalosse (south Landes), where they took four small places, but they failed to attack the region of Soule because of the veto of the count of Foix. Meanwhile, the Anglo-Gascons counter-attacked with their limited means.

The expedition of the constable of France in Limousin and Périgord (August–October 1404)

The duke of Orléans succeeded in convincing the royal government to attack Anglo-Gascon Aquitaine after the Anglo-French truce expired in March 1404. Orléans had the upper hand at the royal court following the death of his rival Duke Philip of Burgundy (27 April 1404), but even before this he had already been nominated captain general in Guyenne under the official authority of the

---

[8] Michael Nordberg, *Les ducs et la royauté. Études sur la rivalité des ducs d'Orléans et de Bourgogne, 1392–1407* (Stockholm, 1964), p. 120, n. 2.
[9] *Royal and Historical Letters during the Reign of Henry the Fourth* [*H IV*], ed. F.C. Hingeston, 2 vols. (London, 1860), 1, appendix IV, p. 446: letters of John Morhay to the bishop of Bath (30 April 1401).
[10] *Chronique du Religieux de Saint-Denys*, ed. M.L. Bellaguet, 6 vols. (Paris, 1839–52), 2, Livre XXI, p. 779–81.
[11] Malcolm Vale, *English Gascony, 1399–1453* (Oxford, 1970), p. 47. Dupuch obtained a letter of remission from the count of Foix on 24 August 1401. I would like to thank Malcolm Vale for his help.

Map 1: The First French Offensive (1404)

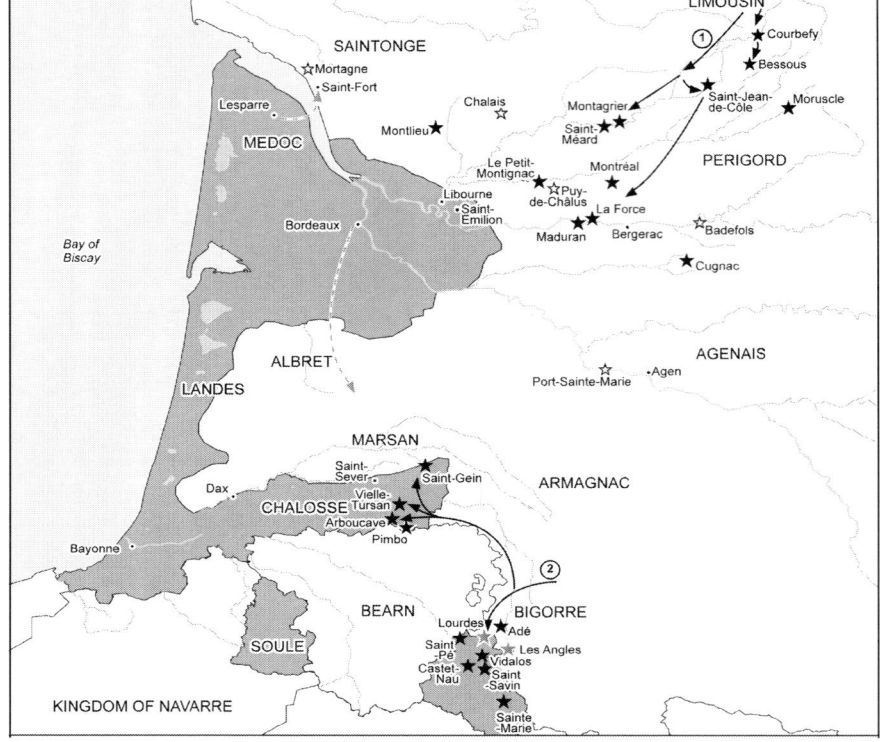

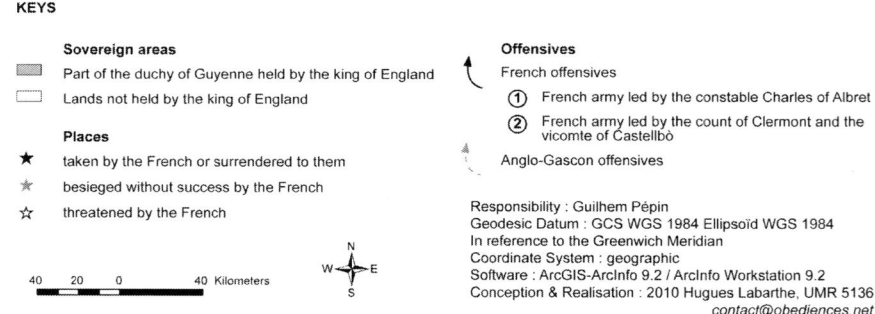

duke of Berry, king's lieutenant in Languedoc and Guyenne (12 March).[12] The first French expedition was led by the constable Charles d'Albret with 1,200 men-at-arms (*bessinetz*) and 300 crossbowmen, his own company being made up

---

[12] B[ibliothèque] N[ationale de] F[rance], MS fr. 20692, p. 178, and Archives municipales de Toulouse AA 46/35. I owe this latter reference to François Couderc.

of 300 men-at-arms and 50 crossbowmen. He targeted Limousin and Périgord, where several fortresses were held by Gascon *routiers* of the English party.[13] In January the constable had summoned men to join him and his company at Limoges on 12 September on penalty of ten silver marks.[14] Charles VI granted Albret a commission on 9 June to obtain the surrender of the castles held by the Anglo-Gascons by any means.[15] From the 1370s fortresses had regularly been taken outside Anglo-Gascon Aquitaine by Gascon *routiers*. The latter acknowledged the authority of the king of England but lived off the *patis* and *sufferte* (ransoms) paid by the region surrounding these fortresses.[16] This forced the French to focus attention and resources on peripheral regions situated outside the core of Anglo-Gascon Aquitaine.

After mid-August 1404 Albret's French army conducted a seven-week siege of the impressive castle of Courbefy, the most important English fortress in Limousin. Because of a tight blockade and an absence of help, the Anglo-Gascon garrison, led by an English captain called Thomas Hervy,[17] negotiated with the constable and was paid two thousand *francs* to leave the place.[18] Subsequently, several other English places were taken in the same manner by the constable in Limousin and in northern Périgord, notably Bessous, St-Jean-de-Côle (occupied by the "English" since 1394) and Montagrier (commanded by the Gascon captain Andriu Andras).[19] In view of this situation, some local lords and captains of the English

---

[13] Figure given in the "Petite chronique de Périgueux (1385–1415)" [henceforward *Pet. Ch. Périgueux*], ed. C.-H. Piraud, *Bulletin de la société historique et archéologique du Périgord* 103 (2003), 299–350, at 329. I thank Claude-Henri Piraud for sending me his edition of this chronicle. For Albret's own company, see BNF, MS fr. 32510, fol. 336 (extract of the accounts of Hémon Raguier, treasurer of the war for the king of France).

[14] BNF, pièces originales [PO] 24, Albret, no. 22 (Paris, 12 January 1404).

[15] BNF, MS fr. 32511, fol. 1r.

[16] On this topic see Guilhem Pépin, "Towards a rehabilitation of Froissart's credibility: the non fictitious Bascot de Mauléon," in *The Soldier Experience in the Fourteenth Century*, ed. A.R. Bell and A. Curry, with A. Chapman, A. King and D. Simpkin (Woodbridge, 2011), forthcoming, and Jonathan Sumption, *Divided Houses. The Hundred Years War III* (London, 2010), pp. 679–722 (chapter XIV. The Gascon March, 1381–1393).

[17] James Hamilton Wylie, *History of England under Henry the Fourth*, 4 vols. (London, 1884–98), vol. 1, 1399–1404, p. 388, n. 10. The other main leaders of the garrison were named Robert Walton and John Hernelines. See Jules Machet de la Martinière, *Les guerres anglaises dans l'ouest et le centre de la France, Poitou, Saintonge Angoumois, Limousin, Périgord (1403–1417)*, unpublished thèse de l'École de Chartes (Paris, 1899), p. 45. A[rchives] N[ationales], AB XXVIII 58. I thank Frédéric Machet de la Martinière for permission to read this. See also the summary of this thesis, "Les guerres anglaises dans l'ouest et le centre de la France, Poitou, Saintonge Angoumois, Limousin, Périgord (1403–1417)," *Positions des thèses*, École Nationale des Chartes (Chalon-sur-Saône, 1899).

[18] B[ritish] L[ibrary], MS Caligula D IV, fol. 79r: "[Corbe]ssin ont a tengut lo seti VII setmanas e […] seti foren tot jorn en treubas e en com […] cum la plassa fos benduda en ayssi cum […] ii milia franxs, lo quau loc es en Lemosin". The *Pet. Ch. Périgueux*, p. 329, asserts that the Courbefy's garrison was paid 6,000 francs to leave the castle with their weapons. Sadly, the English reports now in BL, Cotton Caligula D IV, though very precise, are badly damaged by fire, so some precious information on this offensive has been lost.

[19] *St-Denys*, vol. 3, Livre XXV, pp. 200–209. The captains of these two fortresses, apparently of local origin according to their names (Costereste and Escourian) were paid by the French

party, such as the lord of Montréal, bargained with the French and rallied to them, while others, such as Chopi de Badefols, promised to surrender their castles in Périgord after a certain period of time if no members of the English royal family came to their help with an army.[20] However, it is clear that not all the "English" fortresses were bought off in this way. We know that the constable stormed the castles of La Force and Maduran when he went to Bergerac, forcing the lord of La Force to become French. Similarly, Saint-Méard and le Petit-Montignac were stormed by the French.[21] Finally, the constable agreed a *souffrance* (truce) with the veteran Gascon *routier* Ramonet de Sort, lord of Moncuq, and with the "English" *routiers* on the south of the river Dordogne.[22] The majority of the constable's army remained in the area during the winter 1404/05,[23] essentially in Cognac.[24]

We can assess the importance of these peripheral castles – described as barbicans in 1406 by the archbishop of Bordeaux, in the defence system of the remaining Anglo-Gascon duchy – thanks to a letter addressed on 19 August 1404 by Galhard de Durfort, seneschal of Aquitaine, to the towns of Libourne and St-Émilion.[25] Durfort requested the mayors and communities of these two towns to supply the garrison of Puy-de-Châlus,[26] led by a certain Antony, explaining to them the dangers they could suffer if this fortress were taken. Puy-de-Châlus was the closest castle to these towns situated in the French-dominated area and acted as a shield protecting them. The seneschal had probably heard of the intention of Micheu d'Albret, the French captain of Bergerac, to besiege this place.[27]

in September. See *Berri*, vol. 3, p. 20, n. 4. Courbefy, in com. Bussière-Galant, c. Châlus, arr. Limoges, dép. Haute-Vienne; Bessous, com. Ladignac-le-Long, c. Châlus, arr. Limoges, dép. Haute-Vienne; St-Jean-de-Côle, c. Thiviers, arr. Nontron, dép. Dordogne and Montagrier, ch.-l. c., arr. Périgueux, dép. Dordogne. Bessous and Andriu Andras are mentioned in the *Pet. Ch. Périgueux*, p. 329. Andras is the name of several places in the region of Chalosse (dép. Landes).

[20] After one complete year in the case of Chopi de Badefols. This latter was a *routier* captain active since the 1380s.
[21] BL, Cotton MS Caligula D IV, fol. 79r–v.
[22] *Pet. Ch. Périgueux*, p. 329. In 1383 Ramonet de Sort had succeeded Bertrucat d'Albret, his late uncle, at the head of one of the biggest companies of routiers. Moncuq, com. Pomport, c. Sigoulès, arr. Bergerac, dép. Dordogne.
[23] BNF, PO 24 Albret, no. 85. Order of Charles VI to his general councillors to pay to the lord of Albret, constable of France, what is due to his army as the main part "fait résidence en personne sur le dit pays" since the siege of Courbefy and the other sieges (20 May 1405).
[24] Thesis Machet de la Martinière, pp. 72–73.
[25] Archives municipales de Libourne, EE 1.
[26] Puy-de-Châlus, in com. Montpon-Ménestérol, ch.-l. c., arr. Périgueux, dép. Dordogne.
[27] *Les registres de la ville de Bergerac*, ed. G. Charrier (Bergerac, 1892), p. 140 (10 July 1404). Puy-de-Châlus was seized by the French between 1404 and 1406 as it was included in the Albret/French side in the truce made by Galhart de Durfort, seneschal of Guyenne, with the lord of Albret (22 April 1407), *Archives historiques de la Gironde* [AHG], VI, no. LXXXVII, p. 219.

The expedition of the count of Clermont in Bigorre and the Landes (October–November 1404)

Two letters of Guilhem-Amaniu de Madaillan, lord of Lesparre and Rauzan, then governor of Bordeaux (acting as mayor of Bordeaux although not nominated by the king), were written on 28 November 1404, one in French to King Henry IV, the other in Gascon to his bailiff of Lesparre and sent by him to England. These give us much valuable information on the events of this year.[28] We can complement this with some French chronicles sources as well as some further documents from the British Library Cotton Caligula D IV collection. Madaillan asserted that all the English fortresses in Limousin and Périgord had been taken by the French, which was probably true for the Limousin but an exaggeration for Périgord. He also explained that Jean de Bourbon, count of Clermont, son of the duke of Bourbon, and Johan de Foix-Grailly, vicomte of Castellbò, son of the count of Foix and vicomte of Béarn, had led a French offensive during the summer in southern Gascony against Johan de Béarn, captain of Lourdes and seneschal of Bigorre for the king of England.[29] The latter dominated the south of Bigorre, a region called Lavedan, from the castle of Lourdes that he had held since the early 1370s. Apart from the castles of Lourdes and Les Angles, the French army conquered all the fortresses dominated by the Anglo-Gascons in this region with the help of some local people.[30] Among the places taken we can note the still-extant castles of Vidalos, Castet-Nau and Ste-Marie.[31] The castle of Castet-Nau, or Castelnau, was rendered to Clermont by Guilhem Arieu, its Bigourdan captain, for 1,125*l*. (12 October), while Pè de Cohitte obtained 562*l*. 10*s. tournois* to have permitted the submission of the castle of Ste-Marie and rallied several local lords to the French (16 October).[32] An agreement called *patis general* by Madaillan was

---

[28] T[he] N[ational] A[rchives], E 28/15/90 and SC 1/51/69. Lesparre-Médoc, ch.-l. arr., dép. Gironde and Rauzan, c. Pujols, arr. Libourne, dép. Gironde.

[29] Clermont gathered his army in St-Flour (Auvergne, ch.-l. arr., dép. Cantal), he captured in Quercy the place of Cazals (ch.-l. c., arr. Cahors, dép. Lot), and he went to Agenais where he received the submission of some lords of the English party. Then he went into Gascony and united his army with that led by the vicomte of Castellbò. Clermont, ch.-l. arr., dép. Oise (named in the past Clermont-en-Beauvaisis) and the vicomté of Castellbò (Castellbò in Catalan, Castellbó in Spanish, often Gallicised in Castelbon) was situated in Catalonia in what is now the province of Lleida/Lérida.

[30] BL, Cotton MS Caligula D IV, fol. 83 (24 November 1404). This anonymous letter asserts: "Item le comte de Clarmont et le vicomte de Castelbon ont esté a Lorde et ont pris et occupé touz les lieux que tenoit le capitaine de Lorde en icel pays excepté les Angles, et tous iceulx lieux, il ont eu par traison dez gentz d'icelli pays de Bigourre". Lourdes, ch.-l. c., arr. Argelèst-Gazost, dép. Hautes-Pyrénées and les Angles, c. Lourdes-Est, arr. Argelèst-Gazost, dép. Hautes-Pyrénées.

[31] List of these fortresses in *Chronographia Regum Francorum*, ed. H. Moranvillé, 3 vols. (Paris, 1891–1897), 3:240. All of them are situated in the current département of Hautes-Pyrénées and the arrondissement of Argelès-Gazost: Adé, St-Pé-de-Bigorre, Vidalos (in com. Agos-Vidalos), Castet-Nau (in com. Arras-en-Lavedan), St-Savin and Ste-Marie (in com. Esterre).

[32] *Les mémoires de messire Michel de Castelnau, seigneur de Mauvissière*, ed. J. le Laboureur (Paris, 1659), pp. 14 and 22. Guilhem Arieu is mistakenly called here "Arion" (Arieu is a family name very specific to Bigorre). Pè de Cohitte was a member of the family of the lords of Cohitte (com. Beaucens, arr. Argelès-Gazost, dép. Hautes-Pyrénées).

then agreed with the French by the captain of Lourdes Johan de Béarn. The latter was paid twelve thousand *francs* and one hundred silver marks by the French not to attack them for a year and a month unless he was so ordered by the king or a member of the royal family coming to Guyenne to make war. However, even under such circumstances he had to warn the French fifteen days in advance.[33] According to the *Chronographia Regum Francorum*, Béarn promised to surrender the castle of Lourdes and to rally the French if he did not have any help from the English before the end of the year.[34]

After this the army led by Clermont and Castellbò attacked the region of Chalosse in the seneschalcy of the Landes.[35] But their successes there were far more limited than in Bigorre as they were not able to rely on the support of the local population. This was an area traditionally faithful to the king-duke as is confirmed in a contemporary list describing the allegiance of the noble houses of this region.[36] The French army took only four places of little importance: Pimbo, Arboucave, Vielle and St-Gein.[37] The towns of Chalosse refused to pay a *patis* to the French, declaring they would not give fifty *deniers* and that they had good heart to defend themselves. Even if the seneschalcy of the Landes was at this point without its seneschal, the resistance was organized in St-Sever by the lord of Lescun and Pèr-Arnaut de Béarn, lord of Estang, the brother of the captain of Lourdes. They had gathered up to three hundred horses from their own lands.[38] Some other Landais lords left their lands and fortresses to go to Dax to defend it against the French.[39] Clermont and Castellbò planned to attack the region of Soule, also faithful to the king of England but separated from the Landes by the vicomté of Béarn and the kingdom of Navarre. Béarn was under the authority of Archambaud de Grailly, count of Foix and father of the vicomte of Castellbò, one of the two leaders of the French army, but Archambaud refused to allow access via Béarn as this vicomté had been de facto a neutral lordship since the time of Gaston Fébus. This was not the only reason, as we learn, for example, that Archambaud was paid eight hundred florins by the area of Soule to protect it against the French for one year. This fact underlines the ambivalent attitude

---

[33] BL, Cotton MS Caligula D IV, fol. 83.
[34] *Chronographia*, p. 241.
[35] On 4 October 1404, Galhart de Durfort, seneschal of Guyenne, paid 40 francs to Pey, lord of Campet (com. Campet-et-Lamolère, c. Mont-de-Marsan- Nord, arr. Mont-de-Marsan, dép. Landes), who had been taken prisoner by the French when he went to the Landes to inform the seneschal of the "dominance et ordenances du comte de Clermont et du vicomte de Casteillon et de autres de la partie de France," in *Documents sur la Maison de Durfort*, ed. N. de Peña, 2 vols. (Bordeaux, 1977), 2:818, no. 18 (TNA, E 30/1518).
[36] BL, Cotton MS Caligula D IV, fols. 81r–83r. See Vale, *English Gascony*, map IV, p. 253.
[37] BL, Cotton MS Caligula D IV, fol. 79v. Pimbo (c. Geaune), Arboucave (c. Geaune), Vielle-Tursan (c. Aire-sur-l'Adour) and St-Gein (c. Villeneuve-de-Marsan) are situated in the département of the Landes, arrondissement of Mont-de-Marsan.
[38] Ibid. Estang, c. Cazaubon, arr. Condom, dép. Gers.
[39] Mentioned in TNA, E 28/14/10 (12 July 1405). They were Johan de Caupenne, lord of Mées and the lord of Poyanne. Mées, c. Dax-Nord, arr. Dax, dép. Landes and Poyanne, c. Montfort-en-Chalosse, arr. Dax, dép. Landes.

of Archambaud de Grailly throughout these offensives. Gaston de Foix, lord of Grailly, second son of Archambaud, was present in Cadillac, a town owned by Archambaud, but Madaillan stated that he would not allow him to enter to Bordeaux without an express order of the king. According to the Monk of St-Denis he favoured the English while his elder brother, the vicomte of Castellbò, was a partisan of the French.[40] The French attacks ceased around 11 November when the main lords returned to "France."[41] Clermont's expedition had cost sixty-five thousand *livres*.[42]

The Anglo-Gascon counter-attacks

The Gascons of the English party did not remain inactive, but counter-attacked without the help of England. The seneschal of Guyenne, Galhard de Durfort, went into the Agenais to resist the French offensives. Being lord of Duras, he was one of the most important lords of Agenais and was particularly able to rally the local pro-English nobility around him. He fought together with the lords of Badefols and Lauzun and the men of the lordship of Caumont. They entrenched themselves in the town of Port-Sainte-Marie, close to the regional capital of Agen.[43] Clermont and Castellbò threatened to besiege Durfort there. Madaillan explained in his letters that the king had to send men and money to Aquitaine in order to support them and to avoid losing the whole duchy. As governor of Bordeaux, Madaillan expended his own money to pay one hundred men-at-arms to keep Bordeaux for the king. He stated that his land of Soulac,[44] situated within his lordship of Lesparre, had been burned by the French led by the lord of Pons,[45] the most important lord of the French party in Saintonge, but that in retaliation he burnt St-Fort in Saintonge,[46] a possession of the same lord. Similarly, the men

---

[40] *St-Denys*, vol. 2, Livre XXI, pp. 778–79. In 1401, he would have threatened several times his elder brother to kill him if he became French.
[41] *Pet. Ch. Périgueux*, p. 330. "France" here meant the country roughly situated north of the river Loire, not the kingdom.
[42] BNF, MS fr. 20692, p. 178.
[43] BL, Cotton MS Caligula D IV, fol. 83. Duras, ch.-l. c., arr. Marmande, dép. Lot-et-Garonne; Badefols-sur-Dordogne, c. Le Buisson-de-Cadoin, arr. Bergerac, dép. Dordogne; Lauzun, ch.-l. c., arr. Marmande, dép. Lot-t-Garonne; Caumont-sur-Garonne, c. Le Mas-d'Agenais, arr. Marmande, dép. Lot-et-Garonne; Port-Sainte-Marie, ch.-l. c., arr. Agen, dép. Lot-et-Garonne and Agen, ch.-l. dép., dép. Lot-et-Garonne. Johan de Caumont, lord of Lauzun, officially rallied to the French, represented by the count of Clermont, on 26 December 1404, but had been paid to spy on the Anglo-Gascons on 12 June of this year. See Vale, *English Gascony*, p. 205 n. 5, and 206, n. 1. Bertran de Durfort, lord of Gavaudun, also rallied to the French. He had wanted to give his castle to his kinsman Amaniu de Durfort, an "English" partisan (see BNF, MS Fr. 20692, p. 179). Gavaudun, c. Monflanquin, arr. Villeneuve-sur-Lot, dép. Lot-et-Garonne.
[44] Soulac[-sur-Mer], c. St-Vivien-du-Médoc, arr. Lesparre-Médoc, dép. Gironde.
[45] We learn in the *Registres de la Jurade. Délibérations de 1406 à 1409*, Archives municipales de Bordeaux (Bordeaux, 1873), p. 57, that the lord of Pons had previously burned the town of Soulac (see letter of the mayor of Libourne to the mayor of Bordeaux, 24 September 1406). Pons, ch.-l. c., arr. Saintes, dép. Charente-Maritime.
[46] St-Fort-sur-Gironde, c. St-Génis-de-Saintonge, arr. Jonzac, dép. Charente-Maritime.

of Bordeaux led an expedition to the lands of Albret situated to the south-east of their city where they took fifty prisoners and captured some cattle.

In conclusion, the French successes of the year 1404 were quite important but were not decisive in terms of an attempt to conquer the whole Anglo-Gascon duchy. However, the Anglo-Gascons lost many barbicans protecting the duchy, thereby leaving it open to the risk of direct attack if there was to be another offensive in the future. The fortress of Mortagne remained threatened by the constable of Albret, who was based at Pons in Saintonge, but the increasing tensions existing between the dukes of Orléans and Burgundy worked in Anglo-Gascon favour.

The second French offensive (1405)

Overview

In 1405 the French besieged two "English" castles in Saintonge, Chalais (March to September) and Mortagne (April to June), and obtained their surrender. The main French offensive of the year was led by the count of Armagnac, who, after obtaining the surrender of several places in Agenais and the town of Langon (August), went before the walls of Bordeaux (late September) and tried, in vain, to take it with the help of some Castilian ships coming from the Gironde estuary. From August to October an offensive was carried out by the French against the Landes. Throughout the year a state of endemic warfare existed in Périgord, where the Anglo-Gascons took by storm several places which were subsequently besieged, retaken or threatened by the French. Our information for the military events of this year in Guyenne is based on the Chronicle of the Monk of St-Denis, which has a pro-French bias, although it is possible to complete or correct its narrative by use of some other sources. We also know that there was discussion in Paris on war policy, with two councils held in March 1405: one with the count of Saint-Pol and several Normans and Picards to decide if it was best to march against Calais, the other with people from Limousin and "Langue d'oc" on whether the priority should be to march against Guyenne and Bordeaux.[47] Apparently the latter won the day.

Attacks on the Anglo-Gascon strongholds of Saintonge (March to September)

A series of French operations were organized against Anglo-Gascon Aquitaine. As the exact chronology of the events is lacking, we will describe the different

---

[47] Extract from a letter (7 March 1405) of two Burgundian ambassadors writing from Paris to Margaret of Flanders, duchess of Burgundy, being at Arras (Lille, Archives départementales du Nord, B18824/23910): "Mais si comme nous sceusmes depuis len tint le conseil en deux parties et estoit sur le fait de la guerre, lune partie cest assavoir ou estoient le dit monsieur de saint pol et plusieurs normans picars et autres de ces marches pour savoir sil estoit le plus expedient daler davant calais et lautre partie ou estoient lymosins et autres de la languedoc pour savoir sil estoit plus expedier daler en guienne et devers bordeaux." I thank Chris Ford for giving me this reference and for his help with this article.

Map 2: The Second French Offensive (1405)

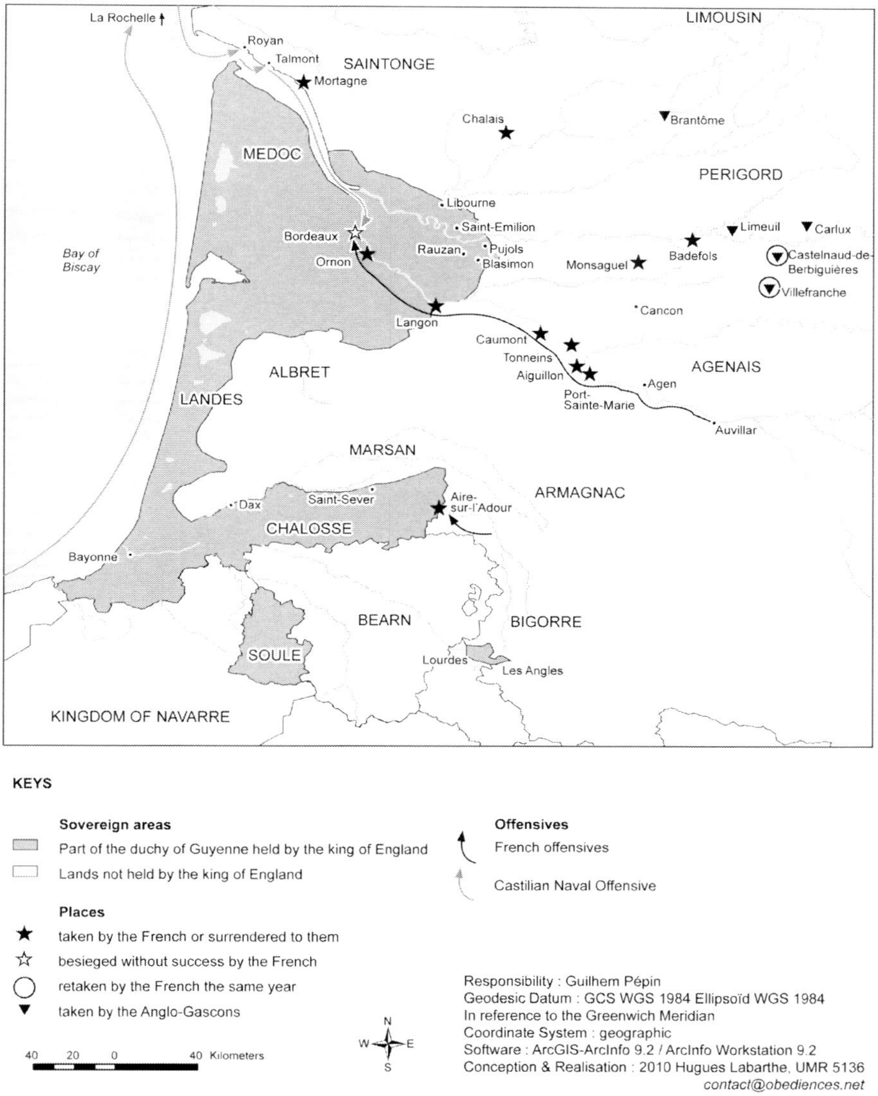

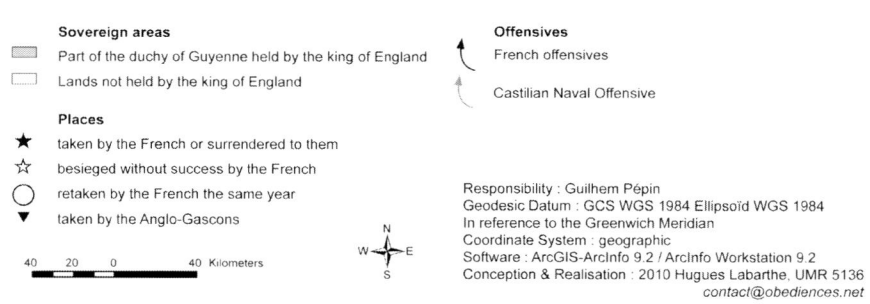

theatres of war. First, the English fortress that was most threatened was Chalais, one of the two remaining English castles in Saintonge. In January 1405 Henry IV promised to his captain, the squire Peyrot Dupuch, that aid and refreshment for his garrison would be provided from England. Pressured since 1401–2 by the French and local allies such as the count of Foix, Dupuch had sent an English messenger named Hopkyn Holm to the king to ask for help,[48] but, sadly, the king's encouragements sent back through Holm were not enough. The castle, besieged since at least March,[49] was finally forced to surrender in October or November to the constable of Albret, who demolished it.[50]

Mortagne, the other "English" castle in Saintonge, was besieged, according to the Monk of St-Denis, for seven weeks from May 1405 by a small army of eight hundred men gathered by the lord of Pons. The garrison, led by an (anonymous) lady, was harassed by the siege engines of the French and finally fled at dawn across the estuary of Gironde.[51] In fact, the terms of the grant of this castle by the king of France to Jacques de Montbron as well as the narrative of the *Petite Chronique de Périgueux* tell us what really happened: Montbron besieged Mortagne for three months (from April to June 1405) at his own expense because his eldest son was married to the legitimate heiress of this castle. The constable was present at this siege during its last month and officially obtained the surrender of the town.[52] It also appears that the real leader of Mortagne's Anglo-Gascon garrison was Ponts, lord of Castillon, who was the castellan of this castle from 1397 on behalf of the duke of York who had obtained this castle and its castellany from his nephew Richard II in that same year.[53] According to the *Petite*

---

[48] TNA, E 28/17/44: letter of Henry IV to Peyroat or Peyronet Dupuch (23 January 1405), and E 28/17/47: letter of Henry IV to the cardinal-archbishop of Bordeaux Francesco Uguccioni (archbishop of Bordeaux from 1389 to 1412) concerning Dupuch and Chalais (24 January 1405). Chalais, ch.-l. c., arr. Angoulême, dép. Charente.

[49] BNF, PO 2535/Rollat no. 3: homages paid to Odin de Rollat, before Chalais (March 1405), in O. Troubat, *La guerre de Cent ans et le prince chevalier, le « bon duc » Louis II de Bourbon, 1337–1410*, 2 vols. (Montluçon, 2001–03), 2:476, n. 3. There are in BNF PO several receipts and musters made before Chalais between 6 July (e.g. PO 2517/La Rochefoucault no. 4) and 22 August 1405 (PO 24/Albret, no. 96). We can suppose it was the peak period of this siege. I thank Jonathan Sumption for these references. There is also a receipt of Pierre de Mornay before Chalais (26 August 1405): see Thesis Machet de la Martinière, p. 56, n. 4 (BNF, Clairambault, 78, fol. 6159).

[50] The constable was besieging the castle of Chalais in August 1405. See *Reg. Bergerac*, p. 142 (25 August 1405). The castle was taken and destroyed as said in the "Petite Chronique de Guyenne jusqu'à l'an 1442," ed. G. Lefèvre-Pontalis, *Bibliothèque de l'École des Chartes* 47 (1886), 64, no. 81. The same chronicle is in the *Livre des Coutumes*, Archives municipales de Bordeaux (Bordeaux, 1890), p. 685–92. The lord of Pons was also present at this siege: BL, MS Caligula D IV, fol. 103.

[51] *St-Denys*, vol. 3, Livre XXVI, p. 275–9. Juvénal des Ursins tells a very similar story and mentions as well the seven-week duration of the siege. Jean Juvénal des Ursins, "Histoire de Charles VI, roy de France," in *Nouvelle collection des mémoires relatifs à l'histoire de France*, éd. J.F. Michaut and J.J.F. Poujoulat, 12 vols. (Paris, 1836–39), 2:435. Mortagne-sur-Gironde, c. Cozes, arr. Saintes, dép. Charente-Maritime.

[52] *Archives Historiques du Poitou* [AHP] 26, pp. 78–80, no. DCCCCX (July 1405) and *Pet. Ch. Périgueux*, p. 331. François de Montbron was married to Louise de Clermont, vicomtesse d'Aulnay. As Jean La Personne, vicomte d'Aulnay, was by marriage lord of Mortagne and rallied the French from 1369, his castle and lordship had been seized by the king of England. Aulnay, c. Moncontour, arr. Châtellerault, dép. Vienne.

[53] On 4 February 1397, Richard II gave for life the castle and castellany of Mortagne to Edmund of Langley, duke of York (TNA, C 61/104, m.3). Thereafter, York nominated Ponts de Castillon as his lieutenant there and the king confirmed this nomination (C 61/105, m.11 and 10 (6 February 1398).

Chronique de Guyenne and the *Petite Chronique de Périgueux* this castle was also demolished.[54]

The main offensive of 1405 led by the count of Armagnac against Bordeaux (August–September)

The main offensive of this year was carried out by Bernat VII, count of Armagnac, son-in-law of the duke of Berry, who was charged in July by King Charles VI to lead an expedition into Guyenne with one thousand men-at-arms and three hundred crossbowmen.[55] In August Bernat had received ten thousand *francs* from the duke of Orléans on behalf of the king to pay these troops.[56] Coming from Auvillar, where he was at the beginning of August,[57] he started to besiege Port-Ste-Marie and on 15 August 1405 obtained from the inhabitants of this town a promise to surrender to the French if they were not rescued before 15 October.[58] The count then continued his expedition, following the valley of the Garonne and taking places including Aiguillon, Tonneins and Caumont.[59] He obtained the submission of the last place, if not the two others, by treaty: Guilhem-Ramon, lord of Caumont, had agreed on 7 August to return to the French obedience.[60] Bernat continued his journey on the Garonne by taking Langon and nominating there as

---

[54] *Pet. Ch. Guyenne*, p. 64, no. 80 and *Pet. Ch. Périgueux*, p. 331. Castillon in Médoc, com. St-Christoly Médoc, c. Lesparre-Médoc, arr. Lesparre-Médoc, dép. Gironde.

[55] *Berri*, iii, p. 83, n. 4. In a letter written in Bordeaux on 11 [October 1405], BL, Cotton MS Caligula D IV, fol. 103, it is asserted that Armagnac "a fait sa monstre de mil et V^c homes d'armez". The same figure is given with 2,000 horses in a letter of the archbishop of Bordeaux to Henry IV (17 April [1405]): "quar le conte d'Arminihac a orez ensemble mil et V^c homes […] de jour en autre, mil et ii^c roussins d'autre part," in *H IV*, p. 439. The *Pet. Ch. Périgueux*, p. 331, gives 1,400 men. The Monk of St-Denis gives a figure of 1,600 men-at-arms and 4,000 men of the militias of the *commune*s, in *St Denys*, 3:354–5 and Juvénal des Ursins of 1,600 men-at-arms and 4,000 crossbowmen, *Ursins*, p. 438: "seize cens hommes d'armes, et quatre mille hommes de traict". It seems that 1,600 men-at-arms and 400 crossbowmen from the south of the kingdom of France is a more credible figure.

[56] Eugène Jarry, *La vie politique de Louis de France, duc d'Orléans, 1372–1407* (Paris and Orléans, 1889), p. 323, n. 3. BNF, PO 93 Armagnac 93, 94 and 95. In July, the king had allocated 25,000 gold francs to Armagnac on the last *aide* levied in the kingdom against Henry IV to pay his army of 1,000 men-at-arms and 300 crossbowmen.

[57] Pierre Durrieu, *Bernard VII, comte d'Armagnac, connétable de France (136?–1418)* (unpublished thesis of the École des Chartes, Paris, 1878), p. 114. I am very grateful to Dominique Barrois for giving me a typed version of this thesis which was recently saved from total oblivion, the only remaining copy having been much damaged. Auvillar, ch.l. c., arr. Castelsarrasin, dép. Tarn-et-Garonne.

[58] BNF, Doat 194, fol. 273 and Archives Nationales, JJ 160, no. 242, fol. 168 (Confirmation of the agreement made on 15 August 1405 between the count of Armagnac and the inhabitants of Port-Ste-Marie following the withdrawal of the "English", March 1406). See Charles Samaran, *La Gascogne dans les registres du Trésor des Chartes* (Paris, 1966), no. 1065, p. 124.

[59] *Pet. Ch. Guyenne*, p. 64, no. 84, and *St-Denys*, vol. 3, Livre XXVI, p. 356–7. Aiguillon, c. Port-Ste-Marie, arr. Agen, dép. Lot-et-Garonne; Tonneins, ch.-l. de c., arr. Marmande, dép. Lot-et-Garonne and Caumont-sur-Garonne, c. Mas-d'Agenais, arr. Marmande, dép. Lot-et-Garonne.

[60] AN, JJ 160, no. 243, fol. 169, see Samaran, *La Gascogne*, no. 1066, p. 124 (confirmation of this agreement in March 1406).

governor one of his most faithful men, Guiraut, lord of Vergoignan.[61] Unlike all the other places mentioned earlier, Langon was situated just at the entry to a region entirely dominated by the Anglo-Gascons.[62] It appeared that Bernat's objective was no less than the city of Bordeaux, capital of Anglo-Gascon Guyenne.

Bernat went on to besiege the small castle of Ornon, situated on the outskirts of Bordeaux. After three assaults the defenders negotiated a surrender (late Sept.).[63] Continuing on, the count's army arrived at the very walls of Bordeaux, staying there for three or four days.[64] According to the Monk of St-Denis, Bernat wanted to provoke the Bordelais in order to defeat them in open battle. To this purpose he knighted one hundred squires, but this did not work. Subsequently he intended to blockade the city, but was finally paid by the burgesses of Bordeaux to give up the siege.[65] However, the Monk does not tell the whole story. We know that the offensive of Bernat against Bordeaux was to be coordinated with a naval offensive of three Castilian galleys led by Don Pero Niño. This double expedition had been decided when Niño met the constable of Albret in La Rochelle.[66] Pero Niño went to the Gironde and called at the French ports of Royan and Talmont-sur-Gironde. Leaving the latter during the night, undetected, he approached Bordeaux at dawn. According to the chronicle relating the life of Pero Niño, the three galleys launched a surprise attack on the port of Bordeaux and pillaged several houses. The Bordelais quickly organized a strong resistance and one hundred boats were sent against the galleys, while volleys of arrows and darts came from the boats and both shores of the Garonne. Niño then withdrew because he was afraid of

---

[61] *Pet. Ch. Guyenne*, p. 64, no. 84. On Vergoignan as captain of Langon for the count of Armagnac in 1411 see AHP, X, no. XXXV, p. 74. Langon, ch.-l. c., ch.-l. arr., dép. Gironde and Vergoignan, c. Riscle, arr. Mirande, dép. Gers.

[62] Excepting Rions and Langoiran (both in c. Cadillac, arr. Bordeaux, dép. Gironde), Vayres (c. Libourne, arr. Libourne, dép. Gironde) and Vertheuil (c. Pauillac, arr. Lesparre-Médoc, dép. Gironde) which acknowledged the French obedience. They were possessions of the lord of Albret as successor of Bérart III d'Albret who died without direct heirs in 1379, having rallied the French side since he had been taken prisoner at the battle of Eymet in 1377.

[63] The Monk of St-Denis curiously names it *Bombatat* and situates it before Langon (*St-Denys*, vol. 3, Livre XXVI, p. 357), but its physical description corresponds to the current remains of the castle of Ornon called the Castéra (in com. Gradignan, ch.-l. c., arr. Bordeaux, dép. Gironde), see Léo Drouyn, *La Guienne militaire*, 2 vols. (Bordeaux and Paris, 1865), vol. 1, pp. LI–LII. The sixteenth-century Bordelais writer Gabriel de Lurbe reported in his *Chronique Bourdeloise* (Bordeaux, 1594), pp. 33–34, that the castle of Ornon was taken towards the end of September 1405 by the troops of the count of Armagnac and was destroyed by them: 'sur la fin du mesme moys [de septembre 1405] le conte d'Armaignac lieutenant du roy de France faict avec son armée le degast iusques aux portes de Bourdeaus, et entre autres choses ruynes et abat le chasteau du conté d'Ornon". In June 1415, the jurats (town's councillors) of Bordeaux wrote to the count of Armagnac that he lately came with his great army in his lordship of Ornon (the commune of Bordeaux bought it in 1409). See *Registres de la Jurade. Délibérations de 1414 à 1416 et de 1420 and 1422*, Archives municipales de Bordeaux (Bordeaux, 1883), p. 175.

[64] Three days in *Pet. Ch. Périgueux*, p. 331, and four days in *St-Denys*, 2:356–9.

[65] Ibid., pp. 356–9. In *Pet. Ch. Périgueux*, p. 331, it is said he knighted 80 men, the first of them being his chancellor Bernat de Goursolle.

[66] Gutierre Díaz de Games, *El Victorial*, ed. Rafael Beltrán Llavador (Madrid, 1994), pp. 316–17.

the arrival of an English fleet in his rear.[67] The reality is simpler. The three galleys did not reach Bordeaux itself because they had been spotted earlier, so they destroyed only some rural properties situated two miles before Bordeaux before being forced to withdraw by the Bordelais both on land and on river. According to an English report this Castilian attack took place on 26 September.[68] The purpose of the attack was doubtless to create a diversion – nobody having ever attacked the port of Bordeaux before – permitting the count of Armagnac to storm the city on another side. The ploy having failed and the count of Armagnac having almost no chance to take such a strong city as Bordeaux, he negotiated his withdrawal in order to pay his men.[69]

The war in Périgord

At the beginning of October the French seneschals of Toulouse, Quercy and Bigorre, probably together with the vicomte of Castellbò, made war in the Landes and forced the submission of two barons and their castles.[70] It is possible that the seneschals had earlier obtained the surrender of the city of Aire-sur-l'Adour in August.[71] Meanwhile, the war of surprise attacks and skirmishes led by the Anglo-Gascon companies of *routiers* since the 1370s was still ongoing in Périgord and the surrounding areas, and the French authorities regularly tried to remove this threat by besieging and taking *routier*-held castles. On 9 January 1405 some "English" seized Villefranche-du-Périgord but the place was retaken by Arnaut, lord of Bourdeilles and the French captain of Montignac, after more than one month of siege.[72] In February the castle of Castelnaud-de-Berbiguières was taken by the English party with, at its head, the Périgourdin noble Archambaud d'Abzac.[73] He

---

[67] Ibid., pp. 356–8. English translation: *The Unconquered Knight. A Chronicle of the Deeds of Don Pero Niño, count of Buelna*, trans. J. Evans (London, 1928 and Woodbridge, 2004), pp. 105–7. French translation: *Le Victorial, Chronique de Don Pero Niño*, ed. A. de Circourt and comte de Puymaigre (Paris, 1867), pp. 266–9.

[68] BL, Cotton MS Caligula D IV, fol. 103 (11 [October 1405 according to the context]): "Et de xv jours ensa trois galees d'Espaigne granddement armé […] asques à ii mille de Bourdeux ou ardirent certains bordius et eussent fait grant domaige ou pais se ne feust le navige qui […] fut mise sur la rive par mer et par terre. Et auscuns des dites gualees didrent quilz cuidoyent trover devant Bourdeux le comte d'Armanhac par terre". The count of Armagnac's army probably did not have any siege engines or enough of them for such a siege. The supplying was probably not planned for a long siege.

[69] Ibid.: "avons pris souffrance avec le dit comte d'Armanhac".

[70] Ibid.: "Et a le roy frances envoyé [… ses sénéchaux de] Thoulouse, de Quersi et de Biguorre son au pais des Landes ou font grant guerre. […] on de leurs chasteaux et autres biens et que par force et défaulte de ayde et secours il se facent d'autre obéissance" and *Pet. Ch. Périgueux*, p. 331.

[71] G. Daumet, *Étude sur l'alliance de la France et de la Castille au XIVe et XVe siècle* (Paris, 1898), no. 53, p. 210 (letter of Olivier de Mauny to Enrique III, king of Castile, Paris, 25 August 1405). Aire-sur-l'Adour, ch.-l. c., arr. Mont-de-Marsan, dép. Landes.

[72] Jean Tarde in his *Chroniques*, ed. G. de Gérard (Paris, 1887), p. 153 (1405 n.st.) and la Martinière, "Les guerres anglaises," p. 85. Bourdeilles, c. Brantôme, arr. Périgueux, dép. Dordogne and Montignac, ch.-l. c., arr. Sarlat-la-Canéda, dép. Dordogne.

[73] On 26 February according to Tarde, *Chroniques*, p. 154, and on 23 February according to

held this castle, as well as that of Cancon, under the authority of Guilhem-Amaniu de Madaillan, lord of Lesparre.[74] Archambaud, together with his kinsman Bertran d'Abzac and Pey de St-Cirq, held the castle against a siege led from 27 June by Jean de Bonnebaut, seneschal of Rouergue. The count of Clermont obtained before 29 July[75] the surrender of the fortress by paying to the three leaders the sum of six thousand gold crowns and eight silver marks, and installed as captain Pons de Beynac, lord of Beynac and Commarque.[76] Bonnebaut had acted there on behalf of Clermont and had borrowed money from the consuls (town councillors) of Sarlat to buy the release of the castle. But two letters of Bonnebaut to Sarlat written on 28 April 1406 tell us that the consuls of Sarlat wanted to execute him and the hostages he had given because he had not repaid to them the borrowed money.[77]

In August Clermont laid siege to the castle of Badefols, held by its lord, Pey de Gontaut, and obtained its surrender in the next month as well as that of Monsaguel.[78] Despite these setbacks, the Périgourdin leaders of the English party counter-attacked. Ramon de Montaut, lord of Mussidan, took the town of Brantôme by surprise on 12 November with a force of four hundred men.[79] Meanwhile, Archambaud d'Abzac treacherously took the castle of Carlux, a possession of the lord of Pons, with just eighty men on 21 November.[80] Around the same time, Johan de Beaufort, son-in-law of the lord of Mussidan,[81] regained his castle of Limeuil which he had previously lost when he rallied to the "English" in February 1405. He installed an "English" garrison under the command of Perrot Fontan, called the Béarnais, a veteran Gascon *routier* leader active from the 1380s, and

---

la Martinière, "Les guerres anglaises ...," pp. 85–6. Castelnaud-la-Chapelle, c. Domme, arr. Sarlat-la-Canéda, dép. Dordogne. Having often the same lord with Berbiguières (c. St-Cyprien, arr. Sarlat-la-Canéda, dép. Dordogne), Castelnaud was called in the late Middle Ages Castelnaud-de-Berbiguières.

[74] Madaillan took Cancon by night c.1395 and appointed Archambaud d'Abzac as its captain. Maurice Campagne, *Histoire de la Maison de Madaillan* (Bergerac, 1900), pp. 62 and 78. Cancon, ch.-l. c., arr. Villeneuve-sur-Lot, dép. Lot-et-Garonne.

[75] *Reg. Bergerac*, p. 141. On 29 July 1405, the count of Clermont requested the town's councillors of Bergerac to have the reimbursement of the 15,000 francs he expended for the siege of Castelnaud-de-Berbiguières.

[76] Tarde, *Chroniques*, p. 154, n. 2. According to a receipt Clermont paid on 28 October 1405 662 *livres* and 10 sous to the two Abzac and St-Cirq. The 1405 expeditions of Clermont had cost 100,000 *livres* (see BNF, MS fr. 20692, p. 178).

[77] "Lettres missives adressées aux consuls et à l'évêque de Sarlat," ed. G. Lavergne, *Bulletin de la société historique et archéologique du Périgord* 55 (1928), 259–61. Sarlat-la-Canéda, ch.-l. arr., dép. Dordogne.

[78] *Pet. Ch. Guyenne*, p. 64, no. 83; *Pet. Ch. Périgueux*, p. 331; Tarde, *Chroniques*, p. 154 and "Les guerres anglaises ...," p. 86. Badefols-sur-Dordogne, c. Le Buisson-de-Cadouin, arr. Bergerac, dép. Dordogne and Monsaguel, c. Issigeac, arr. Bergerac, dép. Dordogne.

[79] *Pet. Ch. Périgueux*, p. 332; La Martinière, "Les guerres anglaises ...," p. 86, and Léon Dessalles, *Histoire du Périgord*, 3 vols. (Périgueux, 1883–85), 2:399. Brantôme, ch.-l. c., arr. Périgueux, dép. Dordogne.

[80] *Pet. Ch. Périgueux*, p. 332. Carlux, ch.-l. c., arr. Sarlat-la-Canéda, dép. Dordogne.

[81] He was married to Margarida de Montaut, a daughter of Ramon de Montaut, lord of Mussidan. See Père Anselme, *Histoire généalogique et chronologique de la Maison royale de France*, 3rd ed., 9 vols. (Paris, 1726–33), 6:322

provided two hundred of them with clothing.[82] In the meantime Johan de Beaufort took refuge with his cousin Ramon de Beaufort, vicomte of Turenne.

A request of Guilhem-Amaniu de Madaillan, lord of Lesparre, before the seneschal of Guyenne Galhart de Durfort and the king's council of Bordeaux (24 September 1405) sheds some light on the border regions situated between the core of the Anglo-Gascon duchy and the predominantly French area.[83] Madaillan was also lord of Rauzan, Pujols, Blasimon and Cancon. All save the last named were situated in the diocese of Bazas, near the border of the small region called Entre-Deux-Mers which was almost entirely "English," and they served as a barbican protecting it.[84] Madaillan explained that the nobles and the people of these places requested that he bring them some help against the "enemies" (*enemixs*) – that is, the French – or to be able to accept a *sufferta* (truce, *soufferte* in French) proposed by them which would last until Pentecost (31 May) 1406. If they accepted it they could not attack the French, but they were able to "arm themselves" before the agreement and serve the king of England with Madaillan or some other people. The lord of Lesparre probably expected that the seneschal and the council would agree with the payment of the *sufferta* to the French, but their answer was in fact to the contrary. They replied that it was not necessary that Madaillan should take this *sufferta* and pay money to the French because these latter could then damage the Entre-Deux-Mers region and its inhabitants. Furthermore, if he took French money it would be a very bad example to all of the lords less important than him. Finally, they asserted that winter was now close and it was a season when nobody could lay sieges as they could in summer. The seneschal proposed to Madaillan that he would send ten, fifteen or twenty men-at-arms and come in person to do his best to help them. Disappointed by this reply, Madaillan retorted that he had enough men-at-arms to hold these places for the king.

The third French offensive (1406–1407)

Overview

Much happened in Périgord in 1406. First, an important French mobilization was undertaken to obtain the surrender of Brantôme (February to May), the 'English' partisan Archambaud d'Abzac took the castle of Commarque by surprise

---

[82] *Pet. Ch. Périgueux*, pp. 330–32; La Martinière, "Les guerres anglaises …," pp. 85–6, and Émile Labroue, *Le Livre de vie* (Bordeaux-Paris, 1891), pp. 219–20. Johan de Beaufort went to Bordeaux in February 1405 and allied with the seneschal of Guyenne, then he returned there with his father-in-law and allied again with the "English" on 6 December 1405. Limeuil, c. St-Alvaire, arr. Bergerac, dép. Dordogne.

[83] Archives départementales du Gers, I 2068, no.10866.

[84] Ibid: "ditz locs son barbacana deu pais dentre dos mas". Rauzan, c. Pujols, arr. Libourne, dép. Gironde; Pujols, ch.l. c., arr. Libourne, dép. Gironde; Blasimon, c. Sauveterre-de-Guyenne, arr. Langon, dép. Gironde and Cancon, ch.-l. c., arr. Villeneuve-sur-Lot, dép. Lot-et-Garonne. The Entre-Deux-Mers is the historical region which was situated between the Rivers Garonne and Dordogne within the diocese of Bordeaux.

Map 3: The Third French Offensive (1406–1407)

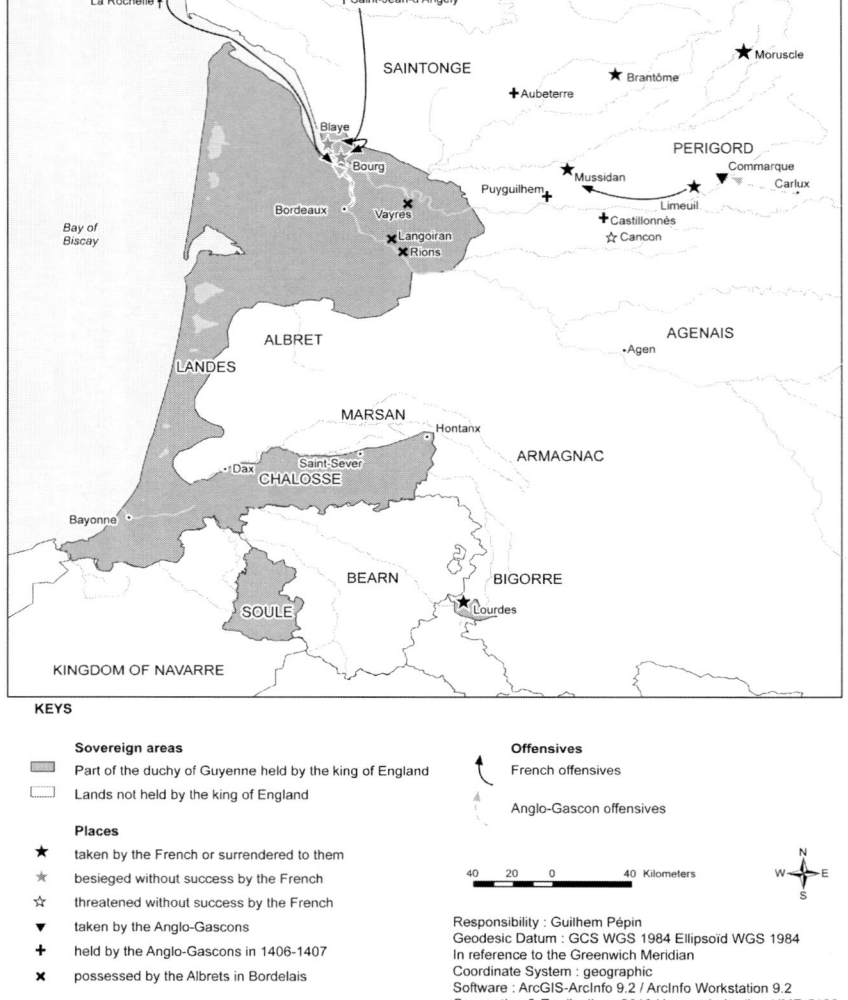

but was taken prisoner in a skirmish with some French lords, the lord of Limeuil and the *routier* leader Ramonet de Sort were forced to rally the French camp in July, and finally the constable of Albret obtained in the same month the surrender of the town of Mussidan from his cousin Margarida d'Albret, the recent widow of Ramon de Montaut, lord of Mussidan and Blaye. However, the main French offensive of this year was led by the duke of Orléans himself against Blaye and, above all, Bourg (October 1406 to February 1407). His efforts failed because of bad weather and a strong resistance led by the commune of Bordeaux. Despite this setback, the close siege of the castle of Lourdes laid from December 1405 continued and the French finally gained its surrender in October 1407.

The siege of Brantôme by the French (February to May 1406)

The local lords of the French party tried to retake the town of Brantôme and laid siege to it. On 23 February 1406, with sixteen of the valets of the lord of Bourdeilles led by a man called Campredon, they took the abbey of Brantôme situated outside of the town on the other side of the river Dronne.[85] Its abbot, Peire III de Puy-Astier, was killed in the process.[86] Soon, the lords of la Rochefoucaud, of Mareuil, of Pérussen and of Pierrebuffière, with some others, as well as four hundred men-at-arms, joined them and started to besiege the town. They were confronted, according to the Monk of St-Denis, with a fierce resistance by the English and Gascons despite the blockade they had organized and the projectiles they continually threw on the town.[87] Eight days later they were joined by the seneschals of Poitou and Saintonge with six hundred men-at-arms and two hundred crossbowmen. Seeing that they were overwhelmed by the French, the Anglo-Gascon troops agreed between 4 and 10 April to surrender Brantôme unless they were strong enough for a planned *journée* set to take place at Pentecost (31 May) or the day after (1 June).[88] According to the Monk of St-Denis there were rumours of the coming of the prince of Wales (future Henry V) to rescue the besieged men, but nothing materialized, and it seems that the other Anglo-Gascon garrisons had neither the means nor the will to help Brantôme. However, the Monk of St-Denis and Juvénal des Ursins assert that a small Anglo-Gascon army came to fight the besiegers and that it was finally defeated by the French who lifted the siege in

---

[85] The town of Brantôme is surrounded by the river Dronne. A *taille* was levied in Saintonge "pour le fait de Brantosme" as explained in the registers of the commune of St-Jean-d'Angely (22 March 1406, n.st.), *Archives historiques de la Saintonge et de l'Aunis*, XXVI, Registres de l'échevinage de St-Jean-d'Angély, II (Paris and Saintes, 1897), p. 146.

[86] *Gallia Christiana*, 13 vols., ed. D. de Ste-Marthe (Paris, 1715–85), vol. 2, col. 1493, no. XXII. It is written there that he had been killed in 1405 during the attack of the French against the abbey occupied by the English. But it is 1405 old style, as the New Year began in Aquitaine on 25 March (day of the Annunciation). According to the *Pet. Ch. Périgueux*, p. 332, the abbot of Brantôme had been killed when the lord of Mussidan took the town on 12 November 1405.

[87] This strong resistance is confirmed by the archbishop of Bordeaux in his letter to Henry IV written on 11 April 1406. See *Registres de la Jurade. Délibérations de 1406 à 1409*, Archives municipales de Bordeaux (Bordeaux, 1873), p. 87: "ne pourtant ilz se sont pourtez tant vaillentment comme gens du monde puissent faire".

[88] *Pet. Ch. Périgueux*, p. 333; *Histoire du Périgord* II, p. 403, n. 1, "Les guerres anglaises …," p. 86–7, *St-Denys*, vol. 3, Livre XXVI, p. 366–9 and 406–15; *Jurade*, 1406, p. 87: "le lieu de Brandome, lequel a este gran temps a assiege, a fayt convenances de soy rendre le jour de Pentecoste, se alors voustre partie n'est plus forte," and *Journal de Nicolas de Baye, greffier du parlement de Paris, 1400–1417*, ed. A. Tuetey, 2 vols. (Paris, 1885), 1:157, the knight Foulques d'Acre was summoned before the Parlement on 21 May 1406 to "assure" Master Oudart Correl, but he went in Parlement on 18 May "car il faloit ledit chevalier partir sur heure et chevaucher nuit et jour pour estre à la besoigne et bataille de Brantosne".

order to fight them.[89] In fact, this troop of two hundred men led by Archambaud d'Abzac had not wanted to help Brantôme but to take Uzerche by surprise.[90] In the event, the men under Abzac were attacked themselves by surprise around the end of May by some nobles of Limousin and Auvergne led by the Auvergnat lords Pons de Langeac and Johan de Randon.[91] Abzac was taken prisoner with fifty of his men while forty others were killed during the fight.[92] If we accept the accounts of St-Denis and Ursins, Perrot the Béarnais was also there and it was the withdrawal of his men that decided the day for the French.[93] Abzac was thereafter forced to accept the surrender of the fortresses he had recently seized (Carlux and Commarque) against sums of money.

This skirmish is not to be confused with the fight that had to take place next to Brantôme to decide the fate of this place. That was scheduled for 31 May or 1 June and the French made all efforts to win the day. Many important French leaders came to this *journée*, including the constable of France, the counts of Clermont, of Alençon, La Marche, Vendôme, and perhaps even the Dauphin as duke of Guyenne, together with three hundred knights and squires. There was no English army to confront them, so the men of Brantôme evacuated the place *vie et bague sauve* according to what was agreed, and thereafter the French demolished the town walls to avoid any future fortification against them.[94] The cost of this siege and other local military actions had to be borne by the local population. A *fouage* was accepted for this purpose on 14 March 1406 by the Three Estates of Périgord.[95] The Anglo-Gascon leaders feared that a seizure of Brantôme would lead to a direct attack on Bordeaux and its region, so they sent the lord of Lesparre, Guilhem-Amaniu de Madaillan, to Henry IV in April to request help. There he met Guilhem Peytabin, who had been sent to England as ambassador by the city of Bordeaux in November 1404,[96] and was still there in January 1407.[97]

The guerrilla warfare of the Anglo-Gascon "irregulars" in Périgord (April–July 1406)

Meanwhile, the guerrilla warfare waged by the Anglo-Gascon "irregulars" continued in Périgord. On the night of 23 April 1406 Archambaud d'Abzac and his men took the strong castle of Commarque, thanks to the treason of the castle's butler, and took prisoner its lord, Pons, lord of Beynac, his wife and children, and

---

[89] *St-Denys*, vol. 3, Livre XXVII, pp. 408–13 and *Ursins*, pp. 439–40.
[90] Uzerche, ch.-l. c., arr. Tulle, dép. Corrèze.
[91] *Pet. Ch. Périgueux*, p. 333.
[92] Tarde, *Chronique*, p. 157, n. 2 (BNF, Périgord, t. I, p. 64). And *Jurade 1406*, p. 89 (on 30 June, the garrison of Carlux had already lost its captain Archambaud d'Abzac).
[93] *St-Denys*, Vol. 3, Livre XXVII, pp. 410–11, *Ursins*, pp. 439–40.
[94] *Pet. Ch. Périgueux*, pp. 332–33, and *Histoire du Périgord* II, p. 403, n. 1.
[95] Thesis, Machet de la Martinière, pièce justificative no. X.
[96] Guilhem Peytabin, burgess of Bordeaux, was in fact forced to stay against his will with Henry IV in England until the latter's death in 1413.
[97] *Jurade*, 1406, p. 154 (26 January 1407). Madaillan returned to Guyenne during this year.

his two brothers.[98] The purpose of this action is not difficult to guess: Beynac had been nominated captain of the castle of Castelnaud-de-Berbiguières when he surrendered this castle to the French the previous year. Abzac would almost certainly seek his revenge or take back by this means his previous castle. On 29 October Pons de Beynac committed himself to pay a ransom of 5,200 gold *francs* for his release.[99] As we have previously seen, Archambaud d'Abzac was taken prisoner by the French in a skirmish around the end of May. He was forced in July to sell the surrender of "his" castles of Carlux and Commarque for twelve thousand or fifteen thousand *francs* in exchange of his freedom and that of one of his men taken prisoner with him.[100] Such a generous agreement was proposed by the French because the garrisons left in these castles would have refused to surrender them without being paid to do so. Albret, the constable of France, wrote at Périgueux on 1 August that the Estates of Périgord had agreed to levy ten thousand *francs* for the release of the two castles and he ordered some local officials to communicate this decision, which they did in making an ordinance on 2 September.[101] Once the garrisons of Carlux and Commarque received the money, they would leave them.[102] The Anglo-Gascon garrison of Moruscle, led by a noble from Quercy, Guiraut de Peyronenc, also negotiated with the French and agreed to leave this castle at Michaelmas.[103]

Johan de Beaufort, lord of Limeuil, was besieged in July in his castle of Limeuil by the constable of France and was forced to submit with all his fortresses to the French before 22 July 1406.[104] Before this, it appears that this lord was closely associated with Archambaud d'Abzac and his garrisons of Carlux and Commarque. For instance, in May he had sent Bertran d'Abzac as his messenger to the Anglo-Gascon's government of Bordeaux.[105] At the beginning of the same month, Ramonet de Sort attempted in vain to take Domme by night but he did

---

[98] Ibid., p. 88 (letter of the archbishop of Bordeaux to Henry IV, 10 May 1406); Tarde, *Chronique*, pp. 155–6, n. 6; *Pet. Ch. Périgueux*, p. 333, and *Histoire du Périgord* II, p. 403, n. 1. Commarque, com. Les Eyzies-de-Tayac-Sireuil, c. St-Cyprien, arr. Sarlat-la-Canéda, dép. Dordogne and Beynac, com. Beynac-et-Cazenac, c. Sarlat-la-Canéda, arr. Sarlat-la-Canéda, dép. Dordogne.
[99] Jean Maubourguet, *Le Périgord Méridional, II 1370–1453* (Paris, 1930), p. 30, n. 3.
[100] *Jurade*, 1406, p. 89 (letter of the archbishop of Bordeaux to Henry IV, 30 June 1406).
[101] Tarde, *Chronique*, p. 155, n. 6 (BNF, Périgord, t. IX, fol. 71). I am grateful to Claude Ribeyrol for photographs of this document.
[102] *Jurade*, 1406, p. 92 (letter of the archbishop of Bordeaux to Henry IV, 22 July 1406).
[103] Moruscle, com. Génis, c. Excideuil, arr. Périgueux, dép. Dordogne. Guiraut de Peyronenc was lord of Loupiac (c. Payrac, arr. Gourdon, dép. Lot).
[104] "Les guerres anglaises …," p. 87 and *Jurade*, 1406, pp. 91 (letter of the archbishop of Bordeaux to Henry IV, 13 July 1406) and 92 (letter of the archbishop of Bordeaux to Henry IV, 22 July 1406). At this date, the lord of Limeuil was besieged by the constable of France and his men and he did not want at this moment to negotiate with the French. The constable had earlier taken another (unknown) castle of the lord of Limeuil where one part of the garrison was killed and the other made prisoner. The lord of Limeuil "turned" English again the following year. For a narrative account of the surrender of Limeuil (to be taken with caution), see *St-Denys*, vol. 2, Livre XXVII, p. 420–23. According to the Monk the siege lasted three days.
[105] *Jurade*, 1406, p. 88 (letter of the archbishop of Bordeaux to Henry IV, 10 May 1406).

succeed in taking some other unnamed places.[106] The vicomte of Turenne, Ramon de Beaufort, in conflict with the inhabitants of Brive, unofficially sent against them Ramonet de Sort and his men. Turenne, though he never officially rallied to the "English" party, exploited such situations for his own purposes.[107] Sort took by treason the neighbouring castle of La Chapelle and settled his men in the vicomte's fortress of Malemort (around April) where they harassed the citizens of Brive.[108] The garrisons of Malemort and la Chapelle were removed in July 1406 by a French troop sent by the constable coming from Limoges. This was composed, according to the Monk of St-Denis, of 360 men, but according to the *Petite Chronique de Périgueux*, of 200 men, who joined the militia of Brive which had already commenced the siege of Malemort in June. This place surrendered on 22 July,[109] but forty "worthless fellows" (*ribaux*), probably from the garrison of la Chapelle, were executed.[110] In June Sort sold Cessac, a place near Cahors that he had seized in the previous March, to the French for 2,500 *francs* because he was allegedly unable to defend it against them.[111] In fact, he probably did this because he had received threats from the count of Armagnac and the lord of Albret that he must become French,[112] as he had been compelled on 26 May to negotiate with the count of Armagnac who besieged him in Parisot and had promised to rally the French party if he was not rescued 15 days after St John's day (9 July).[113] Sort met the constable of France before the 13 July at Montignac,[114] and he rallied to the French, causing his men-at-arms to leave him to join other Anglo-Gascon forces.[115]

---

[106] Tarde, *Chronique*, p. 156, n. 6 (letter of King Charles VI to his seneschal of Périgord, 4 June 1406; BNF, Périgord, t. LII, p. 267), "Les guerres anglaises …," p. 87 and *Jurade*, 1406, p. 88 (letter of the archbishop of Bordeaux to Henry IV, 10 May 1406): "Ramonet de Sort, lequiel a conquiste aucuns lieux desdiz vos ennemis".

[107] *Jurade*, 1406, p. 89 (letter of the archbishop of Bordeaux to Henry IV, 30 June 1406): "mossenhor Ramon de Torena aue metut gens d'armas de nostra part en I. son loc apperat Malamort; losquaus fasen guerre contra aucuns autres ce la part de Franssa, masz non pas per nom d'Anglès expresssament". Brive-la-Gaillarde, ch.-l. arr., dép. Corrèze.

[108] *Pet. Ch. Périgueux*, p. 333. Malemort-sur-Corrèze, ch.-l. c., arr. Brive-la-Gaillarde, dép. Corrèze; la Chapelle-aux-Brocs, c. Malemort-sur-Corrèze, arr. Brive-la-Gaillarde, dép. Corrèze and Turenne, c. Meyssac, arr. Brive-la-Gaillarde, dép. Corrèze.

[109] AN, T 193/43, agreement of the town of Brive with Bernat de Montagnac and Ramon de Beissac, captains of Malemort. On the war between Brive and the vicomte of Turenne, see Henri Delsol, *Le consulat de Brive-la-Gaillarde* (Brive, 1936), pp. 160–67.

[110] "Les guerres anglaises …," pp. 85–6 and for their removal *St-Denys*, vol. 3, Livre XXVII, pp. 416–20; *Pet. Ch. Périgueux*, p. 334.

[111] *Jurade*, 1406, p. 89 (letter of the archbishop of Bordeaux to Henry IV, 30 June 1406). This place is not mentioned there, but see Guillaume Lacoste, *Histoire générale de la province de Quercy*, 4 vols. (Cahors, 1883–86), 3:330. It had been taken by the "English" in 1403 but was probably lost thereafter and taken back by Sort in March 1406 (see *Pet. Ch. Périgueux*, p. 333). Cessac, com. Douelle, arr. Cahors, ch.-l. dép. Lot; Cahors, ch.-l. dép. Lot.

[112] *Jurade*, 1406, p. 90 (letter of the archbishop of Bordeaux to Henry IV, 30 June 1406).

[113] Thèse *Bernard VII*, p. 119 (BNF, Doat 211, fol. 50). Parisot, com. Villeréal, ch.-l. c., arr. Villeneuve-sur-Lot, dép. Lot-et-Garonne.

[114] *Jurade*, 1406, p. 91 (letter of the archbishop of Bordeaux to Henry IV, 13 July 1406). Montignac, ch.-l. c., arr. Sarlat-la-Canéda, dép. Dordogne.

[115] Ibid., p. 92 (letter of the archbishop of Bordeaux to Henry IV, 22 July 1406): "chescun repourte

Around the same time the place of Cancon was besieged by the troops of the count of Armagnac or else was about to be besieged by them.[116]

The seizure of Mussidan by the constable (July 1406)

The town of Mussidan was also threatened by the French armies following the death of its lord Ramon de Montaut at Blaye on 6 July 1406.[117] His wife Margarida d'Albret, a cousin of the lord of Albret who was called "aunt" by him,[118] left Blaye during his illness to go to Mussidan and started to negotiate with his cousin, the constable of France, to prevent Mussidan being attacked by him.[119] It was reported at Bergerac on 20 July that the constable had already laid siege to Mussidan.[120] According to the archbishop of Bordeaux the constable put pressure on his cousin Margarida to marry her daughter, Mariota de Montaut, the heiress of Ramon de Montaut, to his younger brother Lois, lord of Langoiran.[121] Such a marriage was, for the constable, a way to obtain for the French the town of Mussidan, and possibly also the town of Blaye, without the trouble of a siege. According to the Monk of St-Denis the French threatened the inhabitants of Mussidan with the destruction of their cornfields and their vineyards, situated outside the town. Margarida's councillors would have advised her to deal with her son-in-law Jean de Harpedenne, seneschal of Saintonge.[122] This latter acted as a negotiator while the main negotiator was none other than the constable himself. According to the same chronicler, Margarida d'Albret was able to negotiate to leave the town with sixty men-at-arms and to live elsewhere under the authority of the king of England, and keep for life the issues of Mussidan. Following this evacuation the French took possession of the town and its castle, installing their

---

que Ramonet de Sord est accorde avec lesdiz Franceoys; mais en quelle manere, je ne say; et, en senhal de cecy, toutes ses gens d'armes se partent de ly, et vont ailleurs en vostre service". Ramonet de Sort rallied again to the English party the following year.

[116] Ibid., p. 91 (letter of the archbishop of Bordeaux to Henry IV, 13 July 1406). Cancon remained "English" as it was included on the "English" side in the truce made between Galhart de Durfort, seneschal of the Landes and the lord of Albret (22 April 1407). In AHG, VI, no.LXXXVII, p. 217.

[117] *Jurade*, 1406, p. 90 (letter of the archbishop of Bordeaux to Henry IV, 13 July 1406).

[118] She was the youngest daughter of Bérart I, lord of Vayres (d. 1346) and she married Ramon de Montaut in 1365. I thank Jean-Bernard Marquette for this information. For a genealogical tree of this branch of the Albret family with its links with the elder branch (but without mention of Margarida), see the genealogical tree of the Albret family in *Le Trésor des Chartes d'albret. I, Les archives de Vayres, le fonds de Langoiran*, ed. J.-B. Marquette (Paris, 1973).

[119] *Jurade*, 1406, p. 91 (letter of the archbishop of Bordeaux to Henry IV, 13 July 1406).

[120] *Reg. Bergerac*, p. 149. The French captain of Grignols (c. St-Astier, arr. Périgueux, dép. Dordogne) had sent to the constable for this siege 100 "workers" (*cent homes de manobra*), probably for siege works such as the digging of mines and the building of siege engines.

[121] *Jurade*, 1406, p. 92 (letter of the archbishop of Bordeaux to Henry IV, 22 July 1406). This scheme went to nothing.

[122] *St-Denys*, vol. 3, Livre XXVII, pp. 424–5, and *Ursins*, p. 443 (Ursins does not name her son-in-law). Harpedenne had married her daughter Johana de Montaut in May 1404.

own garrison.[123] In reality, the constable granted to Margarida, in exchange for Mussidan, the custodianship of the castle and lordship of Vayres owned by his mother, Marguerite de Bourbon. Margarida was to have the usufruct of Vayres provided that she did not fight against the French party, lived there only with her servants and dealt with the Anglo-Gascon authorities to obtain letters of non-prejudice against Vayres.[124] This was a means of compensating Margarida for the loss of Mussidan and its issues and to protect an Albret possession from the Anglo-Gascons. According to the *Petite Chronique de Périgueux*, the siege of Mussidan – in fact no more than a blockade – lasted only eight days.[125]

The duke of Orléans' failed great expedition against Blaye and Bourg (October 1406–February 1407)

The most important French military offensive of this year was yet to come. It was led by the duke of Orléans himself, the mastermind behind the previous offensives, and was planned to be coupled with another offensive led by the duke of Burgundy, John the Fearless, against Calais, but this never materialized.[126] Apparently, the main goal of Orléans was to take Bordeaux by first capturing some major towns situated around it. Before his arrival, several contradictory rumours circulated in the Anglo-Gascon camp, surely fuelled by the French to cause confusion regarding their real objectives.[127] The campaign of the duke of Orléans in Guyenne has already been described in some narrative secondary works,[128] but these are far from complete and there is the need for a detailed study fully utilizing the rich material in the registers of the Jurade of Bordeaux. Unfortunately, such a study would exceed the aims of this work, so we will outline here only the main events of this expedition.

On 16 September 1406 Orléans left Paris to go to the duchy of Guyenne alongside the counts of Clermont and Alençon, the constable of Albret and the admiral of France.[129] Orléans arrived at St-Jean-d'Angély on 9 October. From there he addressed a letter to the inhabitants of Libourne in which he ordered them to submit to Charles VI and reject the rule of the usurper "Henry of Lancaster."[130] Thereafter, his army laid siege to Blaye on 21 October, the duke arriving himself

[123] Ibid.
[124] *Jurade*, 1406, pp. 10–12. Letters sent to Margarida d'Albret by Charles I, lord of Albret and constable of France, p. 10 (Périgueux, 31 July 1406), and by Lois d'Albret, lord of Langoiran (Périgueux, 31 July 1406), pp. 10–11. Agreement accepted by Margarida d'Albret, pp. 11–12.
[125] *Pet. Ch. Périgueux*, p. 334.
[126] Schnerb, B., "Un projet d'expédition contre Calais (1406)," in *Les champs relationnels en Europe du Nord et du Nord-Ouest des origines à la fin du Premier Empire*, ed. S. Curveiller (Calais, 1994), pp. 179–92.
[127] *Jurade*, 1406, see pp. 40–41, 43–6, 48, 51, 53–4, 56–7, 61, 63, 66, 95, 99 and 105.
[128] Wylie, *Henry the Fourth*, 3, 1407–10, pp. 77–84; Henry Ribadieu, *Histoire de la conquête de la Guyenne par les Français* (Bordeaux, 1866), pp. 87–103, and (though unfootnoted), J.L. Kirby, "The siege of Bourg, 1406," *History Today* 18 (1968), pp. 57–60.
[129] *Calendar of the Close Rolls [CCR], Henry IV, vol. III, 1405–09* (London, 1931), p. 222.
[130] *Jurade*, 1406, p. 110, 15 October.

two days later. This town was situated at a strategic place on the Gironde estuary and constituted one of Bordeaux's key outposts. It had also been chosen because of its weak political situation: its lord Ramon de Montaut had died on 6 July and left only a daughter, Mariota or Maria de Montaut, as heir, and it was supposed that it could be easier to obtain its surrender.[131] But, in the face of such danger, Bordeaux mobilized and strongly supported the town. The seneschal of Guyenne Galhart de Durfort even came there to advise on the defence of the town and to bolster the town's resistance led by Bernat de Lesparre, lord of Labarde, and Johanot de Grailly, the bastard son of the famous captal de Buch Johan III de Grailly.[132] Negotiations between the besieged and the French soon led to an agreement whereby Mariota de Montaut agreed to be married to Archambaud de Foix, one of the sons of the count of Foix (29 October),[133] Johanot de Grailly keeping in the meantime the town for this count and the garrison of Blaye committing itself to not attack the French. According to Monstrelet, there was also a clause by which Mariota agreed to surrender the town to Orléans if he took the neighbouring town of Bourg, but no evidence survives to substantiate such an assertion.[134] On 31 October or 1 November Orléans' army moved on to besiege – this time more seriously – the nearby town of Bourg, defended by Bertran III, lord of Montferrand, one of the most important barons of Bordelais, its castellan Guilhotin de Lansac and the *routier* Peyroat Dupuch, together with 120 men-at-arms and 80 crossbowmen.[135] Bourg occupied a significant strategic point overhanging the river Dordogne and dominating the confluence of this river with the Garonne called Bec d'Ambès. Ownership of this town would deliver complete control over all the river and sea traffic of the northern part of the Anglo-Gascon duchy.

The besieging army was the most important ever brought together by the French during the years 1404–1407, though it is difficult to know its real size. The *Petite Chronique de Guyenne* gives us a figure of fifteen thousand fighters, the *Petite Chronique de Périgueux* gives twenty thousand men, Thomas Walsingham gives no fewer than fifty thousand men, while the Monk of St-Denis and Monstrelet put forward the most reasonable figures of five thousand men-at-arms and six thousand

---

[131] Wylie and Kirby committed an error in asserting that "Auger de Montaut," lord of Blaye and Mussidan, died and left Mariota, his daughter, as heir. In fact, Auger de Montaut was the father of Ramon de Montaut and died in 1359!

[132] Blaye, ch.-l. arr., dép. Gironde; Labarde, c. Castelnau-de-Médoc, arr. Bordeaux, dép. Gironde.

[133] *Jurade*, 1406, pp. 122–4. Archambaud de Foix, future lord of Navailles and third son of the count of Foix, but Mariota de Montaut finally married in 1408 the Navarrese lord Johan de Gramont, lord of Gramont (com. Bergouey-Viellenave, c. Bidache, arr. Bayonne, dép. Pyrénées-Atlantiques).

[134] *Monstrelet*, 1:133.

[135] *St-Denys*, vol. 3, livre XXVII, pp. 453–4, gives 31 October and the *Pet. Ch. Guyenne*, p. 64, no. 85, 1 November. The *Pet. Ch. Périgueux* asserts (p. 336) that the constable went before Bourg on 30 November with 1,000 men-at-arms and the duke of Orléans arrived the day after (31 November) with all his army. Bourg, ch.-l. c., arr. Blaye, dép. Gironde; St-Louis-de-Montferrand, c. Lormont, arr. Bordeaux, dép. Gironde (often known as "Bourg-sur-Gironde" even if Bourg is in fact overhanging the river Dordogne). On the size of Bourg's garrison, see *Pet. Ch. Périgueux*, p. 336.

men-at-arms and archers respectively.[136] Apart from those who left Paris with Orléans, there were several French officials and local lords present at this siege, among them the count of Armagnac and the vicomte of Castellbò, the elder son of the count of Foix.[137] Artillery was deployed and heavily used, mines were made, and Orléans regularly launched assault after assault against the town.[138]

The period of the year when this offensive took place was very unusual. Apparently, many councillors of the French government advised Orléans to wait for a more suitable season (Spring 1407) to launch a major offensive against Anglo-Gascon Aquitaine. The Monk of St-Denis and Juvénal des Ursins provide in their narratives the contrasting pictures of the old seasoned knights advising Orléans to go into winter quarters, whereas his young headstrong friends are eager for an immediate attack to demonstrate their bravery on the battlefield.[139] This picture is probably accurate, but it is possible that Orléans wanted to take the Anglo-Gascons by surprise and attack them when they expected it least. Furthermore, the sending of support by sea from England was far more difficult during winter, so Orléans could feel more confident in dealing with just the Gascons left to their own resources. If so, it was in theory a cunning calculation, but it did not take into account the weather. This winter was particularly wet, cold and windy, and the French camp soon became a form of bog. Because of the rain, the snow and, sometimes, the hail, the men were knee-deep in mud both inside and outside their tents, the foodstuffs began to rot and dysentery killed many.[140] Victuals had to be brought to the camp by sea from La Rochelle, whereas Bourg was well supplied by boats sent from Bordeaux and resisted very well the French assaults despite its old-fashioned thirteenth-century walls (repaired in the fourteenth century).[141]

---

[136] *Pet. Ch. Guyenne*, p. 64, no. 85; *Pet. Ch. Périgueux*, p. 336; *The Chronica Maiora of Thomas Walsingham, 1376–1422*, ed. J. Clark, trans. D. Preest (Woodbridge, 2005), p. 348, *St-Denys*, vol. 3, Livre XXVII, pp. 452–3 and *Monstrelet*, 1:133. It seems that the accurate figure of 5,000 men has been distorted by both the author of the *Petite Chronique de Guyenne* and Walsingham.

[137] Many historians have written, following the *Pet. Ch. Guyenne*, p. 64, no. 85, that the count of Foix Archambaud de Grailly, great-great-uncle of Johanot de Grailly, was with the French among the besiegers. It is an error. Only his son Johan de Foix, vicomte of Castellbò, was there. For a more reliable list of officials and lords present at this siege, see *Jurade*, 1406, p. 162. The count of Armagnac had left the siege of Blaye before 31 November and did not go to the siege of Bourg as he was sick in his town of Rodez (*Pet. Ch. Périgueux*, p. 336).

[138] *St-Denys*, pp. 452–3; Walsingham, *Chronica*, p. 348, and "Chronique ou journal du siège de Blaye et de Bourg," AHG, III, no. LXXII, p. 180: "on meto lo ceti et enginghs gros et feren minas".

[139] *St-Denys*, vol. 3, Livre XXVII, pp. 452–3, and *Ursins*, p. 443.

[140] *St-Denys*, vol. 3, Livre XXVII, pp. 456–7, and Walsingham, *Chronica*, p. 348. Walsingham asserted that 6,000 men died "of various illnesses but especially of dysentery". As the army was probably composed of 5,000 men, figure transformed by Walsingham into 50,000, it is likely that "only" 600 men died during this siege (12% of the total).

[141] Valérian Sanchez, "Histoire des fortifications de Bourg-sur-Gironde: le renouveau aux XIIIe et XIVe siècles," *Les petites villes du Sud-Ouest de l'Antiquité à la Révolution. Colloque d'Aiguillon des 12 et 13 mai 2000*, *Revue de l'Agenais* (2004), 89–95.

During this siege there was a general mobilization at Bordeaux in order to rescue Bourg.[142] As a French fleet tried to blockade this town, Bordeaux planned its own naval expedition, requisitioning all the ships and mariners present at its port. On 23 December the Bordelais fleet, led by Bernat de Lesparre, lord of Labarde, and reinforced by English and Bayonnais ships then at Bordeaux, met a French fleet downstream of Bourg at St-Julien in Médoc.[143] According to the Monk of St-Denis, Ursins and Monstrelet, the Bordelais fleet engaged with a fleet coming from La Rochelle with supplies. The duke of Orléans had sent three hundred men downstream to meet the Rochelais' fleet led by Clignet de Brabant, admiral of France, and brought the supplies to his camp. It would have been when they went together toward Bourg that they met the Bordelais fleet. A tough fight ensued during two hours in the fog and a Bordelais ship was taken by the French and kept by them all night. The following day the fight resumed in front of Bourg and the Bordelais threw at the French fleet a burning old ship filled with pitch and resin, causing turmoil and permitting them to regain the lost ship, to burn one of the French ones and to seize another with its crew. The Bordelais took 367 French prisoners while losing only 32 of their own side to the French. This Anglo-Gascon victory, delivering "English" supremacy in the estuary and a continuity of supply to Bourg, almost certainly impacted on the already low morale of the besiegers. Furthermore, it seems probable that the duke of Orléans was failing to obtain from the king's council the one hundred thousand *francs* per month he demanded for his troops.[144] Nevertheless, it was only on 14 January 1407 at dawn that Orléans lifted the siege to return to "France," to "the great dishonour of him and of all the kingdom of France" as wrote a Bordelais scribe.[145] This failure was felt throughout the kingdom of France and Orléans was blamed for having levied a heavy *taille* for this fruitless expedition.[146] The duke of Burgundy, hardly irreproachable for his aborted expedition against Calais, was most keen to orchestrate the blame on Orléans.

---

[142] See Wylie, *Henry the Fourth*, 3:80–81, and *Histoire de la conquête*, pp. 98–9.

[143] St-Julien-Beychevelle, c. Pauillac, arr. Lesparre-Médoc, dép. Gironde. The French fleet was composed of 18 ships for the Monk of St-Denis, 22 for Monstrelet and 30 for Walsingham (for this latter the Bordelais fleet was 20 ships strong). It is possible that the Rochelais fleet amounted to 18 ships and was later reinforced either at the French port of Royan or Talmont-sur-Gironde by 4 ships coming from Bourg with 300 men. According to the "Chronique ou journal du siège," p. 180, the battle took place at St-Julien of Médoc while the other sources place this battle in front of Bourg. As on 19 December a part of the Bordelais fleet was sent to Castillon in Médoc (com. St-Julien-Beychevelle, in *Jurade*, 1406, p. 145), the other being sent to the Bec d'Ambès, it appears that the Bordelais fleet intercepted this fleet on 23 December in front of St-Julien. The following day, the French fleet succeeded in arriving at Bourg but was attacked there with success by the Bordelais fleet.

[144] *Baye*, pp. 182–3.

[145] *Livre des Bouillons*, Archives municipales de Bordeaux (Bordeaux, 1867), p. 558: "d'aqui en foras s'en anet daban Borc, e aqui estet d'aqui en jeney; d'ont se levet a gran deshonor de siu et de tot lo reyaume de Franssa".

[146] According to Pierre Cochon the duke of Orléans had 800,000 *livres* from this taille on which he would have given only 120,000 to his troops present at Bourg. *Chronique normande de Pierre Cochon*, ed. Ch. de Robillard de Beaurepaire (Rouen, 1870), p. 218.

The siege of Lourdes (December 1405–October 1407)[147]

Since the early 1370s the Anglo-Gascon garrison of Lourdes, led by Johan de Béarn, had been a thorn in the side of the French party as its pillage expeditions and its *patis* spread all over "French" Gascony up to Toulouse.[148] Consequently, the French resolved to get rid of this nuisance that weakened their authority. From Tuesday 22 December 1405 it seems that the French built several bastides or bastilles (temporary fortresses) around the town and castle of Lourdes.[149] Jean de Berry, the king of France's lieutenant in Languedoc and Guyenne, wrote that it had been decided in February 1406 to levy a fouage of 15*s*. by hearth in the seneschalcy of Toulouse to pay the men-at-arms and the crossbowmen keeping the bastides recently made around the town and castle of Lourdes.[150] On 22 July, the archbishop of Bordeaux explained to the English king that four men of the town of Lourdes had come to the city on behalf of the men of Lourdes and described to the seneschal of Guyenne and others how Lourdes suffered from a lack of supplies because of the French bastides surrounding them. If the people did not receive help they had decided to leave the town, but unfortunately, as underlined by the archbishop, it was not possible to send victuals without sending a significant force.[151] Johan de Béarn the younger, constable of the castle of Lourdes and son of its captain, then absent, was sent after 22 October by the garrison to explain its bad situation before Henry IV. As far as we know his pleadings were useless, and the French finally seized the town and immediately blockaded the totally impregnable castle. They were reinforced in January 1407 by some men coming from the siege of Bourg, led by Robert de Châlus, seneschal of Carcassonne.[152] Together with Roger d'Espagne, seneschal of Toulouse, Châlus blockaded the castle and was himself accommodated in the town house of Johan de Béarn, which had been partly destroyed by the French siege engines. But despite the destruction caused to the castle by these men, two French commissaries sent on 31 May by Charles VI to Lourdes noticed that though the castle was highly damaged by these siege engines and the guns it would still not be possible to take it by storm because it was built on a high and strong rock. So, as they were not sure of the success of the blockade because the garrison had enough victuals to hold it until Easter (15 April) 1408

---

[147] This section owes a lot to François Couderc, who kindly gave me his unpublished works on these events.

[148] The "Mémoire contre les Collèges de boursiers" (before 1408) of Toulouse describes the bad situation of Toulousain partly caused by the "garrison of the English of Lourdes". Archives municipales de Toulouse FF 24, fol. 19, extract transcribed in Philippe Wolff, *Commerces et marchands de Toulouse (v. 1350–v. 1450)* (Paris, 1954), pp. 61–2, n. 190.

[149] *Royal and Historical Letters during the reign of Henry the Fourth*, ed. F.C. Hingeston, vol. II, 1405–13 (London, 1860), no. CCLXVII, pp. 346–7 (BL, Ms. Cotton Caligula D. IV, fol. 109), letter of Johan de Béarn the younger, lieutenant of his father and constable of Lourdes written together with the members of the garrison on 22 October 1406. Tuesday before Christmas 1405 was 22 December.

[150] HGL, 10, col. 1928–9 (26 April 1406).

[151] *Jurade*, 1406, pp. 92–3.

[152] *St-Denys*, vol. 3, livre XXVII, pp. 460–63, and *Ursins*, pp. 443–4. The town was "French" at least from February 1407 (AN, JJ 162/182 fols. 141v–142v, letter of King Charles VI).

and there were rumours of the arrival in Aquitaine of a rescue army led by "the son of the king of England," they decided to buy its surrender. On 8 August 1407 the commissaries entrusted a king's councillor and the treasurer of the seneschalcy of Carcassonne to split an imposition of one hundred and thirty-five thousand *l. tournois* on the three seneschalcies of Languedoc (Toulouse, Carcassonne and Beaucaire). This money would be used to buy the castle of Lourdes as well as the nearby lordship of les Angles, to pay the troops surrounding the castle of Lourdes, and to break the *patis* agreed with the "English."[153] Whatever the difficulties, it seems that the garrison of Lourdes succeeded in obtaining some supplies. For example, the city of Bordeaux decided in June to send one cask of wine to help the Lourdes' garrison and to levy a tax on all the casks of wines in part to rescue the same garrison.[154] The French besiegers perhaps over-estimated the extent of supplies kept in the castle. Pey Garlin, a member of the castle's garrison, wrote to Johan de Béarn on 13 September that the castle could resist only three weeks more as they had only two casks of hydromel left that were too musty to be drunk, and one small cask of bad water.[155]

The captain of the castle, Johan de Béarn senior, had been absent from Lourdes since the beginning of its siege and had entrusted the garrison to his son, Johan de Béarn the younger, who was constable of the castle of Lourdes. Johan senior was busy with his other interests outside Lourdes: he was also lord of Hontanx in the Landes and had possessions in Bordeaux and its environs through his late wife Assalhida d'Arsac.[156] Besides, he had successfully petitioned the king in 1405 to become a burgess of Bordeaux – a privileged status normally refused to noble men – because he owned several houses and heritages in this town and had claimed he wanted to stay there for his entire life.[157] The main decisions concerning the castle of Lourdes were therefore taken by Johan de Béarn the younger,[158] who, on 31 July 1407, consented to leave the castle following an agreement which had to be drafted by King Charles III of Navarre and the vicomte of Castellbò, chosen here as arbitrators. The first was the brother-in-law of Johan de Béarn who married in 1397 his bastard half-sister Juana de Navarre and was his suzerain for the barony of Béhorléguy granted to him in 1393, while the second was kinsman of Johan de Béarn and son-in-law of King Charles III of Navarre.[159] The

---

[153] Charles Portal, "Levée d'un subside dans le diocèse d'Albi en 1407 pour le rachat du château de Lourdes," *Annales du Midi* 3 (1891), 71–2.
[154] *Jurade*, 1406, p. 196 (4 June) and p. 205 (24 June).
[155] Ibid., p. 264.
[156] TNA, SC 8/232/11586. Hontanx, c. Villeneuve-de-Marsan, arr. Mont-de-Marsan, dép. Landes. Arsac, c. Castelnau-de-Médoc, arr. Bordeaux, dép. Gironde.
[157] TNA, E 28/20, no. 53 (Reply of the king on 22 April 1405: E 28/20, no. 52 and C 61/110, m. 3).
[158] All the acts concerning the rendering of the castle of Lourdes to the French are copied in AN, J 302/123.
[159] José Ramón Castro, *Carlos III el noble, rey de Navarra* (Pamplona, 1967), p. 395 (Johan de Béarn married in 1397 with Juana de Navarre, daughter of King Charles II of Navarre and Catalina de Esparza), pp. 420–21 (25 May 1393, grant of the lordship of Béhorléguy to Johan de Béarn with the rank of barony), and p. 251 (November 1401: Johan de Foix, vicomte of Castellbò, married Juana de Navarra, apparent heiress of King Charles III). Johan de Béarn was chamberlain of

latter kinsman delegated the decision to two proxies (11 August) and Castellbò, a devoted French partisan who had participated in the siege,[160] did the same (22 September). On 12 October it was decided by these delegates to set the price of the castle's evacuation at 32,500 gold crowns. Eleven thousand crowns had to be paid promptly, with a deadline of 16 October, and the remaining 21,500 crowns had to be delivered in two instalments in Pamplona, where twelve "French" hostages had to be sent. When the first payment was made and the hostage arrived at Pamplona the castle of Lourdes was to be rendered to the French, who were then led by the veteran French knight Gaucher de Passat and the seneschals Châlus and Espagne. This was clearly done, though we do not know the exact date of the surrender of the castle.

Curiously enough, although Johan de Béarn had been negotiating with the duke of Berry via proxies since June 1407 the sale of his lordship of les Angles to the king of France, which took place on 4/5 October for 5,200 gold *francs*,[161] and although he was surely well aware of the negotiations concerning the castle of Lourdes, he officially disagreed with its sale by his son Johan de Béarn the younger. We might suspect that he wanted to prevent the Anglo-Gascon authorities from believing he had agreed to surrender the castle of Lourdes for money, but it is possible that he did not want its surrender because he truly believed the place could be saved. Before 17 September he had met with the Three Estates of the seneschalcy of the Landes gathered at Sorde to request some help for his castle. He also ordered his men at Lourdes not to accept money from the French until he returned to Bordeaux, whence he would alert them to the day that they would be rescued by a relief troop.[162] On 26 October Johan de Béarn had a hearing before the jurats of Bordeaux and the seneschal of Guyenne. It was finally decided that the city would send to Lourdes fifty men-at-arms at its own cost, these men being introduced to Johan de Béarn on 27 October.[163] We do not know if these men went to Lourdes or not. The surrender of his castle probably occurred around this time despite his efforts.

* * *

All of these military operations in Guyenne were part of a massive plan directed by the French monarchy against the crown of England, and all the fronts

King Charles III in 1412–14 and probably died in 1417. Béhorléguy, c. St-Jean-Pied-de-Port, arr. Bayonne, dép. Pyrénées-Atlantiques.

[160] Hélène Biu, "Du panégyrique à l'histoire: l'archiviste Michel du Bernis, chroniqueur des comtes de Foix," *Bibliothèque de l'École des Chartes* 160 (2002), 149, no. 133.

[161] AN, J 302/125⁶. Johan de Béarn nominated his two proxies on 22 July and confirmed them on 22 August. The sale took place on 4 October and was ratified at the gate of the castle of Lourdes by Johan de Béarn the younger on 5 October. The inhabitants of les Angles made an oath to the king of France the same day.

[162] *Jurade*, 1406, p. 264 (letter of Pey Garlin to Johan de Béarn, castle of Lourdes, 13 September 1407), and p. 265–6 (reply of Johan de Béarn, Hontanx, 19 September). Sorde-l'Abbaye, c. Peyrehorade, arr. Dax, dép. Landes.

[163] Ibid., pp. 263–6.

were more or less interconnected. The Anglo-Gascon leaders were aware of this fact, as is shown by a letter of the archbishop of Bordeaux to Henry IV written on 11 April 1406 in which he congratulated the king for the victory of his son in Wales (probably the seizure of Anglesey the previous January) and asserted that he had organized a general procession in Bordeaux to celebrate it.[164] It is further testimony that the Anglo-Gascon duchy of Guyenne genuinely felt itself to be an integral part of the larger polity that included the kingdom of England. This feeling of belonging was regularly re-asserted by receiving the oath of the king-duke's subjects, particularly in periods of crisis such as that in Bordeaux in October 1406.[165]

The human factor

The building of a full chronology of these eventful years has not allowed much focus on the men who were behind the Anglo-Gascon resistance to the French offensives. We have already seen that, as expected, regular communication was maintained between the leading actors of the Anglo-Gascon party in Guyenne and Henry IV. As usual in such circumstances, the king sent letters of support with more or less vague promises of help[166] and his correspondents insistently requested from him serious military and financial assistance. Save for exceptions such as the sending in 1405 of Thomas Swynbourne, nominated as mayor of Bordeaux, with forty-eight men-at-arms and one hundred archers,[167] it seems that the duchy had to rely on its own forces to resist and repel the French offensives of 1404–6. During these years of war English support mainly consisted in the sending of corn to supply the main towns of the duchy, a significant gesture as many areas of the Anglo-Gascon duchy were devastated and the trade in grain and foodstuffs coming from the "rebel land" (the part of Guyenne under French rule) was severely disturbed if not wholly interrupted.[168] It is certain that food shortages or even a famine would have weakened, if not destroyed, all capability of resistance on the part of the Anglo-Gascon duchy. On 17 May 1405 Henry IV learned from the envoys of St-Sever that grain was very expensive in Guyenne and that

---

[164] Ibid., p. 87. For the English expedition to Anglesey, see Robert Rees Davies, *Owain Glyndŵr* (Oxford, 1995), p. 123.

[165] *Jurade*, 1406, pp. 80–83. This oath has to be compared with the oath of the consuls (town councillors) and inhabitants of Bergerac to Charles V on 1 May 1379 while the town already submitted to him in 1377, *Reg. Bergerac*, p. 52.

[166] An example of this kind of letter is the standard letter of support written on 5 November 1404 by Henry IV to his subjects of the duchy of Aquitaine (TNA, E 28/15/40).

[167] TNA, E 101/44/8; Vale, *English Gascony*, pp. 50–51.

[168] See *CCR, Henry IV, vol. II, 1402–1405* (London, 1905), p. 325, licence granted to two Gascons to buy grains and take them to Bayonne as the rebels of Armagnac, Albret, Béarn, Poitou and Brittany have prevented any victuals being brought to the city (6 December 1403). For wheat and victuals sent to Bordeaux see *CCR, 1402–1405*, p. 243 (26 December 1403), p. 263 (5 March 1404), p. 461 (25 June 1405), and *CCR, Henry IV, vol. III, 1405–1409* (London, 1931), p. 42 (6 May 1406). Several references in TNA, C 61/109, C 61/110 and C 61/111.

the shortage of wheat and other victuals made the town particularly vulnerable in case of a French siege. Consequently the king ordered without delay a delivery of two hundred tuns of wheat to the squire Johan Dufau, provost of St-Sever, who was then in England.[169] In July 1405 the king entrusted five hundred marks to Dufau to be used in St-Sever according to local needs.[170]

Despite these difficulties and French pressure, it seems that the loyalty of the inhabitants of the core of the Anglo-Gascon domain towards the king of England, duke of Guyenne, is as noteworthy as it had been in previous periods. We know, for example, that the town of Libourne lent victuals and other materials up to the value of one thousand *francs* to the garrison of the nearby royal castle of Fronsac during the duke of Orléans' offensive of 1406 in order to avoid its surrender, which would have increased the threat to their own town.[171] Regular mentions of rebels in documents show that opinion was not unanimous, although we generally do not know the circumstances of these "rebellions." As far as we can tell, a similar phenomenon existed on the French side. We can assume that on many occasions these "rebels" were simply local inhabitants who owned several properties in different places and who, because of the changing boundaries of allegiance, had a part of their possessions in a different political camp. It is possible they were forced to give up *de facto* the least important part of their patrimony, or the least significant in the context of their social network, staying in their main place of residence with the majority of their goods. Similarly, the inhabitants of a place who submitted to an allegiance and who swore an oath of fidelity to this allegiance were faced with a difficult choice when the other "party" seized their place. These explanations may not be applicable in all cases but could represent a majority of them. Logically, the seized goods of these "rebels" permitted the king to reward his faithful subjects and compensate their losses, and the latter did not hesitate to request such goods or some money allocated to substitute for them, as did in 1405 the Basque squire Anchot d'Espelette, who requested an annual 20 *l.* of the money of England on the goods of rebels in Bordeaux.[172] Similarly, in the same year the squire Ysarn de Rouffignac petitioned to have all the goods of an inhabitant of Floirac who was rebel during his lifetime, and the squire Guiraut de Tartas requested an annual 15 l. sterling of England allocated on the goods of rebels living in St-Macaire and La Réole.[173]

---

[169] TNA, E 28/22/24.
[170] TNA, E 28/14/15. See Vale, *English Gascony*, pp. 51–2.
[171] TNA, SC 8/187/9342. Libourne, ch.-l. arr., dép. Gironde and Fronsac, arr. Libourne, dép. Gironde.
[172] TNA, E 28/20/45 (reply of the king: 21 April 1405, TNA, C 61/110, m.5). *Proceedings and Ordinances of the Privy Council of England*, 4 vols., ed. H. Nicolas (London, 1834–35), 1:254.
[173] TNA, C 81/625/4296, E 28/14/262 and *Proceedings and Ordinances*, 1:254, for Rouffignac (reply of the king: 21 April 1405, TNA, C 61/110, m.4) and E 28/14/263 for Tartas (reply of the king: 21 April 1405, TNA, C 61/110, m.5). Floirac, arr. Bordeaux, dép. Gironde; St-Macaire, arr. Langon, dép. Gironde; La Réole, arr. Langon, dép. Gironde. St-Macaire and la Réole have been "French" since their conquest in 1378 by the duke of Anjou. These Gascons requested to be paid in English money that was then more stable than the local currency. The requested goods

However, it is difficult to explain all political choices as based on material matters even if they were evidently very important to an individual. It is extremely difficult to know the exact motivations behind the expressions of personal opinions, all the more so since these opinions were rarely expressed in a hostile environment. We also know about an extremely rare case of denunciation of seditious talk expressed by a citizen of Bordeaux. In 1404, when the lord of Lesparre was governor of Bordeaux, Johan Bolomere, tailor and burgess of Bordeaux, accused Bertran Usana, merchant and burgess of the same city, of seditious talk before Lesparre and the constable of Bordeaux.[174] Apparently the conflict went back to the first year of the reign of Henry IV between Christmas 1399 and March 1400. According to the narrative of Bolomere, which he gave in his petition to this king, he met Bertran Usana in the "*rue Poitevine*," a street situated just next to the castle of the Ombrière, the administrative centre of Anglo-Gascon Aquitaine, where Usana said: "Master Johan Bolomer, I want to talk to you about a great and marvellous thing, forsooth," and Bolomere replied "I agree with that, so talk to me about what you want to talk." Usana carried on, saying "Truly the English are bad people offending a great deal; lately they were in Margaux and Macau where they cut the trees with their fruits, taking them into their ships. Know you, Bolomere, that we have to leave their lordship." Bolomere asserted that he replied in this manner: 'Saint Mary! Sir, this thing cannot be done as the town [of Bordeaux] has been always in the past so loyal to the Crown of England and still will be by the grace of God from now on; and how could the poor ploughmen and the subjects of the king [of England] our lord live when they would not be able to sell their wines nor have goods from England as it is customary?" Usana retorted: "Leave that, Bolomere, we will live well without them because we will prune half of our vineyards and yield there the double." "Sir," said Bolomere, "do not tell me anything more on this matter as I would prefer to keep quiet than agree to your opinion." Usana allegedly replied, "You will accept it, whether you like it or not, or otherwise you will leave the town, you and all the others who will not accept it." Bolomere came to a conclusion with these words, "I do not want to hear and talk anymore on this matter: I have to make my poor buttons." In his petition, Bolomere asked to prove his case "with God and Saint George's help" by having a duel with Usana. This duel took place before the king and the constable and marshal of England in Nottingham on 12 August 1407.[175]

It is very difficult to say whether such incidents were isolated or common. Certainly, the recent deposition of Richard II, born in Bordeaux in 1367 and probably highly estimated there, may partly explain the remarks of Usana. Furthermore,

---

were situated within the Anglo-Gascon controlled part of the duchy and not in St-Macaire and La Réole.

[174] TNA, C 61/111, m. 10 (8 May 1406).
[175] TNA, C 61/112, m.14 (20 June 1408). Text printed in *Foedera*, viii, pp. 538–40 and, with some misreading, by J.-J. Champollion-Figeac, *Lettres de rois, reines et autres personnages des cours de France et d'Angleterre*, 2 vols. (Paris, 1847), vol. 2, no. CCXXXII, pp. 444–7. Margaux, c. Castelnau-de-Médoc, arr. Bordeaux, dép. Gironde and Macau, c. Blanquefort, arr. Bordeaux, dép. Gironde.

the cohabitation of English and Gascons was not always an easy one. As might expected with people of such different cultures and languages, there was often tension for one reason or another. In July 1406 the archbishop of Bordeaux reported to Henry IV that the Gascons of St-Émilion and Libourne asserted, when thinking about the neighbouring English garrison of the castle of Fronsac, that "the English are brave people in strongholds, but are not inclined to make war, because they are committed with luxury to their pleasures and they do not bear hardships."[176] Another example, in 1407, is the conflict that arose between Guilhem-Amanieu de Madaillan, lord of Lesparre, and the mayor of Bordeaux, Thomas Swynbourne. Swynbourne had a dispute with the lord of Castillon, and Madaillan sided with Castillon against him. The jurats of Bordeaux supported their mayor and decided that if Madaillan came to the gate of the town with his retinue they would refuse his admission if his men did not leave their weapons at the entrance. Madaillan, who had recently been governor of the city, was deeply hurt by this decision and wrote: "I would never have thought that you would want to exclude me from your company because of an Englishman."[177]

Even if some Gascons had mood swings against Englishmen, it never seriously endangered the king-duke's support. Several examples of this surprising (at least for us) loyalty include the words of Galhart de Durfort, seneschal of Guyenne, reported on 29 October 1406 to the jurats of Bordeaux by Naudot, his messenger. The seneschal was then in Blaye besieged by the duke of Orléans. He asserted there that "if he was taken in this place [by the French], the country was lost, notwithstanding he was a man of little importance, and consequently they would receive no honor nor profit from France; they would not be held in esteem, not endowed nor honoured and they would be always oppressed and in great subjection."[178] This statement followed the comments of the count of Armagnac, who was one of the besiegers, to one of Durfort's squires, in which he expressed his surprise to learn that such an important person was present in person in Blaye to defend the town. It seems that Durfort's statement was not mere rhetoric and that he was genuinely extremely committed to defending the Anglo-Gascon cause. It is not surprising that the archbishop of Bordeaux criticized the recklessness of someone in such a position. Indeed, in June 1406 Durfort had fought a troop of Bretons and Armagnacais of forty-five *lances*, thirty of them being "armed," with only twelve men badly armed![179]

---

[176] *Jurade*, 1406, p. 92 (letter of the archbishop of Bordeaux to Henry IV, 22 July 1406): "et disent clerement que les Anglois sont vaillentz gens en les places, mais enclus ne guerez; pour ce qu'ilz voulent fort deliciosament a leur plaisir, et ne pas soustenir leur desayze".

[177] Ibid., p. 267 (letter of Madaillan to the jurats of Bordeaux, 25 December 1407): "et no cutabi pas que per I Anglès me bolgossatz ayssi gitar foras de bos autres".

[178] Ibid., p. 124: "Et disso lodeit Naudot que ed se fet declarar a mossenhor lo senescaut lasdeitas paraulas; loquau disso que lodeit compte ac dise, per so que, si ed era pres deudeit loc, lo pais sere prengut, jassia que ed fos I. petit home; et que d'aqui en auant edz no auren de la partida de Franssa aucuna honor ny proffeyt, ny no seratz presatz, doptatz ny ondratz, antz seren de tot jorn opremutz et en gran subjeccion".

[179] *Jurade*, 1406, p. 90 (letter of the archbishop of Bordeaux to Henry IV, 30 June 1406).

Historians often tend to summarize the motives of the actors of this period in terms of strict self-interest and search for material advantages. Though these motives obviously existed at this time, as from time immemorial, it is a rather simplistic and quite negative view of the motives of the Anglo-Gascons. Feelings of honour, fidelity and commitment to a sovereign, a lord or a "party," whether English or French, existed, as is shown by several unambiguous testimonies. They were mixed, to a greater or lesser degree according to each individual, with more pragmatic goals.

The key role of the Anglo-Gascon *routiers*

We have seen that some Gascon *routier* leaders were very active in the events taking place during this period. This had been the case since the end of the principality of Aquitaine in the early 1370s. In the absence of massive financial and military support from England the Anglo-Gascon government had to rely a great deal on irregular troops outside the core of the part of the duchy still held by the "English" party.[180] It has been stressed that the main motive of the *routiers* in supporting the "English" party was the receipt of the *patis* levied on the countryside situated around the fortress they occupied.[181] According to a French account, the *patis* levied by the "English" garrisons in Limousin and North Périgord amounted to thirty-six thousand *livres* by year.[182] We can mention also the example of Peyroat Dupuch in Chalais, which seems clear on this point.[183] However, as we noted above, we should be cautious about these seemingly unequivocal explanations. It has been rightly said about men-at-arms of this period that "these men may have felt powerful ties of loyalty to authorities within and outside their company; they may have considered themselves knights worthy of the romances of chivalry, forever in search of a just quarrel."[184] Peyroat Dupuch continued to serve the Anglo-Gascon cause, being among those who led the successful defence of Bourg against the duke of Orléans' army. Dupuch's network of spies in Saintonge provided significant information to the Anglo-Gascons on the movements of the French armies.[185] However, he seems to have rallied to the French in 1408,

---

[180] See Sumption, *Divided Houses*, pp. 679–722 (chapter XIV. The Gascon March, 1381–1393).
[181] On the *patis* and *souffertes* see P. Contamine, "Lever l'impôt en terre de guerre: rançons, appatis, souffrances de guerre dans la France des XIVe et XVe siècles," in *L'impôt au Moyen Age. L'impôt public et le prélèvement fiscal fin XIIe – début XVIe siècle. I Le droit d'imposer*, colloque tenu à Bercy les 14, 15 et 16 juin 2000 (Paris, 2002), pp. 11–39, and M. Keen, *The Laws of War in the Late Middle Ages* (London and Toronto, 1965), pp. 251–3.
[182] BNF, Bourgogne 21, fol. 34v (accounts of Jean Chousat). Mentioned in Christopher J. Philpotts, "English Policy towards France during the truces, 1389–1417" (unpublished Ph.D. thesis, University of Liverpool, 1984), p. 322, n. 1. I thank Christopher Allmand and Chris Ford for lending me this thesis.
[183] Vale, *English Gascony*, p. 47, for all the details on Peyroat Dupuch and Chalais between 1401 and 1405.
[184] Neil A.R. Wright, "The *Tree of Battles* of Honoré Bouvet and the Laws of War," in *War, Literature and Politics in the Late Middle Ages*, ed. C.T. Allmand (Liverpool, 1976), p. 19.
[185] *Jurade*, 1406, pp. 93–4 (letter of Peyroat Dupuch to the mayor of Bordeaux, Bourg, 9 October

for unknown reasons.[186] One of his men, named Huguet or Hugues Brouard, a Poitevin who probably stayed on the "English" side from the 1370s, had lost his hereditary possessions, the issues and profits he had in Chalais, but he obtained in compensation from the seneschal of Guyenne the *patis* and ransom of Aubeterre and later, from the king, twenty *livres* from the customs levied in Libourne on the wines coming from the French-dominated area.[187] Obviously, the king and the Anglo-Gascon authorities felt committed to compensate Brouard from his losses, as Chalais was officially a place acknowledging the authority of the king-duke, even if it was not under a "regular" government.

With the prospect of the loss of *patis* if they lost their fortresses, the *routier* leaders had to find a way to continue to make a living from the war. In November 1406 Archambaud d'Abzac still styled himself as captain of Carlux even though he had previously agreed to surrender this castle to the French. Nevertheless, the date of completion of this agreement must have been close as Abzac proposed to the commune of Bordeaux to hire out, if the city required it, fifty men-at-arms, forty armed valets and twenty crossbowmen. He asked the rate of the wages that the commune was ready to pay for each kind of fighter and the total sum they were prepared to offer. Finally, he requested the right to take hostages given by the lord of Commarque, to keep them in Bordeaux, and to be able to free them at will. The desire for profit was an essential motive behind this proposal, but we should not forget that it would have been possible for Abzac to make the same proposal to the French, to be employed by them against the "English." Again, personal connections within the Anglo-Gascon community and a feeling of fidelity towards this "party" may have played its part. In addition, familial links between men fighting for the king-duke could have reinforced the strength of the Anglo-Gascons. We know, for instance, that one of the main military leaders of the Anglo-Gascons, Bernat de Lesparre, lord of Labarde, was married to Catalina de Sort, sister of the famous *routier* captain Ramonet de Sort, lord of Moncuq, and that he regularly kept in close contact with him.[188] Johana de Barbazan, his sister-in-law, wife of Ramonet, even went in pilgrimage to Soulac in 1406, met Labarde on this occasion and talked with him on the current politico-military situation.

The question of allegiance: the ambiguous role of the count of Foix

The testimonies coming from the predominantly "French" areas of Guyenne show that the Anglo-Gascon *routiers* were seen as a disruptive element, a severe

---

1406), and p. 184.

[186] AN, JJ 162, no. 371, fol. 274v. See Samaran, *La Gascogne*, no. 1082, p. 126 (letters of remission of Charles VI to Peyroat Dupuch, captain of a company, and to some others who had held the English party during the wars). As for Ramonet de Sort in 1406, it is likely he had been forced to rally the French.

[187] TNA, C 61/111, m. 11 (21 February 1406) and m. 8 (30 June 1406). Aubeterre-sur-Dronne, ch.-l. c., arr. Angoulême, dép. Charente.

[188] *Jurade*, 1406, p. 66 and AHG, XXIV, no. CI, p. 292.

nuisance to trade and circulation in the area, as well as a hindrance to farming. There are no doubt elements of truth in the assertions of the Monk of St-Denis that local populations requested that the French authorities send military expeditions against the *routiers*, even if there is a lack of direct archival evidence to support that view and there was occasionally some propaganda in the Monk's writings.[189] Many local lords of the French party had ties with their counterparts in the English allegiance but that did not imply they were easily prone to "turning English." In April 1406 the archbishop of Bordeaux reported that the Gascons of the English party believed that the count of Armagnac, who obtained from the French the conquests he made in 1405, would conquer fewer places in the future than the "French of France" because he had a lot of acquaintances and friendships in the region.[190] Yet, despite considering the partisans of the "English party" and himself and his men as being part of the same "nation of Gascony," this linguistic and cultural feeling did not supersede the count's political and military choices.[191] However, there existed, despite everything, a certain amount of support for the "English party" in the "French" regions, as is demonstrated by the case of Peire Gaillard, an inhabitant of Nanthiat in the vicomté of Limoges who was bold enough to cry "Guyenne! Saint George!" at the passing of the vicomte's men who were of the French party (1408), despite the fact that all the Anglo-Gascon garrisons had been removed from the area in 1404.[192]

During these years, the count of Foix Archambaud de Grailly was the Gascon lord who played the most ambiguous role. To be fair, his situation was not an easy one: he had been the main lord supporting the Anglo-Gascon side until 1401, when he succeeded in obtaining his wife's Foix-Béarn heritage. Since then, he had given pledges to the king of France in order to secure this succession. As noted earlier, he rendered the castle of Bouteville to the French in 1401 but tried in the

---

[189] *St-Denys*, vol. 3, Livre XXV, pp. 200–203 (the least credible testimony: the Gascons from Bordelais and even from Bordeaux would have asked the French to deliver them of the English they hated. They would have wanted to submit to the French in the interests of their trade), p. 202–5 (request of the inhabitants of Limousin against the garrison of Courbefy, 1404), pp. 206–9 (the count of Clermont stood in Limousin during the winter 1404 at the request of the inhabitants), Livre XXVI, pp. 274–5 (request of the local inhabitants against the garrison of Mortagne-sur-Gironde, 1404–05), and pp. 366–7 (request of the local inhabitants against the garrison of Brantôme, 1405–06).

[190] *Jurade*, 1406, pp. 87–8. The populations of what is now southern France designated "France" the country roughly situated north of the river Loire and most of the time it was not only the Île-de-France region, this name being rarely used to name the entire kingdom. These populations, at least those acknowledging the king of France's authority, considered themselves as "French" politically because of their allegiance to the king of France, but they did not consider themselves as French in an ethno-linguistic sense.

[191] *Jurade*, 1414, p. 183, letter of Bernat VII of Armagnac to the seneschal of Guyenne Galhart de Durfort, 14 June 1415.

[192] See Guilhem Pépin, "Les cris de guerre 'Guyenne!' and 'Saint Georges!'. L'expression d'une identité politique du duché d'Aquitaine anglo-gascon," *Le Moyen Âge* 112 (2006), 274, n. 64. Hélias de Coudures, sergeant of the vicomte of Limoges, accused Galhart of this crime before the assizes of the vicomté held at Excideuil on 3 December 1408 (Archives départementales des Pyrénées-Atlantiques, E 637, fol. 3). Nanthiat, c. Lanouaille, arr. Nontron, dép. Dordogne.

meantime to maintain a good official relationship with the Anglo-Gascon authorities. This attitude was evidently a means whereby he might keep his possessions in the Anglo-Gascon area, but we should not totally dismiss his attachment to the "English" party, as he fought for it for around forty years. It appears that from 1401 onwards he did not return to Bordeaux, where he possessed the lordship and castle of Puy-Paulin, but dealt with his domains there through proxies.[193] His awkward position between France and England, with a preference for the former because of his important Foix-Béarn domains, surely explains why he did not feel at ease with coming back to meet local authorities who no doubt viewed him with great suspicion. Even so, both Henry IV and the local Anglo-Gascon authorities always dealt with him carefully, continuing to give the impression that they considered him as a member of the "English" party because he was still a vassal of the king of England for his Anglo-Gascon possessions. In a letter written to him on 22 July 1405, Henry IV asserted that Johan Dufau, provost of St-Sever, had reported that his elder son, Johan de Foix, vicomte of Castellbò, fought with the French against his will.[194] On 1 November 1406 the messenger of the town of Bordeaux explained to the jurats of Bordeaux orally on behalf of the count – because the latter feared that the French could read a written message – that he would keep his places for the king of England.[195] In the same message, he gave information on the number of troops his elder son had taken to the duke of Orléans for the siege of Blaye.[196] If the position of his elder son was well known, it was not yet the same case for Gaston de Foix, lord of Grilly.[197] As lord of Lesparre, he was already wondering in 1404 if his entrance to Bordeaux would be accepted if he expressed a wish to go there,[198] and the jurats of Bordeaux still sent messengers to him in 1406 to enquire after his intentions and whether he was ready to help them.[199] Henry IV and the jurats of Bordeaux were not fooled by the count's declarations, but they wanted to prevent him and his second son from providing more troops and help to the French party than had his first son. The jurats of Bordeaux were not at all

---

[193] *Jurade*, 1406, p. 70 (letter of the count of Foix Archambaud to the mayor and jurats of Bordeaux, 22 September 1406): "per relacion de auguns nostres officers, part d'aquera qui nos en an escriut". When in December 1406, Archambaud went to his town of Cadillac (ch.-l. c., arr. Langon, dép. Gironde), he underlined that nobody had to be surprised of his coming there as it was one of his possessions (*Jurade*, 1406, p. 146, 21 December 1406). This remark indicates that he probably did not come to this town for a long period.

[194] TNA, E 28/14/14.

[195] *Jurade*, 1406, p. 127: "que de son locs, a son poder, res de la part du rey d'Anglaterra". Reply to the message of the jurats of Bordeaux sent on 19 October 1406 to the count through Alphonso, the town's trumpet (ibid., p. 98–9).

[196] The vicomte of Castellbò brought 400 "basinets" to the duke of Orléans.

[197] Grilly, c. Gex, arr. Gex, dép. Ain. Graily became a traditional spelling of the family of its lords or issued from these lords.

[198] See TNA, SC 1/51/69. Gaston was then at Cadillac.

[199] *Jurade*, 1406, p. 95 (15 October 1406), and p. 130 (4 November 1406), where the letter had been corrected and was on its way to be sent to Gaston de Foix. Gaston de Foix will be a staunch supporter of the Anglo-Gascon cause since he became captal de Buch, vicomte of Bénauges and Castillon in 1411. He even died in exile in Aragon c.1455 because he did not want to submit to King Charles VII of France.

reassured by the rumours in October 1406 that the duke of Orléans' army was welcomed in all the fortresses of the count of Foix.[200] Consequently, in December 1406, they ordered that no person who had come to Cadillac with the count of Foix could enter their city without examination by the mayor and the jurats.[201] The same decision was taken regarding Johanot de Grailly, the leader of the garrison of Blaye, who was viewed with great suspicion in Bordeaux following the treaty made with the duke of Orléans where Blaye was "neutralized" and Mariota de Montaut had to marry a son of his great-great uncle, the count of Foix.[202]

Conclusion

The failure of the great expedition of the duke of Orléans against Blaye and Bourg was a severe blow to the will of the French to organize and send costly military expeditions to conquer Anglo-Gascon Guyenne. It had shown that methods which were successful against isolated castles and garrisons did not imply inevitable successes against the core of the Anglo-Gascon duchy. That said, it did not mean that the French gave up all hope of conquering places in the English allegiance, as is demonstrated by the siege of Lourdes. The financial capabilities of the French far exceeded those of the Anglo-Gascons, who were then barely supported by Henry IV. Yet the only French military operation of any scale in Guyenne in 1407 was the siege of Lourdes, which had been dragging on since late 1405. Certainly, the final blow to this aggressive French policy against "English" Guyenne was the killing of the duke of Orléans by the men of the duke of Burgundy (23 November 1407). Thereafter, the kingdom of France became too absorbed by the civil war which broke out between the Orleanists–Armagnacs and the Burgundians to put the fate of Anglo-Gascon Guyenne in serious jeopardy in the immediate future.

The lack of support from Henry IV was very much resented by those inhabitants of Guyenne faithful to England.[203] In this context, therefore, the relatively efficient resistance of Anglo-Gascon Guyenne to the French is noteworthy. Was this a result of a lack of interest from Henry IV towards Guyenne? We can argue that the priorities for the king's attention and money were the Welsh revolt of Glyndŵr and any possible revolt in England, while the funds allocated to the king by the English parliament were probably not large enough to mount a serious rescue mission for the duchy. Within these limitations, it seems that during the whole period the king tried to prolong the truce made with France in 1396 despite the clear acts of war made against the duchy of Guyenne and the threats against

---

[200] *Jurade*, 1406, pp. 98–9 (19 October 1406).
[201] Ibid., p. 145 (19 December 1406).
[202] Ibid., p. 147 (22 December 1406). The funeral of Johanot de Grailly, recently deceased, took place in Bordeaux on 6 April 1407 (ibid., p. 173).
[203] BNF, MS Fr. 25708, p. 581. Document mentioned in Thesis Machet de la Martinière, p. 213, n. 3, and *Lettres de rois II*, no. CLXXVI, pp. 321 (letter written to Henry IV from Bordeaux, 18 October 1406).

Calais. The decline of the great French offensives against the Anglo-Gascon duchy meant that local truces were being made even before the death of Orléans, such as those with the count of Armagnac,[204] the lord of Albret,[205] the lord of Pons[206] and other local lords of the French party. In addition, Henry IV negotiated general truces with the French. Despite these agreements, however, a state of guerrilla warfare existed in Périgord even into the 1440s.

For the years 1404–1407 British and French historiography has focused almost exclusively on Calais and on the threats presented by the French to this town; the fate of Guyenne appeared to be peripheral and, in the end, not so important. But a detailed study can show us that even military events highly localized in Guyenne were in fact an essential part of the Anglo-French war at the beginning of the fifteenth century. After all, Calais was never really attacked during these years, whereas the Anglo-Gascon duchy bore the brunt of several important French offensives. As explained earlier, this frontier region was under the influence of the duke of Orléans, who tried to obtain the upper hand in the French government by means of military successes against the English in Guyenne. This policy eventually failed with the expedition he led in person in 1406–1407, but it had been exploited as an essential tool in his power struggle with Duke John of Burgundy. Henry IV, for his part, assumed the title of "king of France" without making any real effort to obtain this throne. In reality, he was more interested in implementing the treaty of Brétigny-Calais, which gave an enlarged Guyenne or Aquitaine in full sovereignty. This is proved by the agreement he made with the Orléans–Armagnac party in 1412. It was his son who changed the direction of English policy away from Guyenne.

---

[204] *Jurade*, 1406, pp. 188–9: the lord of Labarde is sent by the seneschal of Guyenne to the count of Armagnac to deal with him a "general *souffrance*" (*suffrensa generau*), 17 May 1407.

[205] AHG, VI, no. LXXXVII, p. 219 (22 April 1407, truce made with the lord of Albret) and *Jurade*, 1406, p. 263 (19 October 1407).

[206] *Jurade*, 1406, p. 188 (negotiations with the lord of Pons for a *souffrance* requested by him, 14 May 1407. This truce was submitted to the final arbitration of Orléans).

The King's Welshmen: Welsh Involvement in the Expeditionary Army of 1415[1]

Adam Chapman

The "myth"

The victory of the English at Agincourt is still frequently attributed in the popular consciousness to Welsh bowmen in their knitted Monmouth caps. The battle is undoubtedly part of a wider patriotic narrative in both England and Wales. The belief in the English victory being a result of Welsh efforts, though ubiquitous, is almost impossible to reference in a way that might satisfy the editor of an academic journal. A possible origin may lie in Shakespeare's *Henry V* (1599). The garrulous captain Fluellen reminds the king not of the number or importance of Welshmen in *his* army, however, but in that of his great-uncle, Edward the Black Prince, at Crécy.[2] Contemporary accounts of Agincourt make very little mention of Welsh involvement. The Welsh chronicler Adam Usk notes the death of two men, one of them in error, as the first, Sir John Scudamore of Kentchurch, Herefordshire, in fact survived until 1435. The second, Dafydd ap Llywelyn ap Hywel of Brecon, better known as Dafydd or Davy Gam, Usk describes as "David Gam of Brecon." The chronicle of Peter Basset and Christopher Hanson also notes the death of "Davy Gam esquire, Welshman." Although Thomas Walsingham and the Great Chronicle of London also list Gam among the dead, they do not mention his origins or nationality.[3] No chronicle or early history mentions the presence of

---

[1] This paper is based on that given at the Fifteenth Century England Conference held at Aberystwyth in September 2008. I would like to thank Professor Ralph Griffiths, Professor Anne Curry, Professor Adrian Bell and Dr. David Simpkin for their comments on drafts of this paper. I am also grateful to Dr. Dylan Foster Evans for his helpful insights. The majority of the references to muster rolls and letters of protection and attorney are taken from the AHRC-funded database "The Soldier in later Medieval England, 1369–1453," which can be found at www.medievalsoldier.org.

[2] William Shakespeare, *Henry V*, V.vii; K. Buckland, "The Monmouth Cap," *Costume* 13 (1979), 2–16.

[3] *The Chronicle of Adam Usk, 1377–1421*, ed. C. Given-Wilson (Oxford, 1997), pp. 255–6; A. Curry, *The Battle of Agincourt. Sources and Interpretations* (Woodbridge, 2000), pp. 88, 53, 99. For Sir John Scudamore, see Ralph A. Griffiths, *The Principality of Wales in the Later Middle Ages* I: *South Wales, 1277–1536* (Cardiff, 1972), pp. 139–41. Usk's error concerning Scudamore's death is totally inexplicable.

Welsh archers at Agincourt, and nowhere in the extant corpus of fifteenth-century Welsh verse is the battle mentioned.[4]

For much of the six centuries between 1415 and the present Agincourt is the silent battle in Welsh culture. Dafydd Gam seems to be viewed through the prism of Shakespeare, where he is mentioned among the dead presumably because of the playwright's use of Hall and Holinshed. Wylie suggests that Dafydd was also known as "Fluelin," but on what basis is not made clear. Barker, echoing this, goes further, describing him explicitly as "the inspiration for Shakespeare's Fluellen," a link even accepted by the *Oxford Dictionary of National Biography*.[5] Much was made of Gam by the late-sixteenth-century Welsh writer David Powel, who described him as "the great stickler for the house of Lancaster." It is unlikely, however, that Shakespeare knew Powel's work.[6] In the histories of Hall and Holinshed Gam is noted among the battle dead and termed an esquire, but there is no mention of his being Welsh or hailing from Brecon.[7] Gam was undoubtedly a significant figure whose descendents played a role in Welsh society in the fifteenth century, and he will be discussed more fully later in this paper. As we shall see, however, he was far from typical of the Welshmen who actually served in Henry's army in 1415 but who went unnoticed in the chronicles and early histories. The intention of this essay is to address the role of the Welshmen recruited for Henry V's great expeditionary army of 1415 from his Welsh estates and the particular place which they occupied within it. It is not, however, the intention to rake over the role of archers at Agincourt as a whole or the role of the longbow in general, as these topics have been thoroughly addressed elsewhere.[8]

---

[4] I am indebted to Dr. Foster Evans for this observation.

[5] Juliet Barker, *Agincourt: The King, the Campaign, the Battle* (London, 2005), p. 319, citing James Hamilton Wylie and William Templeton Waugh, *The Reign of Henry V: 1413–1422*, 3 vols. (London, 1914–29), 1:188–9. For their source, see *Heraldic Visitations of Wales and Part of the Marches between the years 1586 and 1613 under the authority of Clarencieux and Norroy, two Kings of Arms, by Lewis Dwnn, Deputy Herald at Arms*, ed. Samuel Rush Meyrick, 2 vols. (Llandovery, 1846), 2:56, and *Theophilus Jones, History of Brecknockshire*, ed. G. Davies (Brecon, 1898), pp. 245, 47, 50. T.F. Tout, "Dafydd Gam (*d.* 1415)," rev. R.R. Davies, *Oxford Dictionary of National Biography*, Oxford University Press, 2004; online ed., Jan 2008 [http://www.oxforddnb.com/view/article/10318, accessed 7 January 2011]. More recent study has not addressed the point directly or is explicitly unconcerned with it; for example, Joan Rees, "Shakespeare's Welshmen," in *Literature and Nationalism*, ed. V. Newey and A. Thompson (Liverpool, 1991), pp. 29–30. The essays contained within *Shakespeare and Wales: From the Marches to the Assembly*, ed. Willy Maley and Philip Schwyzer (Farnham, Surrey and Burlington, VT, 2010) are more concerned with the language of the character of Fluellen than his inspiration.

[6] David Powel, *A Historie of Cambria, now called Wales* (1584, repr. Amsterdam, 1969), p. 323.

[7] Curry, *The Battle of Agincourt*, pp. 243, 259. Hall drew on the chronicle of Basset and Hanson and therefore chose to ignore the inclusion of "Welshman" for Gam.

[8] The most recent studies include: *Agincourt 1415. Henry V, Sir Thomas Erpingham and the Triumph of the English Archers*, ed. Anne Curry (Stroud, 2000); Anne Curry, *Agincourt. A New History* (Stroud, 2005); Matthew Strickland and Robert Hardy, *The Great Warbow: from Hastings to the Mary Rose* (Stroud, 2005); Clifford Rogers, "The Battle of Agincourt," in *The Hundred Years War (Part II). Different Vistas*, ed. L.J. Andrew Villalon and Donald J. Kagay

There are four key considerations to address. First, although too broad to be fully discussed here, we need to assess the connections, from a Welsh perspective, between the events of the Glyndŵr rebellion and Henry V's military adventures in France. The second issue concerns the organization of the Welsh contingents recruited from Henry's Welsh estates in 1415, the documents that describe this process, and the motivations of both the authorities and the men concerned. Thirdly, to what extent were these Welshmen important to the 1415 expedition? Finally, what can we make of the subsequent representation of their efforts? Exploration of the reality of Welsh involvement in 1415 has been limited in spite of the large, and generally thorough, historiography of Henry V's adventures in France. H.T. Evans, borrowing heavily from Wylie, reviewed the muster rolls of the Welshmen recruited from the royal demesne in Wales as long ago as 1915, but in light of more recent study of the 1415 campaign and the post-rebellion context of the lands of Wales, a new analysis can, and should, be attempted.[9]

The Welsh inheritance

The burdens of military recruitment from the lands of Wales in 1415 were far from novel. English kings had employed Welshmen in their armies for centuries, but the factors surrounding this campaign were decidedly unusual. The recruitment process played a significant part in the government's response to the end of the Glyndŵr rebellion in the shires and in the March of Wales. While the lands of Wales were more or less at peace by the time of Henry V's accession in 1413, order and governance were far from fully restored. That said, in territorial terms, Henry V's position in the March of Wales was far more significant than that of any earlier English monarch. As king, he retained control of the royal shires in North Wales (Caernarfon, Merioneth and Anglesey), and of South Wales (Cardigan and Carmarthen), which he had held as Prince of Wales. With the lands of the Duchy of Lancaster inherited from his father, Henry dominated southern Wales: in addition to Brecon, one of the largest Marcher lordships, Henry V held the lordships of Monmouth and Three Castles, Hay and Huntington, Ogmore, and Cydweli with Carnwyllion with all their dependent liberties, all of which he incorporated into the royal demesne.

With these estates came significant responsibilities, not least of ensuring that the rebellion, once extinguished, was not re-ignited. It is no surprise that both Henry IV and Henry V made significant efforts not only to ensure that their authority was recognized but also to punish the Welsh communities of both the royal shires and the March for their complicity in the rebellion. The task was accomplished through a combination of judicial action, communal fines and subsidies, and, as

---

(Leiden, 2008), pp. 37–132.
[9] H.T. Evans, *Wales and the Wars of the Roses* (1915, repr. Stroud, 1992), pp. 27–8. See also J.H. Wylie, "Some Notes on the Agincourt Roll," *Transactions of the Royal Historical Society*, 3rd series 5 (1911), 135–6, and the most recent study, Curry, *Agincourt. A New History*, esp. p. 61.

we shall see, unusual military demands. In the March of Wales, some of these actions were exceptional. Communal fines levied by Henry IV in 1413 were arranged directly between the king and the communities of the Marcher liberties. The justification was simple: the revolt was an act of treason against the crown and therefore only the crown could pardon the offenders for their treason. Henry IV levied fines of 180 marks and £50 on the tenants of the Lancaster lordships of Cydweli and Ogmore, and £500 and 500 marks on the Marcher lordships of Glamorgan and Abergavenny immediately before his death. The accession of Henry V in March 1413 brought new and greater demands upon his own lands. By the end of 1414 the new king had raised over £5,000 in collective fines from his Welsh lands, 2,260 marks of which were from the Duchy of Lancaster estates. In part, these fines were part of the usual scheme of marcher government, levied in recognition of the new lord. Their yields compare very favorably with the £1,000 annual revenue which might have been expected from the Principality before the revolt, while only compensating the losses occasioned during that revolt to an extremely limited extent.[10]

The financial burden imposed by the crown was exacerbated by the demands of other Marcher lords. In the earl of Arundel's lordships in north-east Wales, for example, subsidies were granted for the earl's military endeavors in France before 1415 in conjunction with the earl's leadership of the army sent to aid the Burgundians in 1411. These too can be placed in the context of communal re-conciliation with their lord, though such subsidies were not in themselves novel.[11] Other fines were laid upon individual former rebels in return for pardon. The most famous of these individuals was the unrepentant Henry Dwnn, leader of the rebels in the lordship of Cydweli, whose pardon required the payment of a fine of £266 13s. 4d. In the event, nothing was paid by Dwnn and the fine was still being charged upon his grandsons, Gruffudd and Owain, as late as 1439.[12] It is evident from other sources that military service could form part of the process of reconciliation. The well-known correspondence between Gruffudd ap Dafydd ap Gruffydd, Reginald, lord Grey of Ruthin, and the Prince of Wales, now securely dated to 1412, describes the failure of rather covert negotiations involved in one such instance. Here, at the instigation of one of the earl of Arundel's officials, Gruffudd, an unreconciled rebel, had been offered his pardon and offices

---

[10] R.R. Davies, "The Bohun and Lancaster Lordships in Wales in the Fourteenth and Early Fifteenth Centuries" (unpublished D.Phil thesis, University of Oxford, 1966), pp. 310–11; E. Powell, *Kingship, Law and Society: Criminal Justice in the Reign of Henry V* (Oxford, 1989), p. 198; see also R.R. Davies, *The Revolt of Owain Glyn Dŵr* (Oxford, 1995), pp. 306–9, nn. 20–27.

[11] The community of the commote of Nanheudwy in the lordship of Chirk in 1411 made a *donum* to their lord "ad equitanciam suam in partibus Ffrancie." See L. Beverley Smith, "Seignorial Income in the Fourteenth Century: The Arundels in Chirk," *Bulletin of the Board of Celtic Studies* 28 (1978–80), 449. R.R. Davies, *Lordship and Society in the March of Wales 1282–1400* (Oxford, 1978), pp. 82–3. For the context of the army led by Arundel, see A. Tuck, "The Earl of Arundel's Expedition to France, 1411," in *The Reign of Henry IV. Rebellion and Survival 1403–13*, ed. G. Dodd and D. Biggs (Yorks, 2008), pp. 228–39.

[12] Davies, *The Revolt of Owain Glyn Dŵr*, pp. 298, 313, and Griffiths, *Principality of Wales*, pp. 202, 323.

in Arundel's lordships in return for military service with the earl in 1411. That Gruffudd was betrayed by the same officials should not detract from the principle of pardon for military service. There are clear suggestions in the documentation relating to the men raised from the Lancaster estates and royal shires of Wales in 1415 that similar processes were at work.[13]

Despite the processes noted above it must be remembered that in 1415 the king intended to be absent for a whole year and this provoked concern for continued peace in Wales on the part of both the king and his council. The threat of French invasion of England through Wales had often been a concern in the fourteenth century, and French involvement in the recent rebellion, allied to suspicion of the Welsh, served only to heighten this fear. For the most part, the measures taken in Wales were analogous to those taken in England and ordained by the Council at the same time, February 1415. The clergy were arrayed, garrisons were provided for castles and measures were taken to secure the coast. In England, commissions of array were issued in twenty counties for the defense of the realm during the king's absence in 1415.[14] Unlike that to England, however, the threat in Wales was deemed to be predominately internal rather than external. As recently as 1412 Glyndŵr and his followers had been able to kidnap and extort with impunity and both he and his surviving son, Maredudd, remained at large.[15]

In recognition of this, and in anticipation of the king's impending departure for France, on 5 July 1415 Gilbert Talbot, the justiciar of Chester, was authorized to receive Glyndŵr into the king's peace, an offer which appears magnanimous but was merely official recognition of the status quo. While Glyndŵr was no longer a threat militarily, he was equally unlikely to be betrayed. If contact was made Glyndŵr must have refused this offer, as Talbot was issued with similar instructions, this time directed at Owain's son Maredudd, on 24 February 1416.[16] The lords of the March were also ordered to garrison their castles and Henry himself spent significant sums on gunpowder artillery for his own castles in his Principality and duchy.[17] In February, the Council, mindful of the absence of full restoration of law and order in Wales, advised that additional military resources would be

---

[13] J. Beverley Smith, "The Last Phase of the Glyndŵr Rebellion," *Bulletin of the Board of Celtic Studies* 22 (1966–68), 250–60.

[14] For the array of Clergy: *Calendar of Patent Rolls* [*CPR*], *1413–17*, p. 346, *Calendar of Ancient Correspondence Concerning Wales*, ed. J.G. Edwards (Cardiff, 1935), pp. 256–8, and B. McNab, "Obligations of the Church in English Society: Military Arrays of the Clergy, 1369–1418," in *Order and Innovation in the Middle Ages: Essays in Honor of Joseph R. Strayer*, ed. W.C. Jordan, B. McNab and T.F. Ruiz (Princeton, NJ, 1976), pp. 293–314; *Proceedings and Ordinances of the Privy Council of England* [*PPC*], ed. N.H. Nicolas, 7 vols. (London, 1834–7), 2:146–8, 168. The decisions of the Council: *PPC* 2:145–8.

[15] For examples, see references to Dafydd Gam below, n. 76, while for the latter stages of the rebellion, Smith, "The Last Phase of the Glyndŵr rebellion," 255–6.

[16] There is reasonable fifteenth-century evidence that Glyndŵr died in September 1415; J.R.S. Phillips, "When did Owain Glyndŵr die?" *Bulletin of the Board of Celtic Studies* 24 (1970), 59–77. The instructions to Talbot can be found in *CPR, 1413–16*, pp. 342, 404. Owain's last surviving son, Maredudd, eventually accepted pardon on 8 April 1421: *CPR, 1416–22*, p. 335; Wylie and Waugh, *Henry the Fifth*, 1:113–14.

[17] The National Archives [TNA], E 403/623 m. 5.

required for the custody of the Principality and March of Wales while the King was overseas.[18] A force of 60 men-at-arms and 120 archers under Thomas Straunge, sheriff of Merionydd, was to serve in North Wales for a quarter, commencing on 24 March. Thirty men-at-arms and sixty archers were to be stationed at the Cistercian abbey of Cymer near Dolgellau in Merioneth with a similar number at Bala, also in Merioneth. The archers allocated to South Wales were established at another Cistercian abbey, Strata Florida (W. *Ystrad Fflur*), near Aberystwyth, Cardiganshire.[19] The account which confirms this expenditure begins on 24 June 1415, the date on which this period of service ended. From then until Michaelmas 1415, a quarter of a year and six days, one hundred men-at-arms and two hundred archers were to be deployed between North and South Wales under the leadership of Thomas Straunge and John Merbury, chamberlain of South Wales. Finally, a similar number of troops were to be deployed from Michaelmas until the end of December.[20]

There is a second set of payments in the accounts of the chamberlain of South Wales for a force of 60 men-at-arms and 120 archers, rather more than half of the total of 300 proposed by the council. The chamberlain, John Merbury, Richard Oldcastle (constable of Aberystwyth castle) and Sir Robert Whitney of Herefordshire were named as its leaders.[21] These men, whose origins are unknown, were employed for a quarter of a year from 26 August 1415 until 28 November at 12d. per day for the men-at-arms and 6d. for the archers. Provision was also made for a follow-up force of twenty men-at-arms and sixty archers to serve for sixty days from 26 November 1415, around ten days after the king had returned to England.[22] Exactly who made up the force and their mode of operation is a mystery, but the payment from the exchequer to the esquires John Wele, recently steward of Oswestry, and Thomas Straunge of £263 for a similar force guarding (*custodia*) North Wales is recorded in the Issue roll.[23] The emphasis on securing North Wales is understandable: it had been the centre of rebellion and the process of recovery of royal authority proceeded more slowly there. It was for

---

[18] PPC, 2:146–7. The earl of Arundel was sent to carry out the musters (TNA, E 404/621, m. 4).
[19] Very similar precautions were made in 1412, *PPC* 2:35, 38.
[20] *PPC* 2:179. The account printed there, British Library [BL], Cotton Cleopatra F. III fol. 137, runs from 24 June 1415 to 24 June 1416. The total cost of these measures was £1,496.
[21] John Merbury, the chamberlain of South Wales, was also the occupier of many of the most senior positions in the administration of the Lancaster estates: see Griffiths, *The Principality of Wales*, pp. 132–34. For Sir Robert Whitney (d. 1443), see R.A. Griffiths, "Gruffydd ap Nicholas and the Rise of the House of Dinefwr," in idem, *King and Country, England and Wales in the Fifteenth Century* (London, 1994), pp. 195–6.
[22] Curry, *Agincourt. A New History*, pp. 238–40.
[23] TNA, E 403/621 m. 6. Note that the payment for the force in North Wales was not made to the Chamberlain of North Wales, Thomas Walton, but directly to Straunge who, as sheriff of Merioneth, presumably assumed military command. Thomas Straunge was one of four men who entered into a recognisance for the keeping of Chirk Castle in 1420. Smith, "The Last Phase of the Glyndŵr Rebellion," p. 251. Straunge was sheriff of Merioneth in 1415 (see below) and it is possible he served in the military retinue of Richard, earl of Arundel (d. 1397), in 1387 and 1388; TNA, E 101/41/5 and TNA, E 101/40/33. Wele was steward of Oswestry between 1408 and 1415; Smith, "The Last Phase of the Glyndŵr Rebellion," pp. 250–51.

this reason that Henry V made no effort to recruit men from the northern shires of his Principality for his expeditionary army in 1415.

Recruitment

Michael Drayton, in his 1627 poem "The Bataille of Agincourt," described the Welsh presence in Henry V's army: "who no lesse honour ow'd To their own king, nor yet less valiant were, In one strong re'ment [regiment] had themselves bestowed." Drayton was not privy to the surviving documents: his "record" of the Welsh in the English army in 1415 was part of a county-by-county praise of the shires of England and Wales. In Wales these shires were a function of the Act of Union of 1536 and so do not reflect the situation in 1415, but Drayton's notion of a Welsh "regiment" is not so far removed from reality.[24] The means by which Henry recruited his army in 1415 has formed the basis of a recent study,[25] of which the contribution of Henry V's own estates and household naturally formed a part. In common with the royal and duchy estates in Wales, the English royal shires – Cheshire, and, under the Lancastrian kings, Lancashire – provided companies of archers for the royal army. Such companies were not only a feature of the 1415 expedition: the recruitment of companies of archers from the royal demesne in Wales in 1415 followed a precedent set by Richard II, who, for his Scottish campaign in 1385, had recruited 370 Welsh foot archers from his royal demesne in Wales; similar numbers served in Ireland in 1394. Foot archers had not formed a regular part of English expeditionary armies since the resumption of the war in 1369, so their presence was anomalous.[26] Richard had also, infamously, retained archers from his own earldom of Chester as his personal bodyguard during the final years of his reign.[27] He did not recruit companies of archers from Cheshire in 1385 or 1394, but for his fateful second Irish campaign of 1399 he attached to his household a company of 10 knights, 110 men-at-arms and 900 archers from the county.[28] In 1400 Henry IV also recruited heavily from Cheshire for his Scottish campaign, in part, no doubt, as an expression of royal authority over the county most closely associated with Richard. Henry ordered 60 men-at-arms and 500 archers to meet him at Newcastle, and 65 men-at-arms and 488 archers duly

---

[24] Michael Drayton, *The Battaile of Agincourt Fought by Henry the fifth of that name, King of England, against the whole power of the French: vnder the raigne of their Charles the sixt, anno Dom. 1415* (London, 1627), p. 16.
[25] Curry, *Agincourt. A New History*, chapter 3.
[26] For 1385, N.B. Lewis, "The Last Medieval Summons of the English Feudal Levy, 13 June 1385," *English Historical Review* 72 (1958), 1–26, with a reply by J.J.N. Palmer, "The Last Summons of the Feudal Army in England (1385)," *English Historical Review* 82 (1968), 771–5; N.B. Lewis, with reply by J.J.N. Palmer, "The Feudal Summons of 1385," *English Historical Review* 100 (1985), 729–46. For 1394, TNA, E 101/402/20 fol. 39v.
[27] J.L. Gillespie, "Richard II's Cheshire archers," *Transactions of the Historic Society of Lancashire and Cheshire* 125 (1975 for 1974), 1–39.
[28] TNA, E 403/562, m. 16.

turned up.²⁹ In 1400 Henry also utilized his personal estates as Duke of Lancaster. Together, duchy officials recruited at least 3,500 men, which Brown judged was "probably a conservative estimate." Of these, "all but about 200" were archers, and most were from the northern parts of the Duchy. Unfortunately, given the rebellion that enveloped Wales in the subsequent decade, there is no evidence from the surviving documentation relating to this campaign that Henry IV used men from his Welsh estates in this way in 1400.³⁰

We may ask, from a military perspective, what it was that such large numbers of relatively less mobile foot archers were intended to do. In 1385, and possibly on the two Irish campaigns, Richard's armies were intended to impress. Henry IV's expedition may have had a similar intent and, if this is so, such companies of archers bolstered the size of armies. In 1385 Richard was proclaiming himself a martial king, and also an adult. The campaign, however, was brief and, similarly, in the two Irish campaigns in the 1390s the military actions were minor and almost secondary to the main purpose, which was to demonstrate the effectiveness of Richard's power as monarch, both in England and Ireland. In 1400, Henry IV's goal was as much the reconciliation of England to the new king as any military advantage to be won over the Scots and their French allies.³¹

It is true that armies led by kings in person were generally much larger than routine military expeditions and were built around the king's household. Since these archer companies served the king directly they were significant, their presence emphasizing the superior lordship of the crown. Their presence could also alter the overall balance of the army. The mixed retinues brought by Henry's captains in 1415 had one man-at-arms for every three archers. The archer companies from the royal lands in Cheshire, Lancashire and Wales altered that ratio to one man-at-arms to every four archers. In percentage terms this is less stark: an army with 75 per cent archers became one with 80 per cent. Militarily, archers provided bulk and flexibility to Henry's army which, since it was contracted for a year, had probably been envisaged as an army of conquest. Moreover, and especially in Wales, they served a domestic purpose, emphasizing the extent of the royal demesne to the English and reinforcing the power of Henry's lordship in areas of his realm whose loyalty had not, in recent times, been a certainty.

---

29   TNA, CHES 2/74, rot. 9, in *Calendar of Signet Letters of Henry IV and Henry V (1399–1422)*, ed. J.L. Kirby (London, 1978), no. 9; TNA, E101/42/29 provides a list of retinue leaders with the numbers of archers under their command.
30   A.L. Brown, "The English Campaign in Scotland," in *British Government and Administration: Studies presented to S.R. Chrimes*, ed. H. Hearder and H.R. Loyn (Cardiff, 1974), p. 48. The retinues brought by the king's Duchy officials therefore constituted around a quarter of the total number of soldiers on the campaign. However, while they supplied around 30% of the total number of archers, they contributed only around 11% of the total number of men-at-arms. For recent discussion see Anne Curry, Adrian R. Bell, Andy King and David Simpkin, "New regime, new army? Henry IV's Scottish expedition of 1400," *English Historical Review* 517 (2010), 1382–413.
31   For further commentary on these campaigns, see Curry et al., "New regime, new army?"

The documents

The details of the composition and organization of the men raised from the royal demesne in Wales survive in the form of a muster roll attached to indentures for receipt of payment made to this company. These indentures – acknowledgments of receipt of money – are not to be confused with those struck between the crown and its captains for military service. If any of the latter were ever made for these companies of archers they have not survived, and therefore their terms of service are largely unknown. The documents in question, TNA, E 101/46/20, consist of a file of nine indented membranes sewn together recording three separate payments at three apparently separate musters of men recruited from the counties and liberties dependent upon the Principality and those of two of the main Duchy of Lancaster estates, the lordships of Brecon and Cydweli, with their neighboring and dependant lordships.

The indentures were sealed between John Merbury and the men-at-arms (five each from Cardiganshire and Carmarthenshire and ten drawn from the lordship of Brecon) leading the archer companies.[32] The muster of the royal counties of Cardiganshire and Carmarthenshire was taken at Carmarthen. That for the Lancaster lordships of Brecon, Hay and Huntington, as well as other minor lordships then in royal hands, including Llansteffan, St. Clears, Oysterlow and Talacharn, was apparently made at Brecon.[33] These men-at-arms were presumably responsible for co-ordinating the recruitment of the archers. With the exception of the small retinue from Cydweli, the names of the men recruited for service are listed first by lordship and then by *commote* (a Welsh land unit theoretically comprising half or one third of a *cantref*, itself the rough equivalent of an English hundred). From Brecon and other Lancaster lordships there were 10 men-at-arms, 14 mounted archers and 146 foot archers. From the royal shires of South Wales and their dependent lordships came a further 10 men-at-arms and 13 mounted archers with 323 foot archers. The men-at-arms were paid at the usual rate of the time, 12d. per day, while the archers were paid 6d. per day whether mounted or not. The musters taken at Carmarthen and Brecon are dated 26 June 1415, though this smacks of administrative neatness as it is highly improbable that Merbury could have been in both Brecon and Carmarthen, more than forty miles distant, to supervise both of these musters in the course of the same day. With the 3 men-

---

[32] The men-at-arms from Carmarthenshire were John ap Rhys, Henry ab Ieuan Gwyn, Rhys ap Llywelyn ap Gruffudd Fychan, Dafydd ab Ieuan ap Trahaiarn, Gruffudd ap Maredudd ap Henry, from Cardiganshire; Maredudd ab Owain, Owen Mortimer, Owain ap Siencyn Llwyd, Llywelyn ap Gwilym Llwyd, Walter ap Gruffudd ab Ieuan. Those from Brecon; Watcyn Llwyd, Andrew ap Lewis, Ieuan ap Rycard ap Madoc, Gwilym ap Hywel ap Gwilym, Mabe Maredudd ap Rycard, Siencyn ap Meuric ap Rycard, Siencyn ap John ap Rhys, Philip ap Gwilym Bras, Rycard ap Meuric ap Rhys and Richard Boys. Finally, those from Cydweli were Gruffudd ab Ieuan Iscoed, Thomas ap Dafydd ap Thomas and Hywel ab Ieuan ap Hywel. The spelling of these names has been modernized though the distinction between Richard and Rycard has been retained. Details of these payments and indentures of receipt are reiterated in several surviving documents including TNA, C 47/10/33/12 and E 101/45/5 m. 3.

[33] TNA, E 101/46/20 m. 2d and m. 3 respectively.

at-arms, 3 mounted archers and 3 foot archers from the lordship of Cydweli, we have a total of 523 men.

Attached to these indentures of receipt is a warrant for reimbursement to the revenues of the lordship of Cydweli, from the issues of the royal lands of South Wales, for the payment of the nine men from that lordship. Written in French – the remainder of this document is in Latin – this warrant was sealed by Thomas Walter, Merbury's lieutenant as Chamberlain in South Wales, and Hugh Eyton, receiver of the Lancaster lordship of Cydweli (and also, at this date, janitor of the royal castle of Aberystwyth), and was dated 6 April 1415. This warrant shows that the nine men from Cydweli were paid on 20 June to serve for a full quarter commencing on 1 July 1415.[34] The terms of the indentures of receipt recording the musters at Carmarthen and Brecon, however, record the payment of wages for forty-five and a half days' service (half of a quarter of one year) with the king on his expedition to France. Payment of these wages was to begin on 6 July, although no further mention is made of the period of service intended.

At the foot of each indenture are the remains or traces of ten seals on separate tags, which makes it likely that the seals were those of the men-at-arms leading the retinues. Meaningful detail is visible on only two of the surviving seals, however, but the best-surviving bears the initials "RB," identifying it as that of Richard Boys, a man-at-arms from the lordship of Brecon.[35] A minor, but still significant, orthographical point illustrates the linguistic divisions between Welsh and English in these documents. Richard Boys has his name written in the usual Latin manner, an abbreviated rendering of *Ricardus*. His Welsh counterparts, however, both among the men-at-arms and in the lists of archers, have the name spelt out in full as *Rycard* or *Ricard*, hinting at the Welsh form, *Rhisiart*, and the possibility of an oral roll call. Interestingly, and for no readily explicable reason, the musters make no mention of the smaller Lancaster lordships of Ogmore, Monmouth and Three Castles. The sole surviving receiver's account from these lordships, for this year, from Monmouth, provides no elucidation on this point and there are no hints in the other Exchequer accounts that men were ever recruited for similar archer companies from these lordships.[36]

With the exception of the nine men recruited from Cydweli, the companies from the royal estates of southern Wales have the appearance of an afterthought. In 1415 most of the indentures of war were made around mid-April and were generally sealed on 29 April.[37] The first evidence for our force comes from 7 May when £435 was transferred from the Exchequer to the chamberlain of South Wales via the account of the sheriff of Hereford and the hands of William Botiller, a Lancastrian career civil servant and receiver in the lordship of Brecon.[38] As

---

[34] TNA, E 101/46/20 m. 5.
[35] TNA, E 101/46/20 m. 3.
[36] Receiver's accounts for Monmouth, TNA, Duchy of Lancaster 29/615/9844.
[37] Curry, *Agincourt. A New History*, p. 69.
[38] TNA, SC 6/1222/14 m. 7–8. R.A. Griffiths, "William Botiller: A fifteenth-century civil servant," in idem, *King and Country, England and Wales in the Fifteenth Century* (London, 1991), p. 181, n. 4.

noted earlier, there is no evidence that any conventional military indentures were made between the leaders of these companies of Welsh archers and the crown, and thus no indication as to how long they were intended to serve for. This differs markedly from the arrangements made to assemble troops from the royal counties of Cheshire and Lancashire for the same campaign. A total of 247 men was raised from Cheshire and paid from its revenues, although it is possible that 650 were intended. The 500 recruited from Lancashire and paid by the crown were divided into groups of 50, each group under the command of a local knight or esquire. The latter had often also indented directly with the crown to provide a mixed retinue.[39] In comparison with Cheshire, there is no suggestion that the chamberlain of South Wales made any contribution from either his own revenues or from those of any of the Lancaster lordships.

The roles played by Merbury, Botiller, Eyton and Thomas Walter in the recruitment exercise demonstrate the close administrative relationship between the royal shires and the Lancastrian estates in the Welsh March at this date. John Merbury was not only chamberlain of South Wales but, since February 1414, also steward of the lordship of Brecon. He was, in effect, the chief financial and administrative officer for the majority of the estates of southern Wales. He had been in Lancastrian service since at least 1395, and had subsequently served Henry of Monmouth during his time as prince of Wales. He was appointed to the office of chamberlain of South Wales in March 1400, acquired in 1417 the office of steward in the lordship of Cydweli, and was appointed justiciar of South Wales in 1422.[40] In each of the three indentures of receipt from 1415, however, he is described as chamberlain of South Wales. This was evidently the senior position, which indicates that the royal demesne in southern Wales, whether princely or ducal, was governed almost as a single unit under Henry V.

Service

It is certain, however, that not all of the men assembled at Carmarthen left South Wales. Some of the precautions taken in Wales against disturbance during the king's absence have already been noted. In addition to the standing forces specified by the privy council, in the royal lands of South Wales a force of nine men-at-arms with nine mounted archers and thirty-eight foot archers (*valletorum ad pedes*) was retained. Paid 12d., 6d. and 4d. per day respectively, they served between 6 July and 11 November 1415. Four of these nine men-at-arms were named in the chamberlain's account: Henry Gwyn,[41] David

---

[39] Curry, *Agincourt. A New History*, pp. 60–61. A warrant dated 10 Henry V (1422) called upon the sheriff of Hereford to distrain Merbury's goods for failing to account for the £435 paid to the Welsh company, Wylie, "Some Notes on the Agincourt Roll," p. 135.

[40] For full details of his origins and career, see Griffiths, *Principality of Wales*, pp. 181–2.

[41] He was not the Henry Gwyn of Llanstephan who fell at Agincourt fighting for the French, see A.D. Carr, "Welshmen and the Hundred Years War," *Welsh History Review* 4 (1968), p. 36. He

ab Ieuan ap Trahaiarn,[42] Llywelyn ap Gwilym Llwyd[43] and Ieuan Teg.[44] With the exception of Henry Gwyn, all can be positively identified with men in the muster sealed at Carmarthen on 26 June. Since they were paid for service in Wales at the same time that the remainder of the company was heading to Southampton and thence to France we can be sure that these men at least did not leave Wales. Dafydd ab Ieuan ap Trahaiarn, who was included as part of the company intended for France as a man-at-arms from Carmarthenshire, was a former rebel. He is the best-documented of the three since his lands in Cantref Mawr (Carmarthenshire) had been forfeited to Dafydd Gam in November 1401 and presumably he had pardon, as well as mere wages, to gain. Ieuan Teg and Llywelyn ap Gwilym Llwyd had enlisted to serve as archers in France and both later held administrative offices in the royal shires of South Wales. For this period of a quarter of a year plus thirty-six days they were paid £105 10s. 4½ d. in addition to £27 0s. 4½d. paid to them as a regard.[45] The payment of regard in this context is surprising, and there are two possible explanations. The first is the usual reason for such payments: to offset the costs of men-at-arms equipping themselves for military service, in this instance probably with horses, which might also explain why only four of the nine were named: they were the recipients of this payment. Secondly, it is possible that the payment was an attempt to keep the wages of the men serving in West Wales in the account for the financial year which ended at Michaelmas 1415. If, as seems likely, the remainder of this group of men serving in West Wales was recruited from among the men previously recruited to serve in France, it means that only around 450 of the latter would have actually left Wales.

Confirming how many of these Welsh archers actually served in France is complicated by a lack of further references to them as a group after the musters of the 26 June. Some had evidently reached Warminster, Wiltshire, before 24 July, a week before the expedition was due to sail, since the Close Rolls include reference to English and Welsh soldiers refusing to pay for their victuals there.[46] If they had left southern Wales on 6 July, the date at which their pay commenced and a week before the majority of the army were mustered at Southampton, a distinctly leisurely journey towards England's south coast is implied. One possibility, mentioned in decisions taken in March 1416 on post-campaign accounting procedures, is that some men were left behind in England because of a lack of

may, however, have been the man of that name receiving the wages as Forester of Cydweli in 1415–16 (TNA, Duchy of Lancaster 29/584/9243), or possibly Henry ab Ieuan Gwyn, who mustered as a man-at-arms at Carmarthen in 1415: TNA, E 101/46/20 m. 2.

[42] See Griffiths, *Principality of Wales*, pp. 298, 99, 368. He was outlawed in 1397–8 and again for rebellion by 1401: *CPR, 1401–5*, p. 11. He was bailiff itinerant in Cantref Mawr and beadle of Caeo in 1412–13, once more with Rhys ab Ieuan Fychan in 1413–14, and again in 1419–20.

[43] He may be identified with an archer of that name from Ystlwyf (Oysterlow, a dependent lordship of Carmarthenshire) in TNA, E 101/46/20, m. 2. He was Bailiff Itinerant of Cardigan in 1409–10 and held several other offices: Griffiths, *The Principality of Wales*, p. 305.

[44] Ieuan Teg was later reeve of the commote of Perfedd in 1424–5. He is possibly to be identified with Ieuan Teg ap Dafydd Llwyd; Griffiths, *The Principality of Wales*, p. 454.

[45] TNA, SC 6/1222/14, m. 3 and E 101/46/20 m. 2.

[46] *Calendar of Close Rolls [CCR], 1413–19*, p. 223, and Curry, *Agincourt. A New History*, p. 69.

available shipping at the point of embarkation.⁴⁷ Royal policy in this instance was that no financial allowance should be made for those so affected, so that any men left behind would not be included in the campaign accounts if they arrived too late.

It is certain that at least some of the company served at the first action of Henry's campaign, the siege of Harfleur. The unpleasant estuarine conditions at the mouth of the river Seine caused a significant number of casualties among the besieging army, most notably Thomas, earl of Arundel, and Richard Courtenay, bishop of Norwich. Many others also suffered and Allmand calculated that at least 1,687 men were officially regarded as "unfit for service" by the end of the siege.⁴⁸ Some of these men were given license to return to England and several lists of the sick survive. They are not, of course, comprehensive. Adam of Usk noted that there were some who "disgraceful to relate, simply deserted the army, to the king's fury."⁴⁹ One of the lists, however, reveals that some of the Welshmen recruited from the royal demesne in southern Wales made it as far as Harfleur, as they are recorded among the sick.⁵⁰ Evans, citing Wylie, states that fifty-four of the archers also suffered, but detailed examination of the lists and comparison with the initial musters suggests that all is not quite as it seems. The vagaries of English interpretation of Welsh names mean that it is far from clear that all the king's Welshmen on the sick lists also appear in the musters made at Brecon, Carmarthen and Cydweli. Wylie's interpretation is also at fault since it ignores the men with "English" names who appear in both the sick lists and the initial musters.⁵¹ For these reasons, it is impossible to give exact figures of the sick from southern Wales except for the men-at-arms. From those names which can be matched with certainty, however, it is obvious that the attrition rates among

---

47 Curry, *The Battle of Agincourt*, document F9 (BL, Cotton Cleopatra F. III fol. 148), pp. 448–9.
48 Christopher Allmand, *Henry V* (New Haven and London, 1997), p. 211, Curry, *Agincourt. A New History*, p. 131, suggests "at least 1,330."
49 *Chronicle of Adam Usk*, ed. Given-Wilson, pp. 256–7, "quidam ignominiose quia desertores milicie et cum regis indignacione, ad propria remearunt."
50 TNA, E 101/45/1 details the sick from this company. Barker, *Agincourt*, p. 320, is apparently unaware of their presence in this document.
51 Evans, *Wales and the Wars of the Roses*, pp. 26–7 n. 4, suggests that five men-at arms and fifty-four archers were among the sick; these figures are taken from Wylie, "Some notes on the Agincourt Roll," p. 135. By my count, the figure for men-at-arms appearing in both the musters (TNA, E 101/46/20) and the sick lists (TNA, E 101/45/1) is six (Watcyn Llwyd, Andrew ap Lewis, both from Brecon; Rhys ap Llywelyn ap Gruffudd Fychan from Carmarthenshire; Maredudd ab Owain, Walter ap Gruffudd ab Ieuan, Owain ap Siencyn from Cardiganshire). While the number given by Wylie reflects those archers with Welsh patronymics listed as serving with the king in TNA, E 101/45/1, not all can be positively identified in the original musters. In addition, Wylie's count ignores men with "English" names, such as John Wheler, John Body and John Cooke, who appear in both documents and names other names where the clerk omitted the "ap" from the patronymic. Andrew ap Lewis (TNA, E 101/46/20), for example, became Andrew Lewes (TNA, E 101/45/1). John Body was a burgess of Brecon and one of those who witnessed the confirmation of a charter to the town of Brecon 12 May 1415. E. Buckingham, "Charters of the Borough of Brecon, 1276–1517," *Brycheiniog* 25 (1992–3), 46–7.

the men from the royal counties were higher than those among men from Brecon and the other Lancaster lordships. Two of those from Brecon fell ill, compared with four from the Principality, but such a sample is too small to be considered wholly reliable. The fate of those of the Welsh company who remained with the army for the rest of the campaign is also far from clear. Comparison of the initial musters with those surviving for the garrison of Harfleur for the first quarter of 1416 show no names in common.[52] So exactly how many remained? Of the total of 523 recruited, it is probable that 40 never left Wales and that at least 60 of the remainder were given license to return from Harfleur through illness.

Without allowing for any men left behind or possible desertions, a maximum of only 400 could have joined the march to Calais and therefore fought at Agincourt. Whatever the size of Henry V's army at that battle, it is apparent that "his" Welshmen were only a small part of it. It is worth mentioning at this point that Welshmen were extremely rare among the mixed retinues in Henry's army. The king's dominance of southern Wales and his decision not to recruit from the northern shires is one obvious limitation; only very small numbers can be found in the retinues of marcher lords. Of the 470 men in the retinue of Thomas, earl of Arundel, only 40, 3 men at arms and 37 archers, all replacements for men who fell ill at Harfleur, bore Welsh names, as did only 5 of the 60, all archers, led by Sir John de Grey of Ruthin.[53] Among the retinue of the duke of York are 5 men identifiable as Welsh out of 400.[54] The young earl of March's retinue contained but a single identifiably Welsh archer, John Griffith.[55] The largest of the Marcher lordships, Glamorgan, was in the hands of the nineteen-year-old Richard Beauchamp, who remained in England, and thus no recruitment from among its Welsh tenants took place.[56] These penny numbers suggest that the marcher lords either did not trust the Welsh communities of their liberties or did not want to take the risk of disturbing the hard-won peace.

Personnel

Who were the men Henry had recruited from his Welsh estates? Half of the men-at-arms leading the contingent from the shires of South Wales can be identified as former rebels. Dafydd ab Ieuan ap Trahaiarn of Carmarthenshire, as has

---

[52] Muster for the first quarter of 1416, TNA, E 101/47/39. For analysis, see Curry, *The Battle of Agincourt*, pp. 430–31, and *Agincourt. A New History*, pp. 113–14.
[53] TNA, E 101/47/1 and E 101/47/7 respectively.
[54] TNA, E 101/45/2 and E 101/45/19.
[55] TNA, E 101/44/30 piece 1.
[56] Richard (d. 1422) had gained control of Glamorgan by right of his wife, Isabel Despenser, gaining possession of Glamorgan on 28 February 1415: *CCR, 1413–19*, pp. 165–6. It is very likely, however, that Glamorgan men were among the 5,000 assembled at Hanley Castle, Warwickshire against the threat of the Lollard Sir John Oldcastle. T.B. Pugh, "The Marcher Lords of Glamorgan, 1317–1485," in *Glamorgan County History, Volume III: The Middle Ages*, ed. T.B. Pugh (Cardiff, 1971), pp. 186–7.

already been noted, remained in Wales, but the service in France of Jankyn (or John) ap Rhys ap Dafydd, Rhys ap Llywelyn, Gruffudd ap Maredudd ap Henry Dwnn and Maredudd ab Owain can be accounted for.[57] The latter two are the best known of this group, although only Gruffudd Dwnn appears to have remained with the army long enough to serve at Agincourt. The grandson of the notorious and incorrigible rebel Henry Dwnn, Gruffudd had received pardon for his involvement in Glyndŵr's rebellion in 1413. Unlike his grandfather, Gruffudd repented his misdemeanors and put the experience gained in rebellion to good use in the French wars of Henry V and Henry VI. His reward was not only pardon, but favor. He received letters of denizenship granting him full English status in 1421. Most significant of all, even in light of the captaincies he held in France, which included Cherbourg, Carentan, Tancarville, Lisieux and Neufchâtel, was constableship of the castle of Cydweli. Even by 1430, this was an unusual appointment for someone of Welsh birth, and the more so since he had besieged it in his youth.[58]

Unlike Gruffudd Dwnn, Maredudd ab Owain, a relative of the family of the fourteenth-century poet Dafydd ap Gwilym, seems to have confined his activities to his native Cardiganshire after 1415. Though he was granted letters of protection on 12 July 1419, for want of surviving musters from that year, there is no evidence in the surviving musters that he served in France on that, or any subsequent, occasion.[59] Maredudd's possessions had been confiscated by 1406 and he was among the hostages surrendered by the defenders of Aberystwyth Castle in 1407 to confirm a six-week truce between them and Prince Henry. The truce was a fiasco, lengthening both the siege and, with it, Maredudd's imprisonment for nearly a year.[60] He had probably been released by 1409 and, after falling ill at Harfleur, filled a variety of royal offices in West Wales, demonstrating his reconciliation with the authorities. He was granted the important office of bailiff itinerant of Llanbadarn in 1416 and filled numerous other offices until 1439, when he was forced into retirement by the machinations of Gruffudd ap Nicholas and his son Thomas. Despite this reversal he had, by this time, re-established his position in Cardiganshire society and had accumulated a small estate valued at £8 per annum. Even so, this represented a substantial decline in fortunes: the lands he forfeited by rebellion were farmed at £14 per annum in 1406.[61]

---

[57] TNA, E 101/46/20 m. 2; Dafydd ap Ieuan ap Trahaiarn seems to have remained in West Wales; see above, and Griffiths, *The Principality of Wales*, pp. 201–2. Rhys ap Llywelyn and Maredudd ab Owain fell ill at Harfleur and returned home; TNA, E 101/45/1 m. 12. For details of their rebellion, Davies, "The Bohun and Lancaster Lordships," pp. 272–3, Davies, *The Revolt of Owain Glyn Dŵr*, pp. 311–13.
[58] For other references to his life and career see Griffiths, *The Principality of Wales*, pp. 201–2.
[59] TNA, C 67/37 m. 23.
[60] J.E. Lloyd, *Owen Glendower* (Oxford, 1931), pp. 130–33 and *Foedera, conventiones, litterae et cuiuscunque acta publica*, ed. T. Rymer, 10 volumes (3rd ed., The Hague 1739–45), IV, iv, p. 120.
[61] He served as sheriff of Cardiganshire in 1424 and as escheator of the same county in 1437–8 among other offices: see Griffiths, *The Principality of Wales*, pp. 273–4, and also Ralph A. Griffiths, "Gentlemen and Rebels in Later Medieval Cardiganshire," in idem, *Conquerors and*

Joining Maredudd in the army of 1415 was another former Cardiganshire rebel, Jankyn or John ap Rhys ap Dafydd. Jankyn was also among the hostages handed over at Aberystwyth in 1407 and was clearly a man of significant means, as he secured his freedom by making a fine of £233 6s. 8d. in 1410–11 and took out letters of protection for his service overseas in 1415.[62] He was granted further letters of protection in September 1419, in June 1421 and, once more, in July 1432, on this occasion to serve with Sir Walter Hungerford.[63] Between times he engaged in military and administrative activities closer to home. In 1424 he was escheator of Cardiganshire and at various times between 1425 and 1434 he served among the garrison of Aberystwyth castle.[64] As the careers of these men demonstrate, participation in the revolt need not have proved disastrous to the interests of gentry families. There seems little doubt, too, that military service greatly assisted in the oiling of the wheels.

At least four of the archers from the company are known to have been former rebels and further research would probably reveal many more. One indication of this from the musters sealed at Carmarthen are the no fewer than 117 men listed as serving in the place of another named individual. Rebels or not, at the very least this implies that the men who provided substitutes had been summoned in person and it is certainly possible that many of these men were working their way back into favor. Curry suggests that these were in fact substitutes provided on campaign to replace those returning sick from Harfleur.[65] This is very unlikely in the case of the contingent from southern Wales: no dates are given for these substitutions, as is the case for other musters on this campaign where such substitutions are known. It is probable, therefore, that the substitutions were made at the time of muster and were accepted by both Merbury and the men-at-arms whose seals were attached to the indentures. More significant is that the indentures of receipt cover only the first forty-five and a half days' service (from 6 July to 20 August, only two days into the siege). Those occupying official positions were not immune from the obligation to serve, and would have good reason for providing a substitute. One such was Maredudd ap Rhys Fychan, who served as bailiff of the commote of Mabelfyw (Carmarthenshire) in 1415–16, although another officer, Adda ap Maredudd ap Rhys, beadle of Creuddyn (Cardiganshire) in the same year, served in person.[66] Substitutions of this sort do not occur – or at least, were not recorded

---

Conquered in Medieval Wales (Stroud, 1994), pp. 59, 61, and "Gruffudd ap Nicholas and the Rise of the House of Dinefwr," in Griffiths, *King and Country*, pp. 193–4.

[62] TNA, C 76/98 m. 10. This was presumably granted only when he reached Southampton, since the protection is dated 16 August 1415.

[63] *Annual Report of the Deputy Keeper of the Public Records* (London, 1840–), 41:800, 44:627, 48:287.

[64] TNA, SC 6/1288/2. For full details of his extensive administrative career, see Griffiths, *The Principality of Wales*, pp. 326–7, 450, 455, 481, 514–15, 533, 537, 539.

[65] Curry, *Agincourt. A New History*, p. 71. Substitutions from men "oultre le nombre" (outside the number) included in the original muster during the campaign are apparent, with dates, in the muster of the men of the earl of Arundel, TNA, E 101/47/1. For commentary on Arundel's retinue, see Curry, *Agincourt. A New History*, pp. 114, 131.

[66] For Maredudd ap Rhys Fychan see Griffiths, *The Principality of Wales*, p. 382. That Maredudd

– in the musters made at Brecon, and it is noticeable that those men-at-arms from the Lancaster lordships whose careers can be traced were notable for their loyalty rather than for their rebellion.

Suggestions of quasi-legal coercion are reinforced by a number of pardons granted to Welshmen serving in this company in early June 1415, after the money for this force was supplied to Merbury in early May but before the musters took place in June. Nowhere is it spelt out that some of these Welshmen were serving on condition of pardon for their involvement in the Glyndŵr rebellion, but this is the clear implication.[67] Other, darker, inducements may have been at work. In 1418 Hugh Eyton, receiver of Cydweli, told four men that they had been assigned to go as men-at-arms to the siege of Rouen although they could be excused this service on the payment of a fine. This was a common arrangement in the March of Wales and examples can be found in the court rolls of the lordship of Ruthin in the fourteenth century. One of those allegedly selected was aged over seventy, causing the tenants of the lordship to report the receiver for extortion.[68]

Several of the archers serving in 1415 can be demonstrated to have served in the wars against Owain Glyndŵr in the previous decade as well as on later campaigns in France. Laurence Dyer served under Rustin de Villa Nova in the garrison of Cardigan in 1404 before serving as an archer from the commote of Caerwedros (Cardiganshire) in the place of Rhys ap Dafydd ab Ieuan in 1415. He was probably a member of the merchant family of that name from the borough of Cardigan. Owain ap Philip ap Madoc of Traean in the lordship of St. Clears served with Laurence in 1404 and on behalf of Philip Clement in 1415.[69] Another archer who sustained a military career was John ap Herry, alias John Herry, probably of Cydweli, who served as a mounted archer in 1415. He served with Sir Richard Arundell in an expedition against Owain Glyndŵr in 1405 and at sea with the Pembrokeshire knight (although the family is better known for its connections in Devon and Cornwall) Sir Thomas Carew in 1417. Our final reference to him finds him in the retinue of Lewis Powell in 1420 with the same two archers from Cydweli that he served with in 1415, Walter Toucker and Rhys ap Dafydd ap Thomas.[70] Unless Walter Toucker was also the man of that name who served with Guy, lord Brian, as an archer in 1378, neither he nor Rhys have any

---

received two general pardons, in April 1416 and in March 1417, may not be unrelated (ibid., pp. 310, 459, 460, 464). There are two men named Adda ap Maredudd from Uwch Aeron (Cards.) named in the muster; one substituted his son Philip, the other served in person.

[67] For the pardons of Jankyn or John ap Rhys ap Dafydd, Maredudd ab Owain and Gwalter ap Gruffudd ab Ieuan, see TNA, E 368/198.

[68] Curry, *Agincourt. A New History*, p. 61, citing TNA, Duchy of Lancaster 7/1/25 document E.

[69] Clement may well have been a Cardiganshire man, a relative of a family established there after the Edwardian conquest: see, Griffiths, "Gentlemen and Rebels," pp. 53–4. A William Clement also served on behalf of Hywel ab Ieuan ap Llywelyn of Uwch Aeron (Cards.), TNA, E 101/43/20, m. 2d.

[70] A John Henry, or Harry, junior is recorded as a merchant of Cardigan and bailiff of the town in 1407–8 and in 1411–12: Griffiths, *The Principality of Wales*, p. 422. TNA, E 101/46/20 no. 4, m. 1; E 101/44/7 m. 2 (1405); E 101/48/4 m. 8 (1417) and E 101/49/36, m. 12 (1420).

other recorded military service.[71] Another veteran of 1415, Thomas ap Dafydd ap Thomas, who had served as a man-at-arms from Cydweli, appears in this same retinue. Thomas may well have been Rhys's brother and he was probably the notably unsuccessful beadle of Catheiniog between 1428 and 1430. He retired from that office with a debt of £28 19s. 10d and was subsequently imprisoned until Michaelmas 1431.[72] Two further veterans of 1415 can also be found in this retinue: Philip Squire and Dafydd Ferrour.

The presence of the three archers from the lordship of Cydweli serving together in both 1415 and 1420 may suggest that the summoning and selection of specific individuals may have been a common factor in recruitment from royal estates in southern Wales in these and the intervening years. The complaint against the receiver of Cydweli, Hugh Eyton, noted above certainly hints that this was the case in that lordship.[73] The archers raised from the Lancaster lordships and royal shires in southern Wales were recruited in groups by lordship, county and commote, a pattern familiar from the time of Edward I but abandoned with the adoption of fully indentured armies after 1360. Another feature of the 1415 company, common to its fourteenth-century predecessors, was the presence of a chaplain, William Waldebesse of the commote of Yr Allt (the hill or the height) in Brecon. It is probable that he also filled the role of interpreter and was capable of preaching in Welsh.[74] He may be identified with a man who appears several times in the register of Bishop Robert Mascall of Hereford. In November 1410 a William Walkysbache was appointed rector of the church of Middleton in Herefordshire and on April 20 1412 he was appointed to the chantry in the church of Cleobury Mortimer; on each occasion the king, Henry IV, was his patron, although on the second occasion in the place of the young earl of March, then a minor.[75]

Dafydd Gam and the Lancastrian connection

The Lancastrian estates in Wales not only contributed archers to Henry's army in 1415, but two men also served independently with their own retinues. One was John ap Harry, the son of Henry ap John of Oldcourt and Poston, Herefordshire, a prominent official both in the duchy estates in the March and in his home county. In 1399 he was sheriff of Herefordshire and was responsible for transporting Richard II's goods and jewels from Pembroke to London. During the rebellion

---

[71] Brian was also lord of Talacharn/Laugharne just across Carmarthen Bay from Cydweli; TNA, E 101/36/32 m. 2.
[72] Griffiths, *The Principality of Wales*, pp. 202, 373. He should not be confused with his rather wealthier contemporary and namesake from Brecon. See R.R. Davies, "Brecon," in *The Boroughs of Medieval Wales*, ed. Ralph A. Griffiths (Cardiff, 1978), p. 66.
[73] See above, n. 68.
[74] There was also one Hywel ap Y Person (Hywel, son of the parson) of the commote of Caeo (Carmarthenshire).
[75] He was also involved in a dispute over the patronage of Sidbury (Herefordshire) in 1408: *Registrum Roberti Mascall, Episcopi Herefordensis A.D. MCCCCIV–MCCCCXVI*, ed. J.H. Parry (London, 1927), pp. 66, 177, 185.

he commanded the eastern March for the king. Like his cousin Dafydd Gam, John sealed his indenture with the majority of Henry's captains on 29 April 1415 to serve for one year with two men-at-arms and six archers, although his service appears to have lasted only as far as the siege of Harfleur, where he fell ill. His brother, Thomas, was among John's retinue as a man-at-arms, but nothing further is known of his service in 1415.[76] These men were very much representative of the militarization of Wales in the previous decade and a half of rebellion. Welshmen became increasingly prominent in the decades of wars which followed. Their service should perhaps be viewed in the same light as that of others from their locality, such as John Scudamore of Kentchurch, Herefordshire, or Sir John Greyndore of Monmouth, who gained conspicuous benefits from their service in the wars against Glyndŵr.[77]

John's cousin, Dafydd or Davy Gam is, as we have seen, the only Welshman mentioned in any contemporary narrative of the battle.[78] The appearance of Dafydd's name in the contemporary chronicles, with the exception of Usk, who, plausibly, could have known Dafydd personally, may reflect something of his contemporary importance. For his death to have come to the attention of a diverse group of chroniclers it seems probable that his name must have appeared on some official communication of the battle which has failed to survive. What was probably the most immediate notice of the outcome of the battle, however – a newsletter surviving in the archives of the city of Salisbury – does not name him among the dead.[79] That said, the only casualties recorded are the two most prominent men among the English dead: Edward, duke of York, and the young earl of Suffolk. The mention of only these two men of noble birth reflects the newsletter's treatment of the French casualties: only the noble dead were named.

Dafydd entered into an indenture directly with the crown on 29 April 1415 to serve as a man-at-arms with three archers.[80] Quite why his name should have been singled out in the chronicles is not immediately obvious. As retainers of

---

[76] TNA, E 101/69/6/456; 69/3/376; Harfleur, TNA, E 101/45/1 m. 9; Griffiths, *The Principality of Wales*, pp. 234–5, does not include the latter reference. Thomas may also have served in 1418 in the retinue of Edmund, earl of March; TNA, E 101/51/2 m. 7.

[77] This was despite Scudamore's marriage to one of Owain's daughters and allegations concerning his loyalty during the rebellion: see Griffiths, "Some Secret Supporters of Owain Glyndŵr?" in Griffiths, *Conquerors and Conquered*, pp. 102–21. His retinue of four men-at-arms and twelve archers in 1415: TNA, E 101/44/30 no.3 m. 2 (no surviving indenture); Sir John Greyndore's indenture in 1415: TNA, E 101/69/418.

[78] His full name was Dafydd Gam ap Llywelyn ap Hywel Fychan ap Hywel ab Einion Sais. The Welsh cognomen 'Gam' normally refers to some form of physical impairment, possibly in Dafydd's case a squint. See R.R. Davies, "Brecon, Owain Glyn Dŵr and Dafydd Gam," *Brycheniog* 32 (2000), 51–60; Davies, *The Revolt of Owain Glyn Dŵr*, pp. 302, 310; T.F. Tout, revised by R.R. Davies, "Dafydd Gam (d. 1415)," *Oxford Dictionary of National Biography*, www.oxforddnb.com/view/article/10318, accessed 6 January 2011.

[79] Curry, *The Battle of Agincourt*, document D1a (Wiltshire County Record Office, Salisbury Ledger Book A (G23/1/1), fol. 55), pp. 263–5

[80] For Dafydd Gam's indenture, payment and retinue, see TNA, E 101/69/4/404 (indenture), TNA, E 404/31/362 (warrant for issue), E 101/45/5 m. 5 (special issue roll for the campaign). My thanks to Professor Curry for these references. He was also among those receiving jewels in lieu of payment at Winchester on 14 July 1415: E 101/45/23, piece 1.

the house of Lancaster, he, his son Morgan and his brother Gwilym had all been described as king's esquires from early in the reign of Henry IV.[81] It may be that he was deemed more important than others of similar rank who fell, although whether by reason of his long service to the House of Lancaster or because of his capture by Owain Glyndŵr's supporters in 1412 is not clear. Gam's inclusion in the chronicles should perhaps be ascribed, therefore, to a mention in some, now lost, official communication which informed several fifteenth-century English chroniclers. The story of his death and his role in the battle has been much expanded over succeeding centuries from what were brief mentions of him in the list of dead. Dafydd's personal prominence in the lordship of Brecon and the rather wider prominence of the children of his daughter Gwladus (d. 1454) guaranteed his own fame. Despite this, Dafydd's death at Agincourt is not mentioned in any of the Welsh poems which sing his own and his descendants' praises in the fifteenth century. Claims of Dafydd Gam's bravado at the battle appear only in the late sixteenth century in the *Historia Cambriae* of David Powel. They were taken up by Thomas Goodwin in his biography of Henry V. Goodwin, writing in 1704, has Dafydd as the person who relates the size of the French army directly to the king: "May it please you, my liege, there are enough to be killed, enough to be taken prisoner, and enough to run away."[82] Drayton also takes up this story in his *Battaile of Agincourt* (1627). He is more poetic, having Dafydd say: "One part we'll kill, the second prisoners stay, And for the third, we'll leave to run away."[83] The original provenance of the story is lost.

Dafydd's daughter, Gwladus, married into two of the most prominent families in fifteenth-century South Wales. Her first husband was Roger Fychan (or Vaughan) of Bredwardine (Herefs.), who supposedly died with his father-in-law at Agincourt having served as an archer in his retinue. The key problem here, however, is that although we have copies of Dafydd's indenture and Exchequer records which give the size and composition of his retinue, we have no muster or post-campaign retinue list for him. The three sons of Gwladus and Roger Fychan – Walter (or Watcyn), Thomas and Roger (d. 1471)[84] – became staunch supporters of the House of York and great patrons of Welsh poets later in the century. Gwladus' second husband was Sir William ap Thomas of Raglan, progenitor of the Herbert family and another man who is supposed to have served at Agincourt.[85] Though it should be remembered that the surviving musters for the 1415 campaign are far from complete, there is no mention of either Roger Fychan or William ap Thomas in any of the extant musters or financial documentation.

---

[81] King's esquires: *CPR, 1399–1401*, pp. 37, 45, 76.

[82] Thomas Goodwin, *The History of the Reign of Henry the Fifth, King of England* (London, 1704), p. 81, cited in Curry, *The Battle of Agincourt*, p. 372. Goodwin repeats almost verbatim Powel, *A Historie of Cambria*, pp. 321–3.

[83] See n. 70 above; Drayton, *The Battaile of Agincourt*, p. 29.

[84] Sir Roger Fychan was executed at Chepstow following his capture by Jasper Tudor at the battle of Tewkesbury, May 1471. For an account of his career see Griffiths, *The Principality of Wales*, pp. 219–20.

[85] Barker, *Agincourt*, pp. 319–21, reciting Wylie and Waugh, *Henry the Fifth*, 2:188–9.

Moreover, there are several factors which should give us pause in taking at face value the story that Roger Fychan died at Agincourt. First, we find, drawing on muster rolls for Henry V's invasion of Normandy in 1417, a man named Roger Fychan, a man-at-arms in the retinue of the earl of Warwick.[86] While his origins are not specified, Roger was a sufficiently unusual name in a Welsh context for this at least to be noteworthy. If this is a reference to the same man it is unlikely that Roger lived much longer, but no alternative date of death has been suggested. Secondly, there is the survival of a memorial effigy said to be Roger's in the church at Bredwardine. Memorials present several difficulties as sources, not the least of which is that such effigies could have been supplied either some time before, or some time after, the death of the recipient. It is also the case that very little is known of the fates of the bodies of those on the English side killed at Agincourt, including that of Dafydd Gam.[87] What is evident is that the style of armor on this effigy is rather later than that contemporary with Agincourt and is likely to date from around 1450. It has much in common, for example, with that of Sir William ap Thomas (d. 1445), which survives in Abergavenny Priory.[88] Both effigies bear the Lancastrian SS collar, customarily worn by those in royal service. In Roger's case, such a tomb would hardly be in keeping with the status of an archer, but such a fine alabaster tomb would well reflect the status of his widow and, particularly, their children, who were so prominent in the "Herbert decades" of the 1450s and 1460s.[89] Finally, the first written account suggesting that Roger Fychan died at Agincourt appears in Powel's *Historie*, demonstrating that it was current in the second half of the sixteenth century but was unknown before this time. It was later recited in Sir Samuel Rush Meyrick's editions of Dwnn's genealogies, published in the nineteenth century, and it was from there that Nicolas and Wylie took this detail, which has subsequently been taken at face value.[90]

The story that Dafydd Gam was knighted on the field of Agincourt with his son-in-law Roger Vaughan and Watcyn Llwyd of Brecon illustrates why such details given with these genealogies should be treated with extreme caution. As with the death of Roger Fychan, this element of the story is unsubstantiated by any fifteenth-century source. Several chronicles note that casualties of the battle included "two knights, newly dubbed."[91] Although neither Roger Vaughan nor

---

[86] TNA, E 101/51/2 m. 12.
[87] Curry, *Agincourt. A New History*, p. 230.
[88] I owe thanks to Dr. Rhianydd Biebrach, Dave Underhill and Dr. Randall Moffett for their thoughts on the dating of this effigy.
[89] R.A. Griffiths, "Lordship and Society in the Fifteenth Century," in *The Gwent County History* II: *The Age of the Marcher Lords, c.1070–1536*, ed. R.A. Griffiths, A. Hopkins and R. Howell (Cardiff, 2009), pp. 262–3.
[90] Powel, *A Historie of Cambria*, p. 323, *Heraldic Visitations of Wales*, ed. Meyrick, 1:107, n. 1 and N.H. Nicolas, *History of the Battle of Agincourt*, 3rd ed. (London, 1833), Appendix, p. 60.
[91] See *Gesta Henrici Quinti, The Deeds. of Henry V*, ed. F. Taylor and J.S. Roskell (Oxford, 1975), pp. 96–7; *The St Albans Chronicle 1406–1420*, ed. V.H. Galbraith (Oxford, 1937), p. 98. *John Hardyng, Chronicle (to 1461)*, ed. H. Ellis (London, 1812), pp. 389–91 (all cited in Curry, *The Battle of Agincourt*, pp. 39, 53, 85).

Watcyn Llwyd were named in any of these narratives this aside seems a plausible origin for a story which developed in later centuries, but there is no reason to believe that Vaughan and Llywd were the knights concerned. The sick lists show that Watcyn Llwyd was among those invalided home from Harfleur, so his part, at least, in this legend can be discounted.[92] If Watcyn was ever knighted, which seems unlikely, it was on another, later, occasion. A similar tale, also found in Dwnn's heraldic genealogies of the sixteenth century, has been told about Sir Gruffudd Fychan (d. 1447). It is probable that Gruffudd remained in Wales in 1415: he was certainly not the Griffin Fordet found in the duke of Gloucester's retinue, and Glanmor Williams suspected that Gruffudd's elevation to knighthood owed rather more to his involvement in the capture of the Lollard rebel, Sir John Oldcastle, in 1417.[93] It is notable that all of these tales were current in the second half of the sixteenth century but are unknown before this time. These cases rather confirm what Evans said on the subject: "we cannot escape a strong suspicion that these knighthoods have been fathered upon history by [later] family pride."[94]

What is remarkable about fifteenth-century poetic references to the descendants of Dafydd Gam and Roger Fychan is that their service in France (and their definite or apparent deaths) is never recorded. Two generations after 1415 one of Dafydd's grandsons, Philip Fychan, was killed by a cannon ball at the siege of Harlech in 1468: the poet Huw Cae Llwyd in an elegy mentions both Philip's illustrious grandfather and Philip's own service in France. What Huw failed to do, however, was to commemorate Dafydd's death in more noble circumstances at Agincourt.[95] Perhaps this is not surprising given the proximity of Agincourt to the end of a failed national rebellion. Equally, since the majority of their descendants took the Yorkist side in the domestic wars of the fifteenth century, the memory of Dafydd's consistent support of the Lancastrian regime during the rebellion might have been uncomfortable. Even so, Agincourt remains perhaps the only major battle of the Hundred Years War not recorded in Welsh poetry. In light of the evidence discussed above, however, it seems that, for Watcyn Llwyd and Roger Fychan, no grandiose commemoration of their deaths at Agincourt was appropriate: they did not die there.

---

[92] For Walter or Watcyn Llwyd in the muster at Brecon: TNA, E 101/46/20 m. 3; and among the sick at Harfleur: TNA, E 101/45/1 m.7.

[93] For the full details and references, see Rev. W.V. Lloyd, "A Powysian at Agincourt, Sir Griffith Vaughan," *Montgomeryshire Collections* 2 (1869), 139–72, and Glanmor Williams, "Sir Gruffydd Fychan (?–1447)," in *Montgomeryshire Collections* 86 (1998), 17–28. For Griffin Fordon or Fordet, TNA, E 101/45/13 m. 4. This Griffin can be identified with a man-at-arms in the garrison of Montgomery between 1404 and 1407: TNA, E 101/44/6 mm. 3, 6 and E 101/44/14 m. 1.

[94] Evans, *Wales and the Wars of the Roses*, p. 28.

[95] See, for example, *Gwaith Huw Cae Llwyd ac Eraill*, ed. L. Harries (Cardiff, 1953), p. 99 (XXXIX lines 13–20), and D. Foster Evans, "'Tŵr Dewr Gwncwerwr' ('A Brave Conquerors Tower')," in *The Impact of the Edwardian Castles in North Wales*, ed. Diane M. Williams and John R. Kenyon (Oxford and Oakville, CT, 2009), pp. 125–6, n. 34.

Conclusions

Regardless of the veracity of stories which have been told about the Welsh serving in Henry V's army in 1415, it is evident that this famous campaign came at an interesting juncture in the history of later medieval Wales. The motives for service in the army of 1415 must have been many and varied. For some it can be viewed as part of a process of renegotiation of loyalties and fortunes following the failure of their rebellion. It is debatable how much choice some of these men had in the matter. Though Merbury was never implicated in the attempts at extortion from men ordered to serve it is clear that this process was common in the succeeding years, as it had been in the fourteenth century.[96] For others it seems that service in 1415 was an extension of an earlier military career or the beginning of a new one. Some of these careers, notably that of Gruffudd Dwnn, were distinguished, and did much, in English eyes, to atone for earlier misdemeanors in the cause of rebellion. It seems that the company of Welsh archers raised for the French campaign of 1415 was in two parts. Those men recruited from the Duchy of Lancaster estates appear to have had fewer compulsions put upon them than their counterparts from the Principality, where many former rebels appear to have been required to serve or to have provided someone to serve in their stead. None of this service, however, was remembered in Welsh culture. Agincourt remains, despite Shakespeare's characters, a peculiarly English victory, which is a fair reflection of the composition of Henry's army.

The actual contribution of Henry V's Welsh estates to his expeditionary army in 1415 is well recorded, primarily through the efficiency of John Merbury and his officers. As a contribution to the whole, it was hardly extensive: whatever their achievements, these Welsh archers cannot be said to have won the battle of Agincourt for Henry V. We have seen that it is improbable that more than four hundred of these men were still with the army when it left Harfleur for Calais. In light of what is known of military organization in the early years of the fifteenth century this company of Welsh archers, predominately serving on foot, is almost a throwback to the reigns of Edward I, his son and his grandson. In the first half of the fourteenth century Welsh foot soldiers recruited from royal and Marcher estates dominated royal armies. Indeed, it may be that the very scale of Edward I's armies sent to his wars in Scotland, routinely more than ten thousand strong, was made possible only by the resources available to him from the recently conquered shires and the March of Wales.[97] In the context of King Henry's army, the recruitment of this company of archers, as those from Cheshire and Lancashire, makes sense. Whatever Henry's precise intentions were in 1415, some sieges were inevitable. The demands of siege warfare required significant numbers of

---

[96] See Davies, *Lordship and Society*, pp. 81–4, for earlier examples of seignorial extortion on the pretext of military service.
[97] A.J. Chapman, "The Welsh Soldier: 1283–1422" (unpublished University of Southampton Ph.D. thesis, 2009), and idem, "Welshmen in the Armies of Edward I," in *The Impact of the Edwardian Castles in Wales*, ed. Williams and Kenyon, pp. 175–82.

men who could be maintained relatively cheaply, and foot archers made fewer demands on the supply chain or the available grazing during a siege. It may be that, as in 1400, Henry was convinced of the need for the largest possible army and that his experiences in Wales had convinced him of the effectiveness of archers in hostile terrain. Where better to recruit such men than from the royal demesne? Such a process had other benefits to the crown. Through capable officials such as Merbury, valuable military experience gained in the course of the rebellion – on either side – could be harnessed. It seems clear that many of the Welshmen serving in 1415 were former rebels with something to gain. What can be traced of their subsequent careers shows that involvement in rebellion need not have been disastrous. Proportionately, few appear to have forged careers as soldiers, but there seems little doubt that service in 1415 may have eased the process of reconciliation between people and royal authority across southern Wales.

Gunners, Aides and Archers: The Personnel of the English Ordnance Companies in Normandy in the Fifteenth Century*

Andy King

Edward III is widely credited by historians with having presided over a military revolution in English arms; in keeping with this, he was not slow in adapting to technical innovation in the field of war. The English employed guns at Crécy in 1346; and by the time the French war broke out again in 1369 guns were playing an increasingly important role, although mainly at this time in a defensive role in garrisons. The Tower of London was used as an arsenal from which guns were dispatched to English fortresses ranging from Calais to Roxburgh and Berwick.[1] Garrison captains were also authorized to hire guns and gunners themselves on a private enterprise basis. In 1384 Sir Thomas de Beauchamp, the former captain of Carisbrook Castle on the Isle of Wight, was paid £26 5s. by the Crown to reimburse him for the cost of hiring five gunners (*canonarii*) and their cannons, and another gunner with three cannons. They were hired to defend the island against the French galley fleet which had been cruising the channel.[2] Unfortunately, no details are given of the identity of the gunners or the type of firearms with which they were equipped (though the three guns used by one of these gunners may well have been mounted together on a single multiple carriage of the type known as a *ribaudequin*).[3] Nor is it recorded for how long they served – and thus what their wages were. Indeed, while there are plentiful records of the use of guns by the English in the fourteenth century, very much less is recorded regarding the men who actually fired them. The names of a few gunners are known, such as John Arblaster (whose surname was surely occupational), recorded as valet of the king's artillery (*valettus artillerie domini regis*) at Queenborough Castle, Kent, in 1373–5. However, we know rather more about the men who commanded or administered them, such as John Derby, clerk of the office of the king's guns

---

*I would like to thank Prof. Anne Curry and Dr Claire Etty for reading and commenting on various drafts of this paper. This paper has arisen from research for the AHRC-funded project "The Soldier in Later Medieval England," and the record data has been drawn from the project website: www.medievalsoldier.org.

[1] T.F. Tout, "Firearms in England in the Fourteenth Century," *English Historical Review* 26 (1911), 678.
[2] The National Archives [TNA], E 403/505, m. 9.
[3] For *ribaudequins*, see Robert D. Smith and Kelly DeVries, *The Artillery of the Dukes of Burgundy, 1363–1477* (Woodbridge, 2005), pp. 50–51.

(*clericus pro officio gunnorum regis*) in 1372, and William Newlyn, master of guns in the town of Calais (*magister gunnovum de villa Calesie*) in 1375.[4]

It was in the fifteenth century, however, that gunpowder artillery really came into its own, while the voluminous surviving records of the English administration in Normandy means that we are better informed about the people who fired and tended these weapons.[5] After 1415 large guns came to play an increasingly important offensive role in English armies, as the invasion and occupation of Normandy required frequent sieges of French towns. It thus became necessary to organize the artillery on a more regular basis, particularly after the Treaty of Troyes and the death of Henry V left England's minority government with an indefinite military commitment in France. Consequently, the office of Master of the King's Ordnance in Normandy had been established by 1423, with Robert Cottes as its first known incumbent.[6] All together, nine individuals have been identified as holding this office (though with a number of different designations) in the twenty-five years until 1448, and, at times, there were two masters acting concurrently, suggesting that separate ordnance companies might be formed as occasion demanded.[7] Philibert de Moulant and William Gloucester both led ordnance companies at the siege of Louviers in 1431, when Moulant had been appointed by the English crown as a 'Master and surveyor of the king's artillery in France' (*maistre et visiteur de nostre artillerie en France*).[8]

The master filled an administrative rather than a technical role[9] and his office did not, therefore, call for any gunnery expertise. Unfortunately, there is only patchy evidence for men under his command who *did* possess such expertise. Nevertheless, there is a good run of musters for the 1430s and early 1440s which provide good evidence for the composition of the ordnance company during that period. From these, it appears that a core company of seven ordnance personnel was retained at Rouen, together with an escort of a man-at-arms and twelve or eighteen archers. The seven specialists consisted of a master forger (*forgeur*) and his aide, a master carpenter and his aide, a master mason, a master gunner (*artillier*) and a carter. Forgers, or smiths, were employed to maintain and repair the guns.[10] Carpenters were required to construct wooden firing carriages for the artillery, for guns were usually transported separately, without a carriage, which would be constructed on site, although these were sometimes assembled from prefabricated parts. Carpenters would also be employed to construct mantlets,

---

[4] Tout, "Firearms in England," p. 682, 694–5.
[5] Thirty or so gunners accompanied the expeditionary army of 1415, their names indicative of continental origin: A. Curry, *Agincourt. A New History* (Stroud, 2005), p. 60.
[6] He is actually referred to as "Master of ordnances of the artillery of the lord Regent of the realm of France" (*Maistre des ordonnances de lartillerie de monseigneur le Regent le royaume de France*); C.T. Allmand, "L'artillerie de l'armée Anglaise et son organisation a l'époque de Jeanne d'Arc," in *Jeanne d'Arc, une époque, un rayonnement*, ed. R. Pernaud (Paris, 1982), p. 82.
[7] They are listed by Allmand, "L'artillerie de l'armée anglaise," pp. 75, 82–3.
[8] Bibliothèque Nationale de France [BNF], manuscrit français [ms. fr.] 25769/529, 25770/632; Allmand, "L'artillerie de l'armée anglaise," p. 82.
[9] Ibid., p. 75.
[10] Smith and DeVries, *Artillery of the Dukes of Burgundy*, pp. 53–4.

the large swivelling wooden shields which protected the gun and its crew while it was being reloaded.[11] Masons served a vital function for, although cast-iron shot was sometimes used from the early fifteenth century, stone shot remained the usual form of ammunition until after the end of the French wars. Masons were required to cut the stone to size, a task which obviously required a high degree of precision; an example of this role is provided by the commission issued by the Chancery in England to Robert Westerley, mason, in 1431, 'to provide the stonecutters, artificers and labourers required to make stones for the king's cannon; also stones and carriage for the same'.[12] The gunners were responsible for loading and firing the guns. Finally, carters were required to move the guns and the attendant paraphernalia.

What is immediately apparent from the musters is the surprisingly high turnover of personnel in the ordnance company, and of gunners in particular. Philipot Lorin served with the Rouen ordnance company as a master gunner (*maistre artilleur*) for over three years (1435–8),[13] while John Potel served as a master gunner (*maistre canonnier*) on various occasions between 1431 and 1436.[14] Otherwise, few gunners appear to have served for more than a year or two. Nor was this turnover restricted just to gunners.

During the two-year period from January 1345 to December 1437 three master forgers served in succession, with five different aides; these included Guillot Robin, who went on to serve as the aide for his replacement, Thomas Thony, and may have served as a stopgap master forger until Thony could be recruited. There were four successive master carpenters with six different aides (unless Robin Bastard and Robin Bardoul are in fact the same man), three gunners (although William Benoit may just have been a temporary replacement for Philpot Lorin, while the latter was indisposed or otherwise engaged) and five carters. However, one master mason, John Godfrey, served throughout this time. Indeed, despite this high turnover, there were some individuals who served for a considerable period. Thomas de Thony served a seven-year stint as master forger with the Rouen company, although he had five different aides during these seven years.[15] Similarly, the carter William Giroust served for a period of seven years under three different masters.

---

[11] Ibid., pp. 49, 51.
[12] *Calendar of Patent Rolls* [*CPR*], *1429–36*, p. 44; Smith and DeVries, *Artillery of the Dukes of Burgundy*, p. 47. The Crown maintained several quarries near Caen to provide gun-stones; R.A. Newhall, *The English Conquest of Normandy 1416–1424: A Study in Fifteenth-Century Warfare* (New Haven, 1924), p. 263.
[13] BNF, ms. fr. 25772/1016, 25774/1298.
[14] BNF, ms. fr. 25770/632, 25773/1144.
[15] Guillot Robin, Perrin Auffroy, Michael Mahon, Thomas de Mahoyn and Jean Rigault.

Table 1: Personnel of the Ordnance Company based at Rouen, 1435–7[16]

Date	Master Forger	Master Forger's Aide	Master Carpenter	Master Carpenter's Aide	Master Mason	Master Artillerer	Carter
Jan. 1435, Rouen	John le Fevre	Raulin Poucin	Thomas Pourpoint	Peter Surgys	John Godfrey	Raulin Talbot	Jacquet Denneau
Feb. 1435, Rouen	John le Fevre	Piers Auffroy	Thomas Pourpoint	Peter Surgys	John Godfrey	Raulin Talbot	Jacquet Denneau
Oct. 1435, Mantes	John le Fevre	Piers Auffroy	Nicholas Bradway	Robin Bastard	John Godfrey	Raulin Talbot	John Lovell
Nov. 1435	John le Fevre	Piers Auffroy	Nicholas Bradway	Robin Bardoul	John Godfrey	Philpot Lorin	John le Large
Feb. 1436, siege of Meulan	John le Fevre	Robin Deschamps	Nicholas Bradway	John Rassin	John Godfrey	William Benoit	William Johns
Apr. 1436	Guillot Robin	William Harel	Nicholas Bradway	John Gros	John Godfrey	Philpot Lorin	William Giroust
Sep. 1436, Rouen	Thomas Thony	Guillot Robin	Nicholas Bradway	William Poisson	John Godfrey	Philpot Lorin	William Giroust
Jan.–Feb. 1437, Rouen	Thomas Thony	Guillot Robin	John Soissons	William Poisson	John Godfrey	Philpot Lorin	William Giroust
Mar.–July 1437, Rouen	Thomas Thony	Guillot Robin	John Temple	William Poisson	John Godfrey	Philpot Lorin	William Giroust
Dec. 1437	Thomas Thony	Michael Mahon	John Temple	William Poisson	John Godfrey	Philpot Lorin	William Giroust

Table 2: Service of William Giroust, carter, in the ordnance company, 1436–43

Captain	Date	Reference
William Gloucester	Aug. 1436, Rouen	BNF, naf. 8606/53
William Gloucester	Dec. 1437	BL, Add. Ch. 6919
William Forster	July 1438, Espriville, with Lord Talbot's army	BNF, naf. 8602/25
Henry Griffith	Aug 1441	BL, Add. Ch. 12105
[not specified]	1442, siege of Conches	BNF, naf. 8606/89
Henry Griffith	Dec. 1443	BNF, ms. fr. 25777/1665

[16] This period has been chosen because a good run of musters survives. References: Archives Départmentales de la Seine-Maritime [ADSM], Rouen, 100J/33/9, 10; British Library [BL], Additional Charter [Add. Ch.] 6892, 6919, 11875; BNF, ms. fr. 25773/1016, 1075, 1169, 1170, 1172, 1183, 1189, 1200, nouvelle acquisition française [naf.] 8606/53.

Table 3: Service of John Godfrey, master mason, in the ordnance company, 1431–44

Captain	Date	Reference
William Gloucester	Sep. 1431, siege of Louviers	BNF, ms. fr. 25770/632
William Gloucester	Mar. 1432, siege of Chalonel	BNF, ms. fr. 25772/291
William Gloucester	Oct. 1434, Rouen	BNF, ms. fr. 25772/910
William Gloucester	Jan. 1435, Paris	ADSM, 100J/33/9
William Gloucester	Feb. 1435, Rouen	ADSM, 100J/33/10
William Gloucester	Oct. 1435, Mantes	BL, Add. Ch. 11875
William Gloucester	Feb. 1436, siege of Meulan	BL, Add. Ch. 6892
William Gloucester	1436, Rouen	BNF, ms. fr. 25773/1169–70, 1172, 1183; naf. 8606/53
William Gloucester	Oct. 1437, siege of Tancarville, with Lord Talbot's army	BNF, ms. fr. 25773/1144
William Gloucester	Dec. 1437, Pont de l'Arche, with Lord Talbot's army	BNF, ms. fr. 25774/1283
William Gloucester	Jan. 1438, Chartres, with Lord Talbot's army	BNF, ms. fr. 25774/1296
William Forster	July 1438, Espriville, with Lord Talbot's army	BNF, naf. 8602/25
Henry Griffith	Aug. 1441	BL, Add. Ch. 12105
[not specified]	1442, siege of Conches	BNF, naf. 8606/89
Henry Griffith	Sep. 1442, Conches garrison	AN, K 67/12/73
Henry Griffith	1443	BNF, ms. fr. 25777/1658, 1665
Henry Griffith	Jan. 1444	BNF, ms. fr. 25777/1669

Perhaps the outstanding example, however, is John Godfrey, who served with the ordnance company for no less than thirteen years, during which he is known to have served under three masters of the ordnance, William Gloucester, William Forster and Henry Griffith. In fact, his association with the ordnance pre-dated even this, for he had served in the ordnance company of John Harbottle in 1427, as an archer.[17] The master of ordnance retained a permanent escort, listed in a survey of the English forces in Normandy in Michaelmas 1434 as one mounted lance and seventeen archers.[18] And John Godfrey was not the only one of these

---

[17] BL, Add. Ch. 11572; BNF, ms. fr. 25768/245.
[18] *Letters and Papers Illustrative of the Wars of the English in France during the Reign of Henry the Sixth*, ed. Joseph Stevenson, Rolls Series xxii, 3 vols. in 2 parts (1861–64), II, ii, 545.

archers who subsequently served in a technical capacity. Before serving as a master carpenter in William Gloucester's ordnance company, Thomas Pourpoint had served in the same company as an archer; subsequently, he left the ordnance company to serve once again as an archer with Gloucester, in the garrison of Rouen bridge in 1438.[19]

Perhaps surprisingly, however, archers also went on to serve as gunners. William Parent was serving as an archer in the ordnance company under William Gloucester at the siege of Louviers in September 1431. By April 1434, some two and a half years later, he was serving as a valet gunner in an ordnance company detached to serve in the field with the Earl of Arundel (he is described here as a yeoman), and by July he was serving as a master gunner. Indeed, it is possible that men such as Godfrey, Pourpoint and Parent were serving in the ordnance company as archers while they learnt their specialist crafts. Conversely, Nicholas Bradway served as master carpenter for a year, and then for another two years as an archer.[20] Perhaps the most varied career, however, was that of Robin Bardoul, who served as the master forger's aide, then as the master carpenter's aide and finally as an archer. Clearly, these were men with particular skills, such as carpentry, who nevertheless acted in different roles as required.

Table 4: Service of Robin Bardoul in the ordnance company, 1434–6

Date	Function	Reference
Oct. 1434, Rouen	Master forger's aide	BNF, ms. fr. 25772/910
Nov. 1435	Master carpenter's aide	BNF, ms. fr. 25772/1016
Feb. 1436, siege of Meulan	Archer	BL, Add. Ch. 6892
Apr. 1436	Archer	BNF, ms. fr. 25773/1075

This flexibility notwithstanding, there was a striking degree of continuity in the archers who provided an escort for the ordnance company. Raulin Ponchart served for three years,[21] John Acton and John Hamel for five.[22] The appropriately named William Scarlet served as an archer for a year (1435–6), and then for three more years as a man-at-arms (until 1438).[23] Few, however, could match the record of Alain Bryd, who served as an archer at the siege of Chalonet in 1432, and was still serving as that capacity ten years later, in 1442, at the siege of Conches.[24]

[19] ADSM, 100J/30/46; BNF, ms. fr. 25774/1319.
[20] BNF, ms. fr. 25773/1170; naf. 8602/25; and see Table 1, above.
[21] 1436–38; BNF, ms. fr. 25773/1075; naf. 8602/25. He is also listed as an archer of the ordnance company in a muster at Rouen in February 1435, but his name is scored through: ADSM, 100J/33/10.
[22] 1434–38. Acton: BNF, ms. fr. 25772/910, 25774/1324; Hamel: ms. fr. 25772/910; naf. 8602/25.
[23] ADSM, 100J/33/10; BL, Add. Ch. 6892; BNF, naf. 8606/53; ms. fr. 25774/1324.
[24] BNF, ms. fr. 25770/687; naf. 8606/89.

Family connections also seem to have played a role in recruitment. When John le Fevre served as a master smith at the siege of Louviers in 1431, and at Argentan in 1432, his aide was Polet le Fevre; another John le Fevre was serving at Louviers as an archer in the ordnance company.[25] When John Piart served as master carpenter for the ordnance company under the Earl of Arundel in 1434, he was accompanied by John Piart junior, presumably his son.[26] And in 1431, when John Godfrey was serving as a mason at the siege of Louviers, the escort of twelve archers included one Thomas Godfrey, presumably a relative; Thomas is recorded as an archer of William Gloucester's personal retinue on two other occasions.[27]

While the company based at Rouen was maintained on a permanent basis, it could be reinforced as occasion demanded. In this it matched the usual organization of English forces in Normandy, with standing garrisons supplemented by additional retinues and *creus* recruited as required.[28] For the siege of Meulan in 1436 the usual company of seven specialists was strengthened by an additional master gunner and his aid, along with six valet gunners (*valet cannoniers*).[29] Additional companies might also be raised. An ordnance *creu* of five was recruited to serve with the Earl of Arundel in 1434, for sieges and in the field. It consisted of a master gunner, his aide, a valet gunner and two master carpenters (the carpenters being a father and son team).[30] Gunners were also retained on a permanent basis in other parts of France, such as John Collier, in the county of Maine.[31]

Other ordnance personnel remained only on the edge of the military establishment, being employed on a temporary basis, in *creus* or in detachments, although these still remained under the charge of the master of the king's artillery. William Harel served with the English in Normandy over a period of two years. Apart from a brief stint as the forgers' aide in the ordnance company at Rouen, he served as a *valet cannonier* in various temporary companies. John Baker's recorded career as a *valet cannonier* was even briefer, and again confined to temporary companies.

Others remained in the service of the Rouen company for a while and were then employed on a more casual basis. John le Fevre served as a master gunner at the siege of Louviers in 1431. By November 1432 he was serving with the ordnance company at Rouen as a master forger, in which role he served until the siege of Meulan in February 1436.[32] By April of that year he had been replaced at Rouen by Guillot Robin, but he served as a valet gunner in an ordnance detachment serving with Richard Neville, Earl of Salisbury.[33]

---

[25] BNF, ms. fr. 25770/632; ADSM, 100J/30/46.
[26] BNF, ms. fr. 25771/882.
[27] BNF, ms. fr. 25770/291, 687.
[28] Anne Curry, "The Organisation of Field Armies in Lancastrian Normandy," in *Armies, Chivalry and Warfare in Medieval Britain and France. Proceedings of the 1995 Harlaxton Symposium*, ed. Matthew Strickland (Stamford, 1998), pp. 207–31.
[29] BL, Add. Ch. 6892.
[30] BNF, ms. fr. 25771/882.
[31] *Letters and Papers*, ed. Stevenson, II, ii, 556.
[32] BNF, ms. fr., 25770/632; ADSM, 100J/30/46; BL, Add. Ch. 6892.
[33] BNF, ms. fr., 25773/1075; Archives Nationales [AN], Paris, K 64/10/8.

Table 5: Military service by William Harel and John Baker

Date	Service	Function	Reference
William Harel			
Nov. 1434	In the field, with Earl of Arundel	Valet cannonier	BL, Add. Ch. 1021
Apr. 1436	Ordnance company, Rouen	Master forger's aide	BNF, ms. fr. 25773/1075
June–July 1436	Additional ordnance, siege of Cambrai, with Earl of Salisbury	Valet cannonier	AN, K 64/10/6, 8
Sep.–Oct. 1436	Ordnance *creu*, siege of Fecamp, with Duke of York	Valet cannonier	BNF, ms. fr. 25773/1135, 1144
John Baker			
Feb. 1436	Ordnance company siege of Meulan	Valet cannonier	BL, Add. Ch. 6892
June–July 1436	Additional ordnance, siege of Cambrai, with Earl of Salisbury	Valet cannonier	AN, K 64/10/6, 8
July 1436	Ordnance creu, with Earl of Salisbury and Lord Fauconberg	Valet cannonier	BNF, ms. fr. 25773/1124

In the field, the specialists of the ordnance companies would command considerable numbers of assistants. These underlings were treated as labourers, and hired or impressed as occasion demanded. As such, they were not mustered, so unfortunately we have little idea of their numbers or identity. However, by way of comparison, in 1475 the Duke of Burgundy employed more than 100 carpenters, 20 carters and 6 stone cutters, as well as hundreds of sappers and other personnel, for an artillery train which included 45 large guns.[34] A rare illustration of the service undertaken by such additional men is provided by a letter of William Forster, master of the king's ordnance, written in August 1441. In it, he certified the services of John Thierry and John Lucas, two carters from the *vicomté* of Rouen, who had been in his employment from 17 May to 6 August, with two draught horses each. During this time they had helped to carry 'certain ordnances and equipment of war' (*certaines ordonnances et habillemens de guerre*) to Dieppe, in

---

[34] Robert D. Smith, "Good and Bold. A Late Fifteenth-Century Artillery Train," *Royal Armouries Yearbook* 6 (2001), 104.

the company of Lord Talbot, and conveyed some of the *ribaudequins* for Talbot's expedition to Pontoise. They had also been employed by the Duke of York in the Île de France.[35] Nevertheless, they were not employed solely to cart munitions, for they had also been called upon to help with the victualling of Pontoise when it was besieged by the French. In fact, Thierry had previously served as a purveyor for William Gloucester's ordnance company at the siege of Louviers in 1431 (although he is not recorded as serving on any other occasion).[36]

Rates of pay for gunners were not particularly high, despite their specialist skills, although some were paid an annual retainer. In 1433 William Page and his valet, 'English gunners' at Rouen, were paid 150 *livres Tournais* from the revenues of the Duke of Bedford's French lands; Colin Passart and his brother, also gunners, received 120 *livres Tournais* 'pro lez gonnys'; John Temple of Bristol, the master carpenter of the ordnance of artillery (*carpentario principali ordinationis artillerie*), and his servant, got 160 *livres Tournais*; and John Collier, gunner, in the county of Maine, got 75 *livres Tournais*.[37] Collier had previously served as a gunner in John Harbottle's ordnance company in 1427,[38] and Passart would serve with ordnance companies in the field in 1436, under the Earl of Salisbury and the Duke of York.[39] An indication of daily rates of pay is provided by the payment made to the master gunners John Boston and Hankyn Dunkirk, sent to Calais for two months in December 1435, with two *valettii gonnuers* in their retinue. John and Hankyn were paid 8d. and the valet gunners 6d. per day.[40] By way of comparison, mounted archers were customarily paid 6d. a day.

The overall wages bill for the ordnance company is indicated by an estimate of the expenses for the custody of Normandy in 1433–4 preserved by William Worcester.[41] The master of ordnance received 180 *livres Tournais* a year, and his wages were doubled when he rode to war. He was also paid for the wages of 'one master carpenter, one master forger, their aides, one master gunner (*artillier*), one master mason and a carter', at a rate of 55 *livres Tournais* per month, for a total of 660 *livres Tournais* per year. Some indication of the cost of employing the company in action can be gleaned from a receipt for 200 *livres Tournais* paid in February 1427 to John Harbottle for the wages of 'gunners, masons and carpenters, and others necessary for [his] office', for the siege of Pontorson.[42]

Finally, it is worth commenting on the nationality of these artillerymen. Unfortunately, although some muster rolls for English garrisons in France record the nationality of troops, none of the muster rolls for the ordnance companies contain any such details. Some were certainly English, such as William Page and his valet (who were specifically described as 'English gunners' – *Anglice gonners*), while others can be identified as English from their town of origin, such

[35] *Letters and Papers*, ed. Stevenson, II, ii, 463–4.
[36] BNF, ms. fr. 25770/632.
[37] *Letters and Papers*, ed. Stevenson, II, ii, 556.
[38] BNF, ms. fr. 25768/245.
[39] BNF, ms. fr. 25773/1124, 1128, 1135, 1144.
[40] TNA, E 403/722, m. 9.
[41] *Letters and Papers*, ed. Stevenson, II, ii, 562.
[42] Ibid., II, i, 70n.

as the master carpenter John Temple of Bristol. Similarly, John of Boston presumably came from a family originating in the Lincolnshire town of that name.[43] But the very fact that Page was described as 'English' suggests that many of his colleagues were not. From their surnames, men such as Jean le Fevre, Robin Deschamps, Pierre Auffroy, Jean Soissons and Guillaume Poisson were Normans, or Frenchmen, in English service.[44] And men of other nationalities served as well. Jacob d'Allemaigne served as a master gunner at the siege of Cambrai in July 1436, and as a valet gunner at Fecamp two months later; and there is no reason to doubt the evidence of his name that he was German.[45]

In conclusion, the factors that come across most strongly from the study of the personnel of the ordnance company are the high turnover rate and a surprising lack of specialization. Carpenters, forgers and masons must have been recruited from among those who already possessed these skills in civilian life, but nevertheless they were often required to act as jacks-of-all-trades. Expertise in firing guns, however, was something which obviously could not be picked up except in a military context, and this perhaps helps to explain why so many of the ordnance companies seem to have been Normans or Frenchmen, rather than Englishmen, for there was no great call for gunners in the comparatively peaceful conditions of fifteenth-century England (outside of the Scottish marches). Yet even master gunners do not seem to have remained in service for very long periods, which may suggest that their skills were not too difficult to pick up. And even while learning the arcane mysteries of their trade, apprentice gunners seem to have been expected to serve as archers as well.

Rates of pay for the ordnance company probably did work out as higher than those a skilled craftsman could usually command (at least in England), if only because – despite the strictures of the Church – war was no great respecter of religious festivals, and so soldiers had to be paid for every day of the year, whereas craftsmen and labourers would only be paid for working days.[46] On the other hand, service in the ordnance company is unlikely to have presented many opportunities for plunder, and – by the very nature of that service – fewer opportunities for ransoming prisoners; it did not, therefore, offer much in the way of prospects of enrichment. And for martially inclined Englishmen a long career as a gunner, with little opportunity for making a quick fortune, may not have seemed a particularly attractive proposition, particularly for carpenters, smiths and masons who could easily earn a living from their trade at home in a more peaceful capacity – and indeed a more pleasant one. For in addition to the everyday risks of war, gunners

---

[43] See above, nn. 39, 42. Thomas Boston of London, gunner, who took out letters of protection for service in France in 1431, may have been a relative. The protection is recorded only in the writ ordering its revocation; *CPR, 1429–36*, p. 180.

[44] Note that forenames have generally been put in an Anglicised form for this paper; however, they were usually recorded in musters in a French form, and therefore are not a good guide to nationality.

[45] AN, K 64/10/8; BNF, ms. fr. 25773/1135.

[46] In the 1480s wages were typically 6d. a day for a skilled craftsman and 3d. or 4d. for an unskilled labourer; Christopher Dyer, *Standards of Living in the Later Middle Ages. Social Change in England, c.1200–1520* (Cambridge, 1989), p. 227.

worked in a dirty and deafeningly noisy environment. And although the dangers posed by medieval guns to their own crews have undoubtedly been greatly exaggerated, the potential for catastrophic accident – however remote – can have done little to encourage notions of long service.

Defense, Honor and Community: The Military and Social Bonds of the Dukes of Burgundy and the Flemish Shooting Guilds

Laura Crombie

Archery and crossbow guilds are first documented in Flanders in the early fourteenth century, and grew from military origins to become some of the leading cultural and festive groups in late medieval towns. Though the shooting guilds of the fifteenth century maintained a military function, and could become soldiers in ducal armies, they had become social and religious guilds and a vibrant part of late medieval urban culture. The guilds, like religious confraternities, had chapels and paid priests for performing services.[1] And, like craft guilds, the shooters held annual meals, strengthening their unity through commensality.[2] The guilds were an important part of regional festive networks, holding competitions across the Low Countries that could last weeks and bring in hundreds of fully armed competitors.[3] A great deal could be said about the civic and local importance of

---

[1] For confraternities in general see C. Black, "The Development of Confraternity Studies over the Past Thirty Years," in *The Politics of Ritual Kinship. Confraternities and Social Order in Early Modern Italy*, ed. N. Terpstra (Cambridge, 2000), pp. 9–29. For Flemish religious confraternities see P. Trio, "Old Stories and New Themes: An Overview of the Historiography of Confraternities in the Low Countries from the Thirteenth to the Sixteenth Centuries," in *Religious and Laity in Western Europe 1000–1400: Interaction, Negotiation, and Power*, ed. E. Jamroziak and J. Burton (Turnhout, 2006), pp. 357–84; P. Trio, "Middeleeuwse Broederschappen in de Nederlanden. Aan balans en perspectieven voor verder onderzoek," *Tijdschrift voor de Geschiedenis van het Katholiek Leven in de Nederlanden, Trajecta* 3 (1994), 415–26; A. Brown, *Civic Ceremony and Religion in Bruges c.1300–1520* (Cambridge, 2011); A. Brown, "Bruges and the 'Burgundian Theatre-State': Charles the Bold and Our Lady of the Snow," *History* 84 (1999), 573–89.

[2] For the importance of commensality to craft guilds see G. Rosser, "Going to the Fraternity Feast; Commensality and Social Relations in Late Medieval England," *Journal of British Studies* 33 (1994), 430–46; A. Douglas, "Midsummer in Salisbury, the Tailor's Guild and Confraternity, 1444–1642," *Renaissance and Reformation* 13 (1989), 35–51; M. McRee, "Unity or Division? The Social Meaning of Guild Ceremony in Urban Communities," in *City and Spectacle in Medieval Europe*, ed. B.A. Hanawalt and K.L. Regerson (London, 1994), 189–207. For Flanders see P. Stabel, "Organization corporative et production d'œuvres d'art à Bruges à la fin du Moyen Age et au début des temps modernes," *Le Moyen Age: Revue d'histoire et de Philologie* 113 (2007), 91–134, P. Stabel, "Guilds in Medieval Flanders: Myths and Realities of Guild life in an Export-oriented Environment," *Journal of Medieval History* 30 (2004), 187–212.

[3] For shooting competitions see M. de Schrijver and C. Dothee, *Les Concours de tir a l'arbalète des Gildes Médiévales* (Anvers, 1979), and for case studies of one competition, E. Matthieu, "Concour d'arc à main à Braine-le-Comte en 1433," *Annales de la Société Archéologique de*

shooting guilds, but rather than attempt such a huge study here, the focus of this paper will be the military and social interaction between the shooting guilds and the dukes of Burgundy.

Shooting guilds were not unique to Flanders; they are documented across northern Europe.[4] Flanders is, however, the most fitting location for a study of the guilds, firstly because of its numerous detailed archives, from the ducal central archives to town archives to private guild archives, and secondly, because of its urbanized nature: as the most urbanized area north of the Alps, a centre of civic culture and powerful economies, Flanders is an obvious choice for the study of any urban group.

The dukes did not create shooting guilds, but the ways in which the four Valois dukes of Burgundy interacted with the guilds are important. Even before he inherited the county of Flanders from his father-in-law, Louis of Male, in 1384, Philip the Bold had taken part in shoots with guilds, working to win the support of his new subjects. Under his successors, John the Fearless (1405–1419), Philip the Good (1419–1467) and Charles the Bold (1467–1477), such participation became a central aspect of relations between the Valois dukes and their urban subjects; such as can be broadly considered under three headings. First, and perhaps most obviously, the archery and crossbow guilds provided military service to the dukes, either as small elite groups or part of larger militias. Secondly, the dukes of Burgundy issued charters to shooting guilds, granting important rights and privileges to them, often in return for service. The dates and priorities of such charters are revealing. Finally, the guilds and the dukes interacted socially, not only when dukes had themselves enrolled as guild members, but personally, with the dukes joining shooting guilds and taking part in crossbow competitions as active participants in urban festivities.

Military service: defensive

This is not the place to give a full narrative history of all military service provided by Flemish guilds to each of the four dukes of Burgundy; rather, a thematic overview with selected examples will be given. In understanding guild service

l'arrondissement de Nivelles 3 (1892), 100–102; F. de Potter, "Landjuweel van 1497," in *Het Belfort*, ed. A. Siffer (Ghent, undated); A. Brown and G. Small, *Court and Civic Society in the Burgundian Low Countries c.1420–c.1520* (Manchester, 2007), pp. 219–25; J. Vannerus, "Trois documents relatifs aux concours de tir à l'arbalétrier à Malines en 1458 et en 1495," *Bulletin de la Commission Royale d'histoire* 97 (1933), 203–54.

[4] For other areas see E. van Autenboer, *De Kaarten van de Schuttersgilden van het Hertogdom Brabant (1300–1800), stuk 1–2* (Tilburg, 1993–4); *Schutters in Holland-Kracht en Zenuwen van stad*, ed. M. Carasso-Kok and J.-L. Van Halm (Haarlem, 1988); L-A. Delaunay, *Étude sur les Anciennes Compagnies d'Archers, d'Arbalétriers et d'Arquebusiers* (Paris, 1879); A. Janvier, "Notice sur les anciennes corporations d'archers, d'arbalétriers, de coulveriniers et d'arquebusiers des villes de Picardie," *Mémoires de la Société des Antiquaires de la Picardie* 14 (1855); G. LaValley, *Les Compagnies du Papegay, particulièrement à Caen* (Paris, 1881); H. Stein, *Archers d'autrefois; Archers d'aujourd'hui* (Paris, 1925).

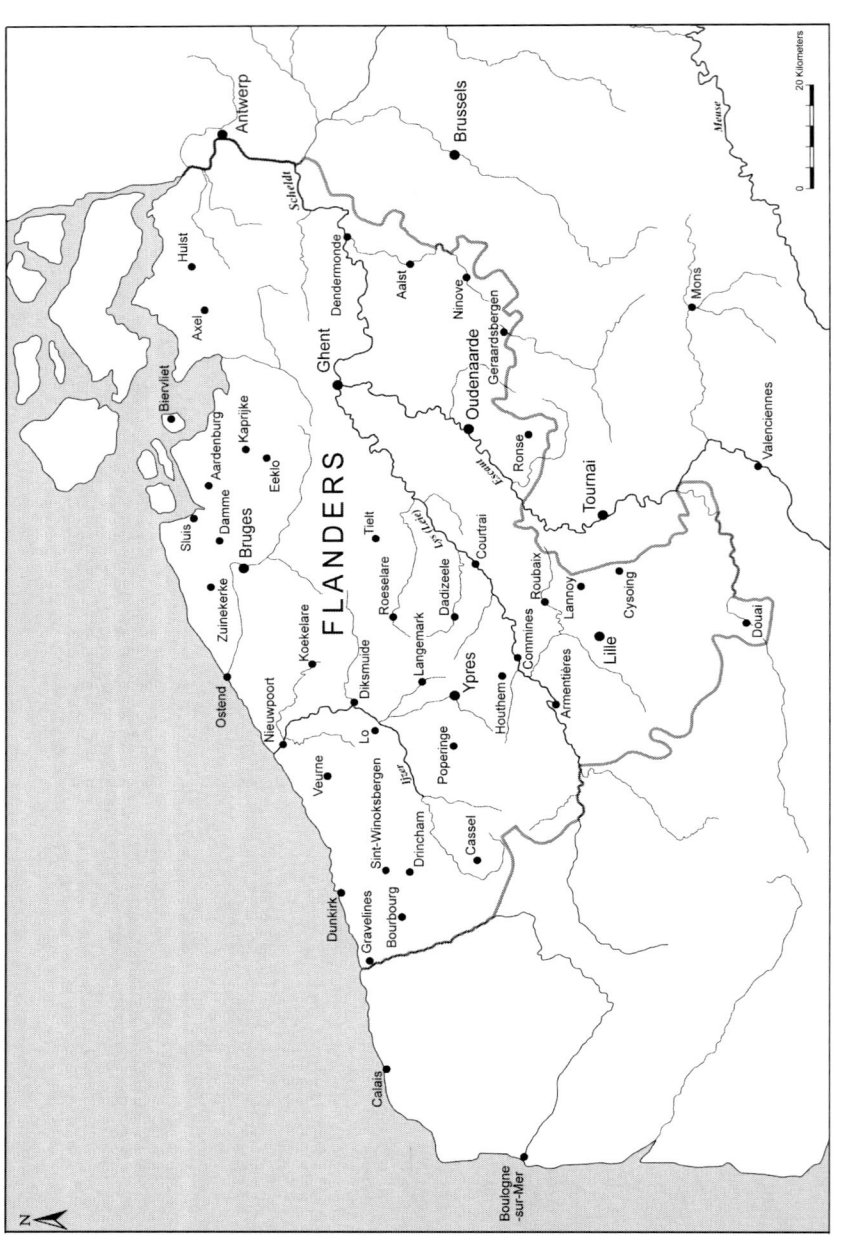

Map 1: Flanders

to the dukes, it is worth emphasizing that the guilds had served the counts of Flanders in the fourteenth century and provided continuous service to all four dukes and their Hapsburg successors. Guilds' primary role was as defenders, not just of their towns but also of Flanders as a whole. Less often, guilds also went out of Flanders in military service to the dukes. Their importance as parts of larger forces in the service of John the Fearless, Philip the Good and Charles the Bold will be demonstrated.

Archers and crossbowmen had been guarding their towns since civic records began, in the 1280s in Ghent and Bruges and from 1301 in Lille.[5] Civic autonomy meant that dukes rarely needed to interfere in town defense, as towns proudly took responsibility for maintaining their own walls and their own defenders. For example, in 1382, on the eve of the battle of Rosebeke, the aldermen of Lille, fearing attack from rebellious Ghent forces, passed ordinances that crossbowmen must watch the walls and must not leave the town.[6] In the same year that such prescriptive legislation was passed the town financial accounts record payments made to the named guildsmen who guarded key areas of Lille's walls.[7] Towns had the power to look after their own defenses, as is well documented in town accounts, but this did not mean that dukes took no interest in the military service provided by the shooting guilds in defending their walls. In 1386 Philip the Bold wrote to congratulate the crossbowmen of Courtrai on their "good and loyal service" in defending the town in the same period of uncertainty.[8]

Archers and crossbowmen defended their town, however, and were often obliged to do so, without any ducal orders. For the defense of Flanders more generally the guilds also played an important role, and one which was more often orchestrated by ducal orders. At the start of his reign, in 1405, John the Fearless was threatened by English forces, and was concerned for the defense of coastal Flanders between English-held Calais and Sluis.[9] In May 1405 English fleets assaulted Sluis and John the Fearless drew forces from across Flanders to defend the coast. Arras sent sixteen crossbowmen from their guild of Saint George to Saint Omer for fifteen days;[10] Douai sent ten crossbowmen and twenty archers to Bruges "for defending the lands against the English;"[11] forty crossbowmen

---

[5] J. Vuylsteke, *Gentsche Stads en Balijuwsrekeningen, 1280–1336* (Ghent, 1900), pp. 41, 46, 52, 62, 67, 69, etc. The town accounts of Bruges, unlike those of Ghent, have not been published but are summarized in E. Gailliard, *Inventaire des archives de la ville de Bruges*, 6 vols. (Bruges, 1871–85), for example 2:376. See also his *Table analytique* (Bruges, 1885), pp. 16–17. The earliest Lille accounts, from 1301, have been published, M.A. Richie, *Compte de recettes et dépenses de la ville de Lille, 1301–2* (Lille, 1894).
[6] Lille, Archives Municipales [LAM], Ordinances des Magistrats, 373, fols. 3v, 6v, 12v, 35.
[7] LAM, Comptes de la Ville 16112, fols. 19v–22v.
[8] Archives Départementales du Nord [ADN], Lille, B1843, 50190.
[9] For background see R. Vaughan, *John the Fearless, the Growth of Burgundian Power* (London, 1966), pp. 20–22; B. Schnerb, *Jean sans Peur, le prince meurtrier* (Paris, 2005) pp. 159–62.
[10] Each man was paid five shillings a day, the constable double, for fifteen days; Arras also paid for 918 bolts and other equipment, pulled in carts by four horses: G. Espinas, *Les Origines du droit d'association, tome* II: *Documents*, 2 vols. (Lille, 1941), 2:112–13.
[11] The Douai accounts reveal that the crossbowmen were led by their constable, Estars Mahieu, the archers by Pierot Moiton, and that all thirty men named were sent out with fine new clothes. The

were requested from Lille for the same purpose, but only twenty-five were sent, although in June the guilds of Lille were sent to guard Gravelines "against the English" and in September a further twenty-four were sent "in service of the duke of Burgundy."[12] Though Gravelines was a small town, with a population of less than three hundred in the fifteenth century, its position on the Flemish border, and on the coast, very close to English lands, meant its defense was crucial in 1405.[13] From across Flanders small groups of archers and crossbowmen went in response to civic requests or ducal orders to defend the coast, showing their importance as defenders of the county.

In 1405 threats came from England, but Flanders' position between France and England meant that danger could also come from the south. In 1411, as tensions within France and in particular between John the Fearless and the Count of Armagnac grew worse, war loomed and guilds were once again required to defend not just their own towns, but Flanders as a whole.[14] In 1411 John the Fearless required the archers and crossbowmen of Lille to watch not just their own walls, but also those of other threatened places.[15] In September 1411 ten crossbowmen of the guild of Saint George of Lille went to Bapaulmes "for the security of that town."[16] After the death of Charles the Bold in 1477, and that of Mary of Burgundy in 1482, France was again a threat to Flanders, and the guilds were once more important in securing the southern border. For example, in the weeks following Charles's death, in the face of approaching French troops, the Hainault town of Valenciennes wrote to Mechelen, asking them to send their guilds, specifically crossbowmen and arquebusiers, for their defense.[17] After Mary's death in 1482 the Flemish guilds aided the defense of Leuven, in Brabant.[18] In the same period the Lille guilds were watching not just their own walls but all "parishes of this castellany of Lille."[19]

Military service: offensive

Archers and crossbowmen provided loyal and reliable defenders to their own towns and even to Flanders as a whole, but they were not always so reliable when they left Flanders as parts of larger ducal hosts. Flemish archery and crossbow

---

archers were paid one shilling a day less than the crossbowmen: Douai, Archives Municipales [DAM], CC 207, fols. 177–81.
[12] LAM, Comptes de la Ville 16146, fol. 32v, 16146 fol. 61v.
[13] P. Stabel, "Composition et recomposition des réseaux urbains des Pays-Bas au moyen âge," *Urban History* 12 (2010), 62–3.
[14] For context, Vaughan, *John the Fearless*, pp. 82–97; G. Small, *Late Medieval France* (Basingstoke, 2009), pp. 131–46.
[15] LAM, Comptes de la Ville 16216, fols. 65–80.
[16] LAM, Comptes de la Ville 16155, fol. 80.
[17] P.-J. van Doren, *Inventaire des archives de la ville de Malines*, 8 vols. (Malines, 1859–94), 3:241.
[18] P. Rock, *Historiek der Tiense Schutterijen* (Toreke, 1982), p. 13.
[19] LAM, Registre des Mandates 16975, n. 114.

guilds had been part of Louis of Male's army in the wars of Brabant succession in 1356,[20] and they continued to serve the Hapsburgs, as at the battle of Guinegate in 1479.[21] Guilds supplied significant soldiers before and after they served the Valois dukes of Burgundy, but service to the dukes is particularly well documented and could be successful in the short term under certain circumstances. The potential, problems and continuity of guild service to the dukes will be shown through three examples: that of John the Fearless in 1411; that of Philip the Good not just at Calais but also in 1453; and that of Charles the Bold at one of his many famous sieges, that of Neuss in 1474.

1411

In 1411 John the Fearless faced open war against the Orleans and Armagnac forces, who were gathered between Coucy and Soissons, just south of Artois, in Picardy. In August of that year John gathered his troops, including nobles, most importantly his brother Anthony, duke of Brabant, in Douai in southern Flanders.[22] John's larger army also included civic contingents, such as 10 crossbowmen from Lille, 11 from Ninove, 120 archers and an unspecified number of crossbowmen from Bruges, as well as contingents from Sluis, Damme, Monikeerde, Hoecke, Muyden, Blankenberghen, Oostende, Dixmuide and the Franc of Bruges.[23] His army enjoyed initial success, moving quickly south and capturing the town of Ham on 14 September; other towns, including Peronne and Nesle, quickly surrendered.

The skill of John the Fearless, and the power of his army, with its significant numbers of bowmen, is striking. It is also interesting to note the opinion of the chronicle of Ghent, which stated in 1411 that: "Ham in Vermandois was conquered by the citizens of Ghent."[24] In a short, fast campaign, the archers and crossbowmen from Flemish towns played an important role, but success did not last and the campaign ended badly. In his analysis of the ducal army, Richard Vaughan is very harsh on the Flemish militias, stating that they "deserted [John] en masse

---

[20] S. Boffa, *Warfare in Medieval Brabant, 1356–1406* (Woodbridge, 2004), pp. 3–9; Bartholomeus de Rantere, *Geschiedenis van Oudenaarde, van 621–1397*, ed. E. Dhoop and M. De Smet (Oudenarde, 1986), pp. 357.

[21] M. Strickland and R. Hardy, *The Great Warbow from Hastings to the Mary Rose* (Stroud, 2005), p. 55; M. Kendal, *Louis XI* (London, 1971), pp. 236–7; J.M. Tyrell, *Louis XI* (Boston, 1980), pp. 167–9; D. Potter, *Renaissance France at War. Armies, Culture and Society, c.1480–1560* (Woodbridge, 2008), pp. 102–3, 199. The only in-depth study is E. Richert, *Die Schlacht bei Guinegate, 7 August 1479* (Berlin, 1907).

[22] Vaughan, *John the Fearless*, pp. 87–96; Schnerb, *Jean sans Peur*, pp. 513–48.

[23] LAM, Comptes de la Ville 16155, fol. 80; Archives Générales du Royaume [AGR], Brussels, Chambre des Comptes, Ville de Ninove, 37085, fols. 10v–11; H. Godar, *Histoire de la gilde des archers de Saint Sébastien de la ville de Bruges* (Bruges, 1947), pp. 89–93; L.A. Vanhoutyre, *De Brugse Kruisbooggilde van Sint-Joris* (Handzame, 1968), pp. 54–6; Brugge Stadsarchief [BSA], Bruges, 210, accounts 1411, fols. 104–118 v. The Bruges crossbowmen were led by their headman Philip van Aerteke; BSA, 385, sint Jorisgilde, registre met ledenlijst enz. 1321–1531, fol. 68; Godar, *Histoire des Archers*, pp. 89–93.

[24] Quoted in Vaughan, *John the Fearless*, p. 144.

on 26 September as soon as its leader had contrived the pretext that there was no enemy to attack."[25] John's campaign of 1411 was far more complex than Vaughan implies, and though John did not hold any significant gains, the power of the Flemish militias, and the power of a mixed noble and bowmen army, had been shown. The guildsmen, like many in the militias, were urban figures; they could not indefinitely remain beyond Flanders, but could provide short-term power when they supported the objectives of their leader and had achievable goals.

Philip the Good: the siege of Calais and afterwards

Philip the Good's attempt to take English-held Calais in July 1436 is well documented and opinions of the viability of such a siege are greatly divided.[26] The size of Philip's army was certainly impressive, implying that he genuinely planned to besiege and take Calais despite many Flemings' commercial bonds with England and suspicion of the French. The force that arrived before Calais on 9 July 1436 included the leading nobles Jean de Croy, Jean de Lalaing and Waleran of Luxembourg, troops from the Low Countries and the two Burgundies and an impressive amount of artillery, perhaps as many as 60 *veuglaires*, 55 *crapaudeaux* and 450 *colveriniers*.[27]

Significant numbers of Flemish shooting guilds were also present at Calais, as were the militias in general; the militias were of course far larger and less well organized. Douai had provided £2,400 as well as the service of its militia and guildsmen;[28] the Bruges contingent included thirty archers;[29] and the crossbowmen too must have been there with the larger militia, but their new guild book, begun in 1437, chose not to mention the siege or its aftermath.[30] Ghent sent its militia, and members of shooting guilds,[31] as did Oudenaarde, with special costs for new

---

[25] Vaughan, *John the Fearless*, pp. 145–8.
[26] J. Doig, "New Source for the Siege of Calais in 1436," *English Historical Review* 110 (1995), pp. 404–7; K. DeVries, "'The Walls come Tumbling Down'. The Campaigns of Philip the Good and the Myth of Fortification Vulnerability to Early Gunpowder Weapons," in *The Hundred Years War: a Wider Focus*, ed. L.J.A. Villalon and D.J. Kagay (Leiden, 2005), pp. 434–7.
[27] M. Sommé, "L'Armée Bourguignonne au siège de Calais," in *Guerre et société en France, en Angleterre et en Bourgogne XIV–XV siècle*, ed. P. Contamine and M. Keen (Lille, 1991), pp. 196–213; R. Vaughan, *Philip the Good, the Apogee of Burgundy* (London, 1970), pp. 74–84; M.R. Thielemans, *Bourgogne et Angleterre. Relations politiques et économiques entre les Pays-Bas Bourguignons et l'Angleterre. 1435–1467* (Brussels, 1966), pp. 65–107; D. Nicholas, *Medieval Flanders* (London, 1992), pp. 327–9.
[28] DAM, EE 4.
[29] Godar, *Histoire des Archers*, pp. 95–101.
[30] The book begins with military service and loyalty to the dukes from 1380, but makes no mention of Calais, or the Bruges revolt that followed: BSA, 385, Sint Jorisgilde, register met ledenlijst enz. 1321–1531.
[31] F. De Potter, *Jaarboeken der Sint-Jorisgilde van Gent* (Ghent, 1904), pp. 58–60. The town accounts are clearer, naming the forty-six men of the guild of Saint George and nine archers of the guild of Saint Sebastian, and other clothes and arms, that formed part the Ghent militia, Ghent, Stadsarchief [GSA], 400, Rekeningen, 15, fols. 43–49v.

weapons and banners for the guilds of Saint George and Saint Sebastian.[32] Even the small town of Ninove sent its shooting guilds as well as militias.[33] Guilds were just a small part of the militias, but they seemed to have been a leading force among them. An ordinance from Ghent, for example, states that no one should stand before the banners of Ghent and Saint George, implying that the crossbow guild of Saint George was leading the militia.[34]

The complex political motives behind Philip's decision to attack Calais and Flemish reluctance to attack their economic ally need not concern us here;[35] important, rather, are the weaknesses and division within the ducal army. Flanders had changed greatly since 1411, with economic tensions between Ghent and Bruges influencing the hegemony of the Flemish army. When the men of Ghent were attacked, they felt that Bruges did not help sufficiently, and withdrew; Bruges, and other Flemish forces, followed.[36] The great force gathered by Philip the Good could not stay together and could not take a strong target. In 1411, when Flemish towns had supported John the Fearless in his quarrels with the Armagnac forces, they had united to leave Flanders and fight a common enemy, taking small and achievable targets. In 1436 an internally divided force that did not support ducal ambition and war with England could not take a fortress as strongly held as Calais. The failure of 1436 cannot be placed entirely on the Flemish militias, still less with the shooting guilds themselves, but they had shown that they were not as durable, as united or as effective as permanent soldiers.

It would be easy to follow Peter Arnade here and simply state that, "after the militias of Bruges and Ghent abandoned Philip the Good," at Calais "the Burgundians drew very selectively on the Flemish archers and crossbowmen."[37] But although Philip certainly had less faith in Ghent and Bruges forces after 1436 he continued to call on guilds from other parts of Flanders in periods of crisis. For example, the ducal army that defeated the rebellious Ghent forces at the battle of Gavere in 1453 included crossbowmen from Lille and archers from Douai.[38]

---

[32] Bartholomeus de Rantere, *Geschiedenis van Oudenaarde, tome 2*, pp. 39–57; Oudenaarde Stadsarchief, Oude Archief [OSAOA], Stadsrekeningen, 1436–1448, microfilm 686, include twelve pounds given to the deken of the Saint George guild, on top of wages and expenses for arms, for his 'good advice' to the town before Calais.
[33] AGR, Chambre des Comptes, Comptes des Villes 37103, fols. 5–7v.
[34] Quoted in P. Arnade, *Realms of Ritual, Burgundian Ceremony and Civic Life in Late Medieval Ghent* (Ithaca and London, 1996), p. 64, but he describes as 'contemporary' with a c.1315 chapel painting. The charter is in an undated cartulary: GSA Witteboek, 97, fol. 2. ter.
[35] J. Haemer's review of S. Rose, *Calais: An English Town in France, 1347–1558* (Woodbridge 2008); Book review from H.-Urban, J. Fris, "Documents Gantois concernant la levée du siège de Calais en 1436," in *Mélanges Paul Fredericq* (Brussels, 1904), pp. 245–58, J. Dumolyn, *De Brugse Opstand van 1436–1438* (Kortrijk-Heule, 1997), pp. 231–66.
[36] Nicholas, *Medieval Flanders*, pp. 326–37, Vaughan, *Philip the Good*, pp. 85–92, 101–9, Arnade, *Realms of Ritual*, pp. 84–5.
[37] Arnade, *Realms of Ritual*, p. 68.
[38] DAM, BB1; LAM, Comptes de la Ville 16194. Mechelen provided gunners, archers, equipment and money: P.-J. Van Doren, *Inventaire des archives de la ville de Malines*, 2:12–17. The chancellor, Nicholas Roulin, wrote to the town to praise the service of these loyal guild brothers: van Doren, *Inventaire des archives de la ville de Malines*, 4:61.

That Philip regarded the archers from Douai as valuable soldiers is made clear in 1455: after committing unspecified crimes, ten archers had been banished from the town by the aldermen, but Philip pardoned them of all crimes and ordered their return to the town in recognition of their "good and loyal service in the wars with Ghent."[39] Although militias were no longer called out *en masse*, small skilled groups of archers and crossbowmen continued to provide support for the dukes on their campaigns, proving their durability and martial value.

Neuss, 1474

Charles the Bold famously reorganized the Burgundian army, introducing more guns as well as regular troops, the so-called "Companies of Ordnance."[40] Though he preferred English archers, or other organized companies of mercenaries, Charles still called guildsmen to his armies. Town accounts from Bruges, Lille and Douai record payments for their archers, crossbowmen and even the newly established gunners' guilds being sent to Charles the Bold's victorious army at Montlhéry, against Louis XI in 1465, and guildsmen were also present in the Liege campaign of 1467.[41]

The best examples of military service of guildsmen to Charles the Bold comes from one of his sieges, that of Neuss. The ducal army that arrived before Neuss on 29 July 1474 had changed greatly from that of Philip the Good, even from that of Montlhéry. Charles's force was based on Companies of Ordnance, and in his analysis of Charles's army Richard Vaughan does not even mention Flemish militias or shooting guilds.[42] The force was not just huge, but international, including at least some English archers.[43] In a famous letter to Georges Chastellain Philippe Croy refers to English and Italian mercenaries,[44] while Olivier de la Marche emphasized the strength of artillery.[45]

Even within Charles's great army, however, Flemish shooting guilds were called upon. Those present included twenty archers from Lille,[46] twenty archers,

---

[39] DAM, affaires militaires EE 14.
[40] C. Brusten, *L'armée Bourguignon de 1465 à 1468* (Brussels, 1995).
[41] DAM, BB 1, f 20; LAM, Comptes de la Ville 16207, fols. 97–97v; Vanhoutyre, *De Brugse Kruisbooggilde*, pp. 56–62, and Godar, *Histoire des Archers*, pp. 80–137; C. Brusten, *L'armée Bourguignon de 1465 à 1468* (Brussels, 1995), pp. 44–9.
[42] R. Vaughan, *Charles the Bold, the Last Valois Duke of Burgundy* (London, 1973), pp. 197–299.
[43] M. Ballard, "An Expedition of English archers to Liège in 1467 and the Anglo-Burgundian Marriage Alliance," *Nottingham Medieval Studies* 34 (1990), pp. 152–74.
[44] Vaughan, *Charles the Bold*, pp. 327–8; for Italian mercenaries in particular see R.J. Walsh, *Charles the Bold and Italy (1467–77). Politics and Personnel* (Liverpool, 2005) pp. 341–66.
[45] Olivier de la Marche, *Collection complète des mémoires relatifs à l'histoire de France*, tome 2, ed. M. Petitot (Paris, 1825), pp. 290–97. For artillery see K. DeVries and R.D. Smith, *The Artillery of the Dukes of Burgundy, 1363–1477* (Woodbridge, 2005) pp. 174–8; J.-M. Cauchies, "Charles le Hardi à Neuss (1474/5): folie militaire ou contrainte politique?" *Publication du Centre Européen d'Etudes Bourguignonnes* 36 (1996), 105–16; P. Contamine, *Guerre, état et société à la fin du moyen âge* (Paris, 1972), pp. 279–89.
[46] LAM, Comptes de la Ville 16212, fol. 130v. They were led by a deputy constable called Jehan de Britanault dit le Holland.

six crossbowmen, six *colveriniers* and two *varlets* from Douai,[47] thirty archers and sixty crossbowmen from Bruges,[48] and contingents from Brabant; all sent more the next year.[49] Worthy of note were the Mechelen crossbowmen, who received a generous new charter in 1474 as thirty-six out of the ninety crossbowmen they had sent to the siege had died.[50] The siege failed not because of disunity of the Flemish militias or shooters, or because they left the field; in contrast, they seemed to support the ducal ambition and were willing to serve in return for privilege. Even with mercenaries, allies, a standing army and gunpowder weapons, therefore, Charles still relied in part on the Flemish shooting guilds and trusted them to provide valuable and meaningful service.[51]

John the Fearless, Philip the Good and Charles the Bold all called upon Flemish shooting guilds to form part of their forces outside Flanders and, although these campaigns were not always successful, the guilds proved themselves to be important soldiers, worthy of being pardoned and granted new tax exemptions. The guildsmen could never provide the mass, long-term service of the English archers, but could be effective in the short term if they supported ducal ambition and were set achievable targets.

Dukes, guilds and privileges: charters

In recognition of military service, or in preparation for it, the dukes issued charters to Flemish archery and crossbow guilds. Across the fifteenth century, ducal charters emphasized that the guilds should provide security and defense for their own towns as well as potential service in armies. Many charters of Philip the Good also make clear the loyalty that was expected from guilds, shown best by his request that the guilds wear his insignia on their liveries. All known charters from the dukes have been set out in Table 1, from which, and from the language of charters, several points emerge.

Philip the Bold spent much of his reign in Paris and issued few charters to guilds, of which only six survive.[52] John the Fearless confirmed a few during his 1405 joyous entries,[53] but most of his charters were issued after he had to

---

[47] DAM, BB1, fol. 41.
[48] Discussed by Vanhoutyre, *De Brugse Kruisbooggilde*, pp. 56–61, and Godar, *Histoire des Archers*, pp. 80–137, with expenses in the towns accounts confirming their numbers, though not Vanhoutyre's detailed description of their uniform as yellow and red. BSA, 210, Rekeningen 1475–6, fol. 137.
[49] P. Jansen, ed., *Om en rond de kruisbooggilden-juwelen, Oplen, Documenten* (Antwerpen, 1981), pp. 9–34.
[50] Doren, *Inventaire des Archives de la Ville de Malines*, 1:158.
[51] Compare to Nicholas, *Medieval Flanders*, p. 393: 'the military fecklessness of the Flemings was as notorious now as their bellicosity had been in the eleventh century. Charles generally avoided using Flemish troops.'
[52] R. Vaughan, *Philip the Bold. The Formation of the Burgundian State* (London, 1962), pp. 39–58.
[53] LAM, pièces aux titres, 15879, fol. 215.

flee Paris in 1408, particularly in 1409 and 1410, while trying to gain Flemish support.[54] None survive from after 1411, after militias disappointed him in his campaign and when his focus was once more on France. Many more charters have been found from the reign of Philip the Good, many of which form part of the thesis and ongoing research of Jonas Braekevelt at Ghent University.[55] The long reign of Philip the Good saw far greater ducal interaction with the guilds, bringing both more status and privileges to the shooters and a greater unity to Philip's lands. Like his father, Philip the Good confirmed the rights of the Lille crossbowmen upon his joyous entry, but no other charters were issued that year.[56] Relative peace came to Flanders in the 1420s, and only four charters issued to shooting guilds are known from this decade. Small numbers of charters were issued up to 1445, but a far larger number in 1446 and 1447. These two years saw seven charters issued to eight guilds, to archers and crossbowmen in large towns and smaller ones. Charters could be simply the rights to bear arms or long and detailed declarations of privileges. In small towns they were often issued at the behest of local lords. For the last decade of Philip's reign, 1457–67, thirteen charters were issued to shooting guilds in Flanders.

Many charters from Philip the Bold and John the Fearless refer to military need as well as civic honor. The first two dukes used guilds to provide themselves with potential soldiers, but also to bolster their support with powerful citizens. In a charter to the crossbowmen of Boezinge in December 1409 John the Fearless granted rights "for the increase, augmentation, growth and maintenance of this (guild), so that they will always be ready for service."[57] In August 1410 a similar charter was issued to the crossbowmen of Croix so that the guilds would be "always ready to serve us or our successors, counts and countesses of Flanders."[58] Like the charters of John the Fearless, many charters of Philip the Good refer to past and future service; but they also reflect greater defensive concerns connected to changing enemies. In the early years of his reign the concern was for the defense of southern towns. In 1419 Philip recognized the "good and diligent" service of the archers of Lille "in many places and areas where they have been;" "in service many of them have been killed and many others injured."[59] In 1423 the focus was Courtrai; in granting rights to the archers there, Philip refers to the "great need and necessity for the security and defense of (Courtrai), having able men sufficient and expert in shooting."[60]

References to border security in ducal charters changed after the Treaty of Arras in 1435, when Philip the Good recognized Charles VII, rather than Henry

---

[54] Vaughan, *John the Fearless*, pp. 74–92.
[55] J. Braekevelt, "Ordinances of Philip the Good for the County of Flanders and Lordship of Malines" (unpublished thesis in progress, University of Ghent).
[56] LAM, registre aux mandates, 16973, n. 90.
[57] Ghent, Rrijksarchief [GRA], raad van Vlaandered 7351, fols. 229v–230r.
[58] LAM, registre aux mandates 16973, fol. 15.
[59] Ibid., fol. 90.
[60] Rijksarchive Kortijk, 478; Register van de gilde van Sint-Sebastiaan fol. 2r–2v.

VI of England, as king of France.[61] Defensive concerns were now focused on the northern and coastal towns. In 1447 the archers of Berghes-Sint-Winnoks received new rights as the town "is located on the frontier of Calais," and "in the times of wars and commotions that have been in our said lands" the guild had been, and would be, necessary for "good fortification" of the town.[62] Similarly, the archers of Biervelt received new privileges in 1446 "as it is on the frontier by the sea" and so "in need of guarding."[63] Defensive concerns continued, but Philip's charters were also designed to encourage honorable, loyal guilds of archers and crossbowmen. The most obvious sign of guild loyalty was Philip's "request" for guilds to wear his emblem. The first surviving charter to refer to ducal insignia comes from 1446. In March that year the archers of Biervelt were granted permission to wear on "their robes our sign of the fusil and of two arrows in a cross of my lord Saint Andrew."[64] Three months later, the archers of Nieuwpoort were permitted to "carry on their robe, hood or cloak, our device … the fusil and two arrows in the form of the cross of Saint Andrew."[65] A month later those of Ypres were permitted to wear "for the finery of the said guild our device of the fusil, of the two arrows, amongst them in the form of the cross of Saint Andrew."[66] The next year guilds in Berghes-Sint-Winnoks,[67] Cassel[68] and Thielt[69] received near-identical charters granting them the right to place the fusil and two arrows in the form of the Saint Andrew's cross on their liveries. By the end of the reign Menin, Cockelare, Douai, Dadizeel and Zuuvekerke had received this special right.[70] It is striking how many of these towns lie in western or coastal Flanders, implying that such charters were connected to providing ready, armed, loyal men in case Flanders was attacked.

Far fewer charters survive from the reign of Charles the Bold, but, as he was absent from Flanders on campaign for most of his reign, this is perhaps not surprising. His 1473 charter, issued with his wife Margaret of York to the crossbowmen of Ghent, may have been a way to attempt to rebuild bonds with the town,[71] and his grant of additional wine to Lille in 1476 was another attempt to bolster support.[72] Charters, in their date and language, provide a glimpse into the important

---

61 For context see Nicholas, *Medieval Flanders*, pp. 327–9; Small, *Later Medieval France*, pp. 148–52, 164–7; Vaughan, *Philip the Good*, pp. 98–120; A. Curry, *The Hundred Years War* (Basingstoke, 2003), pp. 96–9.
62 GRA, Raad van Vlaanderen, 7351, fols. 220–221.
63 Ibid., fol. 239.
64 Ibid., fol. 239.
65 Ibid., fol. 217r–217v.
66 Ibid., fol. 199v.
67 Ibid., fols. 220–221.
68 Archives Municipales de Cassel, AA1, fols. 117–118.
69 GRA, Raad van Vlaanderen, 7351, fols. 222v–223, Original in Stadsarchief Tielt, Oud Archief, n. 846. I am grateful to Jonas Braekvelt for this reference.
70 ADN, B 17696; GRA, Raad van Vlaanderen, 7351, fols. 226v–227; AGR, Chartes de l'audience, n. 219; GRA Raad van Vlaanderen, n. 7351, fols. 230v–231; GRA Raad van Vlaanderen, n. 7351, fols. 205v–206; GSA, Sint Jorisgilde, niet genummerde reeks, 25.
71 GSA, Sint Jorisgilde, niet genummerde reeks, 25.
72 ADN, Lettres reçues et dépêchées, B 17724.

relations between duties and guilds and, along with military records, are the most common sources for studying the dukes and their forces.

The dukes as members of guilds

Guilds served their dukes in war, and were rewarded with privileges. Such military and political bonds are well documented, but important social bonds also existed between dukes and guildsmen. As Peter Arnade has shown, all four Valois dukes of Burgundy were members of the prestigious Greater Guild of Saint George of Ghent.[73] Philip the Bold joined the year after his marriage to Margaret of Male, in 1369, and shot with the guild in 1371;[74] he also shot with the Bruges crossbowmen in 1375.[75] However, as duke, Philip was rarely in Flanders and took little further part in guild social activities.

Philip the Good, like his father and previous counts of Flanders, was a member of the Ghent crossbowmen. Both he and his eldest illegitimate son, Anthony the Great Bastard, were also members of the Bruges Saint George crossbow guild, though their date of entry is not given.[76] Charles the Bold was, as count of Charolaise, also close to the Bruges and Ghent crossbow guilds. For example, in 1446 he was king of the Mechelen crossbowmen, meaning that he had shot the wooden bird, winning their annual competition.[77] As duke of Burgundy he favored Brabant guilds, becoming king of the Brussels crossbowmen in 1471, but it is striking that, as duke, Charles did not shoot with any Flemish guild.[78]

Dukes were not unique in joining guilds; numerous nobles were also active in this way. One of the most famous, Louis of Gruthuse, or Louis of Bruges (d. 1492), joined both archers and crossbowmen of Bruges as well as the crossbow guild of Aalst.[79] This great lord was not just a knight of the Golden Fleece, but also Earl of Winchester and one of the most important figures in Mary's reign, helping to rule Flanders.[80] Membership lists are fascinating, revealing that court and civic cultures were not worlds apart. But lists reveal only that the dukes were

---

[73] Arnade, *Realms of Ritual*, p. 71.
[74] M. Boone, "Réseaux Urbaine," in *Le Prince et le peuple. Image de la société du temps des ducs de Bourgogne, 1384–1530*, ed. W. Prevenier (Antwerp, 1998), p. 247.
[75] Schrijver and Dothee, *Les Concours de Tir*, appendix.
[76] BSA, 385, Sint Joris, register met ledenlijst enz. 1321–1531, fol. 3v.
[77] Schrijver and Dothee, *Les Concours de Tir*, appendix.
[78] A. Wauters, *Notice historique sur les anciens serments ou Gildes d'arbalétriers, d'archers, d'arquebusiers et d'escrimeurs de Bruxelles* (Brussels, 1848), pp. 7–9.
[79] BSA, 385, Sint Joris, register met ledenlijst enz. 1321–1531, fol. 3v; Aalst, stadsarchief, oude archief, 155, Register Sint Joris guild, 1335–1583.
[80] P.J. Martens, ed., *Lodewijk van Gruuthuse. Mecenase en Europees diplomat ca. 1427–1492* (Bruges, 1992); J. Haemers, *For the Common Good. State Power and Urban Revolts in the Reign of Mary of Burgundy* (Turnhout, 2009), pp. 106–13; M. Vale "An Anglo-Burgundian Nobleman and Artistic Patronage: Louis de Bruges, lord of la Gruthuyse and Earl of Winchester," in *England and the Low Countries in the Later Middle Ages*, ed. C. Barron and N. Saul (New York, 1995); M.-P. Lafitte, "Les Manuscrits de Louis de Bruges chevalier de la Toison d'Or," in *Le Banquet du Faisan, 1454: L'Occident face au défit de l'Empire Ottoman*, ed. M.-T. Caron

enrolled in a shooting guild, and though some records of dukes as "shooter-kings" survive these must also be handled carefully.

Dukes and competitions

More useful, and more dramatic, examples of bonds between dukes and shooting guilds are the accounts of ducal participation in shooting competitions. To understand the importance of ducal participation, a brief outline of shooting competitions is necessary. The earliest competition for which records survive, a short event that rewarded shooting skill, was held in Oudenaarde in 1329.[81] Throughout the fourteenth century, despite war, rebellion, even the Black Death, competitions grew and prospered. Two of the most important fourteenth-century competitions were held outside Flanders, in the French city of Tournai in 1350[82] and the Hainault town of Mons in 1387.[83] By the fifteenth century competitions in Flanders were huge. Events could draw in hundreds of fully armed crossbowmen from towns across northern Europe and last as long as three months. They became arguably the largest and most expensive demonstration of urban culture.

At least twice, in 1408 and 1440, the dukes took part and shot with the guilds, but even when they were not actually present their power was made clear, as only they could grant permission for a competition to be held. In 1408 a great shoot was held in Oudenaarde, in central Flanders.[84] In many ways this was an urban event, designed to bring prestige to Oudenaarde and to the guild of crossbowmen. A letter of invitation was sent out addressed to "The honorable, discrete and wise, all those Lords, kings, constables, deans, governors and to all other companions" of sworn guilds "of the noble game of the crossbow in cities, bonnes villes closed and privileged."[85] The letter stated that rural teams would not be welcomed (even supposing that they have guilds): only townsmen were honorable enough to attend Oudenaarde's great civic competition. Honorable men from suitable places were thus invited to play the "excellent, very noble and loved game, and above all other games, the most pure and honorable," which "cannot and must not be bad nor villainous." The letter continues to emphasize the importance of the "very noble game" before moving on to describe the shooting and prizes, setting out the organization of the shoot and the centrality of civic ideals; in contrast, two chronicles that describe the shoot refer to a different source of honor, the participation of John the Fearless. An anonymous town chronicle of Oudenaarde

and D. Clauzel (Arras, 1997); M.P.J. Martens, *Lodewijk van Gruuthuse, Mecenas en Europees Diplomat c.a. 1427–1492* (Bruges, 1992).

[81] Ghent and Lille both paid their guilds to attend: LAM, Comptes de la Ville 16018, fol. 29v.; Vuylsteke, *Gentsche Stads en Balijuwsrekeningen, 1280–1336*, p. 664.
[82] G. le Muisit, *Chronique et Annales*, ed. H. Lemaître (Paris, 1905), pp. 272–3.
[83] L. Deville, "Notice historique sur les milices communales et les compagnies militaire de Mons," *Annales du Cercle Archéologique de Mons* 3 (1862), pp. 169–285.
[84] E. Van Cauwenberghe, "Notice historique sur les Confréries de Saint Georges," *Messager des Sciences Historiques des Arts et de la Bibliographie de Belgique* (1853), pp. 279–91.
[85] Universiteitsbibliotheek Gent, Hs 434, Vredesverdragen, fols. 92–100.

and the chronicle of the nearby monastery of Eename both refer to the wealth of the town, the prestige of the guild and the nobility of the competition, but both give greater emphasis to ducal participation. The chronicle of Eename is written in a simple list format. After brief descriptions of the entries of various teams, the author notes:

> And then the dean of the Saint George guild, and the guild wardens, and the twelve shooters who would shoot in the name of the town, who were all similarly dressed, and all the *poorters* and all the other people of the town, those that were rich, they all had great cloaks of green and white.[86] And then Count John of Flanders, Duke of Burgundy, and my lady the Duchess his wife, were with the shooters. And then Count John shot with the town of Oudenaarde and with him many other noble men, those of the guild of Saint George. And then Count John himself carried his own bow up to his turn ...[87]

The anonymous chronicle of Oudenaarde gives further details: "The Count of Flanders John Duke of Burgundy and my lady his wife were clothed like the shooters and Count John shot with the town of Oudenaarde, like a man of the guild of Saint George of Oudenaarde, and Count John like the rest carried his own bow and won the first prize of two silver jugs (*kannen*)."[88] Ducal motives for this event must have been political – perhaps it was intended to bolster support in Flanders in preparation for the Liège campaign a few months later – but John's actions enhanced the standing of Oudenaarde, of the guild and of the crossbow in general. In the 1408 competition John was acting neither as a distant lord granting privileges, nor as an inactive member simply enrolled in the membership lists. He shot with the guild, dressed like a guild brother, was part of the guild urban community.

Another great crossbow competition was held in Ghent in 1440 by the Greater Guild of Saint George.[89] It has been recorded in incredible detail in contemporary civic accounts, in the surviving invitation and in the book of Pieter Polet, written before 1507.[90] Pieter helped to organize a later Ghent crossbow shoot of 1498, and his book is undoubtedly the most valuable source for analyzing the 1440 competition; its very existence is testament to the way such events were remembered. Exactly when he wrote his description is unclear, but it seems likely that he found out all he could about the 1440 competition before organizing that of 1498.

The shoot of 1440 was planned further in advance than earlier ones had been. Philip the Good gave his consent on 22 February, allowing the event to take place.[91] After more civic planning, the invitations were sent out on 13 March for entrances in June. The invitation again emphasized civic pride and honor, addressing "all good privileged and free towns" and calling them to the "honorable game of the

---

[86] *Poorters* were richer merchants, possibly landowners, who had either been born with or purchased citizenship, and with it important legal rights.
[87] Cauwenberghe, "Notice historique," pp. 281–3.
[88] OSAOA, 241/2, fols. 89–92v.
[89] Arnade, *Realms of Ritual*, pp. 84–93.
[90] Ghent, Universiteitsbibliotheek Gent, Hs G 6112, "*Dit es den bouc vander scutters tobehoorende pieter polet ende ... sint joris gulden te gent.*"
[91] *De Bouc van Pieter Polet*, fols. 32v–33v.

crossbow" by virtue of "their honorable and worthy ancient rights and renown." Crossbowmen are asked to come in friendship, and the letter emphasizes that "this feast of ours is for the good honor of God and his Holy Mother; (we) wish to enhance the common good and bring honor and love to all."[92] This competition made a special effort to emphasize harmony and unity. Just four years after the siege of Calais such ideals were important in Flanders, and hosting a great event helped to bring not just prestige to Ghent but social peace to Flanders. Philip had given his permission for the competition to happen and had been invited to take part with any team he chose, but, unlike his father, Philip did not join in as a guild brother. Rather, he chose to bring his own ducal team, including the lord of Nevers, the knight Mattheus de Brakele and, perhaps most significantly, Jehan Villiers, the lord of l'Isle-Adam, whose father had been killed in the Bruges rebellion a few years earlier, poignantly demonstrating that no permanent gulf had been created between town and court in the bloody events of 1437.[93] Despite the power of such men, and of Philip himself, the ducal team is poorly documented in Ghent sources, unlike the Oudenaarde sources which emphasized John the Fearless's participation. The book of Pieter Polet gives no more space or emphasis to the ducal team than to any other civic team.[94]

Ducal participation in the 1440 competition is significant, and shows that, just four years after his failed siege of Calais, for which Ghent carried at least some of the blame, Philip did not see his town as an enemy. Rather, he cultivated social relations with the town, in particular with the powerful crossbowmen. Just as significantly, the town treated the duke like any other. The competition was a civic event, Philip just another competitor; he did not even win any of the events. Ducal participation did not end with Philip the Good. His great grandson Philip the Fair would continue this tradition, taking part in another Ghent shoot in 1497 with the Ypres crossbow guild.[95] Across the fifteenth century ducal participation in shooting competitions shows a real community developing between the guilds and the dukes, helping to build bonds in periods of crisis and gain support in time of need.

[92] GSA, Sint Jorisgilde, niet genummerde reeks, Charters en diverse losse documenten, 30.
[93] The list of names in GUB, G 6112, *Dit es den bouc vander scutters tobehoorende Pieter Polet*, fol. 34v. The details are transcribed in Moulin-Coppins, *Sint Jorisgilde te Gent*, p. 106, but she misses out the first name. For the shoot see Arnade, *Realms of Ritual*, pp. 91–4. For the death of Jehan Villiers, see Vaughan, *Philip the Good*, pp. 87–94, Dumolyn, *de Brugse Opstand*, pp. 226–30; B. Schnerb, "Jehan de Villiers, seigneur de l'Isle-Adam," in *Les chevaliers de l'ordre de la Toison d'Or au XVe siècle. Notes Bio-biographiques*, ed. R. De Smedt (Frankfurt-am-Main, 1994), pp. 47–9.
[94] *De Bouc van Pieter Polet*, fol. 34 v.
[95] GSA, Fonds Sint Joris, 155, n. 2; P. Van Duyse, "Het groot schietspel en de Rederijkersspelen te Gent in Mei tot Juli 1498," *Annales de la Société Royale des Beaux-arts et de Littérature de Gand* 6 (1865), F. De Potter, "Landjuweel van 1497" in *Het Belfort*, ed. A. Siffer (Ghent, undated).

Conclusion

Guilds of archers and crossbowmen first emerged as urban defenders in the fourteenth century and, though they became far more than this in the fifteenth, their military role never disappeared. They defended their own towns with or without ducal orders, and could go beyond to defend other places on ducal command. Guilds also formed small but important parts of larger ducal forces, in the armies of John the Fearless, Philip the Good, Charles the Bold and even the armies of Maximilian. In return for military service, guilds received tax exemptions and rights to bear arms as well as lands and money. Charters reveal dukes' needs to encourage potential defenders, but also their need to have loyal honorable men, wearing ducal liveries, traveling across ducal lands. Though dukes were the lords of guilds, receiving their service and granting rights, they could also be guild brothers, joining archery and crossbow guilds and, most significantly, taking part in great competitions. Although ducal relations with their towns were not always cordial, ducal relations with the urban shooting guilds were complex and long-lasting, providing honorable, loyal soldiers as well as civic and ducal entertainment.

Table 1: Charters

Issued by	Year	Month	Town	Guild	Subject
Philip the Bold	no original	(No original)	Gerardsbergen	Crossbowmen	Rights and obligations, with Louis of Male
Philip the Bold	1384	No original	Ghent	Crossbowmen	Grant the guild property
Philip the Bold	1387	(No original)	Ninove	Archers	Rights and obligations
Philip the Bold	1389	September	la Bassee	Crossbowmen	Confirmation Charles VI royal ordinance; rights and obligations
Philip the Bold	1394	17 July	Douai	Crossbowmen	New privileges
Philip the Bold	1398	September	Dendermonde	Crossbowmen	Organization, rights and obligations
John the Fearless	1405	20 June (Joyous Entry)	Wattignies and Estrees	Archers and crossbowmen	Organization, rights and obligations
John the Fearless	1405	16 July	Lille	Crossbowmen	Right to bear arms
John the Fearless	1407	(No original)	Bruges	Archers	Rights and obligations
John the Fearless	1408	July	Oudenaarde	Crossbowmen	Right to bear arms
John the Fearless	1409	27 December	Boezigne	Crossbowmen	Organization, rights and obligations
John the Fearless	1410	27 September	Coudekerke	Archers	Organization, rights and obligations
John the Fearless	1410	7 April	Wavrin	Crossbowmen	Organization, rights and obligations
Philip the Good	1419	9 December	Lille	Archers	Right to bear arms bear arms across Flanders
Philip the Good	1421	7 June	Aalst	Archers	Organization, rights and obligations
Philip the Good	1423	9 August	Courtrai	Archers	Organization, rights and obligations

Issued by	Year	Month	Town	Guild	Subject
Philip the Good	1423	11 August	Neiuwpoort	Crossbowmen	Security of the town and new privilege for the guild
Philip the Good	1426	28 February	Mechelen	Archers	Annual grant of money/ support to the guild
Philip the Good	1428	September	Oudenaarde	Archers	Right to bear arms bear arms across Flanders
Philip the Good	1430	30 January	Tielt	Archers and crossbowmen	Organization, rights and obligations
Philip the Good	1430	21 September	Mechelen	Archers	New grant of land and money
Philip the Good	1430	29 July	Wavrin	Archers and crossbowmen	Confirmation of existing rights, and the right to bear arms across Flanders
Philip the Good	1430	7 March	Cysoing	Archers	Organization, rights and obligations
Philip the Good	1431	6 October	Aalst	Archers	Organization, rights and obligations
Philip the Good	1431	16 October	Aalst	crossbowmen	Right to bear arms
Philip the Good	1433	16 June	Douai	Archers	Annual grant of additional wine
Philip the Good	1435	(No original)	Gravelines	Archers and crossbowmen	Organization, rights and obligations
Philip the Good	1439	22 February	Ghent	Crossbowmen	Permission to hold a competition
Philip the Good	1441	27 January	Drincham	Archers	Allow lord of Drincham to set up a confraternity
Philip the Good	1441	2 July	Houtheem	Archers	Confirmation of grant by John the Fearless to bear arms
Philip the Good	1445	4 June	Commines	Archers and crossbowmen	Confirms lord of Commines' right to have guilds

Issued by	Year	Month	Town	Guild	Subject
Philip the Good	1446	20 March	Biervelt	Archers	Allows Loys Witon, ducal chamberlain and captain
Philip the Good	1446	20 July	Ypres	Archers	Ducal emblem
Philip the Good	1446	19 June	Nieuwpoort	Archers	Ducal emblems
Philip the Good	1447	16 January	Elverdinghe and Vlamertinghe	Archers and crossbowmen	Corneil, bastard of Burgundy can establish 2 very large guilds
Philip the Good	1447	5 February	Cassel	Archers	Ducal emblem
Philip the Good	1447	29 March	Sint-Winnoksbergen	Archers	Ducal emblem
Philip the Good	1447	24 August	Thielt	Archers	25 "plus notables et souffisans" wear ducal emblem
Philip the Good	1449	15 September	Koekelare	Archers	New privileges and ducal emblem
Philip the Good	1449	12 July	Zuienkerke	Archers	Allow ducal secretary, Paul des Champs, to establish a guild in his own town
Philip the Good	1451	6 August	Dendermonde	Crossbowmen	Recognition of service, rights
Philip the Good	1452	March	Douai	Crossbowmen	Ducal emblem
Philip the Good	1453	various March and April	Lille	Archers and crossbowmen	Military preparations and rights
Philip the Good	1455	22 April	Douai	Crossbowmen	Rehabilitation of archers in recognition service
Philip the Good	1455	7 March	Loo	Archers and crossbowmen	Confirmation charter form John the Fearless, right to bear arms
Philip the Good	1456	24 October	Zuienkerke	Archers	Ducal emblem
Philip the Good	1458	14 February	Mechelen	Crossbowmen	Permission to hold competition in July

Issued by	Year	Month	Town	Guild	Subject
Philip the Good	1459	24 April	Lannoy	Archers	Allow Jehan de Lannoy to establish guild
Philip the Good	1460	19 March	Cassel	Archers	Rights in recognition of loyal service
Philip the Good	1461	10 June and 15 September	Ghent	Crossbowmen	Payments of death-fees (doothgelt)
Philip the Good	1461	5 June	Gravelines	Archers and crossbowmen	Right to bear arms
Philip the Good	1461	10 September	Oudenaarde	Crossbowmen	Permission to hold shoot
Philip the Good	1463	August	Oudenaarde	Crossbowmen	Confirms charter from John the Fearless to bear arms, as original left in rain
Philip the Good	1463	12 August	Dadizeele	Archers	Jan van Dadizeele can establish archery guild
Philip the Good	1465	9 August	Axelle	Crossbowmen	Lower entrance guild fee, as numbers declining
Philip the Good	1465	7 September	Langemark	Crossbowmen	Organization, rights and obligations
Charles the Bold	1469		Various	All	Orders all guild to declare numbers
Charles the Bold	1475	Not specified	Mechelen	Crossbowmen	Tax exemptions, as 36/90 died at Neuss
Charles the Bold	1475	29 May	Ghent	Crossbowmen	With Margaret of York, gifts to the guild hospital and Chapel of saint Margaret
Charles the Bold	1476	(Damaged, possibly August)	Lille	Archers	Grant of additional annual wine

The Battle of Edgecote or Banbury (1469) Through the Eyes of Contemporary Welsh Poets

Barry Lewis

The battle of Edgecote, also known as the battle of Banbury, was fought in late July 1469. It is one of the least studied and most obscure and poorly understood battles of the Wars of the Roses. Charles Ross, the biographer of Edward IV, spoke of "total confusion amongst contemporary chroniclers" which leaves the events of Edgecote "far from clear today."[1] An examination of the various chronicles which report the events of July 1469 leaves no doubt as to what he meant. They do not agree about the date of the battle, the sequence of events before, during or after the battle, or even whether there was one battle or two. The reason for this is straightforward. The rebel army consisted of northerners. The royalist army was largely Welsh. Most of our chronicle sources, on the other hand, were written in the south of England, or even further afield on the Continent, and most are late. The lines of transmission between what happened in a muddy field in Northamptonshire in July 1469 and the "Warkworth chronicle," probably written at St Albans in the 1480s, or the Burgundian Jehan Waurin, writing in the 1470s, not to mention the Tudor historians Polydore Vergil and Edward Hall, are obscure.

Fortunately, there is an exception to the rule that our sources for the battle of Edgecote are distant in time from the events and lack a clearly identifiable link to the participants. There were contemporary observers who have left us texts and who were in a position to be well-informed about this battle: the Welsh poets of the time. Merely to name them is to suggest why their testimony has had little impact on modern accounts of the battle. Their works are in the Welsh language and are generally not available in a reliable English translation, or in fact any translation at all. Indeed, in some cases the Welsh texts themselves have only recently been published in scholarly critical editions. Moreover, our authors are poets writing poetry, a medium which historians approach with even more caution than other types of source. It is, nevertheless, high time to urge the value of what they have to say, to bring the full weight of their testimony to bear on the events of July 1469, in the hope that, when historians see their potential as a source, they will in future be inspired to make more use of them. Welsh poetry can be of value for facts, for constructing a narrative of events. In the case of the battle of Edgecote, it bears quite centrally on one important matter of fact – the correct date of the battle. But Welsh poetry is usually of more value for its presentation of contemporary reactions to events. It helps us to understand political motivations and opens up the private world of emotional responses. When we read in our history books the

---

[1] Charles Ross, *Edward IV* (Berkeley and Los Angeles, 1974), p. 130.

dry statement that so-and-so died in battle, or that such-and-such was executed, we rarely have the good fortune to be able to read a contemporary reaction which emanates from the family circle of the dead man. In Wales, we often do have that privilege: the reason is the nature of the late medieval poetic tradition.[2]

Late medieval Welsh poetry: a very brief overview

In fifteenth-century Wales, poetry was a profession.[3] Its practitioners were numerous, apparently well rewarded, and underwent extensive training, which was necessary in order to master the complex meters and other conventions. The degree to which their profession was regulated, and through what kind of structures, is uncertain. Nevertheless, the poets' role within gentry society is clear: they were paid to entertain, but most importantly, they were paid to sing praise poems to members of the landowning class of medieval Wales. There are few external accounts of the social setting of the poetry. On internal evidence, poems were performed orally, to the accompaniment of music, before an audience that included the addressee of the praise (except, obviously, in the case of elegies). Poets performed their own work, though professional reciters also existed, their role is difficult to establish. The occasions at which poems were recited are unclear, but they seem to have been associated with feasting and were probably performed at dinner. There was a particular association with the three festivals of Christmas, Easter and Whitsun. In addition, significant events in the life of a patron might bring a poet to his home outside these times: a family marriage, the erection of a new house, a death. Performing an elegy for a dead patron, at the behest of his relatives, was one of the poets' most important roles. Such elegies were probably not given at funerals or in their immediate aftermath, though this is possible in some cases. More likely, they were intended for the month's mind, a ceremony of remembrance held a month after the funeral, or for the year's mind, held twelve months after the funeral. All but two of the poems that will be called in evidence in this article are elegies.[4]

The social role of the poet implies the continuing ascendancy of oral performance. Writing was still not the primary medium for the reception or even the transmission of Welsh poetry in the fifteenth century, but the writing down

---

[2] Still the only extended critical evaluation of the concept of using medieval Welsh poetry as a historical source is that of H.T. Evans, *Wales and the Wars of the Roses* (Cambridge, 1915), chapter 1: "The Historical Value of Contemporary Welsh Literature," pp. 1–15. A new consideration is urgently needed.

[3] The most recent account of the nature and role of the poetic craft in late medieval Wales is in Welsh: Dafydd Johnston, *Llên yr Uchelwyr: Hanes Beirniadol Llenyddiaeth Gymraeg 1300–1525* (Cardiff, 2005), chapter 2: "Y Gyfundrefn Farddol," pp. 18–49. In English, *A Guide to Welsh Literature*, vol. 2: *1282–c.1550*, ed. A.O.H. Jarman and Gwilym Rees Hughes, 2nd ed. rev. by Dafydd Johnston (Cardiff, 1997), is the basic guide.

[4] *Marwnadau* in Welsh (singular *marwnad*). There is no detailed account in English of the social context of medieval Welsh elegies. An important recent treatment in Welsh is Huw Meirion Edwards, "Dwyn Marwnadau Adref," *Llên Cymru* 23 (2000), 21–38.

of poems certainly occurred, both by poets for their own purposes and by poets and others for those patrons who wished to own written copies. Of the poets discussed in this article, Lewys Glyn Cothi was an accomplished scribe who has left two substantial collections of his own works, while Hywel Swrdwal and Huw Cae Llwyd exemplify the other kind of manuscript transmission, since both copied their own poems into collections which appear to have been maintained at the homes of patrons in south Wales.[5] For these poets, therefore, we have autograph copies of the poems that will be discussed in this article. It is notable that patrons' manuscripts are not limited to praise poems of direct interest to the patrons: on the contrary, they collected poems which often had no discernible link to themselves, suggesting that they valued poetry as art and entertainment. This becomes even more marked in the sixteenth and seventeenth centuries, from which time we have many more manuscripts. In this period we continue to see poets making collections for themselves and for patrons; we continue too to see manuscripts being maintained in patrons' houses, with poems being added to them over a long period; and we now also encounter numerous anthologies made by and for interested gentlemen, some of whom were imbued with humanist values which impelled them to collect and preserve Welsh literature in writing.[6] In fact, the majority of fifteenth-century Welsh verse survives in copies which first appear in the century 1550–1650: of the poems to be discussed below, this is true of those by Guto'r Glyn, Dafydd Llwyd of Mathafarn, Bedo Brwynllys and Ieuan Deulwyn.[7] Thanks to the huge collective effort of all those who copied Welsh poetry into manuscripts in the period c.1450–c.1650, perhaps a thousand poems by about a hundred poets of the fifteenth century have survived; even that is probably a smallish proportion of the unquantifiable total composed. Bearing in mind the modest population and relative poverty of fifteenth-century Wales, that must represent a heavy burden of patronage, and we must conclude that the

---

[5] Lewys Glyn Cothi's collections are National Library of Wales [NLW], Aberystwyth, MSS Peniarth 70 and 109. Hywel Swrdwal and Huw Cae Llwyd copied works into, for instance, NLW, MS Peniarth 54. On this latter, see Daniel Huws, *Medieval Welsh Manuscripts* (Cardiff, 2000), pp. 95–6.

[6] The main overview of the manuscript transmission of late medieval Welsh poetry is in Welsh: Daniel Huws, *Cynnull y Farddoniaeth* (Aberystwyth, 2004). There is a case-study in English of the transmission of one poet in Huws, *Medieval Welsh Manuscripts*, pp. 84–103, and cf. Dafydd Johnston, "The Manuscript Tradition" (essay published on website www.dafyddapgwilym.net (accessed 26 April 2011)).

[7] The gap between the date of composition and the date of attestation may trouble some readers. A mixture of oral and written transmission is likely to have preserved each poem in the time between its creation and its first appearance in a surviving manuscript, the precise nature of the mix varying from poem to poem. Earlier written copies may be taken as certain or very probable in the case of all the poems discussed in this article which are not preserved in the poets' own hands: Guto'r Glyn's elegy for William Herbert, for instance, survives in sixty-two copies from various parts of Wales from the mid sixteenth century onwards, but has suffered little of the kind of alteration most typical of oral transmission, namely the dislocation and loss of couplets. Furthermore, the complex internal rhymes and alliteration of Welsh poetry tend towards the preservation of readings. Apart from accidental change during transmission, the possibility of deliberate alteration cannot be ruled out. It is, however, unlikely to have affected any of the points discussed in this article.

social requirement upon Welsh landowners to sustain the traveling poets was a compelling one. In other words, the poets' endorsement mattered. During the 1460s William Herbert of Raglan, the leader of the royalist forces at Edgecote, very deliberately sought that endorsement, making sure that his home became the place the poets would want to be.

What, then, are the credentials of Welsh poems as historical sources? Two aspects should intrigue historians. Firstly, they are virtually contemporary. The elegies which will be discussed below were composed at most a year after the funeral of the man being praised, in some cases probably much sooner. Few of the chronicles of the period are anything like as contemporary as that. Secondly, the authors had direct access to eyewitnesses. The poets will have talked to men who had been at the battle of Edgecote – retainers of the dead men who had fought with them and escaped, men who had traveled with their widows to fetch the bodies home. Moreover, the poems themselves will have been recited in front of these same eyewitnesses, as well as members of the dead man's intimate family: widows and children and other relatives. The poets were at one remove from being eyewitnesses of the battle; but as to the aftermath of the battle in south Wales, they were themselves eyewitnesses. Their testimony regarding the battle of Edgecote deserves far more serious consideration than it has received hitherto.

The Herbert family and the battle of Edgecote, July 1469

The battle of Edgecote destroyed a power bloc that had dominated south Wales throughout the 1460s: the hegemony of William Herbert. When Edward IV took the throne in 1461, William Herbert of Raglan was a prominent gentleman in Edward's marcher lordship of Usk. By 1469 Herbert had been made earl of Pembroke, and Edward had given him charge of just about every office and lordship in Wales that he could obtain for him. Raglan had been elevated into a marcher lordship in its own right, and Herbert had transformed the castle there into a spectacular residence, reflecting his power not only in Wales but also in the border counties of Herefordshire and Gloucestershire. His underage son, also called William Herbert, had married a sister of the queen in 1466 and been given the Somerset title of Dunster. Such high promotion was unique for a man with William Herbert's Welsh lineage, for, notwithstanding his adopted English surname, he was a Welshman on both his father's and his mother's side. His father was Sir William ap Thomas of Raglan, his mother Gwladus Gam, the daughter of Dafydd Gam who died at Agincourt in 1415. No fifteenth-century Welshman, perhaps not even Owain Glyndŵr at the height of his rebellion, ever dominated as much of Wales as did William Herbert by 1469. Herbert owed his rise to the patronage of Edward IV and his close alliance with the family of the queen, the Woodvilles. Nevertheless, he also made use of the structures of power within Welsh society, which, as we have seen, meant cultivating the professional praise poets.

All of William Herbert's empire-building, however, came to a shockingly abrupt end in July 1469. As already indicated, the events of this time are poorly known. What follows is a brief summary of those facts that are clear. Richard Neville, the earl of Warwick, the famous "kingmaker," revolted against the king, in alliance with Edward's discontented brother, George, duke of Clarence. They stirred up a rebellion in Yorkshire, led by a man called Robin of Redesdale, whose real identity is uncertain.[8] The king summoned troops and arrived at Nottingham on 9 July 1469, but he lacked sufficient forces to face the rebels.[9] Warwick and Clarence, meanwhile, reached Canterbury by 18 July and proceeded northwards with an army just as the northern rebels were heading south.[10] The northerners bypassed Edward at Nottingham. At the same time troops loyal to Edward were coming from the west. There was a contingent from the West Country under Humphrey Stafford, the earl of Devon, and another army from south Wales, led by William Herbert. On Monday 24 July 1469 – and this date will receive thorough examination below – the armies of Herbert and the rebels met at Edgecote in Northamptonshire, near Banbury. The Welsh were defeated. There is great confusion as to what the earl of Devon's forces were doing meanwhile – whether they took part in the battle or were even in the vicinity. William Herbert and his brother Sir Richard Herbert were captured and taken to Northampton. There they were tried by a kangaroo court presided over by Warwick and Clarence, and both were beheaded. The execution of William Herbert took place on 27 July, being Thursday. Edward, meanwhile, was still at Nottingham. A letter, which he wrote from there on 29 July, shows no signs that he knew what had occurred at either Edgecote or Northampton.[11] Shortly afterwards he headed south. Somewhere on the road he heard of the outcome of the battle and was deserted by most of his men. Thereupon he was effectively captured by Warwick and Clarence – where and when are not certain, but Edward was taken to Coventry and we know that he was there by 2 August.[12] He was now held prisoner while Warwick and Clarence busied themselves in killing their enemies. The queen's father and brother were taken, probably at Chepstow, and executed outside Coventry on 12 August.[13] Finally, on 17 August, the earl of Devon was lynched by the common people at Bridgewater in Somerset.[14]

The bodies of the Welsh leaders were taken home for burial. William Herbert, earl of Pembroke, was buried at Tintern Abbey. Sadly, but not surprisingly given the ruined state of the abbey, his tomb does not survive, though there is an an-

---

[8] Discussion: Keith Dockray, "The Yorkshire Rebellions of 1469," *The Ricardian: The Journal of the Richard III Society* 83 (December 1983), 246–57.

[9] Ross, *Edward IV*, p. 129. Letters written by Edward from Nottingham on 9 July are printed in *The Paston Letters, AD 1422–1509*, ed. James Gairdner, 6 vols. (London, 1904), 5:35–6.

[10] Cora L. Scofield, *Life and Reign of Edward the Fourth, King of England and of France and Lord of Ireland* (London, 1923), pp. 495–6; a letter written from Canterbury on 18 July by the earl of Oxford, Warwick's brother in law, is printed in *The Paston Letters*, Gairdner, 4:300.

[11] Printed in *The Coventry Leet Book, or Mayor's Register Containing the Records of the City Court Leet or View of Frankpledge, A.D. 1420–1555, with Divers Other Matters*, ed. Mary Dormer Harris, Early English Texts Society (London, 1907–13), pp. 345–6.

[12] Scofield, *Life and Reign of Edward the Fourth*, p. 497, n. 4.

[13] Harris, *Coventry Leet Book*, p. 346.

[14] Scofield, *Life and Reign of Edward the Fourth*, p. 498 and n. 1 (*Inquisitions post mortem*).

tiquarian sketch from the late seventeenth century.[15] His younger brother, Sir Richard Herbert of Coldbrook, was buried at Abergavenny Priory; his tomb can still be seen there in St Mary's church, which survived the dissolution to become the parish church of the town.[16] Their half-brother, Thomas ap Roger Vaughan, who was killed during the battle itself, was buried at Kington in Herefordshire, a short distance from his home at Hergest; the magnificent alabaster tomb which his wife, Elen Gethin, erected for the pair of them remains today in the parish church.[17] A list of the elegies composed for these men, along with two other poems that are also of relevance, follows:

1 Elegy for Thomas ap Roger Vaughan (Lewys Glyn Cothi)
2 The tomb of Thomas ap Roger Vaughan (Lewys Glyn Cothi)
3 Elegy for William Herbert (Guto'r Glyn)
4 Elegy for William Herbert (Hywel Swrdwal)
5 Elegy for William Herbert (Dafydd Llwyd of Mathafarn)
6 Elegy for Richard Herbert (Bedo Brwynllys)
7 Elegy for Richard Herbert (Ieuan Deulwyn)
8 Elegy for William and Richard Herbert (Huw Cae Llwyd)
9 For Rhys ap Dafydd Llwyd, missing after the battle of Edgecote (Dafydd Llwyd of Mathafarn).[18]

Thomas ap Roger received a conventional elegy by Lewys Glyn Cothi (poem 1 above) not long after his death, but perhaps a year or so later the poet then returned to celebrate the completion of his tomb (poem 2). There are three elegies for William Herbert and two for Sir Richard, by various poets, and one for the two brothers together (poem 8). Poem 9 is not a conventional elegy, since the patron is not definitely dead, only missing: it was designed to comfort the man's family, and perhaps as a public act of prayer for his safe return. Now that the material has been introduced, it is time to ask what it can add to our knowledge of the battle of Edgecote and its aftermath.

---

[15] Reproduced in Peter Lord, *The Visual Culture of Wales: Medieval Vision* (Cardiff, 2003), p. 262.

[16] For an image of the tomb, see http://www.stmarys-priory.org/history/monuments.htm (accessed 26 October 2010).

[17] Thomas was the son of Gwladus Gam by her first marriage, to Sir Roger Vaughan of Bredwardine, Herefordshire. She married William ap Thomas of Raglan sometime after the death of her first husband at Agincourt. By William ap Thomas she was the mother of William and Richard Herbert.

[18] All the standard editions are in Welsh. They are: Dafydd Johnston, ed., *Gwaith Lewys Glyn Cothi* (Cardiff, 1995), poems 124 and 125; John Llywelyn Williams and Ifor Williams, eds., *Gwaith Guto'r Glyn*, 2nd ed. (Cardiff, 1961), poem 53; Dylan Foster Evans, ed., *Gwaith Hywel Swrdwal* (Aberystwyth, 2000), poem 7; W. Leslie Richards, ed., *Gwaith Dafydd Llwyd o Fathafarn* (Cardiff, 1964), poems 54 and 55; William Gwyn Lewis, "Astudiaeth o Ganu'r Beirdd i'r Herbertiaid hyd Ddechrau'r Unfed Ganrif ar Bymtheg" (unpublished Ph.D. thesis, University of Wales Bangor, 1982), poems 30 and 31 (Bedo Brwynllys and Ieuan Deulwyn); Leslie Harries, ed., *Gwaith Huw Cae Llwyd* (Cardiff, 1953), poem 5. The works of Guto'r Glyn are being re-edited with a full English translation by the University of Wales Centre for Advanced Welsh and Celtic Studies.

The date of the battle of Edgecote: a case restated

Most historians give the date of the encounter at Edgecote as 26 July 1469. It is a pity that this date has established itself so firmly in the literature, even to the extent of being adopted on the information board that has been erected at the supposed battle site. The sources that give 26 July as the date are the chronicle attributed (probably wrongly) to John Warkworth, which was not written before 1483, and the even later sixteenth-century chronicle of Edward Hall.[19] In a brief article published in 1982 W. Gwyn Lewis, who wrote a very useful Ph.D. thesis collecting all the Welsh poetry addressed to the Herbert family in our period, noted that the evidence of the Welsh poems was not compatible with the commonly cited date of 26 July, but rather favored 24 July.[20] Lewis's note seems to have generally escaped attention, although some people have read it: Michael Hicks, for instance, follows its conclusions in his *Warwick the Kingmaker*.[21] But apart from that it seems to have fallen on stony ground. Nevertheless, Lewis was surely right. Even before we look at the Welsh evidence there are in fact no less than three English sources that tell us that the true date was 24 July, and they have much better claims to be contemporary. The first was also quoted by Lewis: the so-called "Brief Latin Chronicle," apparently a London text written not long after 1471 (that is the date at which it breaks off). It states that the battle took place on the eve of St. James's Day – i.e. 24 July.[22] The other two are less well-known sources and were not cited by Lewis in favor of his argument. A set of annals from Gloucester, about which little is known, gives the same date.[23] These annals extend no further than 1469, and may well be contemporary with the battle. It is a pity that they have not received more attention, even though they were published by C.L. Kingsford as far back as 1913. The other source is the Coventry Leet Book. Here the note on Edgecote occurs immediately after a copy of Edward IV's letter of 29 July 1469, which was mentioned earlier – the letter was addressed to the authorities in Coventry – and it is followed by an account

---

[19] "Warkworth's chronicle" is edited in *Death and Dissent: Two Fifteenth-Century Chronicles*, ed. Lister M. Matheson (Woodbridge, 1999), pp. 93–124 (for the date of Edgecote, see p. 99). The authorship and date of the chronicle are discussed in J.A.F. Thomson, "'Warkworth's Chronicle' Reconsidered," *The English Historical Review* 116 (467) (June 2001), 657–64 (p. 658 for the impossibility of a date before 1483). Hall's Chronicle is edited in *Hall's Chronicle*, ed. H.E. Ellis (London, 1809); see p. 275 for the date of the battle.

[20] W. Gwyn Lewis, "The Exact Date of the Battle of Banbury, 1469," *Bulletin of the Institute of Historical Research* 55 (1982), 194–6; for his thesis, see n. 18 above.

[21] Michael Hicks, *Warwick the Kingmaker* (Oxford, 1998), p. 271.

[22] *Three Fifteenth-Century Chronicles*, ed. James Gairdner, Camden Society (London, 1880), p. 183: "Hoc etiam anno in vigilia Sancti Jacobi Apostoli, facto conflictu militum et belligerorum borealium contra dominum Harberd, ceciderunt hinc et inde multi." For the London associations of the text, see Charles Lethbridge Kingsford, *English Historical Literature in the Fifteenth Century* (Oxford, 1913), p. 159. St. James's Day is 25 July.

[23] Kingsford, *English Historical Literature*, p. 356: "Anno domini M.cccc. sexagesimo nono in vigilia sancti Iacobi Apostoli, tempore Regis Edwardi quarti, fuit bellum apud Banbury inter Anglicos et Wallicos in campo vocato Saxonfelde."

of the Leet or court sessions of September 1469.[24] The editor of the Leet Book regards the scribe as working contemporarily.[25] Again, the date given for the battle is the eve of St. James's Day.

As Lewis argued, it is this date that is supported by the Welsh poems. Fifteenth-century poets were in the habit, if they were talking about particularly dramatic events, of mentioning the day of the week on which they occurred. No less than four of our elegies clearly state that the battle was fought on a Monday. Guto'r Glyn:

> Duw Llun y bu waed a lladd,
> Dydd amliw, diwedd ymladd.[26]
>
> On Monday there was blood and slaughter,
> A day of disgrace, the end of fighting.

Hywel Swrdwal:

> Llu dduw Llun, yn lladd y llaill.[27]
>
> A host on Monday slaying the other.

Dafydd Llwyd of Mathafarn:

> Duw Llun y bu dwyll i wŷr,
> Dydd Brawd a diwedd brodyr.[28]
>
> On Monday there was treachery against men,
> A Day of Judgement and the end of brothers.

And Ieuan Deulwyn, as part of an extended metaphor comparing the events of July 1469 to a game of dice, says that Monday was the day on which the Welsh lost the game:

> Duw Llun, yr wy'n deall, as,
> Yno ternwyd ein teyrnas.[29]
>
> On Monday, as I understand, one on the dice,
> There our kingdom was ruined.

If we consult a calendar for the year 1469, we find that 24 July was indeed a Monday, while 26 July was a Wednesday. And, just to remove any remaining ambiguity, two poets mention the vigil of St. James. Thus Dafydd Llwyd of Mathafarn:

---

[24] *Coventry Leet Book*, p. 346: "Memorandum, quod dominus Herber [sic] fuit captus in bello iuxta Banbery cum Robarto Ryddesdale & sociis suis in vigilia S. Jacobi apostoli, a. r. Edwardi ix°."
[25] *Coventry Leet Book*, p. 846 (hand D).
[26] Lines 5–6. Quotations from Guto'r Glyn will be from the new edition of the poem which I have prepared for the Guto'r Glyn Project (above, n. 18). Other quotations are from the editions listed in n. 18. In some cases I have slightly altered the punctuation. All translations of the Welsh texts are my own.
[27] Evans, *Gwaith Hywel Swrdwal*, poem 7 (line 56).
[28] Richards, *Gwaith Dafydd Llwyd*, poem 54 (lines 1–2).
[29] Lewis, "Astudiaeth," poem 31 (lines 41–42).

> Aeth yn frad weithian y fro,
> Ynys Loegr, noswyl Iago.[30]
>
> The land has now all turned to treachery,
> The kingdom of England, on St. James's Eve.

and Ieuan Deulwyn:

> Ucha'r rhain fu'n nechrau haf,
> A noswyl Iago'n isaf.[31]
>
> These men were most exalted at the beginning of summer,
> And lay lowest on the eve of St. James.

Now, it is understandable that poetry, particularly praise-poetry, should be a medium which historians approach with considerable caution. There is always a temptation to worry whether literary concerns, such as the requirements of meter and poetic diction, might have influenced the choice and arrangement of words to the detriment of strict historical accuracy, not to mention the possibility of bias and tendentious propaganda. But in a straightforward matter of fact like the date of the battle, such worries seem out of place. It is not credible that these poets could stand up in public ceremonies, before not only the dead men's families but also their retainers, supporters and neighbours, men in a position to know the facts, and announce that the fateful battle was fought on Monday, the eve of St. James's Day, if it had actually been fought on Wednesday, the day after St. James's Day.

A complicating factor is the mention by the Tudor chroniclers Polydore Vergil and Edward Hall of two encounters, a lesser one near Northampton and the battle proper at Edgecote/Banbury; the latter is dated to 26 July by Hall, while Vergil gives no date.[32] However tempting, we cannot use their accounts to try to keep both dates, 24 July and 26 July. The Welsh poems are quite emphatic that Monday was the crucial day. Recall Guto'r Glyn's line, quoted earlier:

> Dydd amliw, diwedd ymladd.
>
> A day of disgrace, the end of fighting.

This was "the end of fighting." The words are probably meant both literally to convey that the encounter was concluded on that day, and more rhetorically in the sense that this was "the battle to end all battles." If there were two encounters, which is far from certain given the lateness of the evidence of Vergil and Hall, then the Monday encounter must have been the second and final one, the battle at Edgecote.[33] It is just possible that Ieuan Deulwyn may refer to a preliminary encounter on the Sunday. It will be recalled that he compares the fighting to a

---

[30] Richards, *Gwaith Dafydd Llwyd*, poem 54 (lines 43–44).
[31] Lewis, "Astudiaeth," poem 31 (lines 37–38).
[32] *Hall's Chronicle*, pp. 273–5; *Three Books of Polydore Vergil's English History*, ed. H. Ellis, Camden Society (London, 1844), pp. 122–3.
[33] Philip A. Haigh, "... *Where Both the Hosts Fought ...:" The Rebellions of 1469–1470 and the Battles of Edgecote and Lose-Coat Field* (Heckmondwike, 1997), p. 32, argues that Guto'r Glyn is referring to the first encounter.

game of dice:

> Duw Sul y bu i'r Deau sis,
> A'r Iau'n ôl o ran Alis.³⁴
>
> On Sunday South Wales had a six,
> And on the Thursday it was back with the party of Alice.

"Thursday" refers to the execution of William Herbert (see below); the "party of Alice" means the English, since Alice was Hengest's daughter. It is possible, then, that the Welsh won a victory on the Sunday. On the other hand, the phrase may mean no more than that they were flourishing on the Sunday, the day before their fall.

Is the question of the exact date of the battle of Edgecote an important one? In the great scheme of things, perhaps not: a difference of a mere two days does not affect the outcome of the battle or greatly alter our understanding of how events unfolded. Nevertheless, factual accuracy is important and worth striving for. Between 18 July, when we know that Warwick and Clarence were still at Canterbury, and 27 July, when William Herbert was executed at Northampton, the documentary record fails us. The chroniclers remain, but contradict one another. Only the Welsh poems provide a reliable date for the battle of Edgecote, and they do so unanimously. In fact, the chroniclers are also extraordinarily contradictory on many other aspects of the confused events of July 1469, and we may now turn to the testimony of the poems on some other questions in dispute.

Further aspects of the battle

The role of Humphrey Stafford, earl of Devon, during the battle is irretrievably confused in the chronicle accounts. The early-sixteenth-century chronicle known as "Hearne's Fragment" says that he arrived late for the battle after quarrelling with Herbert the night before concerning their lodgings.³⁵ But, according to the "Warkworth Chronicle," he refused to fight at all for the same reason.³⁶ The Tudor chronicler Hall adds a colorful detail: that the quarrel also involved the innkeeper's daughter.³⁷ The Burgundian chronicler Waurin says that Devon did fight in the battle, but then fled when he thought all was lost.³⁸ To these we can now add Guto'r Glyn, who also says that Devon fled:

---

[34] Lewis, "Astudiaeth," poem 31 (lines 39–40), with a slightly different interpretation of the first line.
[35] Hearne's Fragment is edited in *Thomae Sprotti Chronica*, ed. Thomas Hearne (Oxford, 1719), pp. 283–306; see p. 301.
[36] *Death and Dissent*, ed. Matheson, p. 98.
[37] *Hall's Chronicle*, p. 274.
[38] *Jehan de Waurin: Recueil des croniques et anciennes istoires de la Grant Bretaigne, à présent nommé Engleterre*, ed. William Hardy and Edward L.C.P. Hardy, 5 vols., Rolls Series (London, 1864–91), 5:582.

> Arglwydd difwynswydd Defnsir
> A ffoes – ni chafas oes hir![39]
>
> The lord of Devonshire, his service was worthless,
> Fled – he didn't have a long life!

Apart from the useful point that this dates the poem to a time later than Devon's execution on 17 August, it gives us another perspective on the question of Devon's role in the battle. Unfortunately, the poet does not say when exactly Devon ceased to play a part in the proceedings, nor under what circumstances his forces departed – did he leave during the battle, or sometime before it was fought? What we have here is in fact an opinion about Devon's motives – that he was motivated by fear – rather than a clear statement of what he actually did. So it adds to our repertoire of comment, but does not solve the problem.

The location and action of the battle are reconstructed in detail by Philip Haigh, leaning heavily on the late testimony of Hall.[40] The poems are geographically vague and cannot help us much to confirm or refute the evidence of Hall. The battle is variously known as the battle of Edgecote or Banbury in contemporary and later English sources, but the Welsh never refer to Edgecote: it is always Banbury (*Banbri* in Welsh). Banbury would have been the last town which the Welsh forces would have passed before they reached the battlefield, so this is not surprising. Lewys Glyn Cothi has the additional detail that the enemy army was drawn up on a hilltop:

> Ban fu fatel ein gelyn
> ym Manbri oer ym mhen bryn[41]
>
> When our enemy's battle [i.e. army]
> was at wretched Banbury on a hilltop.

About the action we learn nothing of substance. It is, however, well worth quoting the dramatic opening of Lewys Glyn Cothi's poem, for it does give us an insight into the motivations of the two armies:

> Y maes grymusa' o Gred,
> Ac o wall ef a golled:
> Ym Manbri y bu'r dial
> Ar Gymru deg a'r mawr dâl.
> Yno clywid yn unawr
> Griaw maes rhwng gweywyr mawr:
> Rhai Herbart, rhai'n Edwart ni,
> Iarll Warwig, eraill Harri.[42]
>
> The mightiest field [i.e. battle] of Christendom,
> And through a fault it was lost:
> At Banbury the vengeance was exacted

---

[39] Lines 17–18.
[40] Haigh, *"... Where Both the Hosts Fought ..."*.
[41] Johnston, *Gwaith Lewys Glyn Cothi*, poem 124 (lines 29–30). See Haigh, *"... Where Both the Hosts Fought ...,"* pp. 39–53, for detailed discussion of the location of the battle.
[42] Johnston, *Gwaith Lewys Glyn Cothi*, poem 124 (lines 1–8).

> Upon fair Wales, and the great fine.
> There was heard all at once
> Crying of battle between great spears:
> Some for Herbert, some for our Edward,
> The earl of Warwick, others for Harry.

Harri, of course, is the deposed Henry VI, at that time an involuntary guest of Edward IV in the Tower of London. It is interesting to have an indication that the northern forces at Edgecote were at least partially Lancastrian in sympathy. We might wonder how the earl of Warwick was able to control their expectations, for it does not seem to have been any part of Warwick's intention in July 1469 to depose Edward IV; to that policy he was driven much later, from mid 1470 onwards.[43] Of course, neither Warwick or Clarence was at Edgecote: this was a battle by proxy, fought for Warwick by rebels who were probably attracted by a mixed bag of grievances.[44]

Now, to return to the evidence in the poetry for the sequence of events. The Herbert brothers were taken to Northampton after the battle and beheaded. It is striking that the contemporary and slightly later chroniclers are unanimous on this point, whereas the Tudor writers Vergil and Hall are mistaken.[45] The method of execution is stated in the "Brief Latin Chronicle" and the Coventry Leet Book, and also by Vergil and Hall.[46] It is confirmed by Hywel Swrdwal, who begs rhetorically to be invested with the "miracles of St. Beuno in the way ... he did with Winefride" with regard to their two heads.[47] The reference is to the well-known tale of the resurrection of St. Winefride, patron saint of Holywell in Flintshire. She was beheaded, but St. Beuno succeeded in reattaching her head and bringing her back to life. The Burgundian chronicler Jehan Waurin is thus on his own in suggesting that the two brothers were stoned to death by the mob.[48] One important detail is unique to the Welsh poems: they alone indicate that Sir Richard Herbert was executed the day before his brother, on the Wednesday. Guto'r Glyn:

> Marchog a las dduw Merchyr,
> Mwy ei ladd no mil o wŷr:
> Syr Rhisiart, ni syr Iesu
> Wrthaw er lladd North a'r llu.[49]

---

[43] Ross, *Edward IV*, pp. 145–53.
[44] On which, see Dockray, "The Yorkshire Rebellions of 1469."
[45] Vergil gives Warwick (*Three Books of Polydore Vergil*, p. 123), Hall gives Banbury (*Hall's Chronicle*, p. 274). Guto'r Glyn refers to Northampton, but obliquely (lines 23–24 "The expedition to Northampton will bring about / Fierce fighting on account of the killing of this man.")
[46] *Three Fifteenth-Century Chronicles*, p. 183, "infra breve apud Northampton decapitatus est"; *Coventry Leet Book*, p. 346, "ductus ad villam de Northehampton & ibi erat decollatus, & dominus Ric. Herber [sic] similiter cum aliis," *Three Books of Polydore Vergil*, p. 123; *Hall's Chronicle*, p. 274.
[47] Evans, *Gwaith Hywel Swrdwal*, poem 7 (lines 59–62).
[48] *Jehan de Waurin*, 5:584: "et ainsi furent ces deux bons chevalliers livrez au peuple, qui piteusement les lapiderent."
[49] Lines 9–12.

> On Wednesday a knight was killed,
> Killing him was a greater thing than a thousand men:
> Sir Richard, Jesus won't be angry with him
> For killing the Northerners and the host.

Hywel Swrdwal:

> Ar Iau'dd aeth a urddai wŷr,
> A'r marchog ar y Merchyr.[50]
>
> On Thursday departed the one whom men honored [i.e. William Herbert],
> And the knight on the Wednesday.

And Bedo Brwynllys, who compares the death of Richard Herbert with the crucifixion of Christ:

> Duw Gwener, Grist gwyn i'r Grog,
> Duw Mercher, wedi, marchog.[51]
>
> On Friday, blessed Christ to the Cross,
> On Wednesday, later, a knight.

Every line in a late medieval Welsh poem was required to follow complex patterns of internal rhyme and alliteration (the technical name for which is *cynghanedd* 'harmony'). Even those who cannot read Welsh will surely have noticed that all three poets take advantage of the dense alliteration between *marchog* 'knight' and *Merche(y)r* 'Wednesday.' This was admittedly convenient, but hardly amounts to a reason for doubting the poets' testimony: to adapt what was said earlier about the date of the battle, it is not credible that a poet could stand up at the funeral or month's mind of Sir Richard Herbert and wrongly state the day of the week upon which he died. If Sir Richard had been beheaded on some other day, no doubt an equally effective alliteration would have been found. The evidence that Richard's brother, William Herbert, earl of Pembroke, died on Thursday 27 July is unequivocal, and on that, at least, everybody agrees. Thursday is confirmed as the day by Guto'r Glyn, Hywel Swrdwal and Dafydd Llwyd of Mathafarn.[52] It is also the date of the codicil which Herbert added to his will just before he was executed,[53] and it is confirmed by the *Inquisitions post mortem*.

Perceptions of the battle

Moving away from the battle itself, we may consider some wider implications. The various chroniclers give us a fascinating insight into how the battle was perceived, some at more or less the time itself, and rather more of them at

---

[50] Evans, *Gwaith Hywel Swrdwal*, poem 7 (lines 53–54).
[51] Lewis, "Astudiaeth," poem 30 (lines 53–54).
[52] Guto'r Glyn, lines 7–8; Evans, *Gwaith Hywel Swrdwal*, poem 7 (line 53) (quoted above); Richards, *Gwaith Dafydd Llwyd*, poem 54 (lines 88).
[53] Printed in D.H. Thomas, *The Herberts of Raglan and the Battle of Edgecote 1469* (Enfield, 1994), pp. 109–10. See further, p. 114 below.

a later date, even much later. The Welsh poems greatly add to this perspective by showing us reactions from within the Herbert and Vaughan households in the recent aftermath of the battle and the executions which followed.

In our history books Edgecote is a minor episode in the tortuous high politics of the Wars of the Roses, part of a power struggle within the elite of the kingdom, between the Woodvilles and Herbert on the one side and Warwick and the Neville interest on the other. Fifteenth-century people, in addition to recognizing this, nevertheless also saw it as yet another episode in the age-old struggle between the Welsh and the English. This applies to English observers just as much as Welsh ones. The Gloucester annalist talks of a "battle between the English and the Welsh."[54] The First Continuator of the Croyland Chronicle sums up his view of the battle with a long digression on Welsh prophecy:

> Revera illis in partibus in Wallia celebris ac famosa prophetia est, quod Anglis expulsis reliquiae Britonum iterato regnum Angliae veluti cives proprii debeant obtinere ... unde temporis arridente occasione, diu exoptatam sibi opinantes iam affuisse horam, ad id perficiendum totis viribus operam dabant. Sed hoc alias fieri disponente Deo, adhuc fraudati remanent a desiderio suo.

> The truth is, that in those parts and throughout Wales, there is a celebrated prophecy, to the effect that, having expelled the English, the remains of the Britons are once more to obtain the sovereignty of England, as being the proper citizens thereof ... the present opportunity seeming to be propitious, they imagined that now the long-wished for hour had arrived, and used every possible exertion to promote its fulfillment. However, by the providence of God, it turned out otherwise, and they remain for the present disappointed of the fulfillment of their desires.[55]

For their part, the Welsh poets were even more determined to see the events at Edgecote through this particular lens. Hywel Swrdwal:

> Dwy gynneddf oll, dygnedd fu,
> Ar Saeson a roes Iesu:
> Lolardiaid, traeturiaid hen
> Ŷnt erioed, ânt i'r wden!
> Troasant eiriau Iesu,
> Traeturiaid ŷnt i'r tarw du.
> Ni rôi Sais yn yr oes hon
> Drugaredd i du'r Goron.
> Trech anian ym mhob rhan rhôm
> Nog addysg, ni a'i gwyddom.
> Tebyg iawn at beganiaid
> Ydynt hwy, Waden eu taid.
> Tebyg iawn eto heb gam
> I Dduw eilwaith oedd Wiliam.[56]

---

[54] Kingsford, *English Historical Literature*, p. 356: "bellum apud Banbury inter Anglicos et Wallicos".

[55] William Fulman, ed., *Rerum Anglicarum Scriptorum Veterum*, 1 (Oxford, 1684), p. 543. The translation is that of Henry T. Riley, *Ingulph's Chronicle of the Abbey of Croyland with the Continuations by Peter of Blois and Anonymous Writers* (London, 1908), pp. 446–7.

[56] Evans, *Gwaith Hywel Swrdwal*, poem 7 (lines 19–32).

> Jesus has bestowed just two qualities
> (It was an evil thing) on the English:
> Lollards, traitors of old
> They have always been, they will go to the noose!
> They have perverted the words of Jesus,
> They are traitors to the black bull [Edward IV].
> No Englishman in this age
> Would show any mercy to the Crown.
> Nature is stronger than nurture in all parts,
> Before our eyes, we know it well.
> They are very similar to pagans,
> Woden was their ancestor.
> William, on the other hand,
> Without fault, was very like God.

Guto'r Glyn:

> Ef a'm llas, mi a'm nasiwn
> Yr awr y llas yr iarll hwn.[57]
>
> I was killed, I and my nation too,
> The moment that this earl was killed.

And Bedo Brwynllys sums up the death of the Herbert brothers thus:

> Bwrw tân ar y Brut heno.[58]
>
> Fire cast upon the *Brut* tonight.

The *Brut* was the general term for the prophecy which the Croyland continuator outlined for us earlier, the prophecy of a restored British kingship. It is easy for us to laugh at the prophecy for its utter lack of political realism. It is even easier to ridicule the idea of William Herbert as the deliverer of the Welsh people: William Herbert, with his seat in the house of Lords, his friendship with the English king, his lands scattered across a dozen English counties, his commercial interests in London, his son's royal marriage and Somerset title of Dunster, and his ambitious plans to enrich his family through advantageous marriages to English heiresses.[59] But we ignore contemporary opinion at our peril. Fifteenth-century people really believed in prophecies. That included English people. The Croyland Chronicler is a good example. For all his scoffing at Welsh credulity it is difficult not to detect a hint of relief: "by the providence of God, it turned out otherwise, and they remain *for the present* disappointed of the fulfillment of their desires." In dealing with the fifteenth century, we not only need to treat the actors as calculating politicians, but we must also keep in mind those aspects of fifteenth-century mentalities which do not accord so comfortably with twenty-first-century rationalism, otherwise an important aspect of people's motivations goes missing. The Croyland Chronicler believed that William Herbert was able to call on the Welsh messianic tradition in

---

[57] Lines 67–68.
[58] Lewis, "Astudiaeth," poem 30 (line 8).
[59] See Thomas, *Herberts of Raglan*, pp. 21–53, for Herbert's career as far as July 1469.

order to strengthen his own power. A glance at the poetry composed for Herbert in the 1460s shows that the Croyland Chronicler was right.[60] It is an aspect of Herbert's empire-building in Wales which we should not forget. Edward Hall, writing under Henry VIII, says:

> the whiche battaile [Edgecote] euer synce hath bene, and yet is a continuall grudge betwene the Northemmen and the Welshemen.[61]

For this statement at least, Hall is a contemporary witness. His words are easily verified by a reading of the Welsh poetry of Hall's day. On the eve of the Acts of Union sixteenth-century Welsh poets were still urging the descendants of the casualties of Edgecote to avenge the wrong done in 1469. The motif appears repeatedly in the works of the Glamorgan poet Lewys Morgannwg (fl. c.1520–60). "Let us all go to the place where Gwent's earl was slain," he urges Sir Edward Stradling of St Donat's (d. 1535): "obtain vengeance for Banbury in your lifetime." Likewise, he asks William Herbert, first earl of Pembroke of the second creation, to fight on account of the "unique treachery at Banbury." This William Herbert was the grandson of the William Herbert executed in 1469.[62] Implausible and stereotyped the suggestion of revenge may have been by this time, but it is clear that the events of July 1469 still rankled among the many south Wales families who lost members at Edgecote or Northampton. A particular animus against the northern English, beyond that general dislike of all Englishmen which is the commonest attitude in the poetry, pre-dated the battle of Edgecote, but was probably sharpened by it. "I will never ransom a northerner, if I come across him in his ancient nest," says Hywel Swrdwal: God and St. David will exact judgement upon the men of the north.[63] Guto'r Glyn is convinced that "Jesus will not be angry" with Sir Richard Herbert for killing northerners at Edgecote.[64]

Discordant notes

According to Hywel Swrdwal, William Herbert was "very like God." The likeness to which the poet is drawing attention presumably lies in their both being executed without just cause. The same comparison is made in relation to Sir Richard Herbert by Bedo Brwynllys.[65] It is also, at the very least, implied in Huw

---

[60] The poetry of Hywel Swrdwal and Guto'r Glyn in the period before Edgecote places great emphasis on Herbert's Welshness and the protection which he offered to Welshmen against English oppression. See Evans, *Gwaith Hywel Swrdwal*, poems 4 and 5; Williams and Williams, *Gwaith Guto'r Glyn*, poem 48. The latter envisages Herbert uniting Wales "from the river Conwy to the River Neath," i.e. all of it. Most explicit is Hywel Dafi, in the aftermath of Herbert's triumph at Harlech in 1468: see Lewis, "Astudiaeth," poem 16. Even so, Hywel is careful to subordinate Herbert's new power over a united Wales to the kingship of Edward IV.
[61] *Hall's Chronicle*, p. 275.
[62] *Gwaith Lewys Morgannwg*, poem 1 (lines 31–34); poem 26 (lines 27–28).
[63] Evans, *Gwaith Hywel Swrdwal*, poem 7 (lines 5–6, 47–48).
[64] Above, p. 108–9.
[65] Both passages are quoted above, pp. 110 and 109.

Cae Llwyd's elegy for the two brothers together.[66] Large claims are being made here. It would be unreasonable to expect the behavior of the Herberts, especially during their rapid rise to power in the 1460s, to have been quite as Christ-like as the poets imply. In fact there is quite a lot of evidence that many people thought it was not. It is quite common, at the conclusion of a Welsh elegy, for the poet to pray for the patron's soul. This is perfectly comprehensible in the light of the medieval belief in purgatory and the effectiveness of prayer in lessening the soul's pains in the afterlife: the power of prayer could counter the weight of sin which bound it to purgatorial fire. What is far from common in the Welsh elegy is to imply that some people might not be willing to offer that prayer:

> Na fid Gymro drosto draw,
> O bu dda, heb weddïaw.
> O bu drwm, y byd a red,
> Maddeuent am ei ddäed.[67]

> Let no Welshman there,
> If he [Herbert] was good, be without prayer for him.
> If he [Herbert] was heavy, that's how the world goes,
> Let them forgive him on account of his goodness.

'Heavy lord' was used in the English of the period to denote the disfavor of a lord towards an inferior, and the Welsh *trwm* clearly carried the same meaning. Hywel informs us that the men of Gloucester were "laughing on account of the battle."[68] Dafydd Llwyd of Mathafarn says that it would have been "amazing" for any man to "carry on the way he [Herbert] did, even were he an emperor."[69] In the context of an elegy for Herbert, this must be taken as a compliment, but Dafydd was, like Hywel Swrdwal, aware that Herbert's behavior was not viewed favorably by all:

> O bu ryfygus a balch
> Ennyd awr, benadurwalch,
> Ymbiliwn er mabolaeth
> Â Duw fry, er Difiau aeth.[70]

> If he was arrogant and proud
> Now and again, the hawk-like chief,
> Let us pray on account of his manliness
> To God on high (since Thursday he [Herbert] departed).

Here, again, we have a departure from the generic norms of the elegy: praying for the dead man's soul was normal, implying that he really needed it was not! The authors of the Gloucester annals and the "Brief Latin Chronicle" were blunter: Herbert was "a cruel man, ready for any crime, and, so they said, was intending

---

66 Harries, *Gwaith Huw Cae Llwyd*, poem 5; the imagery of the crucifixion pervades the poem.
67 Evans, *Gwaith Hywel Swrdwal*, poem 7 (lines 65–68).
68 Ibid. (lines 50–51).
69 Richards, *Gwaith Dafydd Llwyd*, poem 54 (lines 57–58).
70 Ibid. (lines 85–88).

to subvert and utterly despoil the kingdom of England."[71] His death was, in the opinion of both, divine justice. The treatment of William Herbert at the hands of modern historians has in general been unfavorable. This is probably due to his relatively humble origins and to his being measured against the outsize figure of Warwick, rather than any particular quality of cruelty or ambition greatly exceeding those characteristic of other political figures of the day. The Welsh poems allow us to see the positive side: Herbert could inspire loyalty, even devotion, for he clearly looked after his own, and that, of course, was the essence of good lordship.[72]

The personal dimension

On the morning of his execution William Herbert was permitted some time to finalize his affairs. He added a codicil to his will, the text of which survives. It concludes:

> Wife, pray for me, and take ye the said ordre that ye promised me as ye had in my life my hert and love. God have mercy uppon me and save you and our children, and our Lady and alle the seints in heven helpe me to salvacion. Amen.[73]

We are forcibly reminded that the Wars of the Roses had a human cost, and that cost could be very high for the losers. The men who were killed in July 1469 left behind wives and children. The final feature of the Welsh poems which will be discussed here is their potential to be a window onto the emotional life of the time; in this instance, a window into the grieving households of the participants at Edgecote in the aftermath of the battle and the executions.

Guto'r Glyn composed a poem of consolation for Ann Herbert after her husband's death. It was not fashioned in the immediate aftermath, but at a quieter and more hopeful time, probably in 1471, and certainly after the battle of Barnet, in which Warwick was killed. It seems to confirm that Ann Herbert took seriously her vow to her husband to remain chaste after his death, to which Herbert referred at the end of his last codicil. She is still in black, and wears the ring which symbolized the widow's chaste devotion to her dead husband.[74] Her role now is to remember William Herbert, and to watch over her underage son, the new earl.

---

[71] These are the words of the Gloucester annalist: see Kingsford, *English Historical Literature*, p. 356 ("homo crudelis erat paratus ad omne crimen, et, vt dicebatur, cogitabat subuertere regnum Anglie et eam totaliter spoliare"). The "Brief Latin Chronicle" calls Herbert "a most heavy oppressor and despoiler of churchmen [or church property] and many others for many years past" ("gravissimus et oppressor et spoliator ecclesiasticorum et aliorum multorum per annos multos)," see *Three Fifteenth-Century Chronicles*, p. 183.

[72] In this regard it should be recalled that there exists a substantial body of poems for the Herberts before the disaster of Edgecote, which allow us a glimpse of the households and supporters of the two brothers in happier times.

[73] Printed in Thomas, *The Herberts of Raglan*, p. 110.

[74] The poem is Williams and Williams, *Gwaith Guto'r Glyn*, poem 52. It has been re-edited for the Guto'r Glyn project. Lines 45–46 refer to the ring and veil of widowhood.

The wife of Thomas ap Roger Vaughan, Herbert's half-brother, was called Elen Gethin. In his elegy for Thomas, Lewys Glyn Cothi recalls:

> Elen Gethin fu'n wylaw
> Ddefni gwlith yn ddafnau glaw.[75]
>
> Elen Gethin was weeping
> Drops of dew, as drops of rain.

These lines were probably written for the month's mind. Later, in his second poem, Lewys recalls seeing the body brought back to Hergest by Elen herself:

> Pan las Tomas letemaur
> Ym Manbri gynt mewn brig aur,
> Dduw Sul ei arglwyddes ef
> I'w dai gwydr a'i dug adref.[76]
>
> When Thomas with the golden buttons was killed
> That time, at Banbury, in golden headgear,
> On Sunday his lady
> Brought him home to his glazed halls.

It was Elen who commissioned and paid for the magnificent tomb for the pair of them which can still be seen in Kington church. Lewys Glyn Cothi gives a long and elaborate description of this tomb, the accuracy of which can be judged by comparing it with the real thing. Only an extract is given here:

> Mae 'sgrifen uwchben y bedd,
> Mae dau o enwau unwedd:
> Enw Domas hael, nid mwy saith,
> Enw Elen yno eilwaith.
> Boparth i'r bedd y gweddyn',
> Byst ar gaer o albawstr gwyn.[77]
>
> There is an inscription above the grave,
> There are two names alike:
> The name of noble Thomas, seven men would not be greater,
> The name of Elen there too.
> On either side of the tomb they are fitting,
> Columns upon a fortress of white alabaster.

The columns are the two fine effigies of Thomas and his wife; the fortress is the body of the tomb. In both of his poems Lewys addresses also the sons of Thomas ap Roger Vaughan and Elen. In the initial elegy they are urged fiercely to take vengeance for their father "before the summer is much older;" where they choose to give battle, God will be fighting alongside them against the English. The tone of the later poem celebrating their father's tomb is quieter. The emphasis is now on the eldest brother and heir, Watkin, who will carry on his father's line. There

---

[75] Johnston, *Gwaith Lewys Glyn Cothi*, poem 124 (lines 41–42).
[76] Ibid., poem 125 (lines 7–10).
[77] Ibid. (lines 15–20).

is no more talk of vengeance.[78]

There is one final poem for a man who followed the Herberts to their deaths, but a quite unconventional one. Its impact is so immediate that it requires little scholarly commentary, and I will simply offer some quotations from it. A man called Rhys ap Dafydd Llwyd, from Newtown in mid Wales, went to Banbury in the army of William Herbert. Weeks later, he had still not returned:

> Os byw'r mab glas o Bowys
> Wedi'r drin, ble'r ydwyd, Rys?[79]
>
> If the vigorous lad of Powys is still alive
> After the battle, where are you, Rhys?

The poet, Dafydd Llwyd of Mathafarn, imagines Rhys returning: he will not have had a chance to shave for weeks:

> Odid dyn a'ch edwyn chwi
> A'th farf, Rys, hyd ar y fron,
> A'r gwallt fal Gwyddyl gwylltion.[80]
>
> Scarcely any man will recognize you,
> Rhys, with your beard down to your chest,
> And your hair like that of wild Irishmen.

The image is almost comic to us, but it can hardly have been received that way at the time. Rhys's wife, Margaret, still waits for him:

> Margred ni chred na boch, Rys,
> Iach a byw – dowch i Bowys![81]
>
> Margaret doesn't believe, Rhys,
> That you are not alive and well – come to Powys!

His family and friends are praying for him. His sisters have sent gold and wax as offerings to the Holy Rood, while the aid of the Virgin Mary and the local parish saint have also been invoked:

> Aeth yma wyth o emys
> I Fair Wen er dy fyw, Rys.
> Y mae garbron Llwchaearn
> Yn ymbil bumil, o'm barn.[82]
>
> Eight horses have been offered
> To the blessed Virgin for your life, Rhys.
> Before St Llwchaearn five thousand
> Are praying, so I believe.

---

[78] Ibid., poem 124 (lines 47–64), poem 125 (lines 47–64).
[79] Richards, *Gwaith Dafydd Llwyd*, poem 55 (lines 11–12). The date is after August 1469, as confirmed by line 17 "Er Awst hyd heddiw," i.e. "from August until today".
[80] Ibid. (lines 38–40).
[81] Ibid. (lines 55–56).
[82] Ibid. (lines 61–64).

Sadly, there is no evidence that Rhys ap Dafydd ever returned to his wife and family in Newtown.

***

The last two decades have seen a huge effort to collect and edit medieval Welsh poetry. That effort is now beginning to encompass the need to provide full and accurate English translations of these fascinating texts.[83] As the works of the late medieval poets gradually begin to be made available in translation, it is to be hoped that they will find a worthy place in historians' thinking and writing about the fifteenth century and its people.

---

[83] The recent electronic edition of the works of Dafydd ap Gwilym (fl. 1340s), with a full English translation, deserves mention here (www.dafyddapgwilym.net). On similar lines, the Guto'r Glyn project will encompass about 120 poems from the fifteenth century, all with full translations (completion date is 2012).

Descriptions of Battles in Fifteenth-Century Urban Chronicles: A Comparison of the Siege of London in May 1471 and the Battle of Grandson, 2 March 1476[1]

Andreas Remy

> ... and [the Swiss] kneeled down in order to pray. But the Burgundians did not let them kneel for long, because they thought they were asking for mercy; they rode with all might to them and cried, "You will get no mercy; you all have to die!"[2]

These words were used by the Zürich chronicler, Heinrich Brennwald, to describe the beginning of the battle of Grandson in 1476. We can ask why the author mentioned this specific act of prayer as the beginning of the actual battle. Why did he present the gesture of prayer, and the reaction of the Burgundians to it, in the way he did? The explanation can be divided into three points. First, it served to portray the Swiss as very pious people, since even on the battlefield they fell on their knees to pray so that God would grant them the victory. This gesture of humility and piety gave them an aura of moral superiority – they deserved to win, because they were so faithful to God. Secondly, the reaction of the Burgundians is telling. They did not recognize the gesture of kneeling as an act of prayer. Rather, they misinterpreted it as a sign of surrender. This stands as a symbol for their own lack of piety and faith: good Christians must recognize a prayer when they see it, yet the Burgundians did not. It also gave the impression of their certainty that the victory would be theirs, otherwise they would not have expected the enemy to surrender before the battle had even started. So, not only were the Burgundians lacking in piety but they were also over-confident, the exact opposite of the humble Swiss who recognized the influence of God on the outcome of the battle by choosing to pray first. Thirdly, the Burgundians are depicted as merciless enemies who would not spare any of the Swiss if they had been victorious. This is shown by their reaction to what they believed was a gesture of begging for mercy. All three aspects combine to give a picture of the two sides. It shows the Swiss as pious fighters who trusted the outcome of the battle in the hands of God, whereas the Burgundians were merciless, over-confident and not very pious fighters.

---

[1] I would like to thank Prof. Malte Prietzel and Prof. Anne Curry for their encouragement and useful advice.

[2] "und [die Schweizer] knüwtend da mit nider in meinung ze beten. Aber die Burgunschen liessend si nüt lang knüwen; den sie meintend, si begertind gnaden und ritend mit aller macht uff si und schruwend: Üch geschicht kein gnad; ir müssend alle sterben!" in Heinrich Brennwald, *Heinrich Brennwalds Schweizerchronik*, ed. Rudolf Luginbühl, 2 vols. (Basel, 1908–10), 2:245.

Through this depiction the chronicler made it obvious to the reader that only the Swiss morally deserved the victory, which, of course, they did obtain. The purpose of this episode is therefore not to describe the start of the battle accurately,[3] but rather to depict both sides in a way in which the chronicler wanted his audience to see them while at the same time giving a justification for the outcome of the battle as a victory for the Swiss. This incident epitomizes a general truth: medieval writers were often strongly in favor of one side taking part in a battle, rather than being unbiased observers. Even if contemporaries or chroniclers tried to provide an objective report about a battle it would rarely have been possible because of the intended purpose of their writing. Most writers were not eyewitnesses of the battles they described. Thus, they relied on information passed on to them, and even their contemporaries sometimes doubted the substance of their sources. For example, in a letter about the battle of Towton, Prospero di Camulio, Milanese ambassador to the French court, wrote to the duke of Milan: "I am ashamed to speak of so many thousands, which resemble the figures of bakers, yet every one affirms that on that day there were 300,000 men under arms."[4] Even being an eyewitness did not guarantee that information about the number of fighters involved, about casualties, or about the proceeding of a battle were precise.[5] Rather than using chronicles simply to reconstruct battles, therefore, it is more useful to examine how battles are presented to us in such writings. In this study the focus is on two battles in which urban communities were heavily involved. It examines how these towns, or more precisely the chroniclers commissioned by or operating within them, described the battle. Which aspects did they stress? No less importantly, which aspects were conspicuous by their absence?

The two examples are the siege of London in 1471 and the Swiss victory over the Burgundians at Grandson in 1476. A study of the accounts of these two engagements shows the similarities and differences in urban-based reflections on warfare in the late fifteenth century. In May 1471, London was besieged and attacked by Thomas Fauconberg. This incident had no impact on the outcome of the struggle between the houses of Lancaster and York and therefore seems far less important than the great pitched battles of the Wars of the Roses, such as the battles of Towton, Tewkesbury or Barnet, where larger numbers of fighters were involved and whose protagonists were more prominent. As a result, the siege of London is often only briefly mentioned in works which concentrate on the military campaigns of the Wars of the Roses.[6] It is remarkable, however, because

---

[3] This does not necessarily mean that the battle did not start like that, but that for the chronicler it was most important to convey the images he wanted his audience to have. What really happened was less important to his purpose.

[4] *Calendar of State Papers and Manuscripts, existing in the Archives and Collections of Milan, vol. 1. 1385–1618*, ed. Allen B. Hinds (London, 1912), p. 55.

[5] For the problems of counting the casualties after a battle see Malte Prietzel, "Der Tod auf dem Schlachtfeld. Töten und Sterben in der Chronistik des Hundertjährigen Kriegs," in *Kriegs/Bilder in Mittelalter und Früher Neuzeit*, Zeitschrift für Historische Forschung Beiheft 42, ed. Birgit Emich and Gabriela Signori (Berlin, 2009), pp. 63–5.

[6] There is one detailed article on the actions of Fauconberg in 1471, in which the siege of London is described: Colin Richmond, "Fauconberg's Kentish Rising of May 1471," *English Historical*

it is well documented within the city itself, with a lengthy report about it in the Great Chronicle of London.[7] The only other chronicle which gives descriptions of battles of the Wars of the Roses and which is comparable in length and detail is the chronicle describing the arrival of Edward IV after his exile in Burgundy.[8] Generally, descriptions of the battles of the Wars of the Roses in contemporary chronicles are short and do not provide much detail about the actual proceedings.[9] The battle of Grandson has attracted more attention from historians as it is one of three major battles between the Swiss Confederacy and Charles the Bold in the Burgundian wars.[10] It has been chosen for this study because the descriptions of the battle establish the most important elements of accounts of battles given by the Swiss.

The siege of London, May 1471

After his short exile in Burgundy, Edward IV returned to England in mid-March 1471 and defeated the Lancastrian forces at the battle of Barnet on 14 April, where Richard, earl of Warwick, died. Edward was also victorious shortly afterwards at Tewkesbury (4 May), where Prince Edward, the son of Henry VI, was slain. The power of the Yorkist king was restored and the Lancastrian dynasty would be wiped out with the murder of Henry VI a short while later (21 May). On 12

Review 85 (1970), 673–92. The prominent works on the Wars of the Roses mostly concentrate on the history of events or the political history and do therefore not focus on detailed accounts of the military events. In the work of J.R. Lander the siege of London is briefly described by citing the account of Warkworth's chronicle and the event is even omitted from the chronological table: see J.R. Lander, *The Wars of the Roses* (Stroud, 2000), pp. 155–8, 265. Christine Carpenter also focuses on the political history and the course of the single military events is not in her focus. Consequently the siege of London is mentioned only in a few sentences: see Christine Carpenter, *The Wars of the Roses* (Cambridge, 1997), p. 180. In Philip A. Haigh, *The Military Campaigns of the Wars of the Roses* (Stroud, 1995), the siege was mentioned only as an aftermath of the battle of Tewkesbury, whereas every other battle of the time was described in detail by the author. As a contrast there are numerous publications – many written for a popular audience – on the more prominent battles of the times, such as P.W. Hammond, *The Battles of Barnet and Tewkesbury* (Gloucester and New York, 1990).

[7] *The Great Chronicle of London* (hereafter *Great Chronicle*), ed. A.H. Thomas and I.D. Thornley (London, 1938), pp. 218–20.

[8] *Historie of the Arrivall of Edward IV in England and the final recouerye of his Kingdoms from Henry VI. A.D. M.CCCC.LXXI* (hereafter *Arrivall*), ed. John Bruce (London, 1838). As the chronicle was written to portray the greatness of Edward IV a detailed description of his deeds on the battlefields of Barnet and Tewkesbury had to be incorporated by the chronicler. This probably explains the great amount of detail given for those battles.

[9] Good examples of the brevity of battle descriptions in most fifteenth-century chronicles are the descriptions of the battles of Northampton, Wakefield, and the second battle of St. Albans in 1461 in the Crowland continuations: *The Crowland Chronicle Continuations: 1459–1486*, ed. Nicholas Pronay and John Cox (London, 1986), pp. 111–13.

[10] See, for example, Walter Schaufelberger, *Der Alte Schweizer und sein Krieg. Studien zur Kriegsführung vornehmlich im 15. Jahrhundert* (Frauenfeld, 1987), or August Bernoulli, *Die Schlacht bei Grandson* (Basel, 1898).

May 1471 the Lancastrian nobleman Thomas Fauconberg,[11] who obviously had not heard the news of the defeats suffered by his party, arrived at London by ship. He wanted to proceed through the city of London to aid his fellow Lancastrians, but the London City Council informed him of recent events – especially the death of the earl of Warwick at the battle of Barnet – and told him that they could not let him pass the city due to an instruction from King Edward IV.[12] Fauconberg had his troops encamped at Southwark and after a few days decided to attack London with his force, which consisted of professional soldiers and – probably to a large part – people from the counties of Essex and Kent. The attack failed and Fauconberg retreated into Kent.[13] He surrendered to Edward IV towards the end of the month and was beheaded in September 1471.[14]

For the Wars of the Roses as a whole the incident was not significant, as the Lancastrian candidates for the throne were already dead or were soon to be so. A victory by Fauconberg would not have changed the fact that the Yorkists had prevailed in the conflict. Thus it seems that the siege of London was not an important event for the realm as a whole, but for London as a community it was the most important military event during this whole struggle because it was the only battle which directly affected the city and its inhabitants. This is clearly demonstrated by two texts of London origin which emanated from the siege.

There are also descriptions of Fauconberg's rising and his attack on London in other chronicles, such as Warkworth's Chronicle[15] and the already mentioned chronicle of the Arrival of Edward IV.[16] Warkworth's Chronicle is quite full on the events that led to Fauconberg's attack on London and the following events, but his description of the actual attack on London is very brief and does not provide any details,[17] so it is not very helpful when one is looking at the way that the battle itself is presented. The chronicle of the Arrival of Edward IV does give an account comparable in detail to the accounts of London, differing from the London accounts only in some important aspects, as will be seen later.[18]

The first London text is the account which is given in the Great Chronicle.[19]

---

[11] An illegitimate son of William Neville, Lord Fauconberg, often referred to by contemporary writers as "the Bastard". For more details on Fauconberg, his role in the conflict and his actions before the siege of London see Richmond, "Fauconberg's Kentish Rising," 673–77.

[12] It is also quite likely that they wanted to avoid any disorder in the city, which surely would have been caused by a large army within the city walls: see Richmond, "Fauconberg's Kentish Rising," 680.

[13] Charles Ross, *Edward IV* (London, 1975), p. 181.

[14] Richmond, "Fauconberg's Kentish Rising," 682.

[15] Printed in *Death and Dissent*, ed. Matheson.

[16] See above, n. 8.

[17] The chronicle mentions only that Fauconberg "losed his gonnys into þe cite & brent at Algate & at Londoun Brygge," in *Death and Dissent*, ed. Matheson, pp. 114–15.

[18] I will use the *Arrivall* to show some of the differences in the description of the battle, but as I am focusing on the accounts given by London itself I will devote more space to the *Great Chronicle*.

[19] The author of the Great Chronicle is not definitely known. It is tentatively ascribed to Robert Fabyan, but it is certain that the author was a citizen of London. See Antonia Gransden, *Historical Writing in England II. c.1307 to the Early Sixteenth Century* (London, 1974), pp. 231–2.

It is the most detailed of any battle of the Wars of the Roses to be found in this text. Even though the battles of St. Albans in 1455 and 1461 and the battle of Barnet in 1471 had been fought quite close to London, their descriptions are not nearly as detailed as the account of the London siege. The second account is an entry in the Common Council Journals about the attack.[20] This takes the form of a short report of how the mayor had strengthened the city's defence prior to the attack, how the attacks were carried out by Fauconberg and which citizens were knighted by Edward IV as a result of the battle. The brief account of the defence of the city and the attacks by Fauconberg lack any narrative element but give a relatively detailed account of where and when the attacks were made: "the 12th day of May […] [rebels] made an attack upon London bridge and on the new gate there and set fire to diverse houses […] the 14th of May […] rebels made an attack with great force and set fire to 13 tenements upon London bridge."[21] The entry states that Fauconberg's forces consisted of about five thousand men.[22] The account goes on to describe how the citizens showed stout resistance and made the aggressors retreat, giving the number of three hundred dead on both sides during the attack.[23] After that it gives a long list of names of those people from London who were knighted after the battle. These dubbings were not only evidence for the bravery shown by the people of London but also proof of the importance of the battle to the city.

The Great Chronicle of London paints a much more lively picture which is due to its being a chronicle rather than a bureaucratic account. This can be illustrated by the contrasting ways in which Fauconberg is depicted. The report in the Common Council Journal of the siege gave no indication that Fauconberg showed particular arrogance towards the city of London. There are also two well-known letters which the Council and Lord Fauconberg exchanged.[24] These were written before the battle and therefore provide no information about the action itself, but they are still of interest because they also do not show any signs of a special enmity between Fauconberg and the city. However, the Great Chronicle states that after the London council sent him word that they would not let him in, his answer was that "he [Fauconberg] wolde Rule the Cyte by the space of a day and a nyght at his pleasure."[25] This wording was chosen to depict Fauconberg as an over-confident noble who underestimated the city's military power. In addition, the pride that was attributed to Fauconberg served to justify the city's victory morally as well as making the use of force legitimate. The chronicler makes it clear that the city of London could not reason with Fauconberg and had therefore no option other than taking the risk of a violent confrontation. The chronicler describes in great

---

[20] A translated transcription of this entry can be found in Reginald R. Sharpe, *London and the Kingdom. A History derived mainly from the Archives at Guildhall in the Custody of the Corporation of the City of London*, 3 vols. (London, 1894–95), 3:391–2.
[21] Ibid.
[22] Ibid., 3:392.
[23] "The citizens, however, sallied out of the gates and made a stout resistance and put them [the attackers] to flight, and nearly 300 fell in battle and in flight," in ibid.
[24] A transcription of these letters can also be found in ibid., 3:387–91.
[25] *Great Chronicle*, p. 219.

detail how Fauconberg despatched his troops to several gates at the same time to "make theyr assawtis alle at oon tyme."[26] There follows detailed information about how the battle worked out, explaining that the attackers were able to "wan the Bullwerk at Algate and drave the Cytyzyns wythyn the portculyows,"[27] and that they were fought off by the stout resistance of the citizens.

Even though the mentioning of individuals and how they influenced a battle was quite common in chivalric tradition, as can be seen in many chronicles of the Hundred Years War, it was not common in descriptions of battles in the Wars of the Roses, which rarely mention the heroic deeds of a single individual. It is significant, therefore, that the author of the Great Chronicle gives us the names of the leaders who were in his opinion most responsible for driving back the enemy force: "Then the aldyrman of that ward [Aldgate] beyng In a blak jak or dobelet of ffens namyd Robard Basset and wyth hym the Recorder of the Cyte callyd Mr. Ursewyk lykewise apparaylid […] Issuyd owth wyth theyr people, and w[ith] sharp shott and ffyers ffyght putt theyr Enemyes bakk."[28] Interesting here – even though not very surprising – is the fact that in the chronicle of the Arrival of Edward IV the most important actors for the defence of the city were named as the earl of Essex and Earl Rivers.[29] With support from "othir Aldyrman & Comoners" and the Mayor, the city won the fight.[30] We are told another alderman's name: "Sir Rauff Josselyn aldyrman wyth a good band of men ffolowyd hym [Fauconberg] along the watyrs syde […] tyll he cam beyond Redclyff."[31] The chronicler gives the names only of those aldermen he deemed most important – the two who defended against the most dangerous attack and the one who chased away Fauconberg. In addition, he does not mention the noblemen who were cited in the chronicle of the Arrival of Edward IV as most important in defending London. The chronicler and his audience probably wanted to describe the battle in a way that gave their city the most credit for winning it and for doing so without much support from noblemen, even if their role might have been important.[32] The mentioning of the names of the aldermen is not due to the fact that they were the

---

26   Fauconberg "sent certayn Capytaynys of his [...] to Algate w^t a multitude of Essex men, and an othir namyd Quyntyn a bowcher was sent unto Bysshoppysgate w^t an othir sort, and two othir unto Aldryshgate and Crepylgate" (*Great Chronicle*, p. 219). The same details are given by the chronicle of the arrival of Edward IV, as it states that Fauconberg's troops "were devided into two partes; one partye went to Algate, wenyng to have entred the citie there, by assaulte; an othar partye went to Bysshops-gate, wenynge to have entred there by an othar assaulte" (*Arrivall*, p. 36).
27   *Great Chronicle*, p. 219.
28   Ibid.
29   "To the citizens, and defence of the citie, cam th'Erle of Essex [...] which had right great diligence in orderinge the citizens, and firste to prepare and ordayne for the defence and surtye of the sayd cittie" (*Arrivall*, p. 36) whereas the Earl Rivers is described as being the one who led the attack on Fauconberg's troops at Aldgate: see *Arrivall*, p. 37.
30   *Great Chronicle*, p. 220.
31   Ibid.
32   It can be assumed that the professional soldiers under the command of these Yorkists strengthened the city's defence considerably and played an important role in denying Fauconberg's attack. See Richmond, "Fauconberg's Kentish Rising," 680–81.

only ones the author of the Great Chronicle knew by name; it is unlikely that he did not know the entry in the Common Council Journal where the scribe named many more citizens who were knighted after the siege. The chronicler chose the names to illustrate the bravery of the leaders of the community because they were involved in what the chronicler thought of as the key moments of the battle. It is telling that chasing away Fauconberg was considered to be one of those key moments. The battle was most likely won by that time, but still the chronicler thought it was important enough to give the name of the alderman involved in the rout. The reason for the importance of the chasing away of Fauconberg is its symbolic value. The flight of the enemy leader was an obvious symbol of victory and as such had to be emphasized by the chronicler.

The chronicler chose to give no details of the number of people involved or of the casualties sustained on either side, even though he most likely knew the figures from the entry in the Journal.[33] He used expressions such as "a multitude of Essex men" who attacked at Aldgate,[34] or "they slew many of the said Rebellys,"[35] and avoided precise figures.[36] The city had been attacked and won the battle; how many attackers there were exactly or how many people had lost their lives was of less interest to either the chronicler or his audience. The reason for this may have been that there was only a relatively small number of enemy slain, and the exact number of casualties could not, therefore, act as an impressive symbol for the size of the victory. It was more important for the chronicler to give a very detailed account of how the battle was fought in order to demonstrate that London had won not by chance, but because of its military ability. Significantly, too, the chronicler also mentions how well the city rulers had prepared for the attack, telling us that the mayor "hadd Garnysshid every place of the Cyte where any peryll shuld be."[37] Surprisingly, there was no mention of any kind of spoils of war the city gained from defeating the attackers, other than the ransom for prisoners taken.[38] It should be remembered, however, that the attackers arrived on ships and were able to retreat relatively quickly after the battle was lost. The opportunities to capture goods or artillery might just have not been there. As there was probably not much, if any, booty, the chronicler could not use it as a symbol of the greatness of the victory for the city.

---

[33] "The Great Chronicle shows considerable knowledge of civc government" (Gransden, *Historical Writing*, p. 231). That knowledge implies that the chronicler at least had access to the city records and the Common Council Journals.
[34] *Great Chronicle*, p. 219.
[35] Ibid., p. 220.
[36] In Warkworth's Chronicle the number of attackers is given as "moe then xx M off goode men well harnessed" (*Death and Dissent*, ed. Matheson, p. 115).
[37] *Great Chronicle*, p. 219. As written above (note 27), the *Arrivall* gives the credit for preparing the city for the attack to the earl of Essex.
[38] "Then such prisoners as were takyn by the Cytyzins were soom of theym Raunsomyd," in *Great Chronicle*, p. 220.

The battle of Grandson, 2 March 1476

The conflict between the Burgundians and the Swiss started when Duke Charles the Bold of Burgundy and Duke Sigmund of Austria concluded the treaty of St. Omer in 1469. The latter gave his land in the upper Rhine valley (Alsatia and Breisgau) into Burgundian administration for the sum of 50,000 Rhenish florins.[39] The cities of the Elsass and Breisgau soon began to complain about the harsh treatment they received from the Burgundian bailiff (*Landvogt*), Peter von Hagenbach, and finally formed a league against him, the *Niedere Vereinigung*. When the traditional enmity between the Habsburgs and the Swiss ended with the signing of a peace treaty (the *Ewige Richtung*) in 1474 – a result of an intervention by the French king Louis XI, who wanted the Habsburgs and Swiss as allies against Charles the Bold – the cities of the *Niedere Vereinigung* called on the Swiss for help.[40] As the Holy Roman Empire was also at war with Charles the Bold – because of the siege of Neuss – Austria and the Swiss Confederacy joined together and declared war on the Burgundians in 1474. Troops of the Swiss raided the Vaud, a part of Burgundian-held Savoy, and conquered many castles and towns, including Grandson. In reaction, Charles the Bold gathered an army and went to defend the territory of his ally against the Swiss. He and his army besieged Grandson, a small town located at the south-western edge of the lake of Neuchâtel. The Swiss sent a relief army which reached Grandson just after the Burgundians had captured the city and executed the whole garrison, which consisted mostly of people from Bern. Both armies met unexpectedly, as all chronicles report, on 2 March 1476. Even though, according to all sources, not many Burgundians were killed, they retreated from the field after a short struggle. The reason for this retreat – at least according to what the Swiss chroniclers tell us – was the surprisingly strong resistance of the Swiss vanguard and the arrival of the main Swiss forces. The Swiss not only liberated Grandson but also captured the Burgundians' enormous artillery park and looted their camp, which was filled with the wealth of one of Europe's richest princes. From a military point of view, the victory of Grandson was probably not as important as the victory of Morat later in the same year. The Burgundian army had not lost many men at Grandson and was quickly reassembled by Charles the Bold to fight the Swiss and their allies again; the armies met at Morat on 22 June 1476. At this battle, about forty miles away from Grandson, according to the chronicles between eight and ten thousand Burgundians died, while the Swiss only lost a few hundred men, effectively ending the attempts of Charles the Bold to fight the Swiss on their territory.[41] In terms of prestige, however, Grandson was a huge defeat for the Burgundians and a great

---

[39] Sigmund also wanted an alliance with the Burgundians against the Swiss Confederacy, but Charles the Bold did not grant him such a promise. Richard Vaughan, *Charles the Bold. The last Valois Duke of Burgundy*, 2nd ed. (Woodbridge, 2002), pp. 85–9.

[40] For more detailed information on the context of the battle of Grandson from a Burgundian perspective, see Vaughan, *Charles the Bold*, pp. 359–98.

[41] For a description of this battle see G. Grosjean, "Die Murtenschlacht. Analyse eines Ereignisses," in *Archiv des historischen Vereins des Kantons Bern* 60 (1976), 35–90.

victory for the Swiss, as the Burgundian army was renowned as one of the most modern and advanced armies on the continent.

In comparison to the siege of London, there are many more accounts of the battle of Grandson. This is mainly due to the fact that most of the Swiss cities that were involved commissioned descriptions of their own. The major accounts I will be looking at for this study are the chronicles of Diebold Schilling the Elder from Bern, Heinrich Brennwald from Zürich and Petermann Etterlin and Diebold Schilling the Younger from Luzern.[42]

Three of these chronicles were directly ordered by the cities to illustrate the increased confidence of the Swiss towns after their successes in the conflict with the Burgundians.[43] In the case of Diebold Schilling the Elder we also know that the council of Bern censored the accounts about the Burgundian wars.[44] The chronicles of Etterlin and Brennwald focus on the whole *Eidgenossenschaft*,[45] but still favour their hometowns when describing important events. The chronicles of Diebold Schilling the Younger as well as that of the Elder are famous for their rich illustrations, which – when they illustrate violence – almost always portray the noble enemies of the Swiss as unfaithful Christians.[46] The earliest chronicle was that of Diebold Schilling the Elder, which was finished in 1483:[47] the other three chronicles were finished between 1507 and 1513, some of the chroniclers being eyewitnesses to the events they described. The descriptions given in these late-fifteenth- and early-sixteenth-century chronicles shaped the picture of the Swiss for a long time.

There are a few central points that were common to all of these accounts which are also found in almost every other account of battles fought by Swiss communes in the fourteenth and fifteenth centuries. An important aspect is the fact that the Burgundians underestimated the Swiss. We have already seen this in the reaction of the Burgundians to the prayers of the Swiss on the field. The Swiss had a particular way of praying before a battle a description of which is incorporated in every major account of Swiss battles from the fourteenth and fifteenth centuries.[48] They fell on their knees, parting their arms in a special

---

[42] For more information on the chroniclers and their life see *Geschichtsschreibung der Schweiz: vom Spätmittelalter zur Neuzeit*, ed. Richard Feller and Edgar Bonjour, 2 vols. (Basel, 1962) 1:39–45, 78–9, 86–8, 89–93. See also in general Jean-Pierre Bodmer, *Chroniken und Chronisten im Spätmittelalter* (Bern, 1976).

[43] The only chronicle where there are no hints at an official order to create a chronicle is that of Heinrich Brennwald. For the other chronicles there are strong hints that they were directly commissioned by the city councils: see *Geschichtsschreibung der Schweiz*, 1:40, 86, 90.

[44] See Bodmer, *Chroniken und Chronisten*, p. 42.

[45] The term *Eidgenossenschaft* is used by the Swiss as a self-definition of their loose federation of cities and is best translated as "Swiss Confederacy".

[46] An analysis of the illustrations of the two chronicles would be valuable for this text, and has already been done: see Michael Jucker, "Die Norm der Gewaltbilder. Zur Darstellung von Opfern und Tätern kriegerischer Gewaltexzesse in Bilderchroniken des Spätmittelalters," in *Kriegs/Bilder in Mittelalter und Früher Neuzeit*, Zeitschrift für Historische Forschung Beiheft 42, ed. Birgit Emich and Gabriela Signori (Berlin, 2009), pp. 121–53.

[47] See Bodmer, *Chroniken und Chronisten*, p. 42.

[48] For a detailed description of this custom and its roots see Peter Ochsenbein, "Beten 'mit zertanen

gesture.⁴⁹ The underestimation of the enemy is a very common feature of other well-known battle accounts of the Swiss. We see it at the battle of Morgarten in 1315, where the invading Austrians were thinking about their return before they even met the Swiss forces, or at Sempach in 1386, where the Austrian nobles were reported promising their duke to bring him for dinner the confederates "cooked and fried however your [the duke's] will is."⁵⁰

Another aspect which can be seen in the Grandson accounts, and which provides a direct link to the account of the siege of London, is the mentioning of certain people from the communes involved and the part they played in the battle. In the case of Grandson it is quite obvious that all chroniclers tried to make the commune which commissioned their work appear as the most important for the victory. There were many descriptions of captains giving decisive orders or comitting heroic acts. For example, an episode describing the death of a Burgundian noble called the Master of Chateau Guyon was mentioned by the Bernese chronicler, Diebold Schilling the Elder, as well as the Luzern chroniclers Petermann Etterlin and Diebold Schilling the Younger;⁵¹ and, whereas the first attributed the heroic act of bringing down the nobleman's flag and killing him to a citizen of his hometown ("there laid dead the master of Chateau Guyon, who was a good noble and he was killed by a citizen of Bern"⁵²), the latter two reported that it was a citizen of Luzern who performed the act.⁵³ The Luzern chroniclers also mentioned the sounds of the Swiss horns, mainly the eerie horn of their hometown,⁵⁴ which scared the Burgundians and played a part in their early retreat. The chronicle of Heinrich Brennwald from Zürich, on the other hand, completely omitted the Luzern horn and the episode about the death of the master of Chateau Guyon, and instead mentioned the citizens of Zürich who had been knighted after the battle.⁵⁵

We have seen that mentioning the heroic deeds of individuals from the communes or good planning by their leading figures was important for the chroniclers, whereas the number of slain enemies was not that important. This was probably due to the fact that there were not that many casualties on either side at Grandson

---

Armen' – ein alteidgenössischer Brauch," *Schweizerisches Archiv für Volkskunde* 75 (1979), 129–72.

⁴⁹ "do knúwt menglich nider mit zertanen armen und rûften den almechtigen got an," in Diebold Schilling, *Die Berner-Chronik des Diebold Schilling 1468–1484*, ed. Gustav Tobler, 2 vols. (Bern, 1897–1901), 1:377; see also Brennwald, *Brennwalds Schweizerchronik*, 2:245.

⁵⁰ "gesoten und gebratten nach dinem willen," in Brennwald, *Brennwalds Schweizerchronik*, 1:407.

⁵¹ For the version from Bern see Schilling, *Berner-Chronik*, 1:378; for the version from Luzern see Petermann Etterlin, *Kronica der loblichen Eydtgnosschaft, jr harkommen und sust seltzam strittenn und geschichten*, ed. Eugen Gruber (Aarau, 1965), p. 252; Diebold Schilling, *Des Lucerners Schweizer Chronik* (Luzern, 1862), p. 77.

⁵² "doch bleip do tot ligen der herr von Tschettegion, der ein rechter fürst was und von von einem burger von Bern umbbracht wart," in Schilling, *Berner-Chronik*, 1:378.

⁵³ "der herr von Chetialgyon, der syn paner selbs in henden hatt, die ouch von denen von Lutzern ritterlichen gewunnen," in Etterlin, *Kronica*, p. 252; "Die [the banner of the master of Chateau Guyon] gewan Heini Elsiner von Lucern," in Schilling, *Lucerners Schweizer Chronik*, p. 77.

⁵⁴ "grusenlich," in Schilling, *Lucerners Schweizer Chronik*, p. 76.

⁵⁵ Brennwald, *Brennwalds Schweizerchronik*, 2:247.

and, therefore, the number of slain enemies could not serve as a proof of the greatness of the victory. It was, however, very important for the Swiss chroniclers after Grandson to mention in detail the extent of the spoils of war they gained after capturing the camp and the artillery park of the Burgundians. In most accounts there are very detailed lists of exactly what the Swiss took from the camp of Charles the Bold.[56] Most chroniclers mentioned personal items of Charles the Bold, such as "the personal seal of the duke Charles of Burgundy,"[57] "the duke's sword, in which hilt there are seven huge diamonds, seven huge rubys and fifteen huge pearls so delightful, its worth can not be well estimated,"[58] and "a diamond as big as half a walnut with three pearls as big as beans, estimated at 60,000 gl."[59] Apart from personal items of the duke the chroniclers also put an emphasis on military goods the Swiss captured. There were "many delightful armors"[60] and "countless numbers of big and small cannons,"[61] which were mentioned by almost every chronicler.[62] As a symbol of victory most chroniclers also mentioned "the flags and banners of the duke and many others" as part of the loot.[63] The Luzern chronicler Diebold Schilling gave a detailed description of the flags, mentioning that they had "the duke's coat of arms on them, with golden letters on each one."[64] The mentioning of the banners is an indication of the pride the cities took in exactly whom they had beaten. They had not been successful against any old opposition but against the duke of Burgundy himself. The banners were a visual proof of the enemy against whom the cities had been victorious and as such they were especially mentioned and sometimes even described in detail. The chroniclers listed the personal items of the duke as a symbol of the scale of the victory: the fact that the Swiss got hold of the duke's personal items emphasized to the reader how hasty Charles's retreat must have been.[65] The artillery is mentioned because, as the most modern weapons, the cannons had been the pride

[56] The two most detailed lists are given in Schilling, *Berner-Chronik*, pp. 387–9, and Brennwald, *Brennwalds Schweizerchronik*, 2:247–9. Less detailed lists can be found in Schilling, *Lucerners Schweizer Chronik*, p. 78, and Etterlin, *Kronica*, pp. 252–3.

[57] "herzog Karlis von Burgund eigen insigel," in Brennwald, *Brennwalds Schweizerchronik*, 2:247.

[58] "des herzogen tegen, sind im hœfte versetzt 7 gros dyamant, 7 gros rubin und 15 gros berlin als kœstlichen, das man es ouch nit wol kann schetzen," in Schilling, *Berner-Chronik*, p. 388.

[59] "einen demund als gross als ein halbi bůmnuss mit trigen berlin als gross als bonen, in einer haften versetzt, acht man für 60 000 gl.," in Brennwald, *Brennwalds Schweizerchronik*, 2:248.

[60] "gar vil kostlichs harnisch," in Brennwald, *Brennwalds Schweizerchronik*, 2:248.

[61] "ouch unsäglich vil grosser und cleiner büchsen," in Schilling, *Lucerners Schweizer Chronik*, p. 78.

[62] They are mentioned by Petermann Etterlin: "büchßen, dera on zal gewunnen ward," in Etterlin, *Kronica*, p. 252, and also by Heinrich Brennwald: "alle sine büchsen; dero kamend vil gen Zürich und insunders der aller grœsten eini," in Brennwald, *Brennwalds Schweizerchronik*, 2:248.

[63] "des herzogen und sunst vil paner und venli," in Brennwald, *Brennwalds Schweizerchronik*, 2:247.

[64] "des hertzogen wapen daran gemachet, und an eim jeglichen mit guldin buochstaben geschriben," in Schilling, *Lucerners Schweizer Chronik*, p. 78.

[65] For the relevance of looting in warfare and its importance as a symbol of victory, see Malte Prietzel, *Kriegführung im Mittelalter. Handlungen, Erinnerungen, Bedeutungen* (Paderborn, 2006), pp. 109–18.

of Charles' army and stood as an important symbol of the military power of the Burgundians. The capture of these cannons showed how mighty the enemy of the Swiss had been, and the captured cannons were now a symbol of the military power of the Swiss.

The accounts of the battle of Grandson describe an ideal type of a battle rather than the actual proceedings. They generated a certain reputation for the Swiss and their style of fighting and also shaped the expectations of their audience, which consisted mainly of people from the cities which were involved. We can also see that the accounts of the battle of Grandson influenced retrospectively the representations of previous, much older, battles, especially in terms of the description of any material gain after a battle. Later accounts seem to have used the accounts given for Grandson as a model. The chroniclers and their audience now expected to read about huge spoils of war, preferably containing artillery, after a famous victory. A Swiss battle description had to include the plundering of the enemy camp at the end as part of an ideal battle.

Comparing the reports about Grandson with other accounts of Swiss battles of the fourteenth and fifteenth centuries, it is obvious that all accounts written after Grandson put a big emphasis on the material gain after a battle. This can be seen most clearly in the accounts of the battle of Sempach (1386). Early accounts of the battle, written before Grandson, put less emphasis on any kind of material gain the Swiss had from that battle, but stress the flags and banners they won,[66] which were also a symbol for the victory against the noble opposition at that time. In almost every account of the Sempach battle composed after the battle of Grandson, however, a large booty is mentioned. Even the capture of artillery was described in one chronicle,[67] despite the fact that it is very unlikely that the Austrian duke, the Swiss enemy at Sempach, had any field ordnance with him in 1386. None of the earlier reports from the Austrian side as well as from the Swiss mentions any kind of artillery for that battle.

Conclusions

This comparison of the descriptions of two battles fought by cities is not in itself enough to make a definitive statement about all battle descriptions given by urban chroniclers in the fourteenth and fifteenth centuries. However, it draws immediate attention to the aspects which were most important for writers from cities in describing the battles in which their inhabitants fought. The (usually noble) enemy was depicted as underestimating the city's military power. The art of warfare had long been in the hands of nobles. Cities were still just emerging as actors of military potency in the fourteenth and fifteenth century. The communes, even at the end of the fifteenth century, seemed to feel that they had to

---

[66] One example of an early description of the battle of Sempach is the account of Conrad Justinger, written around 1420: Conrad Justinger, *Die Berner Chronik des Conrad Justinger*, ed. Gottlieb Studer (Bern, 1871), p. 163.
[67] "ward da gewunnen vil büchßen," in Etterlin, *Kronica*, pp. 144–5.

emphasize the fact that they were military powerful. The illustration of an overconfident enemy is probably meant as a symbol that most nobles were still not giving the cities the credit of being militarily powerful that they – in their own eyes – deserved.

How important it was for cities to stress the fact that they were militarily powerful can be seen by the way actual battles were described by their chroniclers. A striking aspect, especially in the case of the siege of London, but also in the accounts about the battle of Grandson, is the precision with which the proceedings of those battles were described. In both examples the chronicles gave detailed, rational reasons for their victories: the bravery of their own men, good organization and good planning by their captains. It shows that the cities took pride in the way they beat their opponents. The chroniclers made it clear that the cities did not win the battle by chance or because of divine intervention[68] but because of their own military power. The mentioning of individual actors or even heroic figures was also common in reports of battles given by chroniclers from the places involved. This not only emphasized the bravery of the whole commune but also showed that anyone who fought for his home town could become a hero. This may, therefore, have acted as an incentive for others. In case of the Swiss a special custom – the so-called *Schlachtjahrzeiten* – made sure that those who fought for their city were remembered. At these yearly commemoration days on the anniversary of a battle the cities as a whole remembered, in churches and by processions, their casualties of a particular battle.[69] This created a strong sense of community. The message to the citizens was that any sacrifice that was made would not be forgotten by their fellow citizens. In Bern the report of the battle given by Diebold Schilling the Elder was read in the church at every memorial day for the battle of Grandson from the late fifteenth century onwards.[70] These commemorations formed part of the historic self-conception of the Swiss and are still held today.[71]

Many of these aspects are not limited to accounts emanating from urban settings but it is not a coincidence that the descriptions of both the battles examined here put emphasis on them. In all English accounts of the battles of the Wars of the Roses there is rarely a mention of the deeds of a single man.[72] It seems significant that the emphasis was put on individuals in the only battle fought, and reported on, by a city. It is likely that the expectation of reading about heroic figures in

---

[68] Even though the influence of God on the outcome of the battle is at least mentioned in the case of the Swiss.

[69] See Klaus Graf, "Schlachtgedenken im Spätmittelalter. Riten und Medien der Präsentation kollektiver Identität," in *Feste und Feiern im Mittelalter. Paderborner Symposion des Mediävistenverbandes*, ed. Detlef Altenburg, Jörg Janut and Hans-Hugo Steinhoff (Sigmaringen, 1991), pp. 63–9.

[70] See Graf, "Schlachtgedenken", p. 66.

[71] See Klaus Graf, "Erinnerungsfeste in der spätmittelalterlichen Stadt," in *Memoria, Communitas, Civitas. Mémoire et Conscience urbaines en occident à la fin du Moyen Age*, Franica Beihefte 55, ed. Hanno Brand, Pierre Monnet and Martial Staub (Ostfildern, 2003), p. 265.

[72] Other than the already mentioned "Arrivall," which was probably written with the purpose of portraying Edward IV in the best possible light.

the description of a battle was shaped by the many chronicles that were commissioned by noblemen or kings to highlight their personal deeds, but urban writers emphasized what they deemed was important to their audience. A difference between the account of the siege of London given in the Great Chronicle and the accounts of the battle of Grandson given by the Swiss chroniclers is the emphasis the latter put on the spoils of war. Even though material gain was probably more important economically for the Swiss than it was for London, this difference can also be explained to a good degree by the different possibilities for booty after the battles. At Grandson, the Swiss could get hold of the enormous Burgundian artillery park as well as the camp which contained many items of the household of one of Europe's richest princes, whereas London won its battle against a force largely made up by people from the countryside. The spoils of war for the Swiss were an impressive symbol for victory. In the case of the siege of London the loot was not impressive enough to be mentioned. The comparison of these two battles and the way they were reported shows that accounts of battles given by the cities involved, in England as well as on the continent, emphasized many of the same aspects – those which were the most important for their audience. Therefore, they do not give a precise description of what really happened, but rather conveyed the image of a battle that the chronicler, his contemporaries and his audience expected.

Urban Espionage and Counterespionage during the Burgundian Wars (1468–1477)

Bastian Walter

Introduction

On 29 July 1475 the councillors of Strasbourg wrote an enraged letter to their captains in the war theatre in the Free County of Burgundy.[1] The letter opened by thanking them for their last communication in which they had reported the taking of the town of L'Isle-sur-le-Doubs but had failed to talk about their future plans. These, however, could be deduced from a letter of the captains' scribe, written by him to his wife in Strasbourg. As proof, a copy of that letter was attached.[2] The councillors ordered that in future the captains' scribe should write to no one but themselves.[3] In addition, they mentioned the fact that the last messenger coming from the war zone had carried numerous letters written by soldiers to their families reporting of the war against Burgundy. Such *"Nebenschreiben"* were providing irritations and slowing down the city's already greatly overburdened messenger service.[4] In closing their letter, the councillors pointed out that it was problematic if news from the war zone was not to reach it directly and was instead to be talked about on the roads. But which kind of information was to be restricted? The letter of a mercenary captain of Strasbourg, written only two days later to his cousin in the city, provides a first hint. In it he reports bad treatment by the captains, and

---

[1] Archives Municipales et Communautaires de Strasbourg [AMS], *AA 281*, fol. 26.
[2] The author is currently preparing his dissertation for publication. In it, he examines the connections between information, knowledge and power in the sphere of urban foreign policy in the context of the Burgundian Wars: Bastian Walter, "Informationen, Wissen und Macht. Akteure und Techniken städtischer Außenpolitik Bern, Straßburg und Basel im Kontext der Burgunderkriege (1468–1477)" (unpublished Ph.D. thesis, Historical Seminar Muenster, Germany), hereafter cited as Walter, "Informationen, Wissen and Macht").
[3] Frieder Schanze, "Tüsch, Hans Erhard (Johannes Düsch)," in *Verfasserlexikon*, Band 3, lines 1170–1179; N.N., "Légende bourguignonne. Burgundesch Legende. Strasbourg 1477," in *Recueil de pièces historiques imprimées sous le regne de Louis XI reproduites en fac-similé avec des commentaires historiques et bibliographiques*, ed. Emile Picot and Henri Stein (Paris, 1923), pp. 65–90.
[4] For these "nebentgeschrifften" as precursors of military mail see Walter, "Informationen, Wissen und Macht", pp. 312–16.

that he was being given bad food and too little pay. According to him, resistance among the troops was rising, and he was sure to be coming home soon.[5]

I will return to this episode later since it links directly to my subject. These events took place in the middle of the Burgundian wars. From October 1474 the imperial towns of the Swiss Confederation and of the Upper Rhine led by Bern, Basel and Strasbourg acted together against the duke of Burgundy, Charles the Bold. They had been in league since April 1474.[6] In July 1475 they conquered numerous castles and places in Burgundy. That made it all the more important for the councillors to have information about military proceedings reach them alone. Communication routes could be very dangerous, especially in times of war. There was always the danger of rumours being picked up on the roads and used by enemy spies. The councillors knew that especially in times of war any information about the enemy could be valuable.[7] This encouraged the practice of trying to obtain specific information by contacting directly those in possession of that information. But the three cities under consideration – Bern, Basel and Strasbourg – were also employing professional spies in their service. In the first part of this essay I will examine what I term the 'alternative channels' of information used by these cities. I intend to determine here which were the existing channels of information that the councillors used to obtain important information, as well as which professions, groups of people and places were considered for the procuring of such information. In the second part I will discuss the practice of sending out professional spies on purpose. The transfer of information will also be examined. Was the field of spying exclusively oral or are written spy reports to be found? What characterized spies, and what set of skills did they have to

---

[5] After approximately three weeks, the mercenary captain and the troops entrusted to him (from Lichtenberg, a hamlet in the vicinity of Strasbourg) left the theatre of war against the will of the commanders. The mercenary was among the first to do so. The reason for this was a threatened revolt of the Strasbourgian craftsmen who wanted to remain in the field only for the four weeks they had been promised earlier because of the bad weather and the diseases which were rampant. As a result of the quarrels arising from this, it had almost come to a state of revolt within the Strasbourgian army. Only an intervention of the Strasbourgian Ammeister Peter Schott had been able to prevent this. The order of events, their protagonists and the protocols of the interrogation of witnesses can be found in a file assembled by Strasbourgian councillors after the event in order to prepare future suits at law (AMS, *AA 281*, fols. 20–22). There it says, among other things "[...] do zugent über der houbtlüte wille hinweg wider heim Cunrat von Myttelshus mit den Lichtenbergschen" ("against the will of the captains went home Cunrat von Myttelshus with the ones from Lichtenberg." See Walter, "Informationen, Wissen und Macht", pp. 233–5, 312–16.

[6] On the slow process of moving towards unity between the Confederation and the Reichsstädte of the Upper Rhine, see Claudius Sieber-Lehmann, *Spätmittelalterlicher Nationalismus. Die Burgunderkriege am Oberrhein und in der Eidgenossenschaft*, Veröffentlichungen des Max-Planck-Instituts für Geschichte 116 (Göttingen, 1995); for how the war touched the Free County of Burgundy, see Karl Bittmann, *Ludwig, Ludwig XI. und Karl der Kühne. Die Memoiren des Philippe de Commynes als historische Quelle*, Veröffentlichungen des Max-Planck-Instituts für Geschichte 9/II/I (Göttingen, 1970), pp. 863–91; Heinrich Witte, "Zur Geschichte der Burgunderkriege. Das Kriegsjahr 1475: Die Reise gen Blamont," *Zeitschrift für die Geschichte des Oberrheins* 8 (1893), 197–255.

[7] Walter, "Informationen, Wissen und Macht", pp. 318–65.

bring to their tasks? The third part will look at how the councillors communicated secret information to their allies and whether ways of protecting the informers can be found. Finally, in the conclusion I will combine the insights gathered and will attempt to demonstrate more clearly the importance of communication routes using the example of a Burgundian spy named Diebold Benedicti. While some publications about information gathering in the courtly context are extant, this essay fills a gap in the medieval urban history of continental Europe.[8] Information *gathering*, which necessarily preceded its *distribution*, is central, all the more so if we regard the distribution of information as an important element in the legitimizing strategies of rulers.[9] After all, especially in times of war, rulers were in urgent need of information about the enemy.

---

[8] Wolfgang Krieger, *Geheimdienste in der Weltgeschichte. Spionage und verdeckte Aktionen von der Antike bis zur Gegenwart* (Munich, 2003), "Einleitung," pp. 7–19; Christopher Allmand, "Spionage und Geheimdienst im Hundertjährigen Krieg," in *Geheimdienste in der Weltgeschichte. Spionage und verdeckte Aktionen von der Antike bis zur Gegenwart*, ed. Wolfgang Krieger (Munich, 2003), pp. 97–111; for the medieval papacy, cf. Stefan Weiss, "Das Papsttum und seine Geheimdiplomatie," in *Geheimdienste in der Weltgeschichte. Spionage und verdeckte Aktionen von der Antike bis zur Gegenwart*, ed. Wolfgang Krieger (Munich, 2003), pp. 86–97; for France, Heinz Thomas, "Französische Spionage im Reich Ludwigs des Bayern," *Zeitschrift für Historische Forschung* 5 (1978), 1–21; Jean Lelievre, "Espionnage en Beauce à la fin de la guerre de Cent Ans," *Histoire locale Beauce et Perche* 31 (1969), 3–6; Ralph A. Griffiths, "Un espion à Londres, 1425–1429," *Annales de Bretagne et des pays de l'Ouest* 86 (1979), 399–403; for England, Ian Arthurson, "Espionage and Intelligence from the War of Roses to the Reformation," *Nottingham Medieval Studies* 35 (1991), 134–55; Christopher Allmand, "Intelligence in the Hundred Years War," in *Go Spy the Land. Military Intelligence in History*, ed. Keith Neilson and B.J.C. McKercher (London, 1992), pp. 31–47; J.R. Alban and Christopher Allmand, "Spies and Spying in the Fourteenth Century," in *War, Literature and Politics in the Late Middle Ages*, ed. Christopher Allmand (Liverpool, 1976), pp. 73–101; for Burgundy, Werner Paravicini, "Ein Spion in Malpaga. Zur Überlieferungsgeschichte der Urkunden des René d'Anjou und Karls des Kühnen für Bartholomeo Colleoni," in *Italia et Germania. Liber Amicorum Arnold Esch*, ed. Hagen Keller, Werner Paravicini and Wolfgang Schnieder (Tübingen, 2001), pp. 469–89; Mark Ballard, "Etienne Fryon Burgundian Agent, English Secretary and 'Principal Counsellor' to Perkin Warbeck," *Historical Research* 62 (1989), 245–59.

[9] Colin Richmond, "Ruling Classes and Agents of the State Formal and Informal Networks of Power," *Journal of Historical Sociology* 10 (1997), 1–26; idem, "Hand and Mouth Information Gathering and Use in England in the Later Middle Ages," *Journal of Historical Sociology* 1 (1988), 233–52; Walter, "Informationen, Wissen und Macht," pp. 279–82, 294f., 319–65. For exceptions in this context, which to an extent convey the importance of information for the politics of late medieval cities, see Sieber-Lehmann, *Spätmittelalterlicher Nationalismus*, pp. 354–6; Melissa Bullard, "Secrecy, Diplomacy and Language in the Renaissance," in *Das Geheimnis am Beginn der europäischen Moderne*, ed. Brita Rang, Klaus Reichert and Heide Wunder (Hrsg.) (Frankfurt, 2002), pp. 77–97; Gabriel Zeilinger, *Lebensformen im Krieg. Eine Alltags- und Erfahrungsgeschichte des süddeutschen Städtekriegs 1449/50* (Stuttgart, 2007), pp. 129–31; only for Italian cities, such as Venice, can a number of studies be found: Peter Burke, "Early Modern Venice as a Center of Information and Communication," in *Venice Reconsidered. The History and Civilization of an Italian City-State (1297–1797)*, ed. John Martin (Baltimore, 2000), pp. 389–419, and James C. Davis, "Shipping and Spying in the Early Career of a Venetian Doge, 1496–1502," *Studi Veneziani* 16 (1974), 97–105; Filippo de Vivo, *Information and Communication in Venice. Rethinking Early Modern Politics* (Oxford, 2007).

Alternative channels of information

Which channels did the council members use to acquire information? Which places did they visit in order to do this? These questions imply that certain professions, as well as locations, can be identified in the sources for the ease with which they allowed the gathering of information. Let us begin with the group of merchants. When the councillors desired information about the purchases of the duke of Burgundy, for example – this could become particularly important in the context of military confrontations – they fell back upon merchants.[10] Cities such as Strasbourg or Basel could easily use this method of information gathering since their ruling groups consisted of trading families. At markets they had easy access to information relevant to their councils, since it was in such places that the most diverse people and trades met each other. At markets there would be talk about the political situation, rumours were passed on and discussions about the political business of the day were frequent. The additional advantages of merchants were the connections they had with their colleagues, who might be privy to interesting information themselves. Furthermore, the multilingualism of merchants needs to be taken into consideration. It enabled them to acquire important information that was otherwise difficult to obtain by talking to customers or foreign traders at a market, as can be seen in the following example. In the Strasbourg city records, under the heading "News from Flanders," we find notes that belong to the context of the conflict between the duke of Burgundy and the king of France, Louis XI, in the 1470s.[11] It was probably a merchant who put this report in writing. It states that, shortly before, there had been a market in the Flemish city of Ypres. There, servants of the Burgundian duke bought herrings, unsalted fish and meat as provisions for his mercenaries. Since the quantities bought had been so large, the goods loaded onto "70 wagons" had to be accompanied by an armed escort. That proved no obstacle, however, for French mercenaries to stop the convoy shortly afterwards and overpower the Burgundian members of the escort. Furthermore, Charles the Bold was reported to have abolished all tariffs for all markets in Flanders from

---

[10] For the espionage services rendered by merchants, see Allmand, "Spionage im Hundertjährigen Krieg," p. 100; Sieber-Lehmann, *Spätmittelalterlicher Nationalismus*, p. 354; Sigrid Schmitt, "Städtische Gesellschaft und zwischenstädtische Kommunikation am Oberrhein. Netzwerke und Institutionen," in *Historische Landschaft – Kunstlandschaft? Der Oberrhein im späten Mittelalter*, Vorträge und Forschungen 68, ed. Peter Kurmann (Ostfildern, 2008), pp. 299–301; Margot Lindemann, *Nachrichtenübermittlung durch Kaufmannsbriefe. Brief-"Zeitungen" in der Korrespondenz Hildebrand Veckinchusens (1398–1428)*, Dortmunder Beiträge zur Zeitungsforschung 26 (Munich, 1978); Markus A. Denzel, "Wissensmanagement und Wissensnetzwerke der Kaufleute. Aspekte kaufmännischer Kommunikation im späten Mittelalter," *Das Mittelalter* 6 (2001), 73–90; for trade fairs as nodal points of communication see (rudimentally) Jochen Hoock, "Markt und Märkte im frühneuzeitlichen Europa," *Zeitsprünge. Forschungen zur Frühen Neuzeit* 9 (2005), 418–27; Jürgen Schneider, "Die Bedeutung von Kontoren, Faktoreien, Stützpunkten (von Kompagnien), Märkten, Messen und Börsen im Mittelalter und früher Neuzeit," in *Die Bedeutung der Kommunikation für Wirtschaft und Gesellschaft*, Vierteljahrschrift für Sozial- und Wirtschaftsgeschichte, Beiheft 87, ed. Hans Pohl (Stuttgart, 1989), pp. 37–63.

[11] AMS, *AA 266*, fol. 30.

that point in time onwards. This was proclaimed publicly in the market square of Ypres, something which nobody had ever witnessed before, according to our source. Also, the duke was believed to have forbidden his subjects, on pain of punishment, all trade with French merchants or their allies. There was also a rumour that the duke now intended to wait before taking military action.

Other interesting pieces of information came from the merchant Thomas Strubel. In February 1476 he informed the Strasbourg city leadership about things which had happened at the fair in Colombier-Fontaine, about 14km west of Montbéliard, a place which had been allied with Strasbourg against Burgundy since October 1474.[12] According to Strubel, around 200 Burgundian mercenaries entered the place and went to the nearby castle, stabbing eighteen people and capturing two hundred in the process. The captives consisted largely of foreign merchants and local farmers.[13] The mercenaries had also found a woman at the castle who had offered the soldiers a thousand guilders to keep her jewellery. Strubel closes by mentioning that a large quantity of cloth, grain and spices, as well as six hundred head of livestock and two hundred plough-horses, had been captured.

In addition to merchants, taverns and tavern-keepers come to mind when one thinks about information gathering. Taverns were mainly situated alongside important roads, crossings and passes.[14] People ate, drank and slept in them. Here one might recruit mercenaries,[15] question witnesses, discuss contracts, conduct political negotiations and trade news and rumours.[16] Furthermore, taverns served as gathering places for the councillors of the cities when they wanted to continue discussions after their meetings. In this way, taverns were a type of focal point for a great variety of different people, diverse trades and social groups, and were likely to provide an interesting pool of news. It is easy to see why town councils attempted to establish contact with tavern-keepers and even to send their spies

[12] AMS, *AA 292*, fol. 17: Es sy ein jormerckt gewesen in eym flecken, genant Fontany, lige 8 mylen weges von Mümpelgart in Burgund [...].
[13] Deren sy einteil koufflüt von Bisantz, einteil von andern enden uß Burgondie, die dohin weren züm merckt komen, ouch einteil buresüte [...] (ebd.).
[14] Beat Kümin, "Wirtshaus, Reiseverkehr und Raumerfahrung am Ausgang des Mittelalters," in *Strassen- und Verkehrswesen im hohen und späten Mittelalter*, Vorträge und Forschungen 66, ed. Rainer Christoph Schwinges (Ostfildern, 2007), pp. 331–53; Susanne Rau, "Orte der Gastlichkeit – Orte der Kommunikation. Aspekte der Raumkonstitutionen von Herbergen in einer frühneuzeitlichen Stadt," *Zeitsprünge. Forschungen zur Frühen Neuzeit* 9 (2005), 394–418; Beat Kümin, "Wirtshaus, Verkehr und Kommunikationsrevolution im frühneuzeitlichen Alpenraum," in ibid., pp. 376–94; Beat Kümin, "Useful to have, but impossible to govern. Inns and Taverns in Early Modern Bern and Vaud," *Journal of Early Modern History* 3 (1999), 153–203.
[15] Simon Teuscher, *Bekannte – Klienten – Verwandte. Sozialität und Politik in der Stadt Bern um 1500*, Norm und Struktur 9 (Köln/Wien, 1998), pp. 193–5; Ann Tlusty, "The Public House and Military Culture in Germany, 1500–1648," in *The World of the Tavern. Public Houses in Early Modern Europe*, ed. Ann Tlusty and Beat Kümin (Aldershot, 2002), pp. 136–59.
[16] Stefan Selzer, "Trinkstuben als Orte der Kommunikation. Das Beispiel der Artushöfe im Preußenland (ca. 1350–1550)," in *Geschlechtergesellschaften, Zunfttrinkstuben und Bruderschaften in spätmittelalterlichen und frühneuzeitlichen Städten*, Stadt in der Geschichte 30, ed. Gerhard Fouquet, Matthias Steinbrink and Gabriel Zeilinger (Ostfildern, 2003), pp. 73–99.

directly into taverns. That is confirmed by a letter sent by Strasbourg's spies from Breisach to their home town in 1473.[17] When they arrived at Breisach a tavern-keeper gave them a slip of paper, the content of which they communicated to their councillors in a copy. In this text, the tavern-keeper reports that the mayors of the cities of Laufenburg and Seckingen had appeared in his tavern a week earlier for a meal and had asked the councillors of Breisach for urgent advice. The background of this request for help had been the following: shortly before, forty Burgundian mercenaries had appeared before the gates of Laufenburg and asked to be let in. The people from Laufenburg had acceded to this request but when, a few days later, six hundred Burgundians asked for the same right of entry, they denied them passage. This had angered the strangers: they had said that it would be better not to stop them since they were moving to where the Burgundian duke wanted them. So ends the tavern-keeper's slip of paper.

Another group 'predestined' for the task of being informers because of their status was the clergy. Christine de Pizan spoke in her manual of warfare "Livre des fayttes des Armes et Chivalry" (c.1410) about how well suited clergy were to being spies. In the sources there are hints that point to information gathered by clergy and transmitted to the councillors. This becomes explicit, for example, from the evidence of advice given by an ambassador from Lorraine to the Swiss and Upper-Rhine envoys gathered in Strasbourg in September 1475. He suggested monks from a Franciscan monastery as information gatherers, adding that he knew a priest called "Brother Dietrich."[18] That priest was allegedly distinguished by having been in the army of the Burgundian duke as well as in the army of the Emperor. For that reason he possessed contacts with a number of important people he knew from the inner circle around the Burgundian duke. Furthermore, he knew the topography of Lorraine very well.

The observations presented here show that urban leaders tried to embed themselves in networks of information already in existence as well as attempting to find new information networks.[19] It is not always easy to decide whether they approached certain professions on purpose and whether they ordered them officially to gather information. The far-reaching relationships of their own officials must not be overlooked.[20] They also had contacts to fellow councillors, relatives and friends in other cities. Particularly in times of war urban leaders seem to have wanted, if not demanded, an intensification of these contacts.[21]

---

[17] AMS, *AA 264*, fol. 30.
[18] AMS, *AA 261*, fol. 9v (cf. also Sieber-Lehmann, *Spätmittelalterlicher Nationalismus*, p. 355, Anm. 39).
[19] Allmand, "Spionage und Geheimdienst," pp. 101f.; Schmitt, "Zwischenstädtische Kommunikation," pp. 300–302.
[20] For this, compare the dissertation of Klara Hübner (Freiburg i. Ue.), *Im Dienste ihrer Stadt. Boten- und Nachrichtenorganisationen in den schweizerisch-oberdeutschen Städten des Späten Mittelalters*, Mittelalter-Forschungen 30 (Ostfildern, forthcoming 2011). I thank the author for providing me with the manuscript.
[21] Walter, "Von städtischer Spionage," pp. 158–63; Walter, "Informationen, Wissen und Macht", pp. 242–77.

Professional spies

It was a different case, however, with professional spies.[22] The latter found themselves in a employee/employer relationship with their urban leadership that was difficult to define. They were paid for their services and put under an oath before performing them. Hints as to how they were paid in Basel can be found in the *Wochenausgabebüchern*. Every week the same three items appear summarizing expenditures made during the previous week for the judicial system (*judicio*), building (*edificio*) and, finally, for "secret things" (*causis secrete*). The last category is very important, as the funds assigned for this item tended to increase in the context of war. This can be taken as an indication of their being a "special" payment. An indication of the payment of spies in Strasbourg can be found in the statement of the Strasbourg spy Kaspar Michel. He charged the city council three guilders after he had stayed in the duchy of Lorraine from August to October 1476 under orders from the Strasbourgian captains.[23]

Except for this statement, however, no definite details about payment, oaths or exact numbers of spies have been found. The explanation for this is surely the secrecy under which spies were operating. Other sources, however, point to their existence. First, there are letters, and, within them, the so-called "zedulae inclusae" written by the councils to their allies disclosing the activities of their spies. During military conflicts in particular spies were sent into important areas to spy on the enemy. Information acquired by them was transmitted in various ways. Spies might report orally to the respective councillors, who then had the reports put on record; or the spies were already in correspondence with the urban authorities and intermittently relayed to them news about their place of residence and what they had seen and heard; or, possibly, they wrote a form of diary during their missions which was handed over to the councillors after their return. All these possibilities emphasize the importance of literacy and literality in the field of spying.

Letters and reports penned by the spies can help establish under whose orders they were working. In the letters, bearers of town offices (such as the mayor, town writer or military captains) are mentioned, as in the case of the Strasbourgian spy Kaspar Michel, noted earlier, who was very mobile during the Burgundian wars. His letters to the secretary[24] and to the council[25] of Strasbourg are preserved. There is also evidence that he had written to the captains in order to provide them with military information and political assessments.[26] Furthermore, extant sources about Michel contain indications that he gave the councillors spy reports

---

[22] Walter, "Informationen, Wissen und Macht", pp. 342–65.
[23] AMS, *AA 291*, fol. 131. For how the war touched the Duchy of Lorraine, see Heinrich Witte, "Lothringen and Burgund," *Jahrbuch der Gesellschaft für lothringische Geschichte und Altertumskunde* 2 (1890), 1–100, and 3 (1891), 232–93; Heinrich Witte, "Zur Geschichte der Burgunderkriege. Das Kriegsjahr 1475. Verwicklungen in Lothringen," *Zeitschrift für die Geschichte des Oberrheins* 10 (1895), 78–112; 202–66.
[24] AMS, *AA 293*, fol. 90r.
[25] AMS, *AA 293*, fol. 86 (25 March 1477).
[26] AMS, *AA 291*, fol. 131.

composed by himself, and also informed them thoroughly in oral reports. He advised them about the number, the military equipment and the position of the Burgundian troops which he sometimes observed daily and nightly over a time span of several weeks. This reveals the skills spies had to possess.[27] First, they had to be able to write, so that they could compose letters and reports in order to transmit information to the councils. Secondly, it was necessary that they should be closely acquainted with topography, since it was mainly knowledge of the local infrastructure that facilitated their work. Thirdly, it was of advantage if they spoke the language of the country to which they had been sent to gather information. This made it easier for them to be in contact with the local population in order to acquaint themselves with the prevailing mood in the country and to search systematically for specific locations. Knowledge of languages also enabled spies to talk with foreign mercenaries, to inquire of them about possible plans, and subsequently to provide a precise account of place-names heard during the assignment. This is connected, fourthly, to spies having to know local customs and to adapt to them in order to move unobserved through enemy lands. Fifthly, spies had to be able to understand political contexts and events in order to make assessments. It was also very important for them to appreciate the enemy's military equipment. Since they often had to make comparisons between weapons of the enemy and of their own side, this presupposes, sixthly, knowledge of types of weapon. These requirements explain why spies were in high demand in their capacity as specialists and why their work was held in great esteem by political leaders of all kinds. At the same time, they testify to the great trust that the urban leadership placed, and had to place, in their spies.

By virtue of their special knowledge spies were of interest not only to those under whose orders they acted but also to the enemy. It is therefore evident that theirs was an insecure existence: they were always in danger of being discovered and exposed by the enemy. A striking report of the city of Bern to Basel in May 1476, elements of which are reminiscent of James Bond and other spy movies of the 1970s, testifies to this fact. While in the letter the Bernese report only the return of two of their spies, in the "zedula inclusa" they are more explicit. According to the "zedula," one of the spies reported after his return that the Burgundian duke was staying in Lausanne and that he had heard among the troops that the duke planned a move to Murten. Furthermore, he said that in the Burgundian camp there had been altercations between Lombardian and English mercenaries which had claimed thirty lives. The second spy, however, had been impeded from carrying out his orders after having been recognized and stopped by Burgundian mercenaries in Yverdon. These, the report continues, threw him into prison. There he constructed a rope out of the clothes he was wearing and attempted to climb out. Halfway down, the rope tore and he fell from a great height. According to the Bernese, in spite of this he had not been seriously hurt.[28]

---

[27] The following list is derived from several of Michel's reports (AMS, *AA 292*, fol. 24; fols. 6–8; *AA 293*, fol. 90; fol. 87).

[28] Gottlieb Friedrich Ochsenbein, "Die Urkunden der Belagerung und Schlacht von Murten, Freiburg 1876," volume 1, letter no. 289, pp. 206–7.

Protection of informers

Nearly all the information gathered by spies and transmitted to their allies by the cities is not to be found in formal letters but in the "zedulae inclusae" mentioned earlier. This type of writing has been only cursorily investigated in the past. Four possible functions of the "zedulae," which are closely related to each other, have so far been proposed.[29] In some "zedulae" the fact is emphasized that the sender had received new information shortly before the completion of the letter. Since they wanted to transmit this to the receiver, they put it into the "zedulae inclusae."[30] Considering the kind of information they contain, the subject matter of these "zedulae" is also reminiscent of pamphlets or newspapers. That is why they have been analysed previously in a journalistic sense.[31] In contrast to the "zedulae" analysed in this essay, some examples contain the date of composition.[32] Another two functions posited are closely related to the focus of this essay, since the "zedulae" often helped to separate official from personal content.[33] They were also used by communicating partners to exchange the most important, confidential and secret information as well as to give political assessments and to engage in deliberations about tactics.[34] Focus here will be on the last two functions.

The "zedulae" are rarely conserved because of their function of transmitting confidential information. They bear no indications of date, sender or addressee, nor any seals, and, because of their small size, they could be easily destroyed or hidden in case of danger, either by the messenger or by the recipient. The information, thus anonymized, engendered a much higher degree of cohesion between allies than the official letter, since it was based on trust and reciprocity. This observation is boosted by the fact that the letters often contain turns of phrase stressing how secretly the items of information which followed had been won, how confidential they were, and that they were intended for the recipient, the ally, and for no one else. Furthermore, recipients were requested to treat the information with care and to communicate information of their own in return.

To the contemporary reader, the "zedulae" pose a number of problems. Often it is not possible to reconstruct exactly to which letter a "zedula" belonged. This is made even more problematic by the fact that the majority of them were not

---

[29] As discussed briefly in Julian Holzpafl, *Kanzleikorrespondenz des späten Mittelters in Bayern Schriftlichkeit, Sprache und politische Rhetorik*, Schriftenreihe zur bayerischen Landesgeschichte 159 (Munich, 2008), pp. 273–80. He states that the "zedulae" were a particular characteristic of correspondence between nobles (p. 273); Bastian Walter, "Von städtischer Spionage und der Bitte, Briefe zu zerreißen Alternative Kommunikationsnetze von Städten während der Burgunderkriege (1469–1477)," *Diskurs* 2 (2008), 164–6.

[30] Georg Steinhausen, *Geschichte des deutschen Briefes. Zur Kulturgeschichte des deutschen Volkes* (Dublin and Zürich, 1968), p. 33f.

[31] Holzpafl, *Kanzleikorrespondenz*, p. 277.

[32] See, for example, the "zedula" in AMS, *AA 267*, fol. 2 (4 July 1473).

[33] Simon Teuscher, "Bernische Privatbriefe aus der Zeit um 1500. Überlegungen zu ihren zeitgenössischen Funktionen und zu Möglichkeiten ihrer historischen Auswertung," in *Mittelalterliche Literatur im Lebenszusammenhang. Ergebnisse des Troisième Cycle Romand 1994*, ed. Eckart Conrad Lutz (Freiburg/Ue., 1997), p. 374; Steinhausen, *Geschichte des Briefes*, p. 33.

[34] Holzpafl, *Kanzleikorrespondenz*, p. 277, also sees this function of maintaining confidentiality.

written by the writer of the letter but by somebody else. The following example illustrates this. The siege of the city of Neuss on the Lower Rhine, conducted by Charles the Bold from the end of July 1474 onwards, began the Burgundian wars.[35] The archbishop of Cologne, a distant relative of the Burgundian duke, had been evicted by the people of Cologne as the result of a conflict between him and the city. Afterwards, he successfully applied for help from the Burgundian duke. At the same time a gathering of the Upper Rhine-confederation coalition was taking place in Basel. At the end of July 1474 the councillors of Strasbourg sent a letter to their delegates. In it, they told them that, a short time earlier, news had arrived in Strasbourg which they should produce where they deemed it advantageous. They also referred to a slip of paper which, even today, can be found bound to the letter. This slip of paper refers to the information – given in a noticeably different hand from the letter – that a "credible" man from the duchy of Lorraine had told the councillors "in secret" of Charles the Bold's plan to move into the bishopric of Cologne with a large number of soldiers.

However, this example also shows something else concerning the "credible" man from Lorraine. It is to be noticed that, in internal communication, the urban leadership was placing a high regard upon the names of the informants. Furthermore, descriptions of their appearance are often to be found, and the places of meeting are explicitly named. Such details are missing from the letters and "zedulae" written to allies. In the latter it says, for example, that a "good friend," a "credible man" or a "discreet servant" reported this or that. Why, then, were names so important in internal use? First, in this way the urban leadership attempted to keep their sources of information secret and to protect their informers. Secondly, the recording (of names) enabled the councillors always to apply to the same trustworthy persons in order to get information. Thirdly, explicit naming could help prepare the work of spies that were sent out later. It seems possible that the councillors could either hold them to account in case of demonstrable misinformation or simply not make use of them anymore. Against this background, the pleadings of an unnamed informer, who in 1476 was providing the secretary of Strasbourg with many highly detailed pieces of information from the duchies of Bar and Lorraine, can be understood. In all three of his letters he asked the recipient for the following: "Please tear up this letter after you have read it!"[36] Most likely it was the secretary of Strasbourg who indirectly followed that request by simply cutting out the signature underneath the letter.

---

[35] Jens Metzdorf, "Bedrängnis, Angst und große Mühsal Die Belagerung von Neuss durch Karl den Kühnen 1474/75," in "... *wurfen hin in steine – gröze und niht kleine* ..." *Belagerungen und Belagerungsanlagen im Mittelalter*, ed. Olaf Wagener and Heiko Laß, Beihefte zur Mediaevistik 7 (Frankfurt/M., 2006), pp. 167–88; Jean Marie Cauchies, "Charles le Hardi à Neuss (1474/75)," *Pays bourguignons et terres d'Empire* (1996), 105–16; Helmut Gilliam, "Der Neusser Krieg. Wendepunkt der europäischen Geschichte," in *Neuss, Burgund und das Reich*, ed. N.N. (Neuss, 1975), p. 201–54.

[36] AMS, *AA 292*, fols. 29–32.

The Burgundian spy Diebold Benedicti

The councillors of Bern, Strasbourg and Basel knew that the enemy would try everything in order to get important information. Since the conquest of the castle of Hericourt in the first Burgundian wars in November 1474 they had been well aware of this fact. At that point the confederate soldiers had found in the castle a number of letters which the former Burgundian owner had left.[37] The councillors of Basel had the letters, which had originally been written in French, translated into German and sent to their allies.[38] Through them their allies found out about numerous enemy spies who had stayed within their walls and their streets in order to obtain information about their strength, their weapons and the attacks they were planning. Among these spies, the Burgundian Diebold Benedicti stands out. Benedicti was an enemy spy who provided the Burgundian Exchequer in Dijon with a great deal of information.[39] The places mentioned in Benedicti's report make it possible to reconstruct the individual stages of his journey from 27 October to 2 November 1474 through a region which was intently preparing for war. He started on 27 October in Sainte-Croix, which belonged to the duchy of Savoy. Then he travelled to Fribourg/Ue., which was about 65km away from Sainte-Croix and which was allied with the coalition against Charles the Bold. In the morning of the following day he saw 120 soldiers there who were only poorly equipped. These soldiers wanted to join the troops in Bern. Benedicti also mentions in his report that the bearer of a high public office was staying in Fribourg/Ue. in order to examine the troops of the members of the alliance. A day later Benedicti left Fribourg/Ue. and travelled another 20km to Murten. There he was informed of the fact that one group of the confederate troops wanted to meet in Bern, whereas the other group wanted to meet in Basel. In addition, he gained detailed information about the armaments of the troops. As a result, Bern, Basel and Strasbourg would be able to advance with both large ordnance and numerous small weapons. After travelling another 40km to Moudon he stayed there for a short while on 31 October and then rode back to Sainte-Croix, arriving at the latter on 1 November. The last stage of his journey was the Burgundian Exchequer in Dijon, 150km away from Saint-Croix, where he finally handed in his report. Overall, Benedicti covered a distance of almost 320km. From a tactical point of view he did this in a clever

---

[37] For the campaign against Héricourt, see Bittmann, *Ludwig XI*, p. 716–57 (especially p. 732 onwards); Sieber-Lehmann, *Spätmittelalterlicher Nationalismus*, p. 140; at greater length, Walter, "Informationen, Wissen und Macht", pp. 344–51.

[38] That explains why they have been handed down in two different sources. They can be found in the "Abschied" of the assembly at Basel, in the archive of that city, and in the archive of Strasbourg. (Basel Staatsarchiv Basel (hereafter cited as StABas), Politisches G 1, 3 (Burgunderkriege, Abscheide und Richtungen, 1474–1477), pp. 6r–11v; Straßburg AMS, *AA II/9*, Faszikel 1, pp. 6r–11v). For the gathering at Basel cf. Sieber-Lehmann, *Spätmittelalterlicher Nationalismus*, pp. 143–9; Anton P. Segesser, *Amtliche Sammlung der ältern eidgenössischen Abschiede II. Die eidgenössischen Abschiede aus dem Zeitraume von 1421 bis 1477* (Luzern, 1865), no. 769, pp. 518–21.

[39] StABAS, Politisches G 1, 3, fols. 11r and 11v; AMS *AA II/9*, Faszikel 1, fols. 11r and 11v (see the source in the appendix).

way. This becomes obvious from a close look at the map showing the area he had to explore: by his choice of route he could make sure that he was able to see and hear as much as possible. The letters found inside the castle of Hericourt make it obvious that Benedicti was not the only Burgundian spy in the area of the Upper Rhine. For example, there was also another Burgundian bearer of a public office who wrote that he had heard from an informant that the morale of the confederate troops was not high and that they were ready to disobey their captains and kill them if they showed the slightest sign of resistance to the troops' demands.[40] He also wrote that he had ordered a spy to gather information in order to find out which route the confederate troops were to take subsequently. According to him, the ideal place for this endeavor was Strasbourg.

Conclusion

For effective coordination of a joint foreign policy, information communicated by Strasbourg, Bern and Basel to their allies or exchanged among themselves was essential. It also provided for a greater cohesion among the allies. Such information was concerned, for example, with enemy troop numbers, their current location and the kind of weapons they carried. The reciprocity of communication led to greater trust among the allied cities and also to their moving closer together. If we consider the distribution of information a fundamental aspect in the legitimizing strategies of rulers, information gathering, which precedes distribution, assumes a place of central importance. That is especially the case for information gathered by spies, such as the Strasbourg spy Kaspar Michel used above as an example. In communication between allies the information of spies was always encoded and labelled "secret." Against this background, the secrets transmitted through the "zedulae" appear as a means of creating collective identity. They characterize the people sharing them as a group.[41] In this way, spies in the Burgundian wars, who have previously been investigated only superficially, gain a place of special and increased importance, and we can see how important spying was as an element in the formulation and execution of the foreign policy of cities such as Bern, Basel and Strasbourg.

---

[40] StABas, Politisches G 1, 3, fols. 7f; AMS *AA II/9*, Faszikel 1, fols. 7f.
[41] See Alois Hahn, "Soziologische Aspekte von Geheimnissen und ihren Äquivalenten," in *Geheimnis und Öffentlichkeit*, ed. Alois Hahn, Jan Assmann and Hans-Jürgen Lüsebrink (Munich, 1997), pp. 23–39; Alois Hahn, "Geheim," in *Das Geheimnis am Beginn der europäischen Moderne*, ed. Brita Rang, Klaus Reichert and Heide Wunder (Frankfurt/M., 2002), pp. 21–42.

Appendix

Transcript of the report of the Burgundian spy Diebold Benedicti

Versions: 1. Staatsarchiv Basel, Politisches G 1, 3, fol. 11r and 11v; 2. Archives Municipales et Communautaires de Strasbourg AA II/9, Faszikel 1, fol. 11r and 11v.

[fol. 1r] Abgeschrifften allerley briefen hinder den so zů Ellicordt Nidergelegen funden vnd von Welsch zů Tútsch gemacht sind […].

[fol. 11r] Es ist war daz Diebolt Benedicti gieng von Sacra[1] vß uff den xxvii tag octobre lxxiiij° jares[2] ze gon gen Friburg.[3] Vnd zu Friburg stende sache zwentzig vnd hundert gesellen sich rusten morndes zu denen von Bern vnd mit Inen zu ziehen / ouch vß zugent xxiiij gesellen von Moret[4] vnd xij von Paierne[5] vnd was der vogt von Bern[6] zu Friburg vnd fragt den Regierer von Vans was es were darumb der herr von Ramont nit in sin lanndt keme […].

Also schied der selbe regierer In sin stette vnd macht zu rusten die edlen des lanndes vnd tette die stette stercken wan er sich etwaß forchtende sy woltend in das lannd darumb er es emsiglichen bewaren tüt /.

Item uff xxix schied der selb Diebolt von Friburg gonde gen Moret nüwe mer zu erfaren wann er blib zwen tag. / Dahin kam einer vnd sagt daz die tutschen eins teils zu Bern vnd des andern teils gen Basel gesamlet werent by xxvj^m als die seitent die von Inen komen werent / ouch daz sy alle die karrich vnd wagen die sy hetten mogen erfunden vß furtent geladen mit gerusten vnd spisen /.

Item der selb Diebolt seit daz die von Bern hand dar geben ein houptbuchssen die von Basel eyne die von Straßburg ouch eine vnd sint vil kleins geschutzes vnd hattent die von Bern mit ze ziehen hin In durch des Marggrafen von Rotelen[7] lannd

---

[1] Sainte-Croix (Kanton Waadt).
[2] 27 October 1474.
[3] Freiburg i. Ue.
[4] Morat/Murten (Kanton Freiburg).
[5] Payerne (Kanton Waadt).
[6] We are probably dealing with the Bernese "Schultheiss" Nikolaus von Diesbach (1435–1475) here. His stay in Fribourg/Ue. on this day can be confirmed by Bernese sources (Staatsarchiv Bern, Ratsmanual 15, fol. 107, dealing with the session of the Secret Council of Bern on 17 October 1474 where it was decided to send Diesbach to Fribourg/Ue. and where a letter announcing his arrival to the ally was composed.
[7] The source is referring to Margrave Rudolf of Baden-Hachberg (1427–1487). He was connected to Bern through a so-called "Burgrecht" which obliged him to keep his lands open to the Bernese in case of war. It was problematic for him that his son and heir Philipp of Baden-Hachberg had entered the service of the Burgundian duke. For this reason, especially Strasbourg and Basel, the Reichsstädte from the Upper Rhine doubted his loyalty at the beginning of the war against Burgundy. Bern, meanwhile, was convinced of it. Numerous embassies by Bernese officials were necessary to convince the allies of Baden-Hachberg's loyalty and solidarity (Eddi Bauer, *Négociations et campagnes de Rodolphe de Hochberg Comte de Neuchâtel et Marquis de Rothelin Gouverneur de Luxembourg 1427(?)–1487* (Neuchatel, 1928); Petra Ehm, *Burgund und das Reich. Spätmittelalterliche Außenpolitik am Beispiel der Regierung Karls des Kühnen (1465–1477)*, Pariser Historische Studien 61 (Munich, 2002), p. 221–3; for the doubts about his loyalty cf. Sieber-Lehmann, *Spätmittelalterlicher Nationalismus*, pp. 168; 320–22; Walter, "Informationen, Wissen und Macht", pp. 116–23; 269–77).

/ welicher herr erfaren dise mere fugt sich gen Bern vnd bat sy fur sin lannd des er gewar ward vnd ziechent gen Mumpelgart zu als er sagt welicher an mentag letsten tag octobre ließ den genanten Marggrafen zu Bern. Vff den selben letsten tag schied der Diebolt von Moret ze komen gen Mudon[8] vnd morndes als was allerheyligen tag kam er gen Sacra / dennen schied er an mittwochen vnd kam gen Dision[9] uff fritag vierden tag nouembre […].

[fol. 11v] Mer seit der Diebolt daz er die sechs mal zwentzig von Friburg gesehen hat wie vor geseit ist die waren bescheidenlich wol gerust vnd gewapnet mit langen lantzen helbarten hantbuchssen vnd armbrusten vnd sint aber nit gewapnet mit beschhentschuch vnd mit dutschen ysenhuten […].

Translation

[fol. 1) Transcriptions of some letters that were found in the castle of Héricourt and translated from French into German […].
[fol. 11r] It is true that Diebold Benedicti walked from Sainte-Croix on 27 October to Freiburg/Uechtland. There he spied 120 mercenaries who planned to meet the Bernese troops the following day. In addition Diebold spotted 24 soldiers of the city of Murten and 12 of Payerne. At the same time the Bernese mayor stayed in Freiburg/Uechtland and asked an aristocrat from Vans why the count of Ramont did not come back to his territory […]. After that, the aforementioned nobleman left Freiburg/Uechtland and returned home to his territory, and he got the nobility (in his land) to arm themselves and fortify the land because he feared that an invasion was intended, against which he wanted to safeguard (the land).
On 29 October Diebold left Freiburg/Uechtland to spend two days in Murten in order to get some news. There he met someone who told him that part of the coalition troops were going to assemble in Bern and the other in Basle. People who had spotted the troops were saying that there would be 26,000 soldiers altogether, who had loaded all the carts and wagons that they could find with armor and victuals.
Furthermore the same Diebold reported that the Bernese, Basel and Strasbourgian troops were carrying one big gun each and numerous smaller ones. In addition, the Bernese were planning to cross the territory of the count of Baden-Hachberg in order to get to Montbéliard as fast as possible. On 31 October Diebold rode to Moudon and returned to Sainte-Croix on the Feast of All Saints. From there he left on Wednesday for Dijon where he arrived on 4 November.
[fol. 11v] And furthermore Diebold said that the aforementioned 120 mercenaries in Freiburg/Uechtland were badly equipped and had only long lances, halberds, guns and crossbows but no armor at all […].

[8] Moudon (Kanton Waadt).
[9] Dijon (Dép. Côte d'Or).

Urban Militias, Nobles and Mercenaries. The Organization of the Antwerp Army in the Flemish–Brabantine Revolt of the 1480s

Frederik Buylaert, Jan Van Camp and Bert Verwerft

Introduction

In the 1480s Habsburg rule over the Low Countries was faced with its greatest crisis before the Dutch Revolt of the late sixteenth century. After the death of his wife Mary of Burgundy in 1482 Maximilian of Austria had assumed authority over the principalities that constituted the Low Countries as the guardian of Philip the Fair, their under-age son and sole heir to Mary's dominions. This claim did not go unchallenged. The county of Flanders, one of the richest and most populous principalities, was the first to take up arms against Maximilian. The first Flemish revolt of 1482–85 was suppressed but the heavy fiscal demands to fund the Habsburg war against France provoked a new uprising in the city of Ghent in November 1487. In January 1488 the unthinkable happened: the craft guilds of Bruges, the second largest city of Flanders, joined the Ghent revolt and Maximilian, who happened to reside in the city, was taken into custody. He was only released three months later, when he had given his formal promise to respect the political rights of his Flemish subjects. He soon reneged on this promise, however, and declared war on his Flemish subjects. In response, the Flemish towns organized an alternative government to autocratic Habsburg rule and allied themselves with the king of France, who provided military support against the Habsburg armies. The new revolt soon spilled over the borders of the county of Flanders. In the neighbouring duchy of Brabant the cities of Brussels, Louvain, Zoutleeuw, Tienen and Aarschot joined the Flemish revolt in September 1488 and the duchy of Liège followed suit.[1] When the county of Holland fell prey to

---

[1] For a discussion of this revolt, see in particular Wim Blockmans, "Autocratie ou polyarchie? La lutte pour le pouvoir politique en Flandre, d'après des documents inédits, 1482–1492," *Handelingen van de Koninklijke Commissie voor Geschiedenis* 140 (1974), 257–368, and Jelle Haemers, "Philippe de Clèves et la Flandre. La position d'un aristocrate au coeur d'une révolte urbaine (1477–1492)," in *Entre la ville, la noblesse et l'Etat: Philippe de Clèves (1456–1528), homme politique et bibliophile*, ed. Jelle Haemers, Hanno Wijsman and Céline Van Hoorebeeck (Turnhout, 2007), pp. 21–99. The abbreviations used are ACA (Antwerp City Archives), R (military account, 1488–1489) and RA (registers of the aldermen). A Dutch version of this present article is forthcoming: F. Buylaert, J. Van Camp and B. Verwerft, "'t Stad in oorlog. Het Antwerpse stadsleger van Maximiliaan van Oostenrijk (1488–1489)," in *Leven in een groeistad*.

a civil war between two factions (the so-called Cods and Hooks) in November 1488, it was clear to all parties that Maximilian had lost control over the core territories of the Low Countries.[2]

Eventually, the Habsburg state managed to re-establish its authority over the Low Countries by force. Between 1488 and 1492 the revolt was crushed by the Habsburg armies under the command of Albrecht of Bavaria, Maximilian's viceroy.[3] One of the most important operating bases of the Habsburg war machine was situated in northern Brabant. While the cities in the southern part of the duchy had joined the revolt, the northern cities of Antwerp and Malines had declared themselves for Maximilian. Antwerp, in particular, was lavishly rewarded for its loyalty. In June 1488 Maximilian proclaimed an ordinance that encouraged foreign merchants no longer to settle in Bruges, the gateway city par excellence for international trade, but to conduct their business in Antwerp. This decree contributed considerably to the emergence of Antwerp as the dominant commercial metropolis of the sixteenth-century Low Countries.[4]

In this contribution we will focus on the military aid that the city of Antwerp provided to the Habsburg state. In October 1488 the city fielded an army that would remain under arms until August 1489, the moment when the rebellious towns of southern Brabant were forced to surrender to Albrecht of Bavaria. What concerns us is how this army was raised and how it was organized. Next to this, we will also address the issue of whether this army was primarily controlled by the city of Antwerp or by the commanders of the Habsburg state. By engaging with these two matters we hope to contribute to the historiographical debate on warfare in the later medieval Low Countries.

Historians agree that, at the turn of the sixteenth century, the nature of warfare had changed significantly in comparison with the fourteenth or early fifteenth century. Apart from the increasing use of artillery and gunpowder, armies constantly increased in size. Evidently, this "scale-up" was mirrored in the increasing cost of warfare, which forced the princes and cities who engaged in military conflict to develop new fiscal, financial and logistical systems to fund and organize the war effort. However, the implications of this development for pre-existing military traditions continues to be the subject of heated debate. The discussion largely revolves around the importance of the feudal cavalry and urban militias in light of the emergence of new forms of warfare. In twentieth-century scholarship the reign of Duke Charles the Bold, ruler over the Low Countries from 1467 until

---

Privaatrechtelijke akten als spiegel van de Antwerpse samenleving aan het einde van de middeleeuwen, ed. T. Bisschops and P. Stabel (Antwerp, 2011).

[2] For Holland, see Michel J. van Gent, *"Pertijelike saken." Hoeken en Kabeljauwen en het Bourgondisch-Oostenrijkse tijdperk* (The Hague, 1994), pp. 96–7, 348–51, 375–89 and 455–60.

[3] See Wim Blockmans, "Albrecht III, hertog van Saksen," *Nationaal Biografisch Woordenboek* 5 (1972), col. 14–22.

[4] See especially Herman Van der Wee, *The Growth of the Antwerp Market and the European Economy (Fourteenth-Sixteenth century)* (Louvain, 1963), 2:102, as well as Raymond Van Uytven, "Politiek en economie. De crisis in de late 15^e eeuw in de Nederlanden," *Revue belge de Philologie et d'Histoire* 53 (1975), 1147.

1477, has commonly been interpreted as a fundamental watershed in the military history of this region. Charles's attempts to organize a standing army and his penchant for hiring large groups of mercenaries under the command of professional *condottieri* were supposed to have heralded the end of the military relevance of both the urban militias and that of the mounted nobles and fiefholders.[5]

Yet this view has received substantial criticism in the past years. First, it is clear that the importance of the feudal cavalry was not to be underestimated. The commonly held view that the fifteenth century saw a demilitarization of the nobility does not withstand close scrutiny, at least not for Flanders and Brabant. While it is certainly true that this period saw an increase in the tactical importance of infantry vis-à-vis heavily armoured horsemen and that the share of those mounted nobles and important fiefholders in the army as a whole was constantly decreasing, it is also noteworthy that the prince continued to summon them until the middle of the sixteenth century.[6] This observation confirms earlier suspicions that the feudal cavalry was much longer appreciated as a valuable military asset than has often been assumed.[7] Similarly, there is a growing uneasiness with discarding the urban militias as a significant military player. Established historiography assumes that while the militias of the Flemish and Brabantine towns were of considerable military importance in the fourteenth century they must have become obsolete in the fifteenth century with the emergence of the so-called "professional" armies.[8] Yet, as several historians recently noted, this view jars very much with the fact that

---

[5] For this view, see in particular Werner Paravicini, *Karl der Kühne. Das Ende des Hauses Burgund* (Göttingen-Zürich-Frankfurt, 1976), pp. 60–61, and Richard Vaughan, *Charles the Bold. The last Valois Duke of Burgundy* (London, 2002), p. 213. Scholarship on the Low Countries has followed a larger historiographical trend. For a classic discussion, see Charles Tilly, *Coercion, Capital, and European States* (Cambridge, 1994), p. 29, 80.

[6] The muster rolls of the Flemish nobility are recently discovered and edited in Frederik Buylaert, Jan Dumolyn, Pieter Donche, Eric Balthau and Hervé Douxchamps, eds., "De adel ingelijst. "Adelslijsten" voor het graafschap Vlaanderen in de veertiende en de vijftiende eeuw," *Bulletin de la Commission Royale d'Histoire* 173 (2007), 47–187.

[7] See Henk F.K. van Nierop, "Willem van Oranje als hoog edelman: patronage in de Habsburgse Nederlanden," *The Low Countries Historical Review* 99 (1984), 647–48; Paul De Win, "Queeste naar de rechtspositie van de edelman in de Bourgondische Nederlanden," *The Legal History Review* 53 (1985), 244–6; Jan F. Verbruggen, "The Role of Cavalry in Medieval Warfare," *Journal of Medieval Military History* 3 (2005), 46–71 and Paul Janssens, *De evolutie van de Belgische adel sinds de late Middeleeuwen* (Brussels, 1998), pp. 109–10. See also the broader discussion in Matthew Bennett, "The Myth of the Military Supremacy of Knightly Cavalry," in *Medieval Warfare, 1000–1300*, ed. John France (Ashgate, 2006), pp. 171–85; idem, "The Medieval Warhorse Reconsidered," in *Medieval Knighthood V. Papers from the sixth Strawberry Hill conference 1994*, ed. Stephen Church and Ruth Harvey (Woodbridge, 1995), pp. 19–40, as well as the contributions in *Armies, Chivalry and Warfare in Medieval Britain and France. (Proceedings of the 1995 Harlaxton Symposium)*, ed. Matthew Strickland (Stamford, 1998), pp. 315–16, for a critical reassessment of historiographical clichés such as the "infantry revolution" and "the thousand-year rule of the knight."

[8] For this view, see Marc Boone, "Élites urbaines, noblesse d'état: bourgeois et nobles dans la société des Pays-Bas bourguignons (principalement en Flandre et en Brabant)," in *Liber Amicorum Raphaël de Smedt*, ed. Jacques Paviot (Louvain, 2001), p. 68; Bart Willems, "Militaire organisatie en staatsvorming aan de vooravond van de Nieuwe Tijd. Een analyse van het conflict tussen Brabant en Maxmiliaan van Oostenrijk (1488–1489)," *Jaarboek voor Middeleeuwse*

in the revolt of the late fifteenth century the Flemish militias had enough strikepower to hold out for several years against the armies of Albrecht of Bavaria.[9]

In light of the ongoing debate on the presumed "military revolution" in the later medieval and sixteenth-century Low Countries, the Antwerp army of 1488–89 presents a series of interesting questions.[10] Did it concern a militia of Antwerp craftsmen, comparable to the urban militias fielded by Ghent or Bruges, or an army of mercenaries hired by the urban government? One also wonders who exercised daily control over this army during the campaign. Did Antwerp help Maximilian with an autonomous military campaign, or did the political elite limit itself to financing an army that was subsequently handed over to the Habsburg military command? In this context, an in-depth analysis of the Antwerp army of 1488–89 is revealing not only in the context of the debate on later medieval warfare but also for what it reveals about the power relations between the prince and Antwerp, which was well under way to become the largest city in the entire urban Low Countries. Thanks to the survival of records of the army administration it is possible to answer those questions. As such, the Antwerp army of 1488–89 provides an extremely valuable case study, as the sources are usually lacking to study the composition and organization of the armies that were fielded in the Low Countries during the later Middle Ages.

The Antwerp army in the autumn of 1488

Our main source for the Antwerp army is a series of special accounts that the city council of Antwerp commissioned to keep track of all the expenses connected to this army. They are bundled together in a register titled "Accounts of the horsemen and footmen commissioned by the noble city of Antwerp" ("*Rekeningen van den ruytern ende luyde te peerde ende voete geordineert by den edelen stad van Anwerpen*"). For a period of approximately 300 days, stretching from 20 October 1488 to 19 August 1489, Antwerp paid for a relatively large army that would eventually cost the city council the considerable sum of 128,289 artesian pounds (lb. art.).

In this campaign we must distinguish two separate phases, to wit: before and after the early days of January 1489. At that point, the army underwent a thorough

---

Geschiedenis 1 (1998), 261–86, and Sergio Boffa, *Warfare in Medieval Brabant* (Woodbridge, 2004), pp. 74, 146–7.

[9] This critique was voiced in Jan F. Verbruggen, "Flemish Urban Militias against the French Cavalry Armies in the Fourteenth and Fifteenth Centuries," *Journal of Medieval Military History* 1 (2003), 145–69, and Bernard S. Bachrach, "Verbruggen's "Cavalry" and the Lyon-Thesis," *Journal of Medieval Military History* 4 (2006), 137–63. See also Jelle Haemers and Botho Verbist, "Het Gentse gemeenteleger in het laatste kwart van de vijftiende eeuw. Een politieke, financiële en militaire analyse van de stadsmilitie," *Handelingen van de Maatschappij voor Geschiedenis en Oudheidkunde te Gent* 62 (2008), 291–325.

[10] For a historiographical survey, see also David S. Bachrach, 'A Military Revolution Reconsidered: the Case of the Burgundian State under the Valois Dukes', *Essays in Medieval Studies* 18 (1998), pp. 9–14, esp. 11–12.

overhaul. From 20 October 1488 until 5 January 1489 Antwerp's military efforts on behalf of Maximilian of Austria were clearly an exercise in improvisation, echoed in the rather chaotic management of the army expenses in the first part of the accounts. The highly concise nature of the accounts for October, November and December precludes any detailed analysis, but they reveal that the average monthly cost of the Antwerp army then amounted to 6,564 lb. art. These sums were used to field an army that consisted of approximately 180 cavalrymen and 670 infantrymen, this army being commanded by the prominent Brabantine nobleman Jan V van Rotselaar, lord of Perwijs (d. 1496). Next to this, the expenses also covered the maintenance of a small number of soldiers who garrisoned several strategic locations in the duchy of Brabant. Information on the composition of the army in this first phase is rather scarce, but there seems little reason to suspect that the Antwerp army was an urban militia, drafted among the town's craft guilds. The accounts of November and December 1488 mention the existence of a company of respectively 131 and 180 'workmen' (*ghezellen*), but it seems unlikely that it concerned Antwerp craftsmen. The Middle Dutch word *ghezel* could not only indicate the assistant to a guild master but also functioned as a synonym for a footman. In all likelihood, we must understand the use of *ghezellen* in the army account as a military designation, rather than a professional one. Even if it concerned craftsmen, the numerical importance of the Antwerp guild community for the army must have been minute. In November and December those *ghezellen* provide only a small segment of this army of approximately 700 foot soldiers, and they disappear from the accounts from January 1489 onwards. We cannot exclude the possibility that the Antwerp army was partially drafted from among Antwerp's poor, who might have chosen a soldier's life, but, generally speaking, the Antwerp force is likely to have been an army of hired troops, not of armed craftsmen.

We can pursue the issue of the origins of the soldiers with an in-depth study of their commanders. As was common in the later medieval era, the Antwerp military force consisted of a conglomeration of companies, all under the direct command of their own captain. In the first phase of October–December 1488 the army consisted of eighteen companies, and one captain, Jan V van Rotselaar, also functioned as supreme commander of the entire army. The size of the various companies differed widely, a consequence of the fact that, in a mercenary force, the recruitment and equipment of troops was usually the responsibility of the captains hired by the employer. Obviously, a powerful nobleman or a famous mercenary captain could attract a larger band of armed followers than a poorer or less well-known warlord. Given this system of recruitment, and the inevitable toll of desertion, death or mutiny, the size of companies was in a state of perpetual flux.

The composition of the army's high command during the first three months of the campaign is quite clear. At least thirteen of the eighteen captains belonged, in different ways, to the top layers of Brabantine society (Table 1). First, it should be noted that nearly half of the captains belonged to noble lineages whose patrimony was situated in various parts of the duchy of Brabant. Three among them – Filips Butoir, Karel van Immerseel and Jan van Liere – also had family members who

Table 1: The captains of the Antwerp army (October 1488–5 January 1489)

Captain	Size and composition of the company[11]	Social status	Family present in the Antwerp city council between 1477 and 1489
Bauwel, Hein van	33 footmen		
Berchem, Coste van[12]	20 footmen	Nobleman	
Blaesvelt, Jacob van	20–50 cavalrymen; 50–200 footmen	Nobleman	
Butoir, Filips van[13]	6 footmen	Nobleman	Yes
Brant, Augustijn[14]	12 footmen	Nobleman	
Colen, Joos van	30 footmen		Yes
Dielbeke, Wouter van	19 footmen		
Donc, Adriaan van	100 footmen		
Draeck, Walraven	34 footmen		Yes
Glymes-Bergen, Cornelis van	22 cavalrymen	Nobleman	
Immerseel, Karel van	6 cavalrymen; 200 footmen	Nobleman	Yes
Liere, Jan van	n.a.[15]	Nobleman	Yes
Merode, Jan VII de[16]	25 cavalrymen; 100 footmen	Nobleman	
Rotselaar, Jan V van[17]	17–30 cavalrymen; 100 footmen	Nobleman	
Pape, Noël de	12 footmen		
Retie, the bailiff of [?]	6 cavalrymen; 100 footmen		
Weerde, Jan van den	33–40 footmen		
Zandhove, Hein van	33 footmen		

often sat as alderman in the Antwerp city council in the 1480s.[18] In addition, we can assume that Jan van Colen also belonged to the Antwerp urban elite:

[11] The account of 8–31 March 1489, for example, refers to deserting soldiers. The subsequent account of 1–28 April mentions problems with mutinous German mercenaries, who deemed their pay insufficient (ACA, R 1811, section 'Incidental expenses' ("*Diverschen*")). The estimate of the size of the retinue is based on an average of the largest and smallest values mentioned in the accounts.
[12] De Win, *De adel in het hertogdom Brabant in de vijftiende eeuw (inzonderheid de periode 1430–1482)* unpublished MPhil, Ghent University (1979) 2 vols, p. 249.
[13] Ibid., p. 434.
[14] He is referred to as "the lord of Grobbendonk." For this identification, see ibid., pp. 271–2.
[15] Jan van Liere and Jacob van Blaesvelt shared the command over a single company.
[16] He is referred to as "the lord of Petershem." For this identification, see ibid., pp. 410–16.
[17] He is referred to in the accounts as "the lord of Perwez."
[18] The lists of aldermen are published in Floris Prims, *Geschiedenis van Antwerpen, vol. 7, 1ste boek: de politieke orde* (Brussel, 1938–40), pp. 176–83. For a critical appreciation, see Koen

one Jacob van Colen had been alderman in 1478 and 1479. Lastly, there was Walraven Draeck, who had been involved in urban government shortly before 1488. His kinsman Willem Draeck became mayor in 1489.[19] This means that at least five captains had direct connections to the city council. Next to these nobles and members of the urban elite, there were also two local officers in command of a company: Wouter van Dielbeke, bailiff of Malines, and the bailiff of Retie. It was expected that important princely officers such as the bailiff of Malines would levy troops whenever the prince engaged in warfare.[20] The presence of the bailiff of Retie in this list is probably linked to the fact that Jan V van Rotselaar, the army's commander, was lord of Retie and Vorselaar. This suggests that this officer was recruited on the grounds of feudal obligations.[21]

This analysis sheds some light on how the Antwerp army came into being in October 1488. It seems that the city council had contacted local princely officers and those noblemen who were known to be partisans of Maximilian of Austria and who were also noted for their military capacities. Those local aristocrats seem to have been responsible for the first levy of troops, presumably by recruiting men to arms in their seignories and in the neighbouring villages. The bill of such a muster was then submitted to the Antwerp financial administration. The city may also have sent out people to recruit soldiers. Indeed, the army accounts of those first three months often refer to the reimbursements paid to various people 'for the recruitment of soldiers' (*den monster van den luyden van wapene*) in various parts of Brabant (Herentals, Lier, Mol, Turnhout, Bergen-op-Zoom and so on).[22] It is also clear that the city of Antwerp immediately delegated the command over the army that was paid with city funds. The commander, Jan V van Rotselaar, was a member not of the Antwerp city council but of an important noble lineage that had distinguished itself in service of the dukes of Brabant. He was clearly one of

Wouters, "Een open oligarchie? De machtsstructuur in de Antwerpse magistraat tijdens de periode 1520–1555," *Revue belge de Philologie et d'Histoire* 82 (2004), 907. For a study of the Antwerp oligarchy, see in particular Koen Wouters, "De invloed van verwantschap op de machtsstrijd binnen de Antwerpse politieke elite (1520–1555)," *Tijdschrift voor sociale geschiedenis* 28 (2002), 29–56. For the presence of a network in the urban elite that strongly supported the Habsburg dynasty, see Raymond Van Uytven, "1477 in Brabant," in *Le Privilège général et les privilèges régionaux de Marie de Bourgogne pour les Pays-Bas: 1477*, Standen en Landen 80, ed. Wim Blokmans (Kortrijk-Heule, 1985), pp. 264, 266–8.

[19] It is noteworthy that a relative of Walraven Draeck, namely Willem Draeck, was the so-called "*hoodsman*" of the Antwerp crossbow guild (ACA, RA, 102, fol. 136r). Walraven himself became the first dean of the Antwerp arquebus guild that was founded on 17 November 1490 (Prims, *Geschiedenis van Antwerpen*, 7:57–9).

[20] This is discussed in Richard Vaughan, *Philip the Good. The Apogee of Burgundy* (Woodbridge, 2002), pp. 11–16.

[21] See Bart Minnen, "Heerlijke wetgeving in Brabant in de Late Middeleeuwen. De privilegies voor de heerlijkheden Rotselaar, Vorselaar en Retie (1407–1558)," *Koninklijke Commissie voor de uitgave der oude wetten en verordeningen van België* 41 (2000), 104.

[22] ACA, R 1811, account of 20 October – 20 December 1488, section: "travel costs." See also Haemers and Verbist, "Het Gentse Gemeenteleger," pp. 315–17. Most payments start between 6 and 15 November, a period in which a ceasefire was in effect between Maximilian and the rebels. This confirms earlier suspicions that those negotiations were used by both parties as a pretext to recruit additional troops (Prims, *Geschiedenis van Antwerpen*, 7:54).

the more prominent members of the Brabant nobility: he was the only son of Jan IV van Rotselaar, hereditary viceroy of Brabant, and Elisabeth van Horn, and he had married into the Van Boekhoute lineage, hereditary viscounts of Brussels.[23] Despite the fact that Jan V van Rotselaar was not a member of the Antwerp political elite, the aldermen did not need to fear that they would not have any contact with the army during the military campaign. Nearly a quarter of the captains had a direct or indirect link with the city council and even those nobles who did not have a relative in the city council would not have been strangers to the urban elite. In the later medieval Low Countries there was a considerable overlap between the social spheres of the urban elite and the rural aristocracy.[24]

The expansion of the Antwerp army in 1489

The army that was mustered in October 1488 was thoroughly revised in January 1489. It seems that the turn of events provoked a reorganization and expansion of the Antwerp war effort. Jan V van Rotselaar continued to serve in this army but he was now was replaced as supreme commander by Cornelis van Glymes-Bergen, lord of Zevenbergen and Grevenbroek (d. 1508/1509), the youngest scion of what might very well have been the most powerful noble lineage of the Low Countries at the turn of the sixteenth century.[25] In addition, new troops were mustered to increase the strike-power of the army: until now, the army had counted approximately 180 cavalrymen and 670 infantrymen, but this was now expanded to no fewer than 400 cavalrymen and 1,000 footmen. Inevitably, the expenses increased. In October–December 1488 the monthly cost of this army was approximately 6,500 lb. art., but in 1489 the monthly cost would always exceed 10,000 lb. art. In May 1489, the expenses peaked as high as 20,000 lb. art. With the military reorganization of January 1489 the army accounts become much more informative, which allows for a detailed analysis of the financial side of the Antwerp military enterprise.

It is clear that the monthly costs of fielding this expanded force were subject to considerable fluctuations. This was first and foremost a consequence of the fact that warfare was subject to a seasonal rhythm. The army was kept in the field continuously, but military activities were limited during the winter months. This was echoed in the remuneration of the soldiers. With the dawning of spring and

---

[23] An excellent illustration of John's august position is his monumental tombstone, depicting Jan van Rotselaar in full armour with his wife in the parish church of Vorselaar. See also De Win, *De adel*, p. 446.

[24] See Frederik Buylaert, "Edelen in de Vlaamse stedelijke samenleving. Een kwantitatieve benadering van de elite van het laatmiddeleeuwse en vroegmoderne Brugge," *Tijdschrift voor Sociale en Economische Geschiedenis* 4 (2007), 49–56.

[25] The political prominence of the Glymes family is extensively discussed in Hans Cools, *Mannen met macht: edellieden en de moderne staat in de Bourgondisch-Habsburgse landen (1475–1530)* (Zutphen, 2001), pp. 215–16 and in idem, "Les frères Henri, Jean, Antoine et Corneille de Glymes-Bergen: les quatre fils Aymon des Pays-Bas bourguignons," *Publication du centre européen d'études bourguignonnes (XIVe–XVIe s.)* 41 (2001), 123–33.

Figure 1: The financial costs of the Antwerp army (January–August 1489)

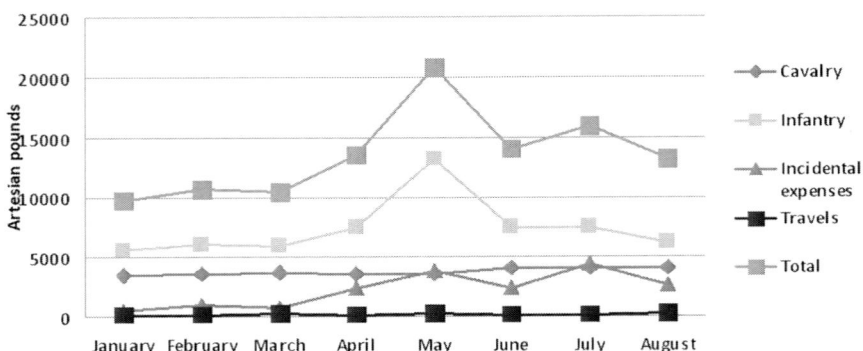

the recommencement of the military season, the soldiers' fee increased.[26] The summer fee of any combatant, whether a cavalryman or an infantryman, exceeded their winter fee by one shilling. The peak in the army expenses during the month of May was caused by the payment of a special fee of 7 lb. 10 s., equivalent to one month of pay, to a battalion of 774 footmen who were now ordered to storm the rebellious city of Aarschot.

Figure 2: The distribution of the expenditures for the Antwerp army (January–August 1489)

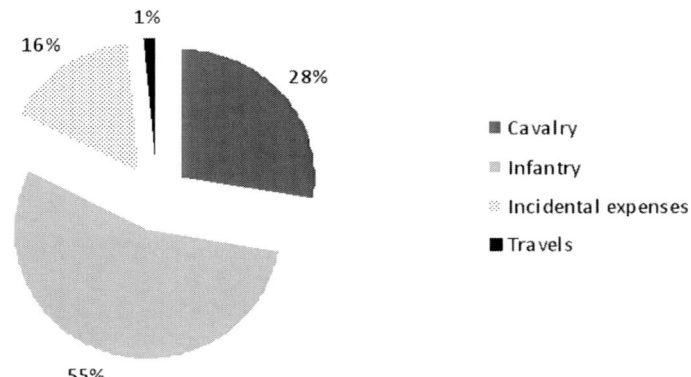

---

[26] For a discussion of the seasonal rhythm in campaining, see Jacob Dekker, "Veldslagen tijdens de Honderdjarige Oorlog. Een kwestie van seizoenen," *Madoc: Tijdschrift over de Middeleeuwen* 15 (2001), 165–71. This was also common practice in the urban economy. See the discussion of the renumeration of journeymen by Etienne Scholliers, *De levensstandaard in de 15de en 16de eeuw te Antwerpen* (Antwerpen, 1960), p. 65.

Those fluctuations in army pay had a decisive influence on the total costs of the Antwerp war because the remuneration of the cavalry and infantry covered no less than 83 per cent of all costs. The lion's share of the military expenses went on the payment of the 1,400 combatants. The four hundred horsemen and the one thousand footmen respectively claimed 26 and 55 per cent of the total budget. That the infantry, providing 70 per cent of all combatants, only claimed half of the pay is caused by the fact that horsemen received a higher fee. In the early spring of 1489 he would receive a daily fee of six shillings while a common soldier received only four shillings (the summer fee of a cavalryman and an infantryman were respectively seven and five shillings). This difference might have been caused by the fact that a horseman was directly responsible for the maintenance of his horse and valet, as well as the fact that the cavalry usually included persons with a higher social status.[27]

What deserves our full attention is that the daily fee of four or five shillings paid to a soldier in this army was a competitive wage compared with that of common labourers. As a point of reference we can take the wages paid to Antwerp bricklayers, as this professional group was the first to adapt its wage to the fluctuating cost of living. The daily wage of those skilled labourers was, in the winter and summer of 1489 respectively, 10,5 Brabantine pennies (d.br.) and 13,5 d.br.[28] Combined with the fact that a soldier's pay was continuous, while bricklayers were not paid on Sundays and another 45 feast-days, this allows us to conclude that the remuneration of a soldier was considerably better than that of a skilled labourer.[29] This confirms that, in 1489, the Antwerp army consisted of professional soldiers rather than urban craftsmen who received a minimal compensation for serving in the urban militia.[30]

The other expenditures of the Antwerp campaign cover the pay of the army commander (400 lb. art. per month), the remuneration of messengers, the leasing of ships and so on. A first set of costs concerned the frequent communications between the city of Antwerp and the army in the field as well as other towns, but this only amounted to 1 per cent of the total costs. Those expenditures were listed in the section "Travels," while the rest was usually listed under "Other expenses" (*Ander uutgheven extraordinaris*). Among others, this included the hiring of carpenters to help with the siege of a city and the lease of five ships from Antwerp shipmen in the autumn of 1488 to transport troops or to provision the garrisons of various castles and cities.[31] The army thus did not work with a permanent logistical staff but instead opted for hired labour for specific tasks.

---

[27] This is discussed in Boffa, *Warfare in Medieval Brabant*, p. 124.
[28] At this time one artesian pound was worth approximately one quarter of one brabantine pound.
[29] For those data, see Scholliers, *De levensstandaard*, pp. 80–81 and 86.
[30] As a rule, the mandatory time for craftsmen to serve in the urban militia was limited to four to six weeks. After this time, one had to discharge them or hire them as common soldiers. This made urban militias highly suited for short campaigns, but not for long-term warfare. For an extensive discussion, see Huub P.H. Jansen and Peter C.M. Hoppenbrouwers, "Military Obligation in Mediaeval Holland. The Burden of the Host," *Acta Historiae Neerlandicae* 13 (1980), 1–24.
[31] That those ships were hired in Antwerp is suggested by the fact that one of the hired shipman, Jan Willems, owned a house in Antwerp (ACA, SR 101, fol. 210v). For the strategic importance of rivers for warfare in late medieval Brabant, see Boffa, *Warfare in Medieval Brabant*, pp. 165–6.

The military command of the Antwerp army in 1489

The indication that we are seeing an army of well-paid mercenaries is confirmed if we focus on the captains of the reorganized army. From January 1489 onwards the accounts differentiate meticulously between the captains who commanded infantry and those who led the cavalry. The newly appointed commander is listed among the forty-seven cavalry officers (Table 2).

Table 2: The cavalry captains of the Antwerp army (January–August 1489)

Captain	Size of the company	Social status	Family present in the Antwerp city council between 1477 and 1489
Alfarado	70–113		
Anspach, Koenraad van	1		
Aveluz, Jan d'[32]	2	Nobleman	
Avonturier, Joris l'	1–2		
Branteghem, Adriaan van	9–22		
Charnu, Claude de	2–3		
Coppewalt, Erhart van	1		
'Croix, monseigneur de'[33]	26–82	Nobleman	
d'Espira, Francisco	38–43		
Dielbeke, Wouter van	4		
Duffel, Boudewijn van	1		
Ee, Filips van der	4	Nobleman	
Famart, Olivier de	4	Nobleman	
Fretin, Antoine de	3–6	Nobleman	
Glymes-Bergen, Cornelis van	23–54	Nobleman	
Hagenau, Michiel van	1–4		
Hauwere, Jan de	2–3		
Harpin/Herpin	48–69		
Heschinger, Koenraad	3		
Immerseel, Karel van	6	Nobleman	Yes
Kabede	2		
Lachat, Jan de ('Spaingaert')	4–5		
Lalaing, Rodriguez de	18–21	Nobleman	
Luzern, Hein van	1		
Lyon, Jan de	3–4		

[32] Cools, *Mannen met macht*, p. 154.
[33] This might concern Philippe de Croÿ, lord of Croÿ (d. 1511), from the august Croÿ lineage from Hainaut, since the account of 1 to 28 April 1489 refers to troops from Hainaut under the command of 'the lord of Croix' (for this family, see Cools, *Mannen*, pp. 197–8, 200–201). Another possibility is that it concerned the noble house of Croix dit de Drumez, lords of the seigniory of Croix in Walloon Flanders (for this family, see Hervé Douxchamps, "Les quarante familles belges les plus anciennes subsistantes: Croix," *Le Parchemin* 319 (1999), 1–12).

Captain	Size of the company	Social status	Family present in the Antwerp city council between 1477 and 1489
Liere, Nicolaas van	2	Nobleman	Yes
Merode, Jan VII de	32	Nobleman	
Metzger, Hans[34]	1		
Montfort	8		
Oliven, Mattheus van	1		
Pinnock, Filips[35]	2	Nobleman	
Pot, Koenraad	4	Nobleman	Yes
Provoost, de [?]	3–4		
Ranst, Jan van	16	Nobleman	Yes
Rochefort, Bernard de	4–5		
Rotselaar, Jan V van	16–33	Nobleman	
Ruttelingen, Hans van	1		
Saint-Simon, Charles de	3		
Salins	25		
Schuyffort, Kilving van	1–2		
Simonet, 'le grand'	1		
Thoisy, the bastard of [?]	3	Nobleman	
Tricht, Paul van	2		
Valkenstein, Peter van	1		
Vaulx, Antoine de	2		
Wijngaerde, Jacob van den	3		Yes
Zurich, Bastiaan van	1		

The captains of the various cavalry companies have a remarkably heterogeneous background. Fifteen of them can be identified as members of noble lineages whose power base was situated in Brabant or in another principality of the Burgundian–Habsburg Low Countries. Of this group, four noblemen – Cornelis van Glymes-Bergen, Jan VII de Merode, Jan V van Rotselaar and Karel van Immerseel – were already active as captains in the Antwerp army in the autumn of 1488. This small group obviously comprises the core of the army's command, since both Jan van Rotselaar and Cornelis van Glymes-Bergen served as the commander of the entire army. This allows us to conclude that this army was not controlled first and foremost by the city of Antwerp but by the Habsburg state. Both the Van Rotselaar lineage and the Van Glymes-Bergen lineage belonged to the high nobility and both families were mainstays of the Habsburg dynasty. Cornelis and his three older brothers are often described by historians as the key

[34] He is mentioned in a chronicle written by one of the military commanders of Maximilian of Austria. See Wilwolt Von Schaumburg, *Die Geschichten und Taten Wilwolts von Schaumburg*, ed. Adelbert von Keller (Stuttgart, 1853), p. 30: "Hans Metger der profos, was ein armer knecht, vieng einen abt in der stat, gab ine zwelf tausent gülden zu schatzung."

[35] It concerned an ennobled family of Louvain patricians (see De Win, *De adel*, pp. 432–23).

figures of the faction which supported Maximilian of Austria in the turmoil of the 1480s and 1490s. But the appointment of Cornelis as supreme commander in January 1489 indicates that it was also considered important to find a commander with excellent relations with the city which paid for an army. Cornelis' oldest brother, Jan III van Glymes-Bergen (d. 1532), was lord of Bergen-op-Zoom, a small city close to Antwerp. The astounding wealth of this noble house was largely based on the increasing popularity of the fair of Bergen-op-Zoom, which functioned as a secondary hub to the Antwerp market. Given this, the noblemen from this lineage must have found it easy to identify themselves with the ambition of Antwerp to assume the role of the Low Countries' primary gateway city for international trade.[36]

The knight Karel van Immerseel, who also belonged to this core group of four captains who remained in command during the entire campaign, had even stronger ties with Antwerp than Cornelis van Glymes-Bergen. He was not a member of the Antwerp political elite and his own possessions in Antwerp were rather limited (he had only a house in Hoboken),[37] but his older brother, Jan van Immerseel, lord of Itegem and viscount of Alost (d. 1506), was very much at home in the top layers of Antwerp society. He regularly served as an alderman in the Antwerp council from 1482 onwards and in 1485 and 1487 – that is, with the start of the Antwerp campaign – Karel van Immerseel was one of the two burgomasters of this town. Next to this, Jan van Immerseel owned at least five houses in Antwerp, as well as a series of properties in the neighbouring villages of Boechout, Kontich and Steenbergen.[38] Next to Karel van Immerseel were three more noble captains with extensive connections with the Antwerp elite. Sir Jan van Ranst, lord of Mortsel and Cantincrode, was the sheriff of Antwerp and margrave of the so-called "Land van Rijen," which made him the direct representative of princely government in Antwerp and the neighbouring countryside.[39] His kinsman Lodewijk van Ranst was a long-standing member of the city council. Indeed, the patrimony of the

---

[36] See Cools, Mannen met macht, pp. 11–14 and pp. 214–22. For the age-old importance of seigniorial taxes on commerce for the revenues of noblemen, see Renée Doehaerd, "Féodalité et commerce. Remarques sur le conduit des marchands Xie–XIIIe siècles, " in La noblesse au Moyen Age. Xie–XVe siècles. Essais à la mémoire de Robert Boutruche, ed. Philippe Contamine (Paris, 1976), pp. 212–13.

[37] ACA, RA 99, fol. 147r; RA 102, fol. 60r and fol. 30v.

[38] ACA, RA 1490–1493; ACA, RA 99, fol. 200r; RA 101, fol. 114v; RA 102, fols. 30v, 68r, 93r, 155v and fol. 206r.

[39] ACA, RA, 102, fol. 112r. The margrave was also commissioned with the supervision of the bailiffs of Herentals, Lier, Zandhoven, Turnhout, Kontich and Waterland (for this office, see Guillaume de Longe, Coutumes du pays et duché de Brabant. Quartier d'Anvers, coutumes de la ville d'Anvers, Compilatae, chapter 2, art. 11, § 10, and Raymond Van Uytven, Claude Bruneel and Herman Coppens, eds., De gewestelijke en lokale overheidsinstellingen in Brabant en Mechelen tot 1795, 2 vols. (Brussels, 2002), 2:627). Jan van Ranst is also supposed to have led a small Antwerp force that occupied the harbour town of Sluis in 1488. This occupation of Sluis allowed to deny the rebellious city of Bruges access to the sea. He was also involved in a successful skirmish against the Flemish militias near Kallo in April 1485. See Floris Prims, "Ons kwaad Ransteken (1410 †1504)," Antwerpiensia 12 (1938), 70–75 and René Van Berchem, La terre et seigneurie de Ranst en Brabant, morcellements et féodalisation (Geneva, 1971), p. 19.

Ranst lineage must be situated in this region. Next to the seigniories of Mortsel and Cantincrode and his properties in Herentals, Turnhout, Putte, Deurne, Hoboken, Oosterweel and Zandvliet (all situated in the vicinity of Antwerp), Jan van Ranst was the owner of six houses within Antwerp's city walls.[40] Sir Koenraad Pot, who commanded four horsemen in May and June 1489, had served as an Antwerp alderman in 1487 and 1488 and owned a house in Antwerp, as well as more extensive properties in Ranst and Rumst.[41] Lastly, there was the nobleman Nicolaas van Liere, who seems to have brought only one combatant to the Antwerp army. He was undoubtedly related to the Jan van Liere who had already served as a captain in the Antwerp force in the autumn of 1488, as well as to Lord Wouter van Liere (burgomaster of Antwerp in 1486) and Hector van Liere, who served in the 1480s as alderman and juror.[42] The available sources confirm that the family patrimony was situated in the Antwerp hinterland, and Nicolaas owned two estates in Schoten and Hildernesse (close to Bergen-op-Zoom).[43] Next to this group of noblemen, we must also note the presence of Jacob van den Wijngaerde among the cavalry captains. He was not a nobleman, but he and his family were firmly established within the Antwerp political elite in the 1480s. Jacob, or a namesake, served as a burgomaster in 1484. He not only owned extensive urban property but also had an estate in the nearby villages of Deurne and Wijnegem, as well as a manor in Loenhout. This seems to have given him sufficient wealth to join the Antwerp army with three armed horsemen.[44]

While it is clear that some captains belonged to the very heart of Antwerp government, it is striking that, in a quantitative sense, only a minority of the cavalry officers had a direct connection to the city that funded this army. Of this group of forty-seven captains, only five came from lineages that belonged to the Antwerp political elite. In short, the city council did not have a strong grasp over the army that was fielded with their financial backing. The sum of all Antwerp politicians, Brabantine nobles and local state officials such as the bailiff of Mechelen who commanded a part of the cavalry detachment amounts to only seventeen of the forty-seven captains. Indeed, the large majority of the captains seems to have been foreign mercenaries. The lists mentions at least sixteen persons whose family name indicates Swiss, German or southern European roots, such as Bastiaan von Zurich, Jannot Lachat (nicknamed 'the Spaniard'), Erhart von Coppewalt and Francisco d'Espira. The origins of the remaining fourteen captains remain enigmatic, since their names are obviously French. They might include French mercenary captains, but also members of the Burgundian–Habsburg aristocracy who came from French-speaking parts of the Low Countries, such as Artois, Hainaut or Liège.

---

[40] ACA, RA 56/1, fol. 78r; RA 97, fol. 36v and fol. 220r; RA 98, fol. 4r; RA 99, fol. 103v and fol. 110r; RA 100, fols. 64r, 99r and fol. 246v; RA 102, fol. 103r and fol. 112r.
[41] ACA, RA 97, fol. 10 r and ACA, SR 97, fol. 10 r; SR 102, fol. 159 r; SR 103, fol. 160 r.
[42] ACA, RA 98, fol. 28 v.
[43] See, in particular, Floris Prims, 'De Van Liere's in de XVe eeuw', *Antwerpiensia* 2 (1928), 279–83 and De Win, *De adel*, pp. 389–92, as well as ACA, RA 98, fol. 61 r; RA 102, fols. 93r–95r.
[44] ACA, RA 97, fol. 20r; SR 99, fol. 105r; RA 101, fol. 41r.

If we take into account that the number of horsemen of each company varied widely, it becomes clear that those foreign mercenaries provided at least about half of the four hundred cavalrymen.[45] The companies that were mustered by local noblemen were also relatively important, which shows that the military importance of the Brabantine nobility in the late fifteenth century should not be underestimated. Conversely, the number of horsemen provided by captains with direct ties to the Antwerp city council was next to negligible. Not only did the Antwerp political elite provide few captains to the army, their companies were relatively small.

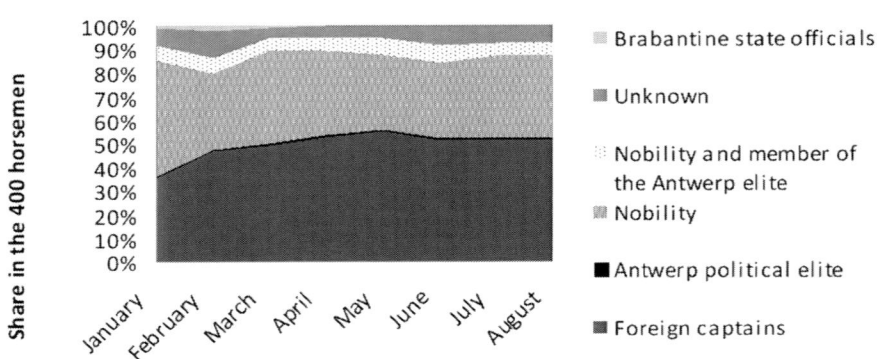

Figure 3: The composition of the cavalry detachment (1489)

This limited involvement of the Antwerp elite in the city's army becomes even more pronounced if we consider the detachment of one thousand footmen fielded after the reorganization of January 1489. Up to this point many captains had commanded a company that included both cavalry and infantry but after the reorganization a stronger division was made between the cavalry and the infantry. Only the highborn noblemen Jan VII de Merode and Karel van Immerseel, as well as a mysterious captain 'Montfort' and the provost – who was responsible for troop discipline – continued to command a mix of cavalry and infantry.[46]

Because the infantry companies were usually much larger than those of the cavalry (their size usually fluctuated around one hundred footmen), the command of the infantry division rested with no more than nineteen captains, among whom the predominance of mercenaries was even more pronounced than it had been for the cavalry (Table 3). No fewer than eleven of the nineteen commanders can be

---

[45] For the use of mercenaries in the years preceding the campaign of 1488–89, see Amable Sablon du Corail, "Les étrangers au service de Marie de Bourgogne: de l'armée de Charles le Téméraire à l'armée de Maximilien (1477–1482)," *Revue du Nord* 84 (2002), 389–412.

[46] For the duties of the provost, see Bertrand Schnerb, *'L'Honneur de Maréchaussée'. Maréchalat et maréchaux en Bourgogne des origines à la fin du XVe siècle*, Burgundica, III (Turnhout, 2001), pp. 160–67.

identified as a captain of a troop of foreign mercenaries, originating from various parts of the German Empire. This suggests that a large majority of the Antwerp army – at least 70 per cent of the infantry – must have consisted of German footmen. Indeed, at the turn of the sixteenth century, German and Swiss infantrymen were widely considered to be the best mercenary troops of Western Europe.[47]

Table 3: The infantry captains of the Antwerp army (January–August 1489)

Infantry Captain	Size of the company	Social status	Family present in the Antwerp city council between 1477 and 1489
Boechout, Filips van	8	Nobleman	
Bruin, Joris	2		
Hablutser, Koenraad	68–71		
Hagenbach	92–96		
Heschinger, Koenraad	92–95		
Immerseel, Karel van	100	Nobleman	Yes
Metzger, Vits	7–11		
Molenere, Hans	87–93		
Molenere, Koenraad	58–62		
Montfort	2		
Oostenrijk, Gerard van	57–77		
Merode, Jan VII de	80–98	Nobleman	
"The provost" [?]	4–8		
Roy, Jennet le	12		
Ruter, Hans	67		
Ruter, Bartholomeus	42–54		
Schafhuyser	123–131		
Straatsburg, Joris van	57–59		
Utrecht, Jan van	84–87		

The only captains with local roots were the noblemen Jan VII de Merode, Karel van Immerseel and Filips van Boechout. Of these, only Karel van Immerseel had close ties to the Antwerp city council. Jan de Merode and Karel van Immerseel both commanded respectable companies of approximately one hundred footmen, but, in contrast, the eight-man company of Filips van Boechout was unusually small. As such, those Brabantine noblemen provided something close to only 20 per cent of the infantry detachment.

[47] See, in particular, Gerhard Kurzmann, *Kaiser Maximilian I und das Kriegswesen der österreichischen Länder und des Reiches* (Militärgeschichtliche Dissertationen österreichischer *Universitäten*, 5) (Vienna, 1985), and Erik Swart, "From "landsknecht" to "soldier": the Low German Foot Soldiers of the Low Countries in the Second Half of the Sixteenth Century," *International Review of Social History* 51 (2006), 75–92.

This prosopographical analysis of the commanding officers of the Antwerp army allows us to make two observations. First, it is clear that the involvement of the Brabantine elite, either noblemen, state officials or Antwerp patricians, must be situated first and foremost in the command of mounted soldiers. The supreme command over the army did not reside with the Antwerp political community, but with highborn noblemen who enjoyed important positions in the entourage of Maximilian of Austria. A second conclusion must be that the expansion and reorganization of the Antwerp army in January 1489 was not matched by a growing participation of the urban and regional elite. Of the eighteen captains who led the Antwerp army in the last months of 1488, thirteen belonged to the social and political elite of the duchy and five of those men had close ties with the Antwerp city council. In the larger army that was fielded in 1489 the involvement of the Antwerp elite and the regional nobility remained quite stable in absolute terms. Sixteen captains belonged to the top layers of Brabantine society, five of whom were involved directly or indirectly in the governance of the city of Antwerp. In a relative sense, however, the importance of this group had diminished considerably, since the number of commanding officers had risen from eighteen to sixty-three. The large majority of the newly recruited captains and the soldiers under their command were clearly foreign mercenaries.

The logistics staff of the Antwerp army

Apart from military commanders, the Antwerp army also required a staff to deal with the considerable logistical challenges that were inherent to warfare at the end of the fifteenth century. Apart from maintaining communications with Maximilian's viceroy, the princely administration or the city of Antwerp, those officers were also charged with the required provisions, equipment and – last but certainly not least – the payment of the hired troops.[48] The financial analysis of this campaign has already shown that the Antwerp expedition of 1488–89 was an extremely costly business. In this light, the persons who had to shoulder the logistical burdens of the campaign deserve our full attention.

The group of twenty-one individuals that took care of the daily functioning of the army had a heterogeneous profile. Two persons explicitly designated as princely servants (*sheeren dienaere* or *sheeren cnaepe*) were most likely minor clerks of the staff of viceroy Albrecht of Bavaria, the commander of Maximilian's army in the Low Countries. On the other hand, there was a rather large group of eight or nine individuals who clearly belonged to the Antwerp political elite. First, there are some members of the urban administration who acted as liaison officers. Gillis van den Broecke had been a *peismaker* (a judge for consensual dispute settlement) and secretary of the city of Antwerp.[49]

---

[48] For a brief discussion of those logistic issues, see Erik Thoen, "Oorlogen en platteland. Sociale en ekonomische aspekten van militaire destruktie in Vlaanderen tijdens de late middeleeuwen en de vroege moderne tijden," *Tijdschrift voor Geschiedenis* 91 (1978), 365.
[49] ACA, RA 100, fol. 60r.

Table 4: The logistics staff of the Antwerp army (January–August 1489)

Logistic manager	Social status	Family present in the Antwerp city council between 1477 and 1489	Duration of commitment (in months)
…, Christiaan ("sheeren cnaepe")			1
Bau, Hendrik	Nobleman		5
Bode, Pieter de			1
Boechout, Gillis van	Nobleman		1
Brimeu, Pieter de	Nobleman		5
Broecke, Gillis van den		Yes	1
Corpt, Jan van		Yes	1
Corpt, Arend van		Yes	3
Desprez, Pierre			1
Draeck, Willem		Yes	3
Hoogstraten, Pieter van			2
Immerseel, Jan van	Nobleman	Yes	3
Kets, Jan van			1
Moeyen, Jermyn van der			8
Molen, Hendrik van der	Nobleman	Yes	2
Pot, Koenraad	Nobleman	Yes	2
Staeck, Nicolaas			7
Staeck, Albrecht			5
Ursel, Lancelot van		Yes	1
Voecht, Nicolaas ("sheeren dienaere")			2
Werve, Nicolaas van den	Nobleman	Yes	6

He also had a respectable property in Antwerp and the surrounding countryside.[50] Arend van Corpt, who had often taken care of the communications between Antwerp and the garrisons in other towns with his brother Jan, had also served as an official in the urban legal apparatus.[51] That the Van Corpt family must be situated in the higher echelons of Antwerp society is confirmed by the fact that Arend owned four houses in Antwerp and a series of houses and properties in the villages of Berlaar and Aartselaar.[52] Master Willem Draeck was even better connected. He undoubtedly belonged to the very heart of the urban political elite: in 1489 he served as one of the two burgomasters of the city and it seems that this

---

[50] ACA, RA 98, fol. 72v and fol. 111r; RA 103, fol. 3v.
[51] It concerned the so-called office of "dienaar van de korte roede." For this office, see Raymond Van Uytven, Claude Bruneel and Herman Coppens, *De gewestelijke en lokale overheidsinstellingen in Brabant en Mechelen tot 1795* (Brussels, 2000), 2:495–6.
[52] For his urban property, see ACA, RA 97, fol. 153v; RA 99, fol. 209 v and RA 101, fol. 69 r. For his rural property, see ACA, RA 99, fols. 209v and 210v; RA 100, fol. 93v.

also implied a certain involvement in the organization of logistics for the army. Lancelot van Ursel can also be described as an Antwerp patrician. His kinsman Reinier van Ursel was one of the leading urban politicians (he was burgomaster in 1480, 1482, 1485 and 1487) and Lancelot himself had served as an inspector of the urban markets in 1480.

That the logistical duties were at least partially fulfilled by important members of the urban elite is confirmed by the presence in this list of four noblemen with strong ties to the city council. First, there was Jan van Immerseel, the previously discussed brother of the cavalry captain Karel van Immerseel.[53] Being lord of Itegem and viscount of Alost, he sat continuously on the bench of aldermen from 1482 onwards, and in 1489 he was partially responsible for the communications between the city and the army in the field. Sir Koenraad Pot provides a similar example: he had served as an alderman in 1487–88 and in 1489 he combined the command over four horsemen with several logistic duties. The third nobleman with Antwerp roots was Sir Hendrik van der Molen, also an important member of the political elite. He had been burgomaster in 1478, 1480, 1484 and 1486 and, during the campaign, he served as an alderman.[54] Last but not least was Nicolaas van den Werve. He did not sit on the city council but no less than three kinsmen were continuously involved in urban government. He served as the bailiff of Bergen-op-Zoom and he possessed an extensive patrimony in Antwerp and the neighbouring villages of Ekeren, Westmalle and Schilde.[55]

Apart from the individuals who belonged to the Antwerp political elite, there were also three logistics officers who belonged to the regional nobility but who did not have official links with the city council: Hendrik Bau, Gillis van Boechout and Pieter de Brimeu. Their involvement in the Antwerp army is not inexplicable. Those three noblemen might have refrained from personal involvement in urban politics but they must have been members of the urban elite in a social sense since their patrimony was situated in the Antwerp hinterland. Hendrik Bau (d. 1513) was a member of an ennobled patrician family from Malines. His seigniory of Vremde was situated in the direct vicinity of Antwerp.[56] The same can be said for Gillis van Boechout, who must have been a relative of Filips van Boechout, the captain of a small detachment of footmen in the Antwerp army, and Pieter de Brimeu (d. 1493/94). Through his marriage with Margaretha van Vriessele, Pieter de Brimeu had become lord of Poederlee, approximately twenty kilometres from the city

---

[53] Cools, *Mannen met macht*, p. 254.
[54] This man had considerable property in the vicinity of Antwerp (in particular in the villages of Ekeren, Westmalle and Schilde). See ARA, RA 97, fols. 48v and 254v; RA 99, fol. 259v and ACA, RA, 102, fols. 5r and 164v–165r.
[55] For his position of bailiff of Bergen-op-Zoom, see ACA, RA 99, fol. 29r. For his rural and urban possessions, see ACA, RA 99, fol. 297r and ACA, RA 98, fol. 118v; RA 99, fol. 11v and 297r, RA 100, fol. 70r). Additional information on this nobleman and his lineage can be found in De Win, *De adel*, pp. 467–8.
[56] Hendrik also had properties in the hamlets of Duffel, Boechout, Kontich and Vremde (ACA, RA 97, fols. 7r and 269r; ACA, RA 99, fol. 159v; RA 102, fol. 61r). For the social status of this lineage, see De Win, *De adel*, pp. 241–5.

of Antwerp.[57] Strikingly, Pieter also must have had excellent contacts with the Habsburg government. He was a bastard member of the extremely powerful De Brimeu lineage, which played a pivotal role at the princely court in the 1470s.[58] As such, he was undoubtedly well-placed to manage the informal communications between the city of Antwerp, the Habsburg state and the army.

Generally speaking, it seems safe to conclude that the persons who were responsible for the logistics of the Antwerp force had a high social status. No fewer than seven of the twenty-one individuals belonged to the regional nobility and nine individuals were active in the urban political arena. Even the six persons who could not be identified may have belonged to the moneyed class.[59] While only a few military commanders of the Antwerp army belonged to the urban elite, the city council seems to have had a strong grasp on the financial and logistic aspects of the military campaign.

Conclusions

First and foremost, an analysis of the Antwerp army of 1488–89 provides a telling illustration of the well-known fact that the daily demands of warfare provided a powerful stimulus for rationalization and the scaling-up of the financial and logistic aspects of the war effort. The wish to improve the military effectiveness of the Antwerp army against the militias of the rebellious Flemish and Brabantine towns led to a major overhaul of this military force in January 1489. The army was expanded considerably with the recruitment of foreign mercenary companies, which inevitably led to a steep rise in costs. In the last months of 1488 the average monthly cost of the Antwerp war effort fluctuated around 6,500 lb. art., but this more than doubled in 1489 to approximately 13,500 lb. art.

This development was certainly not exceptional. A similar evolution can be noted with the armies that were fielded by the rebellious Flemish and Brabantine towns. The Ghent urban militia, for example, was also subjected to a thorough revision in an attempt to increase its strike-power against the Habsburg armies. However, what deserves our full attention is the marked difference in the military organization of the armies of Antwerp and Ghent. Antwerp opted for an army of professional mercenaries but the military force of Ghent was essentially an urban militia of armed craftsmen that was directly controlled by the Ghent city council. In fact, the reorganization of the Ghent militia during the 1480s was supposed not only to increase the military efficiency of the troops but also to secure the

---

[57] His patrimony also included houses and properties in Deurne, Wommelgem, Herenthout, Noorderwijk, Wiekevorst and Oorderen (ACA, RA 97, fols. 26v, 164r, 233v, 236v and 260r; RA 99, fol. 213r).

[58] For an extensive discussion, see Werner Paravicini, *Guy de Brimeu. Der burgundische Staat und Seine adlige Führungsschicht unter Karl dem Kühnen* (Bonn, 1975) pp. 83, 424 and 654–6, and De Win, *De adel*, pp. 278–9.

[59] This is suggested by the respectable properties of Nicolaas Staeck, who owned a house in Antwerp as well as two properties in the hamlet of Hellegat (ACA, RA 97, fols. 127r and 192r; ACA, RA 101, fol. 214v.).

hold of urban government over the militia during the campaign.⁶⁰ This contrasts sharply with the attitude of the Antwerp city council. While the city assumed full financial responsibility for the military campaign, its leading politicians were not particularly eager to fill executive positions within the army. In the first phase of the Antwerp campaign the majority of the eighteen captains were recruited from among the regional aristocracy, but only five captains had close ties to the city council. With the military reorganization of January 1489 nothing was done to maintain this level of participation of the local and regional elite within the enlarged army. Similarly, it must be noted that the high command was not entrusted to an urban politician, but to the high-ranking noblemen Jan V van Rotselaar and Cornelis van Glymes-Bergen, who enjoyed the full confidence of Maximilian of Austria. Thus, while Antwerp was slowly becoming the new demographic and economic capital of the Low Countries, the city was in a political sense still rather docile vis-à-vis the Habsburg state. As such, it followed a tradition that was much more similar to that of the towns of Holland rather than the example set by the large towns of Flanders or southern Brabant.⁶¹

That the city council of Antwerp delegated the military command over an army which was subsidized by their money does not imply that the city's interests were completely ignored. The urban government clearly kept a close watch on the financial aspects of the campaign, since key members of the logistic staff were often leading members of the urban political elite. Next to this, the choice of the military commander indicates that the Habsburg state was fully aware of the city's interests. The decision of Antwerp to support Maximilian of Austria against the rebels was largely motivated by the economic benefits granted by Maximilian; in this light, it is revealing that Cornelis of Glymes-Bergen, the commander of the army in 1489, belonged to a noble lineage whose fortune was largely based on the lordship of Bergen-op-Zoom, a secondary market to Antwerp. In a broader sense, Brabantine noblemen seem to have fulfilled an important role as mediators between the urban elite and the princely administration: many of the noble captains in the army had estates in the Antwerp sphere of influence. Furthermore, the commitment of the regional nobility and their retinue was crucial in the first phase of the campaign. When Antwerp decided to field an army in October 1488 the city council relied first and foremost on local aristocrats to muster troops. In the following year, the city recruited a large number of foreign mercenaries, but those troops were hired not so much to replace the existing army as to reinforce it. As such, the case of the Antwerp army of 1488–89 suggests that feudal recruitment and the hiring of mercenaries were more complementary in the later medieval Low Countries than has often been assumed.

---

⁶⁰ Haemers and Verbist, "Het Gentse gemeenteleger," pp. 296, 307–8, 320–21 and 324–5.
⁶¹ Compare with the analysis provided in Hanno A.J. Brand, "Urban Elites and Central Government; Co-operation or Antagonism? The case of Leiden at the end of the Middle Ages," *Publication du centre Européen d'études bourguignonnes (XIVe–XVIe s.)* 33 (1993), 49–60.

Military Equipment in the Town of Southampton During the Fourteenth and Fifteenth Centuries

Randall Moffett

The provision of ships from port towns such as Southampton is a well-known aspect of urban military obligation to the crown in late medieval England. This ancient right was imperative to the king in his wars. In all but one decade in two hundred years between 1300 and 1500 Southampton provided ships to the king for transportation of troops or naval activity.[1] Less well studied is the military equipment which such towns held, and its deployment to serve both urban and royal needs. The crown, the civic government and individual townsmen all played a role in the provision of equipment used in a town to fulfil its obligations to the crown and to sustain its own military organization.[2]

Southampton is a good example to use for a study of military equipment. From the Anglo-Saxon period onwards the town grew in importance in maritime activity – trade and transportation – because it possessed a deep and well-protected harbour as well as a double tide daily, allowing extra departures. Its proximity to the continent made it a frequent point of departure for English armies but also a target for French raids. The most famous occurred in 1338 and triggered subsequent royal orders for the building of a complete circuit of stone walls as well as a temporary transfer of the town to direct royal control over a keeper in order to ensure its defence.[3] On the whole, however, the town was self-governing, with a

---

[1] R. Moffett, "The Military Organization of Southampton in the Late Medieval Period, 1300–1500" (unpublished Ph.D. thesis, University of Southampton, 2009). I would like to thank a number of people who greatly helped in this research: Eddie Stevens, Southampton's "Town Gunner," for allowing me to spend inordinate amounts of time at God's House Tower and sharing my enthusiasm regarding Southampton's martial history; A-Space Art Gallery for their kindness in tolerating my often short-notice intrusions at Bargate; Dr. Andy Russell, Head of Southampton City Council's Archaeology Unit, has spent much time exploring medieval Southampton with me and sharing his comments and thoughts on the monuments; Dr. Adam Chapman, a fellow Ph.D. student, for discussing the various aspects of this topic that I was constantly mulling over; my two Ph.D. advisors, Professor Anne Curry and Professor Matthew Johnson, for their endless help in driving me to constantly improve my ideas and research on this theme; and, lastly, L. Arthur Burgess, who not only founded the generous Burgess Studentship which gave me the opportunity to study but was the founder in many ways of my research in Southampton, having translated and edited sources and written on medieval Southampton.

[2] For further information on the military organization of late medieval Southampton see Moffett, "Military Organization of Southampton," pp. 7–25.

[3] Building began in the twelfth century but was not completed until 1377. See *Calendar of Patent Rolls* [*CPR*] *1377–1381*, pp. 4, 7 and 9; C. Platt, *Medieval Southampton: The Port and Trading*

mayor, steward, twelve aldermen and a number of other civic officers.[4] We have a considerable amount of information on the provision and ownership of weapons and armour in the town thanks to the rich survival of urban administrative records.[5] These show that the civic government was fully engaged in military organization through its own acquisition and maintenance of military equipment. Artillery – initially traditional war engines such as trebuchets and springalds and later gunpowder weaponry – played a part in defending the town from attack.[6] The town also maintained a supply of personal armour and weapons, presumably to be used by individual townsmen as need arose. In addition, townsmen were expected to provide themselves with arms and armour for their own protection and to fulfil their military obligations to the town as well as to the crown. This led to the responsibility to own arms and armour. In England this was mandatory from at least Henry II's reign, if not earlier.[7] As can be seen by several royal statutes, ownership of arms and armour was a requirement for all adult males.[8] Yet these royal commands do not by themselves prove conclusively the holding of weapons by individuals. While relatively few personal inventories survive for the

Community, A.D. 1000–1600 (London, 1973); p. 122; H.L. Turner, *Town Defences in England and Wales: An Architectural and Documentary Study AD 900–1500* (London, 1971), p. 50. For further information on the town fortifications see L.A. Burgess, "Introduction," in *The Southampton Terrier of 1454*, ed. L.A. Burgess, Southampton Record Series (London, 1976); R. Kenyon, *Medieval Fortifications* (Leicester, 1990) p. 195; D.M. Palliser, "Town Defences in Medieval England and Wales," in *The Medieval Military Revolution*, ed. A. Ayton and J. Price (London, 1995), pp. 109, 110, 113; Platt, *Medieval Southampton*, p. 40; A.D. Saunders, "Hampshire Coastal Defence," *Archaeological Journal* 123 (1967), 136; Turner, *Town Defences*, p. 47.

[4] H.W. Gidden, "Introduction," in *The Charters of Southampton. Volume One 1199–1480*, ed. H.W. Gidden (Southampton, 1909); "Introduction," in *The Book of Remembrance of Southampton 1440–1620. Volume 1* (Southampton, 1927); and "Introduction," in *Steward's Book of Southampton 1434–1439* (Southampton, 1939). All of these volumes were published by the Southampton Records Society.

[5] These are all held in the Southampton City Archives housed in the Civic Centre, Southampton. Many have been published by the Southampton Records Society and by its successor, the Southampton Records Series. For a full discussion of these records see Moffett, "Military Organization of Southampton," pp. 7–25. Southampton Record Series, http://www.soton.ac.uk/history/research/records_series/.

[6] For general discussion see J. Liebel, *Springalds and Great Crossbows*, trans. J. Vale (Leeds, 1998), pp. 1–2; J. Bradbury, *The Medieval Siege* (Woodbridge, 1994) pp. 159, 165, 173, 268, 290; M. Bennett, J. Bradbury, K. DeVries, Ian Dickie, P.G. Jestice, *Fighting Techniques of the Medieval World, AD 500–1500: Equipment, Combat, Skills and Tactics* (Staplehurst, 2005) pp. 47, 59, 61, 63–5; P. Contamine, *War in the Middle Ages*, trans. M.C.E. Jones (Oxford, 1985), pp. 146, 194–5, 199–202.

[7] *Statutes of the Realm* (London, 1963), 1:246, 259; A. Ayton and P. Preston, *The Battle of Crécy, 1346* (Woodbridge, 2005), pp. 183–4; A. Brown, *The Governance of Late Medieval England* (London, 1989), pp. 90, 93–4; Contamine, *War in the Middle Ages*, pp. 67, 83 and 86; M. Powicke, *Military Obligations in Medieval England* (Oxford, 1962) pp. 192–6; M.C. Prestwich, "Was There a Military Revolution in Medieval England?," in *Recognitions: Essays Presented to Edmund Fryde*, ed. C. Richmond and I. Harvey (Aberystwyth, 1996), p. 25.

[8] *Calendar of Close Rolls* [*CCR*] *1288–1296*, p. 439; *CCR, 1296–1302*, pp. 112, 388, 395; *CCR, 1302–1307*, p. 86; *CCR, 1313–1318*, pp. 122, 201; *CPR, 1324–1327*, pp. 219; *CCR, 1343–1346*, p. 450; *CPR, 1343–1345*, p. 427; *Statutes of the Realm*, 1:259.

townsmen of Southampton in this period, we can draw on various urban records to demonstrate the variety of the military equipment individuals possessed.

The civic government and individual townsmen were not the only participants in Southampton's military organization who provided military equipment. Given the key strategic position of the town, and its importance in both defensive and offensive strategies during the Hundred Years War, the king and his representatives played a key role in the *matériel de guerre* that the town used to fulfil its military responsibilities. The crown might directly provide the town with arms, armour and artillery to be employed in fulfilling military obligations. It also maintained a royal castle in the town which had equipment placed in it for its own security as well as for the defence of the town as a whole. Chancery enrolments (the Patent and Close Rolls) contain many references to the intended defensive strategies employed by the king for the town and the region: particularly valuable here are the instructions to the king's ministers in the town, the keepers of Southampton, not least in the aftermath of the raid when the town was placed under direct royal control. The Chancery enrolments also provide evidence of numerous letters sent across the period to civic leaders regarding the king's wishes on how they fulfilled military obligations.

This essay will examine the military equipment of Southampton over the fourteenth and fifteenth centuries. The arms, armour and other martial equipment provided and owned by the town, townspeople and royal castle provide evidence of Southampton's military capabilities. A consideration of a two-century period also enables us to assess change over time, in particular with regard to the chronology of gunpowder weaponry. Furthermore, we can also link the evidence of arms and armour to the defensive structures of the town, which are substantial. Not only the standing structures but also the findings of excavations can be analysed. Late medieval Southampton offers a unique opportunity to combine documentary and archaeological research into urban military provision.

The fourteenth century: town equipment, artillery and guns

Prior to the French raid of 1338 there is little information on what manner of artillery or other equipment the town had for its own defence. It is probable that military equipment was in the town's possession before the raid, as the town leadership had been involved in military activity previous to this event,[9] but since no inventory exists at this early date it is impossible to know exactly what military equipment the civic government possessed. No sooner had the king taken over the military and other functions of the town following the disastrous raid of 1338 than he began sending provisions, specifically military equipment. This suggests that Edward III felt that the town was unprepared for further assault. Whether

---

[9] The National Archives [TNA], E 101/5/2 and E 101/5/12. These two manuscripts describe the construction and provision for war service of a ship that was required of Southampton for Edward I's use. It goes into great detail both about the ship itself and the equipment that was provided in it by the town.

this was because Southampton had insufficient equipment or because some of it had been destroyed during the raid remains an open question. At the start of 1339 the king had sent a large amount of military equipment: "all manner of furniture of engines, springalds, bows, arbalests, targets, lances, and all manner of other engines, shall remain in the said town for the safe keeping of the same."[10]

An item that is often listed in several different sources is springalds. These weapons were a type of traditional artillery that was commonly employed in high to late medieval town defence.[11] These low trajectory pieces were placed upon gates or walls, though some appear to have been mobile, presumably being employed by townsmen to shoot at enemies at a distance.[12] While the Southampton records are unclear as to exactly the size and design of these pieces, other records shed further light on the subject and their use in England. One such record from December 1324, as Edward II was preparing for war in France, details a great number of these springalds being gathered for his use in war.[13] In one request for nine springalds to be sent for the king's use, five of them were used to shoot projectiles three-quarters of a yard long, while four of them loosed projectiles of five-eighths of a yard, both with iron tips. Along with these springalds came one thousand quarrels, half of each type. Edward ordered several hundred of these springalds and thousands of quarrels for both types, indicating that these weapons were employed often in the period, though with no real detail of how they were used. They were similar to large crossbows in appearance, as their projectiles clearly indicate a similarity to crossbows but on a larger scale. The order of 1339 concerning equipment sent to Southampton also implies that at least two sizes of springald quarrels were sent to the town; later records of the town's equipment continue to show this variety in projectile sizes but no precise lengths are given in either of these accounts.[14] Since they are coming from the king it is possible that they were of similar lengths to those of Edward II in the 1320s – three-quarters and four-fifths of a yard.

Alongside this large missile artillery the king sent in 1339 other standard weapons intended for individual use, including crossbows.[15] There were two types, as shown by the two sizes of bolt which accompanied them, though no exact measurements are given.[16] The crossbows referred to were probably one- and two-foot crossbows. Liebel asserts that these measurements refer not to the number of feet needed to span the device but the length of the bolts in use.[17] Later documents regarding this equipment in Southampton prove this, as they

---

[10] *The Sign Manual and the Letters Patent of Southampton to 1422. Volume One*, ed. H.W. Gidden, Southampton Record Society 18 (Southampton, 1916), p. 49.
[11] Liebel, *Springalds and Great Crossbows*, pp. 2–53.
[12] Ibid., pp. 4–5, 19.
[13] *CCR 1323–1328*, p. 246.
[14] TNA, E 101/ 22/16,17; *CCR, 1339–1341*, pp. 288, 304–5, 340; *Calendar of Inquisitions Miscellaneous preserved in the PRO [CMI] Volume 3, 1348–1377* (London, 1937), p. 38.
[15] *CCR, 1339–1341*, pp. 288, 304–5, 340; *CMI, 1348–1377*, p. 38.
[16] TNA, E 101/ 22/6, 17; *CCR, 1339–1341*, pp. 288, 304–5, 340; *CMI, 1348–1377*, p. 38.
[17] Liebel, *Springalds and Great Crossbows*, pp. 59–60.

note two sizes of bolt for these crossbows.[18] In the same account from December 1324, Edward II commanded both one- and two-foot crossbows to be gathered alongside the springalds.[19]

When Southampton formally regained control of its military responsibilities in 1341, the king gave to the town for its defence much of the equipment he had had sent there.[20] Although there may have been additional pieces provided since the town was taken into royal hands this provides some idea of what might have been sent in 1339. At this point we know that the town possessed 3 springalds, 33 arbalests (crossbows), 9 arbalest belts (devices used to span the crossbows), 62 lances, 31 bows, 49 sheaves of arrows, an assortment of quarrels for the springalds and 2 sizes of bolt for the arbalests.[21] Additional evidence of town military equipment can be found in an royal inquisition from 1353.[22] Here are listed two great mangonels and smaller tripogets (trebuchets) in good order and ready for use. It is possible that these weapons, too, had been in Southampton since 1339.[23] This inquest of 1353 also found 12 one-foot crossbows with 300 quarrels, 12 bows with 300 arrows, 12 springalds with 300 bolts, 24 shields and 24 lances.[24] Over half the crossbows from Edward III's earlier donations had perhaps been taken into private hands, most likely by locals, acquired by the castle garrison, or been broken. By 1353 the town had 9 springalds additional to those acquired from the 1339 contribution. These may have been present in the town before the raid, or could have been purchased subsequently by the town, or were perhaps a later royal gift: unfortunately no sources have been found to clarify this. By the third quarter of the fourteenth century, therefore, the town had a number of springalds that rivaled that of London.[25] At this same point, London possessed between 13 to 15 springalds.[26] From Spain to Eastern Europe these weapons were common to town arsenals, so it is no surprise that a town as vulnerable to attack as Southampton had such a large number of them.[27] At this time, therefore, Southampton had a great supply of military equipment, due in no small part to Edward III's shipment of arms and armour there in 1339.

There is further evidence regarding the positioning of this artillery within the town. God's House Gate, the principal tower at the south-east of the town beside Southampton Water, was upgraded in the mid fourteenth century to a strong for-

[18] TNA, E 101/ 22/ 16, 17; *CCR, 1339–1341*, pp. 288, 304–5, 340; *CMI, 1348–1377*, p. 38.
[19] *CCR, 1323–1328*, pp. 603, 640.
[20] *CCR, 1339–1341*, pp. 288, 304–5, 340.
[21] TNA, E 101/ 22/ 16, 17; *CCR, 1339–1341*, pp. 288, 304–5, 340.
[22] *CMI, 1348–1377*, p. 38.
[23] TNA, E 101/ 22/ 16, 17; *CCR, 1339–1341*, pp. 288, 304–5, 340 (equipment in Southampton previous to 1353); *CMI, 1348–1377*, p. 38 (1353 inquest); Platt, *Medieval Southampton*, p. 122.
[24] *CMI, 1348–1377*, p. 38.
[25] *Calendar of Letter Books of the City of London*, ed. R.R. Sharpe, 11 vols. (1899–1912), *Book F*, p. 1; *Calendar of Plea and Memoranda Rolls Preserved among the Archives of the Corporation of London, 1323–1482*, ed. A.H. Thomas and P.E. Jones, 6 vols. (Cambridge, 1926–61), 1:176.
[26] R. Moffett, "London at War: The City of London's Involvement in Warfare From 1330–1400" (unpublished MA Dissertation, University of York, 2006), p. 45.
[27] Liebel, *Springalds and Great Crossbows*, pp. 4–5.

Figure 1: God's House Gate

tification, having being built earlier in the century as a small gate (Figure 1).[28] The large addition to the south of the building towards the sea had a number of windows which are relatively wide for embrasures and dissimilar to most of the arrowloops found elsewhere in the town fortifications. These may be simply small windows to allow for light but the design of the room suggests a different use. The structure is such that the semi-rectangular room is terminated in a triangular shape that points south towards Southampton Water (Figure 2). This unusual shape would allow an additional degree of movement for missile weapons. This suggests that it may have housed weapons such as giant crossbows or springalds. It is important to note that the two gunports on the south-east and south-west faces of God's House are post-medieval, and had previously been similar to the other embrasures.[29] If this structure was intended for such weapons, which, as we saw, existed in great numbers in Southampton, this would indicate a significant precedent for fortifications designed specifically for artillery in the area of God's House long before the major adjustments made for firearms in the next century. It is also probable that some of the large artillery pieces were used to defend the southern waterfront of the town, as it was the first defence of the town from the sea. As construction of the town wall was underway this deployment may have been necessary to defend the western perimeter until the wall was completed

---

[28] P.A. Faulkner, "The Surviving Medieval Buildings," in *Excavations in Medieval Southampton 1953–1969 Volume One: the Excavations*, ed. R. Coleman-Smith and C. Platt (Southampton, 1975), p. 62.
[29] Ibid., pp. 62–3.

Figure 2: Peak of God's House Gate

sometime in the 1370s.[30] One such weapon, called a mangel or manganel, was placed outside Westgate, the site subsequently bearing the name "Mangel" for at least a hundred years.[31] As further evidence, ammunition for such a device was found in excavations near the site in question.[32]

A development that took place in the late fourteenth century was the introduction of firearms. Early cannons or guns were usually quite small, weighing no more than 20 to 40lbs.[33] From the mid fourteenth century the size of cannons increased, in great part upon realizing that guns were of limited value on the battlefield but were more useful against fortresses.[34] In addition, firearms were employed by the late fourteenth century in maritime military activities both in coastal fortresses against ships and by ships against coastal fortresses.[35] The first evidence of guns in Southampton is from 1382, when the town purchased one

---

[30] C. Platt, "Introduction," *Excavations in Medieval Southampton 1953–1969. Volume One: the Excavations [Excavations vol. 1]*, ed. R. Coleman-Smith and C. Platt (Southampton, 1975), p. 37.
[31] Faulkner, "The Surviving Medieval Buildings," p. 37.
[32] Ibid.; C. Platt "Excavations 1966–1969," *Excavations vol. 1*, p. 297.
[33] P.E. Russell, "Introduction," in *Castles and Cannons: A Study of Early Artillery Fortifications in England*, B.H. St. John O'Neil (Oxford, 1960) p. xv.
[34] Liebel, *Springalds and Great Crossbows*, pp. 1–2; Bradbury, *The Medieval Siege*, pp. 159, 165, 173, 268, 290; Bennett et al., *Fighting Techniques of the Medieval World*, pp. 47, 59, 61, 63–65; Contamine, *War in the Middle Ages*, pp. 146, 194–5, 199–202; R. Smith and K. DeVries, *The Artillery of the Dukes of Burgundy 1363–1477* (Woodbridge, 2005), pp. 16–20.
[35] Russell, "Introduction," p. xvi.

Figure 3: The Arcade

gun for 5s. 8d.[36] Judging by the sum paid, it was probably small in size. This is the only gun that can be attributed to town ownership until the second quarter of the fifteenth century, but its inclusion in Southampton's defence alongside more traditional missile weapons shows the town's eagerness and willingness to experiment with new weapons for war. Indeed, it may be that the documentary records give us an under-estimate of the early use of gunpowder artillery in the town. Archaeology gives more support to Southampton's use of firearms in the fourteenth century. One important structure here is the Arcade, on the western side of the town (Figure 3). This fortification, coupled with God's House Tower, has received the most study of any of Southampton's fortified structures.[37] The arcade was formed from existing stone houses, with pre-existing arches forming machicolations. This structure possesses several of the earliest keyhole gunloops in Europe (Figure 4). Scholars have dated these gunports to various points during the late fourteenth century.[38] Saunders concluded that the openings were blocked in the 1360s and that the gunloops were added later in the century after the French raids of the late 1370s which overran the Isle of Wight.[39] O'Neil assumes

---

[36] O'Neil, *Castles and Cannons*, p. 10; Turner, *Town Defences in England and Wales*, p. 84.
[37] O'Neil, *Castles and Cannons*, p. 6; D.F. Renn, "The Southampton Arcade," *Medieval Archaeology* 8 (1964), 226–8; T. Robey, "Southampton, The Arcades, Western Esplanade," in *Archaeology in Hampshire: Annual Report* (Winchester, 1987), pp. 22–3; Saunders, "Hampshire Coastal Defence," *Archaeology Journal* 123 (1967), 136; A.D. Saunders, "The defences of Southampton in the later Middle Ages," in *The Southampton Terriers of 1454*, ed. L.A Burgess, Southampton Record Series 15 (Southampton, 1976), pp. 20–34, and idem, "Southampton: The Introduction of Gunpowder Artillery to the Town's Defences," *Europa Nostra Bulletin* 53 (2000), 53–8. Saunders, "Hampshire Coastal Defence," 136.
[38] Platt, "Introduction," *Excavations vol. 1*, p. 38.
[39] Saunders, "Hampshire Coastal Defence," 137.

Figure 4: Arcade Gunport

that the passages were blocked in the 1360s to 1370s, with the gunloops being contemporary.[40] The closest English contemporary gunports are at the Westgate of Winchester, dated to around 1392–94, and at Carisbrooke Castle, dated to the 1380s.[41] Saunders makes a possible connection with Henry Yevele, a well-known late medieval architect who worked in and around Southampton, regarding the inclusion of gunports.[42]

The existing gunports in the Arcade have deteriorated (see Figure 4). Many appear to have been asymmetric upon their creation, possibly indicating they were added into existing stone work, perhaps in haste, where function constituted more of a priority than aesthetics. There are three gunloops remaining, with others now sealed during various stages of repairs to the walls.[43] According to Renn the Arcade at one point was pierced with multiple gunloops thirty to forty feet apart, making the wall defensible from twenty yards away, which left the men on the wall to protect the remaining area.[44] All three of the surviving loops appear to have some restoration, one recently. It is probable that these loops were intended for early

---

[40] O'Neil, *Castles and Cannons*, p. 7.
[41] Saunders, "Hampshire Coastal Defence," 137.
[42] Ibid.
[43] Saunders, "The defences of Southampton in the later Middle Ages," p. 23.
[44] Renn, "The Southampton Arcade," 226–28.

hand cannons, as O'Neil and others have stated, as they would have been unusable for bows and crossbows;[45] from the outside it does not appear that it would have been difficult to use a crossbow or bow, but inside these three-foot-tall slits are very steep, with only twenty-two to twenty-four inches available from side to side at the very back, a mere two-inch opening at the front and a five- to six-inch circular opening at the bottom. Such an embrasure would seem somewhat daunting to an archer with a bow or crossbow, though it should be noted that, in Renn's testing of arrowloops, a much smaller slit could be used for traditional missile weapons such as bows and crossbows.[46] However, the somewhat confined nature of the loops in the Arcade would appear to limit their angle of fire significantly, and it is obvious, therefore, why many scholars assume these were for firearms.[47] The Arcade thus probably includes one of the earliest gunports in England, which may imply a much greater use of guns than documents suggest.

During many decades of the fourteenth century Southampton was heavily armed with both traditional and newer weapons, both large and small. The civic government, with assistance from the king, acquired and maintained a wide array of weapons for the town's protection. To a great degree this was in response to the king's increased attention to the town's defence after this had failed in the raid of 1338. While it is doubtful that the town was unprepared in arms, armour and artillery before the raid, it is certain that thereafter it was strengthened substantially.

Military equipment, artillery and guns in the royal castle at Southampton

Before the raid of 1338 Edward III began sending arms and equipment to defend his possessions in Southampton, primarily the royal castle, which was supposedly built by William the Conqueror.[48] It appears that Edward had significant armaments there, as in March 1336, amidst French attacks to the south coast, he sent sixty stones for his engines of war to his castle in Southampton.[49] Edward was aware of the need to equip his castle there, but perhaps was not concerned enough to justify large expenses, or may have felt that it was sufficiently prepared. Thus, while the king did organize his castle with arms and armour it was not until after

---

[45] O'Neil, *Castles and Cannons*, p. 7.
[46] P.N. Jones and D.F. Renn, "The Military Effectiveness of Arrow loops. Some Experiments at White Castle," *Château Gaillard* 9–10 (1982), 445–56; O. Creighton and R. Higham, *Medieval Town Walls: An Archaeology and Social History of Urban Defence* (Stroud, 2005), p. 111.
[47] O'Neil, *Castles and Cannons*, p. 7.
[48] J. Speed, *Speed's History of Southampton*, ed. Elinor R. Aubrey, Southampton Record Society 8 (Southampton, 1909), p. 15.
[49] *CCR, 1337–1339*, pp. 15–16.

the raid that his attention was fully turned toward the military equipment of the town, particularly the state of his own castle.

After the raid Edward III began large-scale efforts to strengthen the town, including his own castle there. A large part of this was done through his keeper, who commanded a garrison of royal troops.[50] Edward also sent great numbers of artillery such as springalds and engines, arms, aketons (a padded textile armour), lances, arbalests, shields and armour for the town and castle's defence.[51] Engineers were also sent to construct large and powerful engines of war to protect Southampton and the castle. The king continued sending munitions, with another shipment in April of more springalds, arbalests, quarrels, bows with arrows, lances and breastplates.[52] An account of 16 April included three hundred quarrels for two-foot arbalests and springalds, and one thousand one-foot quarrels for lesser arbelests sent to Southampton.[53] In May, June and July more engines, springalds, bows, lances, other weapons and armour were still being delivered from the king.[54] Between 12 May and 11 August the king spent £206 4½d. on the manufacture and repair of springalds and other engines of war in the castle and town.[55] When the king began to return rights and authority to the townsmen, he also began to gift them artillery, arms and armour for their own defence. However, not all this equipment was surrendered; much was kept, probably for the castle.[56] Clearly Edward III decided after the raid that the need outweighed the costs for the defence of his castle in Southampton.

In the last quarter of the century, after Richard II refortified much of the castle, firearms were recorded in Southampton Castle for the first time. In 1386 three guns were sent for its defence, probably some six years after the new castle's completion.[57] In July 1386 Thomas Tredyngton was made cleric of the castle's chapel, and in addition to preparing the divine services he received a position over the armaments owing to his skill with guns and artillery.[58] These services were renewed under Henry IV in 1399.[59] Thereafter few specific mentions are made of firearms being in the castle, though doubtless they were there. Other possible changes might also have been masked by the fact that the king was not directly overseeing the castle for a large part of the fourteenth century, as it had passed to various keepers and owners as gifts from the king.

Apart from the continuance of the king's chaplain who was placed in charge of the king's military equipment in the castle in 1386, there is little more evidence of

---

[50] Platt, *Medieval Southampton*, pp. 108–14.
[51] *CCR, 1339–1341*, p. 64; *The Parliament Rolls of Medieval England 1275–1504. Volume 4, 1337–1377*, ed. M. Ormrod (London, 2006), p. 253; Platt, *Medieval Southampton*, p. 113.
[52] *CCR, 1339–1341*, pp. 64, 82, 83,189.
[53] Ibid., p. 64.
[54] Ibid., pp. 82–3, 161.
[55] TNA, E 101/22/11; Platt, *Medieval Southampton*, p. 114.
[56] TNA, E 101/ 22/ 16 and 17; *CCR, 1339–1341*, pp. 288, 304–5, 340.
[57] O'Neil, *Castles and Cannons*, p. 10.
[58] *CCR, 1385–1389*, pp. 162–163; *CPR, 1385–1389*, p. 196; Platt, *Medieval Southampton*, p. 130.
[59] *CPR, 1399–1401*, p. 144.

military equipment in the castle for the late fourteenth and fifteenth centuries.[60] As far as can be ascertained, almost continuously from 1386 to 1470 a line of chaplains in the castle had this responsibility.[61] From 1386 to 1405 Thomas Tredyngton was named as chaplain and paid £10 yearly to celebrate divine services in the king's castle as well as for the care of the artillery, armour, arms and guns housed there.[62] All held the same responsibility to keep the castle defensible both in structure and equipment and maintain the artillery, guns, arms and armour of the castle.[63] While little can be said about specific weapons placed in the castle after 1383 the military position held by the chaplains for close on 100 years attests to their existence there.[64]

The fourteenth century: equipment held by individual townsmen

Ownership of arms and armour was not considered abnormal or a luxury in England during the late medieval period, but, rather, was the responsibility of all males. From the time of Henry II there are clear indications of adult males being required by the crown to own arms. This responsibility continued throughout the period in question, from 1300 to 1500, and applied to the inhabitants of Southampton as much as to those anywhere else in the country. For instance, Edward II required arrayed men with specific items such as aketons, hauberks, pairs of plates and bascinets. In 1326 he reissued clarification for the required weapon ownership by wealth, including ownership of a horse and arms, and the provision of either themselves or another capable in their place when called, by those with £10 to 15.[65] Similarly, Edward III made both specific demands for armour and men as well as general statutes for arms and armour ownership. In January 1345, with constant war before him, an updated system was pronounced for the arms, armour and other equipment required, as before by annual wealth: those with 100s. were mounted archers, with £10 hobelars, and with £25 men-at-arms.[66] Those with more than £25 yearly were incrementally to provide additional men with the proper equipment: those with £50 were to provide themselves as a man-at-arms as well as another; with £100 once more to provide themselves as a man-at-arms with three others; and beyond £100 to be assessed for more men-at-arms in accordance with their wealth. Arms and armour were expected according to rank: that of the hobelar, for instance, a haqueton, a visor, a burnished palet, iron gauntlets and a lance (*cum aketona pisario, paletto*

---

[60] *CCR, 1402–1405*, p. 44; *CPR, 1405–1408*, p. 103; *CPR, 1408–1413*, p. 246; *CPR, 1422–1429*, p. 48; *CPR, 1436–1441*, p. 548; *CCR, 1435–1441*, p. 424; *CPR, 1452–1461*, p. 20.
[61] *CCR, 1402–1405*, p. 44; *CPR, 1405–1408*, p. 103; *CPR, 1408–1413*, p. 246; *CPR, 1422–1429*, p. 48; *CPR, 1436–1441*, p. 548; *CCR, 1435–1441*, p. 424; *CPR, 1452–1461*, p. 20.
[62] *CPR, 1385–1389*, pp. 196, 198; *CCR, 1402–1405*, p. 44; *CPR, 1405–1408*, p. 103.
[63] *CCR, 1402–1405*, p. 44; *CPR, 1405–1408*, p. 103; *CPR, 1408–1413*, p. 246; *CPR, 1422–1429*, p. 48; *CPR, 1436–1441*, p. 548; *CCR, 1435–1441*, p. 424; *CPR, 1452–1461*, p. 20.
[64] O'Neil, *Castles and Cannons*, p. 10.
[65] *CCR, 1313–1318*, pp. 122, 201; *CPR, 1324–1327*, p. 219.
[66] *CPR, 1343–1345*, p. 427.

burnito, cirotecis ferreis et lancea). In this way Edward III created a well-armed defence force for his kingdom that included all adult males as well as a pool of manpower he could rely on for equipped soldiers for his armies abroad. With the increasing use of plate armour and the clear value that came from it, it is no surprise that Edward saw this as a way to give his armies an advantage in combat. Utilization of these weapons was a different matter to simple ownership. In June 1363 the king ordered all men on feast days to practice with their bows.[67] They were commanded to avoid all other games "of no value" on pain of imprisonment. The king's message reasoned that in great part the archer had brought victory to the English in war. Two years later this was once again ordered, and was to be enforced by the sheriffs of all counties in England,[68] evidence which has been used to indicate a laxity in the training of the warbow, though at this date it might be more due to a lull in the demands of war than English disinterest in the weapon. While these royal orders do not apply only to Southampton but to the whole realm, it would have been one of the aspects of the town's enforcement of "the king's ordinances."

Indications of weapons available to men of Southampton can be identified directly, where the arms can be shown to have been in their possession, and indirectly where weapons can be demonstrated to have been available and accessible to them. While direct evidence shows definite ownership of these military items, such sources make up only a small fraction of the evidence base, making it impossible to gain a clear understanding of the types of armaments the townsmen would have possessed. Only a few inventories from fourteenth-century Southampton survive, including that of Richard Mey from 1392. In his will he left Ralph Mey, almost certainly a relative, a bascinet, a breastplate and pair of plate gauntlets.[69] This account demonstrates how a townsman might have been fairly well equipped in respect of their military obligations. It also shows an important way in which arms and armour were transferred between generations of men in a family, increasing the probability that townsmen would be armed. An inquisition of 1360 by the town keeper, Sir Henry Peverel, not only demonstrates the manpower available but also indicates equipment held by individual soldiers. It lists thirty well-armed men, thirty other armed men, thirty archers, and two hundred men called "clubmen."[70] It also shows that there was a perceivable difference between those described as well armed and the others. The archers would have had bows and arrows at the least, and the clubmen probably had only a personal arm and perhaps little or no defensive armour. This small report shows the variety of military equipment owned by the townsmen of Southampton as individuals.

Another source demonstrates that townsmen not only provided arms and armour for themselves but also for others in their employ. In May 1398 a ship of Henry Sondey of Southampton was listed as having nine cannons, armaments and

---

[67] *CCR, 1360–1364*, p. 534.
[68] *CCR, 1364–1368*, p. 181.
[69] *The Black Book of Southampton 1388–1414, vol. 2*, ed. A.B. Wallis Chapman, Southampton Record Society 14 (Southampton, 1912), p. 26.
[70] *CMI, 1348–1377*, pp. 154–5; Platt, *Medieval Southampton*, p. 123.

Figure 5: Southampton Breastplate

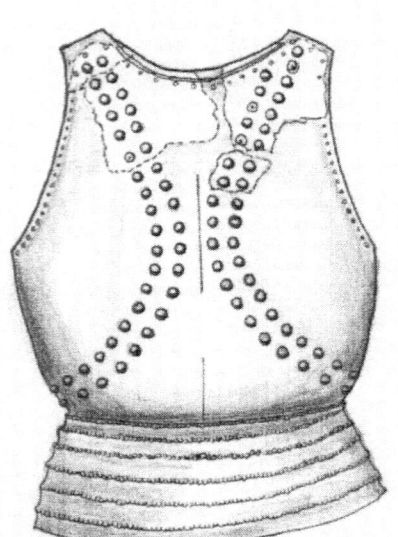

harnesses.[71] While it is possible that the cannons were the ship's cargo, since it would have been unusual for so many cannons to be used on a ship at this time, the other arms and armour were stated as being for the defence of the ship.[72] This indicates that townsmen, particularly wealthy ones such as Henry Sondey, might have owned a great deal of arms and armour, which might even have included gunpowder weapons, and that such weapons were available to the men of the town, whether for sale onwards or for the defence of their ships. Townsmen might also accumulate arms and armour by somewhat illicit means. In 1322 townsmen, included the town bailiff, John le Barber, and the mayor, Richard Frost,[73] acquired arms and armour illegally from a merchant of Genoa,[74] seizing arms and armour, including harnesses (implying complete sets) for some sixteen people. This armour was inventoried as pairs of plates, bascinets, collarets, gauntlets, cuisses, greaves and other armour.[75]

Archaeology provides other evidence of equipment with which the townsmen were armed and armoured. During excavations in the mid twentieth century many military objects were recovered. While ownership of these items is always in question, the fact they were often found among other more common objects of town life lends validity to the idea that these items were owned by inhabitants of

---

[71] *CMI, 1377–1399*, p. 93.
[72] I. Friel, *The Good Ship* (Baltimore, 1995), pp. 150–53.
[73] *CPR, 1321–1324*, p. 250.
[74] Ibid., p. 251.
[75] Ibid., pp. 251, 453.

the town. Throughout the century the coat-of-plates or pair of plates was one of the most common types of body armour from knight to commoner. Four plates of this kind of armour were discovered at the Cuckoo Lane excavation alone.[76] While these may date from the late thirteenth century it is clear that the use of such armour continued afterwards. Other items found on Cuckoo Lane include three similar plates dating to around 1350.[77] The most interesting find from this site is a top plate either to a coat-of-plates or even perhaps an early single piece breastplate, dating c.1350, which would make it a unique survival (Figure 5). Not only would this have been a very early example of rigid breastplate, but it shows that the townsmen had possession of, or at least access to, the most up-to-date armour of the day.[78] Excavations on High Street found six more plates (probably from coats-of-plates) which were dated to between 1300 and 1350.[79] A buckle commonly used for armour harnesses was also found in one of the High Street excavations.[80] This large number of plates and other items associated with armour found in Southampton suggests that armour was commonplace in the town, as do the few inventories which exist from men of Southampton. Weapons that have been dated to within the late medieval period have also been found in excavations in Southampton. A magnificent sword of a type used in the second half of the thirteenth and into the fourteenth century was found in the excavations off Cuckoo Lane.[81] If this sword was indeed owned by an inhabitant of the town he must have been wealthy, judging by the materials, craftsmanship and design of the weapon. The majority of weapon finds, however, have comprised the remains of a longbow and a massive number of arrowheads and crossbow quarrel heads.

Demands on Hampshire and Southampton for military equipment, and commercial activity in the same, also demonstrate the accessibility of weapons and armour in the town. Such demands were common throughout the fourteenth century. In December 1352 commands were sent to the mayor and bailiff of Southampton to ensure fair payment for bows, arrows and bowstrings to the men preparing to go to war and to keep the townsmen from selling arms and armour to the king's enemies.[82] The king ordered the officials to arrest these items and to certify that their sales had been made to legitimate persons alone.[83] From this record a number of facts can be gleaned. First, townsmen were buying and selling arms and armour locally. Second, the townsmen were selling to people forbidden by law and "unjustly" raising the prices for the king's men. The first aspect is by far the most important, that some townsmen owned stocks of large amounts of arms and armour. Further evidence of this appears in November 1360, when the king ordered Hampshire to provide three hundred painted bows or equivalent

---

[76] Y. Harvey, "The Iron," in *Excavations in Medieval Southampton 1953–1969. Volume Two: the Finds*, ed. R. Coleman-Smith and C. Platt (Southampton, 1975), p. 279.
[77] Ibid., p. 285.
[78] Ibid.
[79] Ibid., p. 282.
[80] Ibid., p. 287.
[81] Ibid., p. 279.
[82] *CCR, 1349–1354*, p. 335.
[83] Ibid., p. 335.

payment.[84] In February 1371 six hundred sheaves were ordered as well.[85] Of the twenty-six counties with similar requests only four counties provide more.[86] In April 1371 six hundred sheaves were again commanded, while Surrey and Sussex were to provide one thousand combined, and Somerset and Dorset another one thousand together.[87]

Trade in Southampton not uncommonly included the exchange of weapons and armour, both from urban tradesmen and abroad. The local industry of arms and armour coupled with outside commerce created an environment in which Southampton played a part and accessed military items of every nature to fulfil its military needs, providing also a local market for townsmen in their acquiring of these materials. Customs ordinances in Southampton reveal further goods involved in the town's commerce. In the Oak Book several military items, including bow staves, bows for arbalests and hauberks, appear in a list created around 1300 for custom charges on common goods entering the town.[88] While much of the evidence for the arms and armour owned by townsmen is indirect, it is still substantial. The examples of Richard Mey and Henry Sondey certainly indicate that individual men could arm themselves, and at times others, well. When this evidence is complemented with that for the amounts of military equipment being used, bought and sold in the town, it is clear that Southampton had no lack of military equipment for its inhabitants.

The fifteenth century: town equipment, artillery and guns

During the fifteenth century the town continued to acquire weapons, armour, guns and other equipment for defence, much as it had the century before. More traditional weapons remained in use as the primary means of protection for the town and its fortifications, but the rise of gunpowder weapons was to become an integral part of this aspect of the town's military organization especially during the second quarter of the fifteenth century and after. At first such weapons were added alongside traditional artillery, but subsequently they slowly began to replace them. After 1454 the town makes no mention of mangonels located on the mangonel site.[89] According to Platt, this lacuna in the terrier of 1454, coupled with the fact that it had been some time since any traditional artillery had been mentioned in the town records, indicates that the town was no longer using traditional artillery.[90] Yet this might not necessarily be the case, as *no* weapons are mentioned in this

---

[84] *CCR, 1354–1360*, p. 601.
[85] *CCR, 1368–1374*, pp. 208–9.
[86] Ibid., pp. 208–9.
[87] Ibid., p. 292.
[88] *Oak Book of Southampton c.1300. Volume 2*, ed. Paul Studer, Southampton Record Society 10 (Southampton, 1910), pp. 6, 8.
[89] *Steward's Book of Southampton* [*SBS*] *1456–1457*, ed. Berry N.D. Chinchen (Eastleigh, 1980), p. 8; *SBS, 1457–1458*, ed. Berry N.D. Chinchen (Eastleigh, 1980), p. 5; Platt, *Medieval Southampton*, p. 174.
[90] Southampton City Archives [SCA] 13/1; Platt, *Medieval Southampton*, p. 174.

Figure 6: God's House Tower and Gate

terrier, not even guns. A 1434 inventory shows that some non-gunpowder artillery was still in use at that time, making up a part of the town armament.[91] Whether this was still the case by the mid fifteenth century, however, is debateable.

During the first three decades of the fifteenth century there is little evidence of gunpowder weapons in Southampton in civic or royal documents but there is strong archaeological evidence for the increased use of firearms in the town. During the 1410s God's House Gate was strengthened with the addition of a large tower (Figure 6). The new structure, God's House Tower, bolstered the defences of the gate and the south-eastern approach to the town from the sea. The tower was first mentioned in 1417, although must have been finished earlier, as the account of 1417 related to repairs being made to it.[92] The Tower had many features that indicate the town's keen understanding of military engineering and technology. Like other town fortifications, it had machicolation. The tower's position, along with the neighbouring wall to the north, coupled with the existing God's House Gate structure, gave reciprocal flanking cover, creating a location of great strength in a potentially high-danger area of the town. Watergate and the quays below it to the south would all have benefited from the construction of God's House Tower as a defence. So while the tower of God's House received protection from its surrounding fortifications it greatly enhanced their protective qualities.

---

[91] *The Steward Book of Southampton. Vol. 1, 1428–1434*, ed. H.W. Gidden, Southampton Record Society 35 (Southampton, 1935), p. 91.
[92] *CPR, 1416–1422*, p. 109; Turner, *Town Defences in England and Wales*, p. 175.

Figure 7: God's House Tower's Gunport

One key feature of God's House Tower was its adoption of innovations for firearms, continuing the earlier developments which we noted for the Arcade. The tower had a number of keyhole gunports, particularly in the main tower at the east end (Figure 7). What is unusual about these is they have long vision slits at thirty-two inches.[93] It is assumed by many scholars that the guns used here were larger than those of the Arcade because of the larger apertures.[94] The guns used in the Arcade would have needed to have been significantly smaller than the ten-inch-diameter embrasure to allow movement. O'Neil considered that some of the gunports in God's House Tower were of the original construction, though many do not appear in old photos and illustrations of the structure.[95] One of the main issues with the gunports at the east end of the tower is that they leave blind

---

[93] *The Southampton Terrier of 1454*, ed. L.A. Burgess, Southampton Record Series 15 (Southampton, 1976), p. 23.
[94] Saunders, "Hampshire Coastal Defence," 137. Saunders assumes that the longer slit was used because they were bigger guns, though he also states the slits were for sighting, which seems confusing since, no matter how long the slits, you cannot fit a larger gun into the round section at the bottom.
[95] O'Neil, *Castles and Cannons*, p. 11.

spots. The east tower has at the north-east, south-east and south-west corners two gunports each at ninety degrees to each other. Their placement in the wall slopes allowed the guns to be pointed straight forward or away from the centre of the walls in which they were located. This would have left most of the tower walls as dead angles. In addition to these gunports the tower may have had rooftop guns.[96] This has been assumed because of the tower's wide crenellations and roof design.[97] If so, then the tower would have housed a number of guns of a variety of sizes and possible uses.[98] The introduction of structures adapted for firearms shows the town's willingness to use new military technology.

A second fortification was built in Southampton specifically for firearms during the fifteenth century. This fortification, Catchcold Tower, was newly made during the 1430s. The first mention of it dates to April 1438, but it is uncertain whether the reference is to an initial building or to maintenance.[99] Since several works that seem to be repairs follow this initial entry, it is likely that it was built earlier; thus, it may be assumed that somewhere in the mid to late 1430s it was built and completed.[100] Catchcold Tower, like God's House Tower, was a very important development in urban military technology as it was a specially built artillery tower. It is located in the north-west of the town, south of Arundel's Tower. It has three keyhole gunports of eleven-inch apertures with eleven-inch vertical slits.[101] However, the north gunport faces directly toward Arundel's Tower and the southern gunport faces dead on the town wall, so, depending on the size of the gun's barrel, it would be nearly impossible from these to hit anything besides the town or castle walls! The centre gunport is the only one not directed toward town defences, being aimed, rather, directly over the sea. The alignment of these gunports could be for a number of reasons, and the type of shot and size of gun used are vital in determining these. If a large gun, around seven to ten inches in diameter, was in use, it would lose much of its range of fire and only be able to fire ahead, possibly damaging the defender's own fortifications.[102] It is possible that such a gun could have used some type of grapeshot but use of such ammunition at this time with firearms is poorly evidenced. A medium to small gun would have a larger range of fire and the shot would not damage the town's own fortifications, which perhaps indicates it was specifically used for flanking fire to Arundel's Tower and the other fortifications around it. It is also probable that a larger rooftop gun was present on the top of Catchcold Tower.[103] Though we have no evidence of firearms being stationed in either of these fortifications for a decade after their construction, the fact that they were created for the use of

---

[96] Creighton and Higham, *Medieval Town Walls*, p. 116.
[97] Faulkner, "Surviving Medieval Buildings," *Excavations vol. 1*, pp. 56, 67.
[98] O'Neil, *Castles and Cannons*, p. 11.
[99] *The Steward Books of Southampton vol. 2, 1434–1439*, ed. H.W. Gidden, Southampton Record Society 35 (Southampton, 1935), p. 83.
[100] Ibid.; Turner, *Town Defences in England and Wales*, p. 175.
[101] O'Neil, *Castles and Cannons*, p. 31; Saunders, "Hampshire Coastal Defence," 137. Catchcold Tower received gunports at the same time as Polymond's Tower.
[102] Turner, *Town Defences in England and Wales*, p. 66.
[103] Creighton and Higham, *Medieval Town Walls*, p. 111.

firearms makes it highly improbable that they were left unarmed for long after their completion.

Around the time of the Catchcold Tower's completion we have written evidence that the town of Southampton owned firearms, exemplifying the types of military equipment these fortifications were designed for. When town stewards left office they left a list of the goods in their care to the next steward who would receive them, and for 1434 such a list exists in the Steward's Book of Southampton. A number of the weapons that the town owned at the time are given: one great iron cannon, two brass cannons, two small cannons or pellet guns, one of iron, the other of brass, and both with wooden tillers, one trypict or trebuchet, one iron rod for the cannons, two chambers for the cannons, two unweighed barrels of gunpowder and a number of stones for the assorted guns that are unnumbered.[104] It is interesting that the trypict (trebuchet) was still in service, as this may be one of the pieces of artillery delivered during the royal keepership and described as being in good order in the 1353 assessment.[105] It is clear, therefore, that some traditional artillery was being used alongside the newer firearms that were steadily becoming more numerous in Southampton. While it is uncertain when non-gunpowder artillery was discontinued for the town defence, it is apparent by the increased number of guns listed in town records that firearms were becoming the main part of town protection.

By the second quarter of the fifteenth century the town had acquired enough guns to make the provision of ammunition a fairly lengthy procedure that took several days to accomplish. Peter Liell (Lyle), a labourer, was paid 10d. for carrying gun stones to God's House Tower over two days in 1433.[106] The same Peter Liell also hauled gun stones to the tower of the castle for two days and was paid a further 10d.[107] Neither the quantity nor the size of the gun stones is listed, but it can be assumed that a man could transport a large number of gun stones over the space of two days. Although Peter was also stocking the castle with ammunition, which would have been the king's responsibility, the town was the body that gave him instructions and paid him, implying that either the town did what was necessary for its own protection when needed or the king delegated this task; but we have no record of the latter.[108]

From the mid fifteenth century onwards mentions of guns and gunpowder weapons in town records increase greatly. This trend apparently indicates that the town government increased the number and use of firearms in the town. In 1450 a list of pieces of artillery along with details of repairs to them is given in the town's Steward's Books concerned with the town-owned equipment for war.[109] One Harry Gunner appears to played an active role in the town's firearms, making

---

[104] *SBS, 1428–1434*, p. 91–3.
[105] *CMI, 1348–1377*, p. 38.
[106] *SBS, 1428–1434*, p. 53.
[107] Ibid., p. 111.
[108] Ibid.
[109] *The Steward Books of Southampton 1449–1450*, ed. Berry N.D. Chinchen (Eastleigh, 1980), pp. 33–7.

one large cannon chamber and sixteen standard gun chambers and repairing tens of chambers and six guns.[110] Others were also part of the town outfitting of firearms in 1450: John Piper sold two pestles and John William one pestle to pulverize the town gunpowder;[111] Will Willery made two chambers for the organ guns; and, later in the year, John Franklin, a carpenter, made a cart for one of these organ guns, a firearm equipped with multiple barrels which could be fired simultaneously.[112] John Wayte made repairs to the guns kept in Bargate.[113] The powder appears to have been prepared for use and stored in portable leather bags, as two such bags were bought for 4d.[114] John Swaynsey made six dozen gun stones for various town guns.[115]

By 1450 there is little doubt that Southampton had fully adopted firearms into their defensive strategy. Powder, guns, chambers, carts, firearms and specialists could all be found in the town and were kept at the ready. Also by the mid fifteenth century it is clear that larger cannons were beginning to be placed on carts with wheels for mobility. Southampton adapted some of their large guns with these.[116] Firearms and other gun-related paraphernalia continue to be found in the town's inventories after 1450. During the mid to late 1450s one Saunders Lokyer was heavily engaged with making many of the accessories and carrying out many of the repairs for the town firearms, providing in the period 1456–57 bolts, bands, forlocks, pouches, staves and *touches* (igniters).[117] He also cleaned a gun at God's House Gate, including a new touch hole, and bound two guns, with four iron bands each, to their staves.[118] As can be seen from Saunders Lokyer, the town had craftsmen who provided much, if not all, of the firearms-related equipment needed for urban defence. The town also purchased sieves for "sifting gunpowder," an important aspect of the powder's preparation.[119] For transport and use of the gunpowder a hogshead and another six white leather bags were purchased at 6d. for the hogshead and 14d. for the white bags.[120] Unless the leather bags sold in 1457 were much larger than those sold in 1450 it seems that the price of gunpowder remained about the same, at around 2d. a bag.

As is evident, Southampton by the mid fifteenth century was no stranger to firearms, and as their numbers increased so too did demands for the essential materials. John Wayte made six hundred tampons for the guns of the town around the mid 1450s, actions probably tied to increased preparations for French attacks.[121] These devices were important, especially for larger guns, as the tampons stopped

---

[110] Ibid., p. 33.
[111] Ibid., pp. 33, 37.
[112] *SBS, 1449–1450*, pp. 33, 37.
[113] Ibid., p. 57.
[114] Ibid., p. 33.
[115] Ibid.
[116] *CPR, 1452–1461*, p. 564.
[117] *SBS, 1456–1457*, ed. Berry N.D. Chinchen (Eastleigh, 1980), pp. 21, 24, 27.
[118] Ibid., p. 27.
[119] Ibid., p. 22.
[120] Ibid.
[121] Ibid., p. 24.

up the hole and allowed gases to create the force needed to shoot the ball, which was large but often, nevertheless, much smaller than the barrel. Such a quantity of tampons clearly shows how significant the town's needs were. In addition, Burgess Smith made several articles needed for a great gun that weighted 43lbs.[122]

In 1460 the Corporation of the Town of Southampton petitioned the Council of Lords for aid with their defence.[123] One concern the town conveyed was that the number of artillery it possessed at the time was insufficient. The town leaders claimed that they owned of the "town's stuff twenty-five guns great and small." They also stated that, owing to the condition of many of the fortifications being weakened, they would need at least sixty guns to protect the town sufficiently, a number financially impossible for them to acquire. Why the civic government thought that sixty guns of various types would be the optimum figure is not explained, but it is evident from this account at least that they felt that the town's twenty-five guns were insufficient for their defence. As Southampton had 1.75 miles of walls it is probable that they simply felt that twenty-five guns could not protect so much area efficiently, sixty guns meaning one for every 154 feet of wall, while the twenty-five they had would mean one to every 370 feet.[124] While this is merely an estimate, as a higher density of firearms, especially the larger ones, would be required at the gates, towers and bulwarks, some would have been placed on the walls for defence. Compared with other towns, however, even those greater than Southampton, sixty guns would have been a substantial number in the period. York, for example, had only four guns at the start of the sixteenth century.[125] Once again, as Southampton was petitioning for financial aid they were probably exaggerating their weakened state. However, "twenty-five guns great and small" does not seem far from accurate as several town inventories of that time, particularly those of 1468, contain a similar number of guns.[126]

The 1468 Steward's Book contains numerous entries regarding town artillery. "Thomas with the Beard," the town's great cannon and first named piece of artillery in Southampton (presumably that of 1434 still in use), was repaired and then deployed upon the walls.[127] The smith, William Frye, was to repair the bolts, forlock, match and make a new bed to make it serviceable. William also repaired the town's "gun cart." Another entry from the 1468 Steward's Book details a list of the guns and their positioning in the town defences. This is useful for knowing the exact number of firearms employed in the town in 1468, where they were stored and where they were employed in conflict as part of the town defence. It also gives details as to the designs and types of gun that the town

[122] Ibid., p. 27.
[123] *Letters from the Fifteenth and Sixteenth Centuries from the Archives of Southampton*, ed. R.C. Anderson, Southampton Records Society 22 (Southampton, 1921), p. 21.
[124] J.R. Kenyon, *Medieval Fortifications* (Leicester, 1990) p. 195.
[125] *York Chamberlains Rolls*, ed. R.B. Dobson, Surtees Society (Woodbridge, 1979), pp. 130, 135, 139; R. Moffett, "The Urban Military Organization of York in the Second Half of the Fifteenth Century," *The Medelai Gazette, Loyal To The Truth* 14 (1) (April 2007), 8.
[126] *SBS, 1428–1434*, pp. 91–3; *SBS, 1467–1468*, ed. Berry N.D. Chinchen (Eastleigh, 1980), pp. 34–6.
[127] Ibid., p. 23.

had in its possession, listing some twenty-eight firearms with varying levels of description and locations:[128]

> Bargate one brass gun chambered of himself.
> Bargate 2 guns with 5 chambers and trestles
> Bargate 2 guns without chambers the two which two guns lay in two towers "which are next to the said bargate Eastward to St Denys tower"
> St Denys tower one gun without chamber
>
> One great gun upon wheels "was wont to stand at bargate at John Roosy's door the which at the deliverance there of stood at the kings custom house door by the Watergate. Chamber for gun stored at Gods House Tower"
>
> Tower next westward from Bargate two guns with two chambers
> Pylgrym's Pyt 1 gun with 3 chambers
> Tower next to playhouse one gun without chambers
> Watchtower one gun with 3 chambers
> God's House Tower – One broken gun
>   Two whole guns and one serpentine
>   Eleven chambers for guns and serpentines
>   Spruce chest with 19 chambers to organ gun after specified.
>   ¾ of a barrel of powder
>   Diverse sorts of gun stones
>   Broken iron pondery
>   In the cheney two chains of iron and the hangers of iron pondery
>   2 iron great stakes and 3 ladders
> Millhouse
>   2 cart guns
>   1 peys organs in a cart
>   9 guns
>   1 great gun
>   1 gun upon trestles chambered of himself
>   2 windows of the same house with 2 guns
>   6 gun chambers
>   1 great broken chamber for the cannon Thomas with the beard
>   2 whole chambers for them with 8 gunstones and 8 tampons delivered the 30th day of
>   1 little Rondelet with gunpowder
> Tower next to Gods House Tower in the East part 2 guns with 3 chambers
> Gebon cornmonger's tower 2 guns with chambers
> Mechell Luk's tower 2 guns with 6 chambers.

From this 1468 inventory several important aspects of the town's use of firearms are evident. First, the town had a large number and assortment of guns from small handguns to massive bombards placed strategically around the town for defence. Secondly, the locations where these firearms were stored and used was not always the same place. Locations for use were not given for some guns as they were intended for mobile use, presumably where the town was most heavily threatened. It is clear that many of the guns were used in towers and gates,

[128] Ibid., pp. 34–5.

and even on the town walls. When not in use most were amassed in places such as Bargate and God's House Tower.[129] This inventory demonstrates the way in which the town systematically employed firearms for increased protection as part of their general defence. The town had a clear plan for where the guns would be employed in defence. Movement and positioning of the town guns can often be found in the Stewards' Books. In 1457 men were busy at work laying the guns out for the defence of the town: William Taylor laid guns at the bulwarks in preparation for attack[130] while John Myles, carpenter, and one man, "Sympkyn," were working on the quay laying one of the town's great guns there.[131] Evidence from 1472 indicates that the town was busy deploying and redeploying the town guns for use, repair and storage with some on the quays, to Watergate and some stored in God's House Tower.[132] Throughout the late fifteenth century artillery played an increasingly important part in the town's defence, and it is clear that there were few places that guns were not employed in the town defence on the walls, towers, gates, bulwarks and quays.

The town continued to develop the use of gunpowder weapons during the 1470s with new items and repairs. Repair of existing guns was most common, only one gun being bought in 1470 for the whole of the following decade.[133] Repairs were done, several taking place in 1470, 1471, 1474 and 1475,[134] often for several guns at one time. These ranged from vague mentions of repairs to very specific entries relating to, for example, the making of trestles to rest the guns upon, carts to make them mobile, stocks for handheld guns, forlocks, bands to attach the carts, stocks, beds or other rests to the barrels. In some situations we know where these works were carried out and what was done. In 1471 the trestle at Friary Gate was repaired. In July 1475, once repaired, the cannons were returned to the town quays to be ready for defence.[135] In January 1475 "Thomas with the Beard" was repaired again and, in July of the same year, it received a new cart. This cart must have been rather large as it took nearly two weeks to complete.[136] Repairs were also carried out on the organ gun chambers in January 1475.[137] The maintenance of the smaller guns was not overlooked; repairing of bands, chambers, chains, forlocks, stands and stocks seems to have been done often, as in July 1474 and again in January 1475.[138] Not only townsmen were used in this effort; in 1471 John Reynolds of London, one of the men from the earl of Salisbury's company in the town, was employed mending the town guns.[139] Most of the activity of the

[129] *SBS, 1467–1468*, pp. 23, 34–5.
[130] *SBS, 1456–1457*, p. 22.
[131] Ibid., p. 23.
[132] *SBS, 1472–1473*, ed. Berry N.D. Chinchen (Eastleigh, 1981), p. 13.
[133] *SBS, 1469–1470*, ed. Berry N.D. Chinchen (Eastleigh, 1980), p. 22.
[134] Ibid., pp. 22–3; *SBS, 1470–1471*, pp. 31–3; SCA 5/1/1, Southampton Book of Fines, 1488; SCA 5/1/15, *SBS, 1474–1475*, ff. 24. 26r.
[135] *SBS, 1470–1471*, pp. 32 and 33; SCA *5/1/15, SBS, 1474–1475*, f. 26r.
[136] Ibid., f. 26r.
[137] Ibid.
[138] Ibid., ff. 24, 26r.
[139] *SBS, 1470–1471*, p. 31.

1470s demonstrates the town's preoccupation with firearms, clearly indicating the town's increase in the use of state-of-the-art military technology.

Tampons and ammunition continued to be made in large numbers for the town. In 1471 John Wayte was hired to make one hundred tampons for town guns.[140] In 1475 the town paid men to make gun tampons and even provided them with additional ale for their efforts.[141] The stock of gun stones needed for the town defence was not neglected, the town's store of projectiles apparently being fairly large at this time. Late in the 1470s the store of gun stones was restored, and in 1478 the town paid for a man to spend an entire day hauling gun stones to the store house.[142] Southampton was aware of the need for preparation, and the gathering of tampons and ammunition in large quantities for storage shows a great deal of planning in this aspect to maintain sufficient accessories for their stock of firearms.

During the last two decades of the century this activity changed. While the 1470s was a time of repairs and maintenance the 1480s saw an increase in new guns in the town, with little maintenance known. In 1485 the town purchased a number of guns and gun chambers from the earl of Arundel.[143] The 1490s would have remained quiet had not the situation in the country changed in 1497, with dangers mounting from the Cornish rebellion and contention with the Scots. On 20 November 1497 42lbs of gunpowder was purchased, and on 7 December an additional 112lbs was acquired to prepare for the Cornish and Scottish contentions.[144] On the same day the mayor sent a ship and barge on the king's service, providing bread, meat, beer, bow strings, "bow rings," candles, beer pots, and three-quarters of a hundredweight of lead pellets worth 3s.[145] The town's ability to equip itself for home defence and for the king's uses abroad show the town's organizational abilities. The town also bought two hundred gun tampons in June 1498 and repaired a serpentine, the first time this type of firearm is mentioned in Southampton.[146]

The making of gunpowder in Southampton was also part of the town's defence as a military organization. The Steward's Book of 1456–57 contains not only various payments for men to make powder under the town gunner but also details on how this was done. Some fifteen people were involved for two to four days at a time in the creation of gunpowder supplied for the town, and were paid 11s 4d for labour.[147] One man designated as a labourer was specifically stated to have earned his wages for "beating coal" for the gunpowder.[148] It is obvious how much of a production this creation of gunpowder was. It started with men breaking raw materials into more manageable parts, sifting the material, then crushing it further

[140] Ibid., p. 32.
[141] *SBS, 1474–1475*, f. 27.
[142] *SBS, 1478–1479*, ed. Berry N.D. Chinchen (Eastleigh, 1981), p. 11.
[143] SCA 5/1/2, *Southampton Steward's Book 1485–1486*, f. 4r.
[144] *SBS, 1497–1498*, ed. Berry N.D. Chinchen (Eastleigh, 1981), p. 3.
[145] Ibid., p. 6.
[146] Ibid., pp. 4, 5.
[147] *SBS, 1456–1457*, pp. 21–2, *SBS, 1474–1475*, f.27.
[148] *SBS, 1456–1457*, p. 21.

with aforementioned pestles and stamps, and lastly mixing the materials together. During one short production of powder in 1475 three men made 222 lbs.[149] This all appears to have taken place under the supervision of the town gunner who, as well as his daily pay, was well provided for with bread and beer by the town.[150] This work was not without hazard, as John Brenne was paid 12d. for "burning his clothes" while engaged thus.[151] The town sensibly kept materials on hand to make gunpowder for their supplies; thus, throughout the period coal, saltpetre and sulphur were often acquired by the town in large measures, usually quarters of hundredweights, for future use in the preparation of gunpowder probably by townsmen under the town gunner.[152] Apparently the town also knew where to find some of the materials naturally, as in 1475 two men were sent by the town to "find" saltpetre for gunpowder over five days.[153] This also indicates that the town kept amounts of both ready to use as well as the raw materials to make more. Here the town's preparations show the time and expenses the town incurred as a military organization. This town supply of gunpowder was for use in protecting not just the town but also the town's interests: several accounts of the 1470s indicate the use of gunpowder from the town supply outside Southampton. In 1471 the town sent 22lbs of gunpowder with John Denine on his voyage to Jersey for protection.[154] Again in 1472, by command of the mayor, some 12lbs of gunpowder were given to John Walker for his crossing as well.[155] Clearly the town was able to provide gunpowder, whether on official town business or given out to townsmen for their own use, for use at home and away.

The town also kept a store of arms and armour on hand for townsmen or other troops to use. The steward's inventory in 1468 lists one linen banner with the king's arms, another unidentified, three old poleaxes, six lead mallets, five pavaises and rusty, broken harnesses.[156] John Payn of Southampton bought several brigandines in 1470 costing 6s. 8d. for the town armoury.[157] In 1481 the town paid to have three loads of weapons brought from Christopher Ambroise's house.[158] The town was also able to "inherit" goods of deceased individuals in certain situations. While it is hard to discern why the town was able to acquire these items, this took place on a number of occasions. A bill found at the house of John Walker and a sallet found in the house of John Chandeler were acquired in this manner, though later sold.[159] The town also had other means of acquisition, even claiming ownership

---

[149] *SBS, 1474–1475*, f. 27.
[150] *SBS, 1456–1457*, p. 22.
[151] Ibid.
[152] Ibid., pp. 22, 23; *SBS, 1472–1473*, p. 39; *SBS, 1474–1475*, f. 26r.
[153] Ibid., f. 26r.
[154] *SBS, 1470–1471*, p. 61.
[155] *SBS, 1472–1473*, p. 13.
[156] *SBS, 1467–1468*, p. 34.
[157] *SBS, 1470–1471*, p. 1.
[158] *SBS, 1481–1482*, p. 19.
[159] *The Book of Remembrance of Southampton 1485–1563 [BRS]*, Volume 3, ed. H.W Gidden, Southampton Record Society 30 (Southampton, 1930), p. 3.

of and then selling a sword that had been left at the town court.[160] It certainly had sufficient arms and armour to lend them to men both inside and outside the town: so in March 1484 Henry Brathwayte, one of the collectors of the king's customs, borrowed a pair of brigandines from town, while on the last day of the same month Robert Wilson was loaned a pair of brigandines for 10s. and a sallet for 2s. 6d; a sallet was also delivered to Walter Litthum for 12d.[161] It is clear, therefore, that the town had at the least a small cache of arms and armour for their use and enough to lend out to others. While many of these military items appear old or in need of repair, the town kept them on hand to augment the equipment the townsmen themselves possessed as individuals.

By the fifteenth century the town of Southampton had a large store of military equipment. While this is perhaps more apparent than in the fourteenth century because of better survival of primary sources it does seem that there were some major changes taking place from the late fourteenth century into the fifteenth century. This is most obvious in the increase in both the types and the deployment of gunpowder weapons. During the fourteenth century there is limited evidence for the ownership and use of firearms, but during the first half of the fifteenth century, especially from the 1430s, the use of gunpowder weapons increases greatly, although for much of the century in combination with other forms of arms. While firearms increasingly have a key place in Southampton's military equipment, the employment of traditional equipment, especially personal arms and armour, remains steady, demonstrating Southampton's adaptability and eagerness to incorporate, and to a degree experiment with, new technologies to complement their existing military equipment.

The fifteenth century: equipment held by individual townsmen

While there are still few inventories of the weapons and armour which townsmen owned during the fifteenth century, there are more than in the fourteenth century, and there are more relevant sources in general. Records of trade in the town remain important and, with more extant for the fifteenth century, are an excellent tool to identify how large the arms trade in Southampton was, indicating the accessibility of such items.

An inventory of Richard Thomas, a town merchant, written in 1447, contains an interesting collection of goods, including instruments of war, which may be typical of those that a wealthy townsman may have owned.[162] Thomas appears to have been very wealthy, owning at least two ships, "the *Mary*" and "the *James*," which he sold prior to his death.[163] His arms included seventeen lances or spears,

---

[160] *BRS, 1303–1518, volume 2*, ed. H.W Gidden, Southampton Record Society 28 (Southampton, 1928), p. 69.
[161] *BRS 1485–1563*, p. 3.
[162] *Southampton Probate Inventories. Volume One 1447–1575*, ed. Edward Roberts and Karen Parker, Southampton Record Series 34 (Southampton, 1992), p. 2.
[163] Ibid., p. 8.

four pole axes, one dagger and a baselard.[164] He also owned four handguns, but these were listed among the goods of the respective vessels, probably for use at sea, although they would have been available to Thomas at his need.[165] While Thomas's inventory gives an example of the type of military equipment a townsman might possess, it is also obvious that all these arms were not intended solely for his personal use but also for others serving under him. There are a few other isolated evidences of personal ownership of arms and armour in Southampton.[166] One is that of Gabriel Flemings, who owned a brigandine valued at 40s. which was given to John White, who married Gabriel's widow. John Chandler owned a sallet worth 2s. 6d.; John Walker owned a bill that was worth 16d. On multiple occasions when townsmen apparently brought their arms, including swords, to town court they were promptly confiscated then expeditiously sold.[167] While these examples are rather disjointed, they demonstrate the theme in question: that many townsmen owned weapons and armour. It is also difficult to say when these incidents took place, as while they were all recorded in 1484 little other specific information is available.

The Southampton Book of Fines for 1488–1540 sheds further light on military equipment owned by townsmen.[168] A summary from the late fifteenth century, presumably for fines issued for men lacking equipment, indicates some of the townsmen's arms and armour at the time. Unfortunately the opening page is now difficult to read but what is legible shows a large quantity of military equipment: 162 harnesses, 23 hauberks, 9 jacks, 120 pikes and more are listed. Extrapolating from the types of soldiers listed, there were nearly 300 bills, between 30 to 100 bows with arrows and 17 handguns.[169] It seems the weapons listed were in addition to those men named as there are only 2 pikemen listed and 120 pikes. This document, while difficult to interpret, indicates a large number of both arms and armour present in the town in the late fifteenth century.

In 1441 a list of equipment used in acts of piracy within the liberty of Southampton, probably including by townsmen, gives an impression of some of the equipment that was being used in the area and aboard ships.[170] These men were armed with "swords, crossbows, bombards, pollaxes, *gysarmes*, *platys* [probably a pair of plates or brigandine] and palets [helmets]."[171] It is interesting to note the lack of bows in this list and even more interesting to note how the men were both armoured and armed well, including with large firearms to assault other ships at sea. Clearly men of the area could be well equipped for many types of military activities, licit or illicit.

---

[164] Ibid., pp. 2–4.
[165] Ibid., p. 8.
[166] For the examples which follow see *BRS, 1485–1563*, p. 3.
[167] *BRS, 1303–1518*, p. 69.
[168] SCA 5/1.
[169] Unfortunately the number of archers listed is very difficult to read. There are at least thirty, but probably more.
[170] *CPR, 1436–1441*, p. 575.
[171] Ibid., p. 575.

Town fines also demonstrate ownership and employment of arms, in these cases for illicit uses. In 1472 the Mayor of Southampton, Thomas Payne, was attacked by a Spaniard who drew his sword on him.[172] John Barbour was fined 1s. for drawing a sword on John Adams and insulting him.[173] Lewis Aymer was arrested in 1486 for using a sword and wearing a sallet in this assault;[174] he was later fined 4d. twice, once for the use of the sword and once for the sallet, indicating that it was just as much of a crime to be in a fight with armour as with arms.[175] A surviving record from 1481 details fines for similar attacks. John Smith was fined 9d. for fighting and drawing a blade on a common woman at the stews side (i.e. the brothels).[176] John Rose's son drew a sword and beat a butcher above Bar Street and was fined 6d.[177] An unnamed townsman was fined 20d. for fighting and drawing a sword.[178] While fights between townsmen were less common than those involving galleymen or others from outside the town, these instances show that townsmen did possess arms and found occasion to employ them as both aggressor and victim. Galleymen seem to have had a notorious reputation for brawling in this period and those in Southampton were no exception; by and large, many of these affrays were related to the large populations of sailors in town. One galleyman was arrested and fined 8d. for carrying a "land knife" about the town. Another galleyman was arrested for actually drawing his blade in a fight and fined 2s.[179] There are pages of incidents involving galleymen in the town records, many of which involve swords, daggers and other weapons.[180] In 1487 there seems to have been quite a large fight, as a number of galleymen were fined 20s together.[181] To combat the number of fights that took place in town, especially by outsiders with townsmen, strict civic laws were enabled, in 1457 an order being made that no "stranger" or non-townsman should bear weapons in the town.[182] Though the wearing of blades, particularly swords, was often prohibited inside the town, it is clear that large numbers of weapons were in fact carried about by townsmen and others dwelling there.

Another indication of the availability of arms and armour in the town is trade. The arms and armour economy in and through Southampton is evident from records of transactions and the taxes placed upon trade goods by the civic authorities. The Portage and Brokage Books of Southampton as well as other accounts from the town during the fifteenth century provide evidence of large-scale commerce of bows and bowstaves through the town. These also prove that

---

[172] *SBS, 1472–1473*, p. 4.
[173] *BRS, 1303–1518*, p. 72.
[174] SCA 5/1/2; *SBS, 1485–1486*, f. 7.
[175] Ibid.
[176] *The Assize of Bread Book of 1477 to 1517*, ed. R.C. Anderson, Southampton Record Society 23 (Southampton, 1923), p. 31.
[177] Ibid., p. 33.
[178] Ibid., p. 42.
[179] *BRS, 1303–1518* p. 69.
[180] *BRS, 1485–1563*, pp. 69–71.
[181] *SBS, 1487–1488*, p. 9.
[182] *SBS, 1456–1457*, p. 19.

Southampton had many bowyers and other tradesmen in the town. Starting in the early fifteenth century, 100 bowstaves in a typical shipment appears to be average.[183] From the 1435–1436 Port Book of Southampton loads of 100 bowstaves appear still to be average, although this varied, with Paul Morel bringing in 1,240 in one shipment.[184] The numbers of bowstaves and shipments increased later in the decade. In the Port Books of 1439–1440 loads of 100 bowstaves are common, increasing to shipments of 200, 550 and up to 1,500.[185] The Brokage Books of the same years, 1439–1440, show loads from 50 bowstaves or more, with 100 being an average.[186]

The mid fifteenth century saw a near-constant flow of bowstaves into the town. In 1441 one bowyer, Thomas Gerard of Romsey, was charged duty of £1 on his finished bows alone.[187] While it does not give the specific number it is worth noting how much Thomas was charged considering a finished bow perhaps cost 8d. to 12d. This suggests a fairly substantial number of bows leaving the town.[188] In the Brokage Books of 1443–1444 shipments of 200 bowstaves are average, 300 being the upper limit.[189] Some were not numbered; Richard Gonner had two cartloads of bowstaves and shortly after William Hekle had the same.[190] Later in the 1440s shipments of 100, 200, 350, and 400 bowstaves were common, and included finished bows in addition to the staves.[191] Arrows for bows were also recorded as having entered into the town.[192] All these records show just how large the market for bowstaves, and to a lesser extent finished bows, was in Southampton, with between 5,000 to 10,000 bowstaves passing through the town from 1440 to 1449.

The second half of the fifteenth century continues to show evidence of a great deal of trade in bowstaves in Southampton. Although this took place in fewer shipments, these were larger on average. From the evidence of the Port Books of 1469–1471 Aungell Corpore arrived in Southampton with 50 staves,[193] while

---

[183] *BRS, 1303–1518*, p. 22.
[184] *The Local Port Book of Southampton, 1435 to 1436*, ed. Brian Foster, Southampton Records Series vol. 7 (Southampton, 1963) pp. 62–3, 84–5.
[185] *The Local Port Book of Southampton, 1439 to 1440*, ed. Henry S. Cobb, Southampton Records Series vol. 5 (Southampton, 1961), pp. 11, 12, 28, 61, 62, 93.
[186] *The Brokage Book of Southampton [BBS], 1439–1440. Volume 1*, ed. Barbara Bunyard, Southampton Record Society 40 (Southampton, 1941), pp. 10–11, 32–3, 57, 85.
[187] *SBS, 1441–1442*, p. 4.
[188] Ibid.; R. Hardy and M. Strickland, *The Great Warbow: From Hastings to the Mary Rose* (Stroud, 2005), p. 24.
[189] *BBS, 1443–1444. Volume 2*, ed. Olive Coleman, Southampton Record Series 4 (Southampton, 1961), pp. 192, 205, 207, 208, 210, 212, 240, 311–12.
[190] Ibid., pp. 205, 212.
[191] *The Southampton Port and Brokage Books, 1448–1449*, ed. Elisabeth A. Lewis, Southampton Record Series 36 (Southampton, 1993), *p. 94, 180, 184, 196, 203 and 209*.
[192] Ibid., p. 203.
[193] *The Port Books, or, Local customs Accounts of Southampton for the Reign of Edward IV, 1469–1471 [PBS], Volume 1*, ed. D.B. Quinn, Southampton Record Society 37 (Southampton, 1937), p. 94.

one Nicholas de Peysero brought to Southampton 2,000 bowstaves not long afterwards.[194] Finished bows also continued to be brought into the town, as Thomas Lemoyn arrived with 24 bows and 12 sheaves of arrows and Jeffrey Salmon with 12 bows.[195] Later in the fifteenth century Thomas Overay, a prominent town official and at one point mayor, brought 100 bowstaves to Southampton as part of his wares.[196] It seems that in the second half of the fifteenth century, especially the last decades, trade slowed, with perhaps only a few thousand bowstaves, probably fewer than 3,000, and fewer than 100 finished bows, being traded in that period.

Bows, arrows and bowstaves were not the only military items traded. One de Marco Negr', perhaps an Italian, paid 6s. 8d. for bringing one habergeon into port during the late 1430s.[197] Brokage Books of 1443–1444 show brimstone and five swords being taxed,[198] while those of 1439–1440 show a few other items that were of military use: barrels of saltpetre and sulphur, ingredients used in the mixture of gunpowder. The town also bought materials for military purposes, including, in one instance, 2,000lbs of iron ore; although its exact purpose is unknown it is likely that it would have been used for the repairs of the town gates, guns and other equipment.[199] Other items of a military nature from the Port Books of 1469–1471 included 50lbs of crossbow thread or cable.[200] Armour, such as hauberks and other pieces of armour, and even full suits, was also included in the town trade. Aungel Catan arrived in port with thirty-five white harnesses.[201]

While the Port Books offer a valuable view of the commerce taking place in the port and town of Southampton, as well as items townsmen could have possessed, this was not the only evidence of this nature. The Brokage Books of Southampton record the items that had customs paid upon entering the town from the landward side. These records also are full of military equipment, especially bowstaves in their hundreds, perhaps thousands, but also finished bows and other arms, such as swords, entering and leaving the town.[202] As before, these records show a great flow of arms and armour and indicate that some of this industry may have been based locally; several men, for instance, were named bowyer.[203] Royal commands for military equipment and their constituent materials offer further evidence of the arms and armour economy of Southampton and Hampshire. In February 1417 the king ordered his sheriffs in a number of counties, including Southampton, to take six feathers from every goose in the county for the production of arrows. This was for his archers in his war with France. As Henry's letter

[194] Ibid., p. 46.
[195] Ibid., pp. 90–91.
[196] *BRS, 1303–1518*, p. 79.
[197] *PBS, 1439–1440*, p. 80.
[198] *BBS, 1443–1444*, p. 251.
[199] *BBS, 1439–1440*, pp. 141, 142, 163.
[200] *PBS, 1469–1471*, p. 49.
[201] *Assize of Bread Book*, p. 34; *The Southampton Port and Brokage Books, 1448–1449*, p. 197; *PBS 1469–1471*, p. 49, 93, 94.
[202] *BBS, 1443–1444*, pp. 192, 205, 207, 208, 210, 212, 240, 311–12.
[203] *BBS, 1443–1444*, pp. 251, 311.

reads, "God gave him victory by his archers, among others with their arrows."[204] In July 1421 Henry ordered 40,000 feathers to be collected from Hampshire.[205] Just like much of England, Southampton would have had local tradesmen making arms and armour, and it appears that bows and arrows were made as well. In May 1474 Edward IV commanded payment to fletchers, arrowhead makers, bowyers and stringers for making their respective products in the counties of Norfolk, Suffolk, Cambridgeshire, Huntingdonshire and Hampshire. This was for goods he had pressed for his wars in France. Specifically mentioned in Hampshire was Southampton for its contribution.[206] In March 1475 the king ordered Thomas Asshe and Nicholas Long of Southampton to "take" the men called brigandine makers and all gear and materials needed for them to make brigandines.[207] This work was being done to prepare for Edward's war with France later that year. This example demonstrates the existence of yet another industry of military equipment in Hampshire. These industries, brigandines and archery supplies in particular, can be seen in and around Southampton, making the fact that many such items and related materials are being found in excavations in the town more relevant.

While the town government owned a large supply of guns by the mid fifteenth century, it is hard to clarify if the same was true for individual townsmen. We have seen that at least one inhabitant, Richard James, owned four firearms in 1447. Though he was one of the richer inhabitants, it would be hard to imagine that he was an isolated case. However, the number of handguns used by townsmen might never have been very large during the fifteenth century, as even in the 1556 muster of Southampton only twenty handguns were listed in the whole town.[208] Although Southampton's men probably were not always armed and armoured in the best or most up-to-date equipment, they clearly were armed and armoured sufficiently for their needs. Sadly, most inventories and wills have been lost, which diminishes our understanding of how they were equipped. What is clear, however, is that the townsmen had access to and owned a wide number of weapons and armour, enabling them to fulfil their military obligation both to the king and to the town.

Conclusion

Over the whole period, the arms, armour and artillery owned by the town and by individual townsmen, and provided by the king for the town, were vital for town defence and military obligation. All parties played roles of varying importance in the equipment that the town had access to within the late medieval period. The role of the civic government in this system revolved mainly around the larger devices used for town protection. In the fourteenth and into the fifteenth century,

---

[204] *CCR, 1413–1419*, p. 336.
[205] *CCR, 1419–1422*, p. 166.
[206] *CPR, 1467–1477*, p. 462.
[207] Ibid., p. 524.
[208] SCA 13/2/2, 4, 5a, Southampton Muster Book 1556; Platt, *Medieval Southampton*, p. 174.

traditional siege engines, mangonels and springalds played a key part in defensive provision. These items were maintained and administered by the civic leadership for the safekeeping of the town. The greatest change to take place in military equipment employed in Southampton was in this category, and concerned the adoption of firearms. From the late fourteenth century onwards, at first with installations at selected points and subsequently with specially constructed fortifications and eventually a large arsenal of fixed and moveable guns which could cover all the weakest points in the town, Southampton demonstrated itself ready and willing to adapt to new weapons of war. The town also kept on hand smaller items of military equipment, personal arms and armour that could be used by those lacking their own, as well as equipment to be employed for a specific purpose. From the town and royal records the number, types and uses of equipment controlled by the civic government can be ascertained. These various tools of war were a major means by which the town leaders increased the effectiveness of the town's military organization. The changes and adaptations of equipment show the attitude of the town leadership towards military preparedness. As we have seen, they proved wholly adaptable as gunpowder artillery developed. While on an individual level it is harder to explore ownership of weapons, it is clear that many types of arms and armour were available to the townsmen, and the town was fully involved in arms manufacture and trade. It is also important to note how the town and its inhabitants were increasingly self-sufficient in the provision of both large and small weapons and armour. Only in the aftermath of the raid of 1338 was the crown was the main force in supplying the town with military equipment, but this initial supply of equipment was a huge aid to the town's ability to protect itself and formed the basis of its arsenal of traditional artillery. There is no evidence, however, that the town relied on royal provision of gunpowder artillery. Ever improving and acquiring more and more equipment was one way in which the town of Southampton was able to fulfil its military obligation by strengthening all military aspects of the town.

Journal of Medieval Military History
1477 545X

Volume I

1. The Vegetian 'Science of Warfare' in the Middle Ages – *Clifford J. Rogers*
2. Battle Seeking: The Contexts and Limits of Vegetian Strategy – *Stephen F. Morillo*
3. Italia – Bavaria – Avaria: The Grand Strategy behind Charlemagne's Renovatio Imperii in the West – *Charles R. Bowlus*
4. The Composition and Raising of the Armies of Charlemagne – *John France*
5. Some Observations on the Role of the Byzantine Navy in the Sucess of the First Crusade – *Bernard S. Bachrach*
6. Besieging Bedford: Military Logistics in 1224 – *Emilie M. Amt*
7. 'To aid the Custodian and Council': Edmund of Langley and the Defense of the Realm, June–July 1399 – *Douglas Biggs*
8. Flemish Urban Militias Against the French Cavalry Armies in the Fourteenth and Fifteenth Centuries – *J.F. Verbruggen (translated by Kelly DeVries)*

Volume II

1. The Use of Chronicles in Recreating Medieval Military History – *Kelly DeVries*
2. Military Service in the County of Flanders – *J.F. Verbruggen (translated by Kelly DeVries)*
3. Prince into Mercenary: Count Armengol VI of Urgel, 1102–1154 – *Bernard F. Reilly*
4. Henry II's Military Campaigns in Wales, 1157–1165 – *John Hosler*
5. Origins of the Crossbow Industry in England – *David S. Bachrach*
6. The Bergerac Campaign (1345) and the Generalship of Henry of Lancaster – *Clifford J. Rogers*
7. A Shattered Circle: Eastern Spanish Fortifications and Their Repair during the 'Calamitous Fourteenth Century' – *Donald Kagay*
8. The Militia of Malta – *Theresa M. Vann*
9. 'Up with Orthodoxy': In Defense of Vegetian Warfare – *John B. Gillingham*
10. 100,000 Crossbow Bolts for the Crusading King of Aragon – *Robert Burns*

Contents of Previous Volumes

Volume III

1 A Lying Legacy? A Preliminary Discussion of Images of Antiquity and Altered Reality in Medieval Military History – *Richard Abels and Stephen F. Morillo*
2 War and Sanctity: Saints' Lives as Sources for Early Medieval Warfare – *John France*
3 The 791 Equine Epidemic and its Impact on Charlemagne's Army – *Carroll Gillmor*
4 The Role of the Cavalry in Medieval Warfare – *J.F. Verbruggen*
5 Sichelgaita of Salerno: Amazon or Trophy Wife? – *Valerie Eads*
6 Castilian Military Reform under the Reign of Alfonso XI (1312–50) – *Nicolas Agrait*
7 Sir Thomas Dagworth in Brittany, 1346–7: Restellou and La Roche Derrien – *Clifford J. Rogers*
8 Ferrante d'Este's Letters as a Source for Military History – *Sergio Mantovani*
9 Provisions for the Ostend Militia on the Defense, August 1436 – *Kelly DeVries*

Volume IV

1 The Sword of Justice: War and State Formation in Comparative Perspective – *Stephen F. Morillo*
2 Archery *versus* Mail: Experimental Archaeology and the Value of Historical Context – *Russ Mitchell*
3 'Cowardice' and Duty in Anglo-Saxon England – *Richard Abels*
4 Cowardice and Fear Management: The 1173–74 Conflict as a Case Study – *Steven Isaac*
5 Expecting Cowardice: Medieval Battle Tactics Reconsidered – *Stephen F. Morillo*
6 Naval Tactics at the Battle of Zierikzee (1304) in the Light of Mediterranean Praxis – *William Sayers*
7 The Military Role of the Magistrates in Holland during the Guelders War – *James P. Ward*
8 Women in Medieval Armies – *J.F. Verbruggen*
9 Verbruggen's 'Cavalry' and the Lyon-Thesis – *Bernard S. Bachrach*
10 Dogs of War in Thirteenth-Century Valencian Garrisons – *Robert I. Burns*

Volume V

1 Literature as Essential Evidence for Understanding Chivalry – *Richard W. Kaeuper*

Contents of Previous Volumes

2 The Battle of Hattin: A Chronicle of a Defeat Foretold? – *Michael Ehrlich*
3 Hybrid or Counterpoise? A Study of Transitional Trebuchets – *Michael Basista*
4 The Struggle between the Nicaean Empire and the Bulgarian State (1254–1256) : towards a Revivial of Byzantine Military Tactics under Theodore II Laskaris – *Nicholas S. Kanellopoulos and Joanne K. Lekea*
5 A 'Clock-and-Bow' Story: Late Medieval Technology from Monastic Evidence – *Mark Dupuy*
6 The Strength of Lancastrian Loyalism during the Readeption: Gentry Participation at the Battle of Tewkesbury – *Malcolm Mercer*
7 Soldiers and Gentlemen: The Rise of the Duel in Renaissance Italy – *Stephen Hughes*
8 'A Lying Legacy' Revisited: The Abels-Morillo Defense of Discontinuity – *Bernard S. Bachrach*

Volume VI

1 Cultural Representation and the Practice of War in the Middle Ages – *Richard Abels*
2 The *Brevium Exempla* as a Source for Carolingian Warhorses – *Carroll Gillmor*
3 Infantry and Cavalry in Lombardy (11th–12th Centuries) – *Aldo Settia*
4 Unintended Consumption: The Interruption of the Fourth Crusade at Venice and its Consequences – *Greg Bell*
5 Light Cavalry, Heavy Cavalry, Horse Archers, Oh My! What Abstract Definitions Don't Tell Us About 1205 Adrianople – *Russ Mitchell*
6 War, Financing in the Late-Medieval Crown of Aragon – *Donald Kagay*
7 National Reconciliation in France at the end of the Hundred Years War – *Christopher Allmand*

Volume VII

1 The Military Role of the Order of the Garter – *Richard W. Barber*
2 The Itineraries of the Black Prince's *Chevauchées* of 1355 and 1356: Observations and Interpretations – *Peter Hoskins*
3 The *Chevauchée* of John Chandos and Robert Knolles: Early March to Early June, 1369 – *Nicolas Savy*
4 'A Voyage, or Rather an Expedition, to Portugal': Edmund of Langley's Journey to Iberia, June/July 1381 – *Douglas Biggs*
5 The Battle of Aljubarrota (1385): A Reassessment – *João Gouveia Monteiro*
6 'Military' Knighthood in the Lancastrian Era: the Case of Sir John Montgomery – *Gilbert Bogner*

Contents of Previous Volumes

7 Medieval Romances and Military History: Marching Orders in Jean de Bueil's *Le Jouvencel introduit aux armes* – *Matthieu Chan Tsin*
8 Arms and the Art of War: The Ghentenaar and Brugeois Militia in 1477–79 – *J. F. Verbruggen*
9 Accounting for Service at War: the Case of Sir James Audley of Heighley – *Nicholas Gribit*
10 The Black Prince in Gascony and France (1355–6), According to MS78 of Corpus Christi College, Oxford – *Clifford J. Rogers*

Volume VIII

1 People against Mercenaries: the Capuchins in Southern Gaul – *John France*
2 The Last Italian Expedition of Henry IV: Re-reading the *Vita Mathildis* of Donizone of Canossa – *Valerie Eads*
3 Jaime I of Aragon: Child and Master of the Spanish Reconquest – *Donald Kagay*
4 Numbers in Mongol Warfare – *Carl Sverdrup*
5 Battlefield Medicine in Wolfram's *Parzival* – *Jolyon T. Hughes*
6 Battle-Seeking, Battle-Avoiding or Perhaps Just Battle-Willing? Applying the Gillingham Paradigm to Enrique II of Castile – *Andrew Villalon*
7 *Outrance* and *Plaisance* – *Will McLean*
8 Guns and Goddams: Was there a Military Revolution in Lancastrian Normandy 1415–50? – *Anne Curry*
9 The Name of the Siege Engine *Trebuchet*: Etymology and History in Medieval France and Britain – *William Sayers*